The Slaughter-House
of Mammon

LOCUST HILL LITERARY STUDIES
NO. 8

The Slaughter-House of Mammon

An Anthology of Victorian Social Protest Literature

Edited by
Sharon A. Winn
Lynn M. Alexander

With a Foreword by
Joseph A. Kestner

LOCUST HILL PRESS
West Cornwall, CT
1992

Library of Congress Cataloging-in-Publication Data

The Slaughter-house of Mammon : an anthology of Victorian social
 protest literature / edited by Sharon A. Winn, Lynn M. Alexander ;
 with a foreword by Joseph A. Kestner.
    344p.   cm. -- (Locust Hill literary studies ; no. 8)
    Includes bibliographical references.
    ISBN 0-933951-41-8 : $32.00
    1. Social problems--Fiction. 2. English fiction--19th century.
 3. Protest literature, English. I. Winn, Sharon A. II. Alexander,
 Lynn Mae. III. Series.
 PR1309.S63S57
 823'.8080355--dc20   92-7269
                                                        CIP

Printed on acid-free, 250-year-life paper
Manufactured in the United States of America

For
Nina H. Winn
Milly M. Wolfe
Cleo W. Alexander
—with love.

Contents

Acknowledgments

Many people helped make this book a reality and the editors would like to express our appreciation for their assistance. We thank the Department of Faculty Development, University of Tennessee at Martin, Janie Hinds, Kate Meyers, Sally Mitchell, Barbara Quinn Schmidt, Joseph Kestner and the Research Society for Victorian Periodicals for their guidance. We also thank the wonderful faculty and staff at Lee College for their unflagging encouragement. We especially want to thank Kay Tiller, Linda Jayne, Jerry Hamby and Gary Ervin for the moral, editorial and computer support they gave us. Above all, our eternal gratitude goes to Debbie Earnest and Laurie Portrey without whose proofreading and computer skills this book would not have been completed.

Sharon A. Winn
Lynn M. Alexander

Foreword

During the 1980s there was a considerable growth of interest in the Victorian social problem novel. Scholars such as Catherine Gallagher, Joseph Kestner, and Rosemarie Bodenheimer reinvestigated social protest narratives, arguing that they embraced their own modes of discourse, had strong affiliations with questions of gender in Britain, and redirected readers' attention to conditions requiring amelioration lest anyone not recall Thomas Carlyle's exhortations in *Chartism* and *Past and Present*. These critical studies discussed a number of texts not considered "canonical" in the conventional histories of Victorian literature, works by such writers as Charlotte Tonna, Elizabeth Stone, Frances Trollope, George W.M. Reynolds, and Julia Kavanagh.

While these critical studies of the 1980s refocused attention on these authors, for scholars in Victorian literature and those interested in the cultural poetics of Victorian society, the major difficulty was the lack of the primary texts. Although such presses as Virago have done much to bring the work of lesser-known women writers to a wider public, presses in general have not performed the essential task of getting these works into editions accessible to students and scholars. It is this work that the two editors, Sharon A. Winn and Lynn M. Alexander, have initiated in this very important anthology.

The selections included in this anthology represent a wide spectrum of social protest writing. One major advantage of this collection is its focus on neglected writers. For example, Harriet Martineau's work is known to scholars of the *Illustrations of Political Economy*. Few individuals have read her earlier—and crucial—formulations of idea in her novellas *The Rioters* (1827) and *The Turn-Out* (1829), the latter now appearing in print for the first time since its publication. The availability of such a text will enable current scholars to trace the origins of the social protest that informs the better-known stories of *A Manchester Strike* or *The Hill and the Valley*.

Similarly, an anthology such as this also brings to light writers whose work is totally unknown. Camilla Toulmin, for example, whose *The Orphan Milliners* (1844) is published here for the first time since its appearance, also wrote the later *A Story of the Factories* (1846). *The Orphan Milliners* is a trenchant exposé of dressmaking conditions during the forties, even as *A Story of the Factories* analyzes the plight of factory "hands" who leave the poverty of the agricultural districts. As significant as these analyses are, however, perhaps more striking is the fact that these narratives are written by a woman. In the instances of both Martineau and Toulmin, one sees female writers addressing the new conditions created by the Industrial Revolution, appropriating new modes of discourse and thereby enlarging the creative range of women writing during this era.

Some of the writers had specific ideological positions to advance, as is the case of the Radicals G.W.M. Reynolds and Ernest Jones who are represented by three selections in this anthology. In his *Reynolds's Miscellany,* Reynolds attacked a wide range of social abuses, imbued with a Chartist/reformist spirit and often addressing specifically working-class readers. Jones published in the Chartist periodical, *The Northern Star,* and his work reflects Chartist ideology as well. Here again, Winn and Alexander's anthology performs another important function in allowing the Victorianist to have readily available texts that instruct the reader in an innovative form for specific political, ideological agendas. In the works of Toulmin, Martineau, Reynolds and others included in this collection one sees the broad objectives of the social protest narrative to expose abuses and promote legislative reform.

Although one thinks of the major achievements of the social protest narrative to be from the 1840s and 1850s, this anthology usefully reminds readers that the origins of the social protest narrative exist in earlier decades. For example, Hannah More's stories "Village Politics" (1795) and "A Lancashire Collier Girl" (1795) demonstrate the focus on political ideology and individual suffering at the end of the eighteenth century. The novels of Maria Edgeworth, notably *Castle Rackrent* (1800) and *The Absentee* (1812), concentrating respectively on the abuse of tenants and the evils of absentee landlordism in Ireland, demonstrate the objective of the social protest writer to educate the complacent reader.

The decade of the 1830s is particularly crucial in the evolution of the social protest narrative. It was a period in which memoirs and social investigative reporting established the evidentiary basis of these novels and tales. Winn and Alexander have included examples of both these elements with *A Memoir of Robert Blincoe* (1828) and excerpts from John Fielden's The *Curse of the Factory System* (1836). The *Memoir* was reprinted in Manchester in 1832, the same year as the publication of the Sadler Committee *Report* on children's employment. The *Memoir,* in turn, was used by Frances Trollope for some of the most scathing pages of her novel, *Michael Armstrong, the Factory Boy* (1840). Having such a work available again permits one to analyze source material, evaluating its incorporation into social problem narrative. Similarly, Fielden's investigation was used as a source by Charlotte Tonna in the pages of *The Christian Lady's Magazine* and spurred her to write *Helen Fleetwood* (1839-41) and *The Wrongs of Woman* (1843-44), advancing the social protest she had undertaken with the anti-slavery *The System* (1827) and the labor movement study of *Combination* (1832). The fact that Fielden became a key advocate of the Ten Hours' Movement increases the value of the selections provided here.

Social protest fiction may be approached through certain sub-categories, especially by the occupation or trade analyzed in the respective narratives. For example, some texts concentrate on the condition of the seamstress in such narratives as *The Wrongs of Woman* by Tonna, *The Young Milliner* (1843) by Stone, and *Rachel Gray* (1856) by Kavanagh. The metals trades were the focus of Disraeli's *Sybil* (1845); mining was the central subject of Fanny Mayne's *Jane Rutherford* (1853); the textile industries were exposed in *A Story of the Factories, Michael Armstrong*, and *Helen Fleetwood*, while the tailoring sweatshops preoccupied Kingsley in *Alton Locke* (1850). This emphasis on specific trades permitted the writer to concentrate the reader's attention on a single abuse, addressing specific avenues of remediation in terms of hours, working conditions, sanitation, and occupational hazards.

While this anthology makes available key primary texts of the social protest tradition, an additional benefit of this collection is its demonstration that both major and less canonical writers shared common concerns. The seamstress, for example, was a primary focus of Elizabeth Gaskell's tale in Ruth (1853) and figured in novels by Dickens such as *Nicholas Nickleby* (1838-39). The condition of factory "hands" is part of Charlotte Brontë's focus in *Shirley* (1849). The mores of the factory town are central to Gaskell's *Mary Barton* (1848), while the Captain of Industry who figured in such works as Stone's *William Langshawe* (1842) or Geraldine Jewsbury's *Marian Withers* (1851) is a protagonist in Gaskell's *North and South* (1854-55). Thus, the less canonical works included in this collection can illuminate the context of social protest in which a Dickens, Gaskell, or Brontë was writing.

The inclusion of Kipling's "The Record of Badalia Herodsfoot" and Greenwood's "A Night in a Workhouse" in this anthology indicates that, while the social protest narrative is particularly identified with the 1840s and 1850s, the tradition was to endure in the work of subsequent writers. George Eliot in *Felix Holt, the Radical* (1866); George Moore in *Esther Waters* (1894); Arthur Morrison in *Tales of Mean Streets* (1894), *A Child of the Jago* (1896), and *The Hole in the Wall* (1902); and Somerset Maugham in *Liza of Lambeth* (1897) demonstrated the enduring power of the previous practitioners. In America as well, social protest was to thrive in such works as Stephen Crane's *Maggie: A Girl of the Streets* (1893) and Rebecca Davis's *Life in the Iron Mills* (1861).

The legacy is evident in George Orwell's inter-war memoirs *Down and Out in Paris and London* (1933) and *The Road to Wigan Pier* (1937).

Sharon Winn and Lynn Alexander, in bringing these texts to new readers in the 1990s, challenge received notions concerning gender in writing, the formation of the canon, and the function of fictional literature in legislative reform. In his Preface to the *Stanford Companion to Victorian Fiction*, John Sutherland has observed that "the Victorian novel ... has effectively become a lost continent of English literature," noting that "not all the Victorian novels we neglect are worthless." Winn and Alexander, themselves explorers, compel all advocates of cultural poetics to explore that "lost continent."

Joseph A. Kestner
McFarlin Professor of English
The University of Tulsa

Introduction

In G.W.M. Reynolds's *The Mysteries of London*, one of the main characters is "The Resurrection Man" whose crimes included bodysnatching. Most resurrection men sold corpses to hospitals for medical research and without those bodies the search for the scientific basis of disease might have been thwarted. The present editors are following in the footsteps of Reynolds's Resurrection Man, but we are disinterring literary texts in order to make them available to scholars and students in hopes of understanding the principles of the societal "diseases" that afflicted England during the early industrial era.

There are several reasons for resurrecting these texts, the foremost being to help fill a gap that exists in the canon of Victorian literature. Generally, when we speak of the Victorian novel, the works of authors such as Charlotte Brontë, Charles Dickens, and George Eliot come to mind. Nevertheless, these novelists, often considered representational of the best of their age, are anomalies. Although these authors deal with social issues in a nominal way (e.g., *Jane Eyre* with women's education, *Oliver Twist* or *A Christmas Carol* with the poor, and *Middlemarch* with the opportunities open to women), rarely are they grounded in specific social problems of the day. What then constituted typical Victorian fiction? Commentators such as Catherine Gallagher in *The Industrial Reformation of England*, and Joseph Kestner in *Protest and Reform*, have demonstrated that the social protest novel represents a major stratum of Victorian literature.

Social protest fiction, the "novel with a purpose," grew in response to the social and economic pressure created through population growth and industrialization. The recognition and response to the genre was immediate. In *The Westminster Review*, the author of "Novels with a purpose" notes:

> The current of public feeling at present sets in favor of prose fiction.... The author seems to have written, not because he or she felt inspired to tell a story, but because certain meditations, or convictions, or doubts, on some subject connected with human society, seemed to find convenient and emphatic expression through the medium of a work of fiction. In each of these books the philosophical critic of humanity, the social reformer, or the social accuser, stands behind the story-teller and inspires and guides his utterance.... In all alike the story is not the end, but only the means.[1]

Notable not only because writers such as Brontë (*Shirley*), Dickens (*Hard Times*), and Eliot (*Felix Holt*) felt the need to contribute, but also for its impact on Victorian society, social protest fiction and allied non-fiction have presented contemporary scholars with a wide offering of material for study. The only problem has been accessibility.

For the most part, social protest literature has been uncatalogued and available only on microfilm from the British Library. To obtain copies for study was time consuming and expensive, placing the works outside the reach of many scholars and most students. It is our intent to offer a sampling of social protest literature, representing a variety of viewpoints about the social ills that plagued the Victorians, for classroom use. In making our selections we considered factors such as author, genre, topic, and time period, intending to create a sampling which could be used as a reader in a variety of courses, as well as a source for students of Victorian literature and history in general. The works selected represent the major genres of the time—the essay, autobiography, and serial novel—as well as the social classes involved, the working, manufacturing, and upper classes. The literature is presented chronologically beginning with Robert Blincoe's *Memoir* and concluding with Rudyard Kipling's "The Record of Badalia Herodsfoot."

Harriet Martineau wrote *The Turn-Out* at the request of a group of factory owners in Nottingham and Derby who noticed the useful way her earlier novel, *The Rioters,* had conveyed the message that strikes were not only futile, but had long-range negative effects. *The Turn-Out,* published in 1829, combines elements of both the industrial novel and the social tract as it presents the story of the Gilbert brothers, Henry and James. In the first chapter Henry Gilbert delivers a speech inciting the mill workers to strike and then tries to convince his brother to join the strike. The second chapter balances the workers' strike with the presentation of the mill owner's perspective through a conversation between James and Robert Wallace, a stance emphasized by its restatement in the following chapter by another mill owner. Because no agreement is reached between workers and owners, a strike follows which lasts over three months on the strength of financial support from trade union organizations in neighboring areas. However, as winter approaches the workers' enthusiasm begins to flag and the strike is eventually called off without achieving the goal of higher wages. In the course of the story, workers are encouraged to save their wages, consider apprenticing their children in different occupations, and to postpone marriage until the couple is economically established. Martineau's story presents the major arguments of political economists in the early part of the century though Martineau says she never read anything about political economy until after she wrote the novel. Despite this disclaimer, it is clear that she understood the tenets of political economy very well, and she is able to explain the laissez-faire system of supply and demand with a clarity that is rarely seen in economic texts. Martineau's political stance is opposed to that of other writers in this book, but *The Turn-Out* is included so that students will not only be familiar with political economy, but that it will be seen that even those writers who opposed the political or economic activities of the workers still felt sympathy with them.

A Memoir of Robert Blincoe, first published serially in 1828, was the first and arguably most influential of the apprentice stories that were popular during the 1820s and '30s. The memoir was written by John Brown, a journalist, who assumes the role of social psychologist within the course of the work. Beginning with the title page, Victorian readers were presented with messages of veracity (the story is a "memoir" in "minute detail") and emotion (Blincoe is "an orphan boy" who "at seven years of age" must "endure the Horrors of a Cotton-Mill"). According to publisher Richard Carlile's preface, a work such as Blincoe's memoir filled a void in early social protest literature:

> But such a Memoir as this was much wanted, to hand down to posterity, what was the real character of the complaints about the treatment of children in our cotton mills .... An amended treatment of children has been made, the apprenticing system having been abandoned by the masters of the mills; but the employment is in itself bad for children—first, as to their health, and second, as to their manners and acquirements, the employment being in a bad atmosphere;.... If a remedy be desired, it must be sought by that part of the working people themselves, who are alive to their progressing degradation. It will never be sought fairly out, by those who have no interest in seeking it.

In Chapter I, Brown establishes the time of his interview with Blincoe, 1822-24, and Blincoe's present condition. Brown uses this first chapter primarily to establish the validity of his narrative, but also to create sympathy for Blincoe. With the second chapter, Brown moves from Blincoe's early childhood as a ward of the parish and an inmate of the Saint Pancras workhouse to apprenticeship at Lowdham Cotton Mill. Through the child's eyes, readers are introduced to the poor food, long hours, and wretched conditons which constituted life in the early factories. Brown chronicles the savage brutality of factory owners and overlookers and equates the children's condition with that of American slaves, saying that the slaves actually have better conditions. The memoir closes with Blincoe's completion of his indenture, and his attempts at various business ventures up to the time of publication. Blincoe's memoir is, perhaps, one of the most important social documents of the early Victorian period. The truth of its allegations must have been clear to the Victorians because the memoir served as the basis for several other literary works, including Fielden's *The Curse of the Factory System* and Frances Trollope's *Michael Armstrong, the Factory Boy*.

The publication of John Galt's "The Seamstress" in *Tait's Edinburgh Magazine* in1833 brought a new figure into the world of social protest literature, a figure which would soon gain prominence: the seamstress. The story, labeled "a reminiscence of our youth," is to be read as an illustration of the subtle distinction between the English "industry" and Scottish "eydency," with its "employments of a feminine and sedentary kind," and "industry free from labour." The brief story centers on Miss Peggy Pingle, a victim of "pinched gentility," forced to earn her own living following the early death of her father. Galt carefully establishes the conditions in which Miss Pingle lives and tells of her brief engagement at 36, broken when, following the advice of friends, she asks her suitor about his financial status. The story concludes with Miss Pingle's aging, decline and death. Of particular interest is an authorial comment made midway in the story: "We make this important distinction between the wheel and the needle, because, although we have often overheard malcontent murmurings against the former, yet we do not recollect, in any one instance, the latter spoken of either with complaint or disparagement." There is a certain irony to Galt's statement since a few women's magazines were already beginning to voice concerns about the working conditions faced by seamstresses, and within a decade the seamstress would be one of the most popular symbols of suffering in social protest literature. And yet even Galt may have been aware of some of the problems later associated with needlework. For he notes that following her mother's death, Miss Pingle rose to work earlier and was forced to work with a smaller candle, and while the other women note the "new stinting in her narrow means," it is with "a kind-hearted hypocrisy" that they invite her to tea.

The 1836 publication of John Fielden's The *Curse of the Factory System*, arguing for a Ten Hours Bill, created a furor among mill owners, for here was an essay attacking the factory system in no uncertain terms—written by a successfull mill owner. Fielden had worked in his father's cotton mill as a child and knew first hand the conditions faced by mill workers:

> I well remember being set to work in my father's mill when I was little more than ten years old: my associates, too, in the labour and in recreation are still in my memory. Only a few of them are now alive; some dying very young, others living to become men and women; but many of those who lived have died off before they attained the age of fifty years…. For several years after I began to work in the mill, the

hours of labour in our works did not exceed *ten* in the day, winter and summer, and even with the labour of those hours, I shall never forget the fatigue I often felt before the day ended....

His essay is a powerful indictment of the factory conditions both of the 1830s and of a period thirty years earlier. Fielden strongly argues that the conditions had not improved with time, but had, in fact, deteriorated: the working hours were no fewer, but were often even more; the amount of exertion called for had grown; and the danger had risen as the speed and intricacy of the machinery increased.

Fielden's monograph took up many of the concerns of the day, and his stance was more radical than that of the majority of reformers. While many reformers felt that the Ten Hours Bill was a strong statement regarding child labor, Fielden argued that a ten hour day was too long for any worker, adult or child. He also attacked attempts by Poor Law Commissioners to transfer large numbers of laborers from the agrarian South to the industrial North. To Fielden, this policy was little more than a means of supplying unscrupulous manufacturers with cheap, unprotected labor. To convince his readship of the undesirable economic, as well as moral, ramifications of this policy, Fielden established a cause and effect scenario, which is the portion included in this anthology: lower wages lead to lower purchasing power, which will eventually deprive manufacturers of adequate markets for their goods. Fielden's work is particularly effective because he was an extremely successful manufacturer while incorporating all the reforms he advocated for factories at large. Thus he could answer charges that industrial reform would either bankrupt owners or make English manufacturers vulnerable to foreign competitors.

Camilla Toulmin's *The Orphan Milliners: A Story of the West End,* published in 1844, is a short novel illustrating the need for young women to establish economic independence. The narrative centers around two sisters, Henrietta and Anne Standford, who are apprenticed to a dressmaker, Madam Dobière, following the death of their mother. From the beginning Toulmin makes her position clear: because of their lack of education and money, the girls have no employment alternatives other than needlework. And the responsibility for their predicament is placed directly on their mother, who blithely assumed her daughters would marry and "thus be provided for, and protected." Toulmin tells readers, "Too many mothers, who think little, think thus; and so neglect to cherish in those they love a spirit of self-reliance, or to place within their reach the means of self-dependence."

As with most literature portraying needlewomen, much of *The Orphan Milliners* concerns the working and living conditions of young milliners. The long hours and harsh conditions faced by these women is a primary concern, one which Toulmin compounds through the age of the protagonists—while Henrietta is nineteen, Anne is only fourteen years old. Toulmin wishes to shock her readers with the youth and suffering of her protagonists since, like many of her fellow activists, she places much of the responsibility for suffering on the thoughtlessness of the women who patronize the shops. Although Henrietta and Anne are able, with the help of a cousin, to start their own establishment after serving their apprenticeship, Anne's health has been irretrievably damaged and she dies. Henrietta's fate is less determined; at the close of the novel Toulmin only suggests that Henrietta will marry, and thus be relieved of self-support.

G.W.M. Reynolds's *The Mysteries of London,* published in multiple volumes by John Dicks in 1850, is an exhaustive, and exhausting, study of the inhabitants of London, ranging from the highest social classes to the lowest. Two selections from Reynolds's opus have been included in this anthology, "The Rattlesnake's History" and "Crankey Jem's History." Both are products of Reynolds's outrage at the Victorian sociopolitical system in general though each deals with a specific facet of abuse of the lower classes at the hands of the upper and middle classes.

"The Rattlesnake's History" details the miserable conditions of coal miners. The Rattlesnake is the daughter of a female coal miner, and she describes the misery and degradation of her life growing up as a child worker in the mines. Reynolds sensationalizes the information from the 1842 *Report of the Children's Employment Commission* by emphasizing the most lurid aspects of the workers' condition. Reynolds covers the long hours, brutality, and immorality of the mines, and also the continued exploitation of miners above ground in tommy shops, areas that Disraeli also examines in *Sybil.* The Rattlesnake escapes the mines, commits a crime and discovers that conditions in jail are so much better than among the miners that she opts for a life of crime. Reflecting Reynolds's radical political stance, the Rattlesnake's story is an indictment of mine owners and a society that allows such exploitation and suggests that government intervention in the mining industry is a moral necessity.

In "Crankey Jem's History," Reynolds follows a prisoner who is transported to Australia. The author indulges in a brief, but hilarious, description of Crankey Jem's early life as the son of a religious charlatan. Mistreatment by his stepmother forces Jem into a life of crime, and, arrested for theft, he is transported to Australia. Jem is first sent to Port Macquarie where conditions are so bad that prisoners, who haven't the nerve to commit suicide, murder someone so that the state will execute them and, thus, relieve them of their misery. Crankey Jem and other prisoners escape, giving Reynolds the chance to describe the Australian bush as well as add sensational incidents involving cannibalism and a giant snake. Crankey Jem is recaptured and sent to Norfolk Island, a paradise which has been converted "into a perfect hell on earth." Jem escapes once again and, after overcoming storms and shark attacks, returns to London where his story ends with a vow to seek vengeance on the Resurrection Man. "Crankey Jem's History" exposes the excesses of the penal system and allows Reynolds to call for a more humane method of punishment for criminals.

In *Lucy Dean; the Noble Needlewoman*, Eliza Meteyard illustrates the efficacy of emigration as a solution to "the woman question" which centered around the excessive number of unmarried women in Victorian England. Sidney Herbert's plan to send these superfluous women to various colonies is explored as Lucy Dean, an impoverished seamstress, emigrates to Australia. Meteyard shows Smilesian self-help in action as Lucy works, under the aegis of her mentor Mary Austen, to earn enough money for the passage. Characters like Mr. Twiddlesing and the heartless Mrs. Moss add a Dickensian note to the narrative, and Australia is seen as a veritable paradise, populated by stalwart but love-starved men. One of the most remarkable aspects of the tale is Mary Austen's ability to change conditions for distressed needlewomen through the power of her pen. Ostensibly the epitome of the "Angel of the House," Mary Austen is a powerful, courageous figure and, as such, emphasizes the strength of Victorian women, especially when such strength is allied with moral rectitude. The role of emigration in reclaiming fallen women is illustrated in the transformation of Lucy's sister, Nelly, from an unwed mother cast upon the street to a blooming wife and mother in Australia. Meteyard uses the iconic seamstress to explore alternatives for women and in praising emigration, she illuminates one of the primary social schemes of the era.

Ernest Jones's *Woman's Wrongs*, published in the Chartist periodical *The Northern Star*, was an ambitious scheme to illustrate women's problems in all of the social classes. Unfortunately, Jones did not finish all four projected stories, apparently due to his activities as a leader of the Chartists. The section included in this anthology, "The Working-Man's Wife," is an example of Chartist sympathy for women's issues. The original Charter called for universal suffrage, and, though the later Charter included only manhood suffrage, Jones clearly respected the domestic and economic influence of working class women and found it expedient to recognize women's issues. Heavily influenced by Reynolds, Jones's tale illustrates the brutality of working class men toward their women as well as the privations working class wives and children suffered due to employers' machinations against workers.

Beginning with Margaret Haspen in the throes of childbirth, Jones chronicles her fall into utter penury as her husband is denied work, physically abuses

Margaret and her children, and eventually descends into crime which, ironically, frees Margaret from her abominable marriage and allows her to become an innkeeper. However, her husband returns, murders her employer and precipitates Margaret's fall into the hands of the law. Though innocent, she is charged for the murder and hanged, Jones's final ironic comment on the lack of justice for the poor. Margaret Haspen's world foreshadows the brutal cosmos of Zola, but Jones implicitly charges the government and higher classes with responsibility for the horrors Margaret suffers. In doing so, Jones make a case for government intervention in the plight of the poor, especially that of working class women.

Influenced by Henry Mayhew, many young reporters in the 1860s, wrote investigative reports on the condition of the poor in London. James Greenwood was among the earliest investigative reporters, and his "A Night in a Workhouse" is among the best of the articles generated by what P. J. Keating calls "Urban Explorers." Greenwood, dressed as a poor man, spends a night in a workhouse and details his experiences. Though conditions in workhouses had improved since the 1830s and '40s, Greenwood is still appalled by the filth, immorality and discomfort in the workhouse he visits. Yet his indignation is aimed less at the men who operate the workhouse and the "respectable" denizens of the place than at the ruffians like a young man, Kay, and his friends who are noisy, rude and blasphemous. Greenwood's moral scruples reflect the Victorian distinction between the respectable poor and the non-respectable element consisting of vagrants and criminals. Greenwood's sympathy with an old man who loses his hat only to find that the ruffians have destroyed it is as evident as his disdain for the rowdies who mistreat the respectable group. His report covers the regulations, provisions, sleeping arrangements and population of a workhouse at the time of Luke Fildes's famous *Houseless and Hungry* (1896), a painting which, like Greenwood's report, depicts the real distress of the poor in the 1860s.

The final selection in the anthology is Rudyard Kipling's "The Record of Badalia Herodsfoot," published in the *Detroit Free Press* (London) in 1890. Seemingly a radical departure from his usual soldiers' stories, Badalia's tale is actually of a piece with Kipling's cockney soldiers since in all of these stories, he explores the relationship of working class people to their world. Badalia's story is part of the renascence of public interest in the poor of the East End of London that marked the final decades of the century. Much attention was focused on the East End due to the depredations of Jack the Ripper in that area in 1888, but a large number of missionaries and social reformers had been at work there throughout the 1880s. Kipling was in England in the later '80s, and "The Record of Badalia Herodsfoot" is his contribution to the books and stories about the East End that were so popular.

Focusing on attempts at social reform by missionaries, Kipling illustrates the idea of the poor controlling charitable funds themselves in order to make sure that the money is given only to those who deserve it. The Reverend Eustace Hanna appoints Badalia Herodsfoot as trustee for dispensing charity, and Badalia performs the job admirably, keeping meticulous accounts. But her husband, who has married another woman, returns and beats her to death for the money she has in her keeping. Kipling emphasizes the brutality of the East End in order to show the reader the uselessness of the efforts of the "do-gooders" to alleviate the problems of the poor. The East End is a senseless, cruel world that, Kipling intimates, cannot be reformed despite the best efforts of both its own denizens and outsiders. "The Record of Badalia Herodsfoot" shows that even social protest fiction was not immune to the malaise that overtook the world's first industrialized nation at the end of the nineteenth century.

Many of the works in this anthology are well-written, riveting accounts of the sufferings of the nineteenth-century laboring classes, yet virtually all of these works have disappeared during the last century. Some readers have complained that social protest literature lacks the extremes of romanticism and pathos found in some of the more famous Victorian novels, yet few works could equal *A Memoir of Robert Blincoe* for pathos, even Dickens rarely draws his suffering more broadly, and many of the novels focusing on women, such as *Lucy Dean,* conclude in romance. So, why then has social protest fiction disappeared? Part of the problem may be that the emphasis is on social reform rather than entertaining through romance or pathos. For many modern readers the reason for a lack of interest in this literature is historical in nature, rather than literary: many readers feel that Victorian social protest literature is dated because of its reliance on contemporary issues, statistics, and Parliamentary papers. To these readers the social and moral issues faced by Victorian society seem to bear little relevance to the twentieth century. When the literature is viewed as dealing with the issues specifically raised by the transition from an agrarian to an industrial economy, or as restricted to a particular special interest group such as miners, needlewomen, or factory children, many modern readers assume that it will be of little interest to the general reader. After all, we have laws establishing minimum ages and wages for workers, and we have codes and inspectors to protect worker safety—why should we be interested in the Victorian reaction to the problems which sparked the British forerunners of these laws?

Ironically, we are currently going through a transitional period parallel to the Industrial Revolution—the High-Tech Revolution. Again people, especially the working class, are finding themselves unprepared and ill-equipped for new employment opportunities; again, there are fears of displacement of workers by machines and of foreign competition. So the study of Victorian social protest literature is quite timely and the lessons these authors taught may be applicable today.

Another problem for many modern readers is the overt didacticism of the literature. As the novel has evolved during the last century there has been a movement away from the didacticism in which the Victorians seemed to revel. Modern novels tend to present lives without comment, occasionally presenting models for behavior but more often leaving any situational reactions strictly to the impulse of the reader. In contrast, the majority of social protest novelists were writing not only to inform readers of the conditions faced by the working poor, but to motivate readers to specific actions. In these texts authors are more concerned with enlightening readers as to the actual working and living conditions of people, particularly women and children, forced to earn a living under harsh conditions than with entertaining or amusing their readership. Thus twentieth-century readers frequently come to Victorian social protest literature with false expectations and are startled, even repulsed, by the strong moral activism which confronts them.

But the moral emphasis found in social protest literature provides the key to an understanding of how the authors succeeded in focusing public attention on these problems. One of the foundations of a moral system is care for others. Recognizing this, Victorian social protest writers appealed to their readers' finer feelings in an effort to raise consciousness about the tribulations of large segments of the society. The authors' works were calculated to provoke pity which was transformed into moral indignation leading, in turn, to a public outcry for redress of the grievances of those members of society who were being mistreated. Social protest writers exhibited a sophisticated ability to manipulate social attitudes and the results were that both Parliament and business interests took steps to rectify the problems. The Victorian era is notable for the number of laws passed to protect citizens from legal and financial abuses. In fact, the protective laws that we take for granted might not exist if the Victorians had not examined the excesses of their social system and demanded change.

The study of Victorian social protest literature allows us to follow the methodologies used by the Victorians to alleviate social problems. Beginning with the almost unbelievably inhumane working conditions in factories and mines, social protest writers vehemently demanded improvements. Using government documents as sources, they transformed dry statistics and incoherent testimony into cogent, dramatic stories and essays that illustrated the necessity for enforceable laws that would regulate industry and weed out the excesses that were destroying their fellows. Many social protest writers were less than enthusiastic about the self-aggrandizement that formed the basis of political economy and the self-help philosophy of Samuel Smiles. They saw that the *laissez-faire* approach to economics, while creating untold wealth for a few, condemned the majority to lives of unremitting, unremunerated toil. They wondered in print why the wealthiest nation in the world had so many people who were starving or barely able to make ends meet, and they noted the huge disparity between the wealthy and the poor. These issues have reappeared in our own era and, once again, people fear for the moral, economic and political health of the nation, so the study of how previous generations handled these issues may help us solve our own dilemmas. Thus, the resurrection of these works of social protest may serve much the same purpose as the corpses that Reynolds's Resurrection Man supplied to medical science—they may give us further insight into the workings of the body politic which may help ensure better lives for us all.

Notes

[1]"Novels with a Purpose," *Westminster Review* 82 (1864), pp. 24-29.

About the Text

Wherever possible original texts have been used. Editing has been limited to correcting only the worst grammatical and typographical errors. In the interest of promoting easier reading, notes have been kept to a minimum. Footnotes appeared in the original texts, and endnotes are used for citation of secondary sources. An extended bibliography of secondary sources is included to assist research in social protest literature.

A Memoir of Robert Blincoe,

An Orphan Boy,

Who, with others, was sent from the Workhouse of Saint Pancras, London,
to one of the horrible cotton-mills and cotton-masters in Nottinghamshire.

John Brown
(1828)

The earliest cotton spinning factories in England were not located in cities
but in the country. Because the machinery was driven by water wheels,
factories had to be built near sources of water. Due to the remote locations of
these mills, the labor pool was small, but the manufacturers solved this problem
by importing child labor, in the form of parish apprentices, from city workhouses. The plan not only supplied labor for the mills but removed large
numbers of pauper children and orphans from the workhouses, which were
supported by parish taxes. Thus, taxes were lowered; the mills were supplied
with cheap labor, and the children supposedly learned a skill during their
"apprenticeships," thereby securing the greatest good for the greatest number.

In practice, the plan worked well for the parish overseers and the
manufacturers, but the children, some as young as five years old, were horribly
abused. John Brown's A Memoir of Robert Blincoe, one of the earliest exposés
of conditions in early cotton mills, was written in hopes of goading Parliament
into instituting reforms to protect child workers. At the time the memoir was
published in 1828 in The Lion, parish apprentices were no longer the primary
source of child labor. Since the steam engine allowed factories to be
established in populated areas, millowners hired local children in order to
sidestep the 1802 Health and Morals of Apprentices Act, and conditions in the
factories again degenerated to the point that children worked fourteen to
sixteen hours a day under extremely adverse circumstances.

Blincoe's memoir is part of the agitation that led to the Factory Act of
1833, which restricted children's hours to twelve, banned children under nine
from all mills except silk mills, and provided for two hours a day of school.

A Memoir of Robert Blincoe is perhaps the most important early publication detailing the mistreatment of factory apprentices. Both the author and
publisher took pains to double check Blincoe's tale to verify its veracity, and

1

*the story of the hideous conditions in which factory children lived and worked
is well calculated to appal even the most phlegmatic reader. The factual basis
of the book, and its references to Parliamentary committees, presages the types
of fiction and non-fiction that constitute the bulk of Nineteenth Century social
protest literature. In fact, the memoir was a primary source for both John
Fielden's* The Curse of the Factory System *and Frances Trollope's* The Life
and Adventures of Michael Armstrong, the Factory Boy. *Blincoe's memoir sets
a precedent for later social protest literature that is grounded in documentary
evidence of man's inhumanity to man.*

THE PUBLISHER'S PREFACE
TO BLINCOE'S MEMOIR

The various Acts of Parliament, which have been passed, to regulate the
treatment of children in the Cotton Spinning Manufactories, betoken the
previous existence of some treatment, so glaringly wrong, as to force itself upon
the attention of the legislature. This Cotton-slave-trade, like the Negro-slave-
trade, did not lack its defenders, and it might have afforded a sort of sorry
consolation to the Negro slaves of America, had they been informed, that their
condition, in having agriculturally to raise the cotton, was not half so bad, as
that of the white infant-slaves, who had to assist in the spinning of it, when
brought to this country. The religion and the black humanity of Mr. Wilberforce
seem to have been entirely of a foreign nature. Pardon is begged, if an error is
about to be wrongfully imputed; but the Publisher has no knowledge, that Mr.
Wilberforce's humane advocacy for slaves, was ever of that homely kind, as to
embrace the region of the home-cotton-slave-trade. And yet, who shall read the
Memoir of Robert Blincoe, and say, that the charity towards slaves should not
have begun or ended at home?

The Author of this Memoir is now dead: he fell, about two or three years
ago, by his own hand. He united, with a strong feeling for the injuries and
sufferings of others, a high sense of injury when it bore on himself, whether real
or imaginary; and a despondency when his prospects were not good. Hence his
suicide. Had he not possessed a fine fellow-feeling with the child of misfortune, he had never taken such pains to compile the Memoir of Robert Blincoe,
and to collect all the wrongs on paper, on which he could gain information,
about the various sufferers under the cotton-mill systems. Notes to the Memoir
of Robert Blincoe were intended by the author, in illustration of his strong
personal assertions. The references were marked in the Memoir; but the Notes
were not prepared, or if prepared, have not come to the Publisher's hand. But,
on enquiring after Robert Blincoe, in Manchester, and mentioning the Memoir

of him written by Mr. Brown, as being in the Publisher's possession, other papers, by the same Author, which had been left on a loan of money in Manchester, were obtained, and these papers seem to have formed the authorities, from which the notes to the Memoirs would have been made. So that, though the Publisher does not presume to make notes for the Author, nor for himself, to this Memoir, he is prepared to confirm much of the statement here made, the personalities of Robert Blincoe excepted, should it be generally challenged.

Robert Blincoe, the subject of the Memoir, is still living somewhere in Lancashire. The Publisher was anxious to see him, in the autumn of last year; but received information, on enquiry, that, having engaged in some kind of shop, he had become insolvent, and was, or had been, confined in Lancaster Castle for debt. The Publisher having no knowledge of Robert Blincoe, but in common with every reader of this Memoir, can have no personal feelings towards him, other than those of pity for his past sufferings. But such a Memoir as this was much wanted, to hand down to posterity, what was the real character of the complaints about the treatment of children in our cotton mills, about which a legislation has taken place, and so much has been said. An amended treatment of children has been made; the apprenticing system having been abandoned by the masters of the mills; but the employment is in itself bad for children; first, as to their health; and second, as to their manners and acquirements; the employment being in a bad atmosphere; and the education, from example, being bad; the time, that should be devoted to a better education, being devoted to that which is bad. The employment of infant children in the cotton-mills furnishes a bad means to dissolute parents, to live, in idleness and all sorts of vice, upon the produce of infant labour. There is much of this in Lancashire, which a little care and looking after, on the part of the masters of cotton-mills, might easily prevent. But what is to be done? Most of the extensive manufacturers profit by human misery and become callous toward it; both from habit and interest. If a remedy be desired, it must be sought by that part of the working people themselves, who are alive to their progressing degradation. It will never be sought fairly out, by those who have no interest in seeking it. And so long as the majority of the working people squanders its already scanty income in those pest-houses, those intoxicating nurseries, for vice, idleness and misery, the public drinking houses, there is no hope for them of an amended condition.

* * *

CHAPTER I.

By the time the observant reader has got through the melancholy recital of the sufferings of Blincoe and his associates in cotton-mill bondage, he will probably incline to an opinion, that rather than rear destitute and deserted children, to be thus distorted by excessive toil, and famished and tortured as those have been, it were incomparably less cruel to put them at once to death—less cruel that they had never been born alive; and far more wise that they had never been conceived. In cases of unauthorized pregnancies, our laws are tender of unconscious life, perhaps to a faulty extreme; whilst our parochial institutions, as these pages will prove, after incurring considerable expense to *preserve* the lives of those forlorn beings, sweep them off by shoals, under the sanction of other legal enactments, and consign them to a fate, far worse than sudden death.

Reared in the most profound ignorance and depravity, these unhappy beings are, from the hour of their birth, to the last of their existence, generally cut off from all that is decent in social life. Their preceptors are the veriest wretches in nature!—their influential examples all of the worst possible kind. The reports of the Cotton Bill Committees abundantly prove, that, by forcing those destitute poor to go into cotton-mills, they have, in very numerous instances, been consigned to a destiny worse than death without torture. Yet appalling as are many of the statements, which, through the reports of the Committees, have found their way before the public, similar acts of delinquencies, of a hue still darker—even repeated acts of murder, have escaped unnoticed. Much of the evidence brought forward by the friends of humanity, was neutralized or frittered away by the timidity of their witnesses, or by the base subserviency of venally unprincipled professional men, who, influenced by rich capitalists, basely prostituted their talent and character as physicians, surgeons, and apothecaries, to deceive the government, to perplex and mislead public opinion, and avert the loud cry raised against the insatiate avarice and relentless cruelty of their greedy and unfeeling suborners.

It was in the spring of 1822, after having devoted a considerable time to the investigating of the effect of the manufacturing system, and factory establishments, on the health and morals of the manufacturing populace, that I first heard of the extraordinary sufferings of R. Blincoe. At the same time, I was told of his earnest wish that those sufferings should, for the protection of the rising generation of parish children, be laid before the world. Thus assured, I went to inquire for him, and was much pleased with his conversation. If this young man had not been consigned to a cotton-factory, he would probably have been strong, healthy, and well grown; instead of which, he is diminutive as to stature, and his knees are grievously distorted. In his manners, he appeared remarkably gentle; in his language, temperate; in his statements, cautious and consistent. If, in any part of the ensuing narrative, there are falsehoods and misrepresentations, the fault rests solely with himself; for, repeatedly and earnestly, I admonished him to beware, lest a too keen remembrance of the injustice he had suffered should lead him to transgress the limits of truth. After I had taken down his communications, I tested them, by reading the same to other persons, with whom Blincoe had not had any intercourse on the subject, and who had partaken of the miseries of the same hard servitude, and by whom they were in every point confirmed.

Robert Blincoe commenced his melancholy narrative, by stating, that he was a parish orphan, and knew not either his father or mother. From the age of four years, he says, "till I had completed my seventh, I was supported in Saint Pancras poorhouse, near London." In very pathetic terms, he frequently censured and regretted the remissness of the parish officers, who, when they received him into the workhouse, had, as he seemed to believe, neglected to make any entry, or, at least, any to which he could obtain access, of his mother's and father's name, occupation, age, or residence. Blincoe argued, and plausibly too, that those officers would not have received him, if his mother had not proved her settlement; and he considered it inhuman in the extreme, either to neglect to record the names of his parents, or, if recorded, to refuse to give him that information, which, after his attaining his freedom, he had requested at their hands. His lamentations, on this head, were truly touching, and evinced a far higher degree of susceptibility of heart, than could have been expected from the extreme and long continued wretchedness he had endured in the den of vice and misery, where he was so long immured. Experience often evinces, that, whilst moderate adversity mollifies and expands the human heart, extreme and long continued wretchedness has a direct and powerful contrary tendency, and renders it impenetrably callous.

In one of our early interviews, tears trickling down his pallid cheeks, and his voice tremulous and faltering, Blincoe said, "I am worse off than a child reared in the Foundling Hospital. Those orphans have a name given them by the heads of that Institution, at the time of baptism, to which they are legally entitled. But I have no name I can call my own." He said he perfectly recollected riding in a coach to the workhouse, accompanied by some female, that he did not however think this female was his mother, for he had not the least consciousness of having felt either sorrow or uneasiness at being separated from her, as he very naturally supposed he should have felt, if that person had been his mother. Blincoe also appeared to think he had not been nursed by his mother, but had passed through many hands before he arrived at the workhouse; because he had no recollection of ever having experienced a mother's caresses. It seems, young as he was, he often inquired of the nurses, when the parents and relations of other children came to see his young associates, *why no one came to him,* and used to weep, when he was told, that *no one had ever owned him,* after his being placed in that house. Some of the nurses stated, that a female, who called soon after his arrival, inquired for him by the name of "Saint;" and, when he was produced, gave him a penny-piece, and told him his mother was dead. If this report were well founded, his mother's illness was the cause of his being removed and sent to the workhouse. According to his own description, he felt with extreme sensibility the loneliness of his condition, and, at each stage of his future sufferings, during his severe cotton-mill servitude, it pressed on his heart the heaviest of all his sorrows—an impassable barrier, "a wall of brass," cut him off from all mankind. The sad consciousness, that he stood alone, *"a waif on the world's wide common;"* that he had no acknowledged claim of kindred with any human being, rich or poor—that he stood apparently forever excluded from every social circle, so constantly occupied his thoughts, that, together with his sufferings, they imprinted a pensive character on his features, which probably neither change of fortune, nor time itself, would ever entirely obliterate. When he was six years old, and, as the workhouse children were saying their Catechism, it was his turn to repeat the Fifth Command-ment—"Honour thy father and thy mother, &c.," he recollects having suddenly burst into tears, and felt greatly agitated and distressed—his voice faltering, and his limbs trembling. According to his statement, and his pathetic eloquence in reciting his misfortunes, strongly corroborated his assertion. He was a very ready scholar, and the source of this sudden burst of grief being inquired into by some of his superiors, he said, "I cry, because I *cannot* obey one of God's commandments, I know not either my father or my mother. I cannot therefore be a good child and honour my parents."

It was rumoured, in the ward where Robert Blincoe was placed, that he owed his existence to the mutual frailties of his mother and a reverend divine, and was called the young *Saint,* in allusion to his priestly descent. This name or appellation he did not long retain, for he was afterwards called Parson; often, *the young Parson;* and he recollected hearing it said in his presence, that he was the son of a parson Blincoe. Whether these allusions were founded in truth, or were but the vile effusions of vulgar malice, was not, and is not, in his power to determine, whose bosom they have so painfully agitated. Another remark-able circumstance in his case, was, that when he was sent in August, 1799, with a large number of other children, from Saint Pancras workhouse, to a cotton-mill near Nottingham, he bore amongst his comrades, the name of *Parson,* and retained it afterwards till he had served considerably longer than his FOUR-TEEN YEARS, and then, when his Indentures were at last relinquished, and not till then, the young man found he had been apprenticed by the name of Robert Blincoe. I urged the probability, that his right indenture might, in the change of masters that took place, or the careless indifference of his last master, have been given to another boy, and that to the one given to him, bearing the name of Blincoe, he had no just claim. This reasoning he repelled, by steadily and consistently asserting, he fully recollected having heard it said his real name was Blincoe, whilst he remained at Saint Pancras workhouse. His indentures were dated the 15th August, 1799. If, at this time, he was seven years of age, which is by no means certain, he was born in 1792, and in 1796, was placed in Pancras. With these remarks, I close this preliminary matter, and happy should I be, if the publication of these facts enables the individual to whom they relate, to remove the veil which has hitherto deprived him of a knowledge of his parentage, a privation which he still appears to feel with undiminished intensity of grief.

Two years have elapsed, since I first began to take notes of Blincoe's extraordinary narrative. At the close of 1822 and beginning of 1823, I was seized with a serious illness, which wholly prevented my publishing this and other important communications. The testimony of as respectable a surgeon, who attended me, as any in the country, even ocular demonstration of my enfeebled state, failed to convince some of the cotton spinners, that my inability was not feigned, to answer some sinister end; and such atrocious conduct was pursued towards me, as would have fully justified a prosecution for conspiracy. Animated by the most opposite views, the worst of miscreants united to vilify and oppress me; the one wanting to get my papers, in order, by destroying them to prevent the enormities of the cotton masters being exposed; and another, traducing my character, and menacing my life, under an impression that I had basely sold the declarations and communications received from oppressed workpeople to their masters. By some of those suspicious misjudging people, Blincoe was led away. He did not, however, at any time, or under any circumstances, retract or deny any part of his communications, and, on the 18th and 19th of March, 1824, of his own free will, he not only confirmed all that he had communicated in the spring of 1822, with many other traits of suffering, not then recollected, but furnished me with them. It has, therefore, stood the test of this hurricane, without its authenticity being in any one part questioned or impaired. The authenticity of this narrative is, therefore, entitled to greater credit, than much of the testimony given by the owners of cotton-factories, or by professional men on their behalf, as will, in the course of this narrative, be fully demonstrated, by evidence wholly incontrovertible. If, therefore, it should be proved, that atrocities to the same extent, exist no longer; still, its publication, as a preventive remedy, is no less essential to the protection of parish paupers and foundlings. If the gentlemen of Manchester and its vicinity, who acted in 1816, &c., in conjunction with the late Mr. Nathaniel Gould, had not made the selection of witnesses too much in the power of incompetent persons, Robert Blincoe would have been selected in 1819, as the most impressive pleader in behalf of destitute and deserted children.

CHAPTER II

Of the few adventures of Robert Blincoe, during his residence in old Saint Pancras workhouse, the principal occurred when he had been there about two years. He acknowledges he was well fed, decently clad, and comfortably lodged, and not at all overdone, as regarded work; yet, with all these blessings in possession, this destitute child grew melancholy. He relished none of the humble comforts he enjoyed. It was liberty he wanted. The busy world lay outside the workhouse gates, and those he was seldom, if ever permitted to pass. He was cooped up in a gloomy, though liberal sort of a prison-house. His buoyant spirits longed to rove at large. He was too young to understand the necessity of the restraint to which he was subjected, and too opiniative to admit it could be intended for his good. Of the world he knew nothing, and the society of a workhouse was not very well calculated to delight the mind of a volatile child. He saw givers, destitute of charity, receivers of insult, instead of gratitude, witnessed little besides sullenness and discontent, and heard little but murmurs or malicious and slanderous whispers. The aged were commonly petulant and miserable—the young demoralized and wholly destitute of gaiety of heart. From the top to the bottom, the whole of this motley mass was tainted with dissimulation, and he saw the most abhorrent hypocrisy in constant operation. Like a bird newly caged, that flutters from side to side, and foolishly beats it wings against its prison walls, in hope of obtaining its liberty, so young Blincoe, weary of confinement, and resolved, if possible to be free, often watched the outer gates of the house, in the hope, that some favorable opportunity might facilitate his escape. He wistfully measured the height of the wall, and found it too lofty for him to scale, and too well guarded were the gates to admit of his egress unnoticed. His spirits, he says, which were naturally lively and buoyant, sank under this vehement longing after liberty. His appetite declined, and he wholly forsook his usual sports and comrades. It is hard to say how this disease of the mind might have terminated, if an accident had not occurred, which afforded a chance of emerging from the lifeless monotony of a workhouse, and of launching into the busy world, with which he longed to mingle.

Blincoe declares, he was so weary of confinement, he would gladly have exchanged situations with the poorest of the poor children, whom, from the upper windows of the workhouse, he had seen begging from door to door, or, as a subterfuge, offering matches for sale. Even the melancholy note of the sweep-boy, whom, long before day, and in the depths of winter, in frost, in snow, in rain and sleet, he heard pacing behind his surly master, had no terrors for him. So far from it, he envied him his fortune, and, in the fulness of discontent, thought his own state incomparably more wretched. The poor child was suffering under a diseased imagination, from which men of mature years and elaborate culture are not always free. It filled his heart with perverted feelings—it rendered the little urchin morose and unthankful, and, as undeserving of, as he was insensible to, the important benefits extended to him by a humane institution, when helpless, destitute and forlorn.

From this state of early misanthropy, young Blincoe was suddenly diverted, by a rumour, that filled many a heart among his comrades with terror, viz. that a day was appointed, when the master-sweeps of the metropolis were to come and select such a number of boys as apprentices, till they attained the age of 21 years, as they might deign to take into their sable fraternity. These tidings, that struck damp to the heart of the other boys, sounded like heavenly music to the ears of young Blincoe:—he anxiously inquired of the nurses if the news were true, and if so, what chance there was of his being one of the elect. The ancient matrons, amazed at the boy's temerity and folly, told him how bitterly he would rue the day that should consign him to that wretched employment, and bade him pray earnestly to God to protect him from such a destiny. The young adventurer heard these opinions with silent contempt. Finding, on farther inquiry, that the rumour was well founded, he applied to several menials in the house, whom he thought likely to promote his suit, entreating them to forward his election with all the interest they could command! Although at this time he was a fine grown boy, being fearful he might be deemed too low in stature, he accustomed himself to walk in an erect posture, and went almost a tip-toe;—by a ludicrous conceit, he used to hang by the hands to the rafters and balustrades, supposing that an exercise, which could only lengthen his arms, would produce the same effect on his legs and body. In this course of training for the contingent honour of being chosen by the master-sweeps, as one fit for their use,—with a perseverance truly admirable, his tender age considered, young Blincoe continued till the important day arrived. The boys were brought forth, many of them in tears, and all except Blincoe, very sorrowful. Amongst them, by an act unauthorised by his guardians, young

Blincoe contrived to intrude his person. His deportment formed a striking contrast to that of all his comrades: his seemed unusually high: he smiled as the grim looking fellows approached him; held his head as high as he could, and, by every little artifice in his power, strove to attract their notice, and obtain the honour of their preference. While this fatherless and motherless child, with an intrepid step, and firm countenance, thus courted the smiles of the sooty tribe, the rest of the boys conducted themselves as if they nothing so much dreaded, as to become the objects of their choice, and shrunk back from their touch as if they had been tainted by the most deadly contagion. Boy after boy was taken, in preference to Blincoe, who was often handled, examined, and rejected. At the close of the show, the number required was elected, and Blincoe was not among them! He declared, that his chagrin was inexpressible, when his failure was apparent.

Some of the sweeps complimented him for his spirit, and, to console him, said, if he made a good use of his time, and contrived to grow a head taller, he might do very well for a fag, at the end of a couple of years. This disappointment gave a severe blow to the aspiring ambition of young Blincoe, whose love of liberty was so ardent, that he cared little about the sufferings by which, if attained, it was likely to be alloyed. The boys that were chosen, were not immediately taken away. Mingling with these, some of them said to our hero, the tears standing in their eyes:—"why, Parson, can you endure the thought of going to be a chimney-sweep? I wish they would take you instead of me?" "So do I, with all my heart," said Blincoe, "for I would rather be any where than here." At night, as Blincoe lay tossing about, unable to sleep; because he had been rejected, his unhappy associates were weeping and wailing, because they had been accepted! Yet, his heart was not so cold as to be unaffected by the wailings of those poor children, who, mournfully anticipating the horrors of their new calling, deplored their misfortune in the most touching terms. They called upon their parents, who, living or dead, were alike unable to hear them, to come and save them! What a difference of feeling amongst children of the same unfortunate class! The confinement that was so wearisome to young Blincoe, must have been equally irksome to some of his young associates; therefore, the love of liberty could not have been its sole cause,—there was another and a stronger reason—all his comrades had friends, parents, or relations: poor Blincoe stood alone! no ties of consanguinity or kindred bound him to any particular portion of society, or to any place—he had no friend to soothe his troubled mind—no domestic circle to which, though excluded for a time, he might hope to be reunited. As he stood thus estranged from the common ties of nature, it is the less to be wondered at, that, propelled by a violent inclination to a rambling life, and loathing the restraint imposed by his then condition, he should indulge so preposterous a notion, as to prefer the wretched state of a sweeping-boy. Speaking on this subject, Blincoe said to me, "If I could penetrate the source of my exemption from the sorrow and consternation so forcibly expressed by my companions, it would probably have been resolved by the peculiarity of my destiny, and the privation of those endearing ties and ligatures which cement family circles. When the friends, relatives, parents of other children came to visit them, the caresses that were sometimes exchanged, the joy that beamed on the faces of those so favoured, went as daggers to my heart; not that I cherished a feeling of envy at their good fortune; but that it taught me more keenly to feel my own forlorn condition. Sensations, thus excited, clouded every festive hour, and, young as I was, the voice of nature, instinct, if you will, forced me to consider myself as a moral outcast, as a scathed and blighted tree, in the midst of a verdant lawn."

I dare not aver, that such were the very words Blincoe used, but they faithfully convey the spirit and tendency of his language and sentiments. Blincoe is by no means deficient in understanding: he can be witty, satirical, and pathetic, by turns, and he never showed himself to such advantage, as when expatiating upon the desolate state to which his utter ignorance of his parentage had reduced him.

During Blincoe's abode at St. Pancras, he was inoculated at the Small Pox Hospital. He retained a vivid remembrance of the copious doses of salts he had to swallow, and that his heart heaved, and his hand shook as the nauseous potion approached his lips. The old nurse seemed to consider such conduct as being wholly unbecoming a *pauper child;* and chiding young Blincoe, told him, he ought to "lick his lips," and say thank you, for the good and wholesome medicine provided for him at the public expense: at the same time, very coarsely reminding him of the care that was taken to save him from an untimely death by catching the small-pox in the natural way. In the midst of his subsequent afflictions, in Litton Mill, Blincoe declared, he often lamented having, by this inoculation, lost a chance of escaping by an early death, the horrible destiny for which he was preserved.

From the period of Blincoe's disappointment, in being rejected by the sweeps, a sudden calm seems to have succeeded, which lasted till a rumour ran through the house, that a treaty was on foot between the Churchwardens and Overseers of St. Pancras, and the owner of a great cotton factory, in the vicinity of Nottingham, for the disposal of a large number of children, as apprentices, till they became twenty-one years of age. This occurred about a twelvemonth after his chimney-sweep miscarriage. The rumour itself inspired Blincoe with new life and spirits: he was in a manner intoxicated with joy, when he found, it was not only confirmed, but that the number required was so considerable, that it would take off the greater part of the children in the house,—poor infatuated boy! delighted with the hope of obtaining a greater degree of liberty than he was allowed in the workhouse,—he dreamed not of the misery that impended, in the midst of which he could look back to Pancras as to an Elysium, and bitterly reproach himself for his ingratitude and folly.

Prior to the show-day of the pauper children to the purveyor or cotton master, the most illusive and artfully contrived falsehoods were spread, to fill the minds of those poor infants with the most absurd and ridiculous errors, as to the real nature of the servitude, to which they were to be consigned. It was gravely stated to them, according to Blincoe's statement, made in the most positive and solemn manner, that they were all, when they arrived at the cotton-mill, to be transformed into ladies and gentlemen: that they would be fed on roast beef and plum-pudding—be allowed to ride their masters' horses, and have silver watches, and plenty of cash in their pockets. Nor was it the nurses, or other inferior persons of the workhouse, with whom this vile deception originated; but with the parish officers themselves. From the statement of the victims of cotton-mill bondage, it seems to have been a constant rule, with those who had the disposal of parish children, prior to sending them off to cotton-mills, to fill their minds with the same delusion. Their hopes being thus excited, and their imaginations inflamed, it was next stated, amongst the innocent victims of fraud and deception, that no one could be *compelled* to go, nor any but volunteers accepted.

When it was supposed at St. Pancras, that these excitements had operated sufficiently powerful to induce a ready acquiescence in the proposed migration, all the children, male and female, who were seven years old, or considered to be of that age, were assembled in the committee room, for the purpose of being publicly examined, touching their health, and capacity, and what is almost incredible, touching their *willingness* to go and serve as apprentices, in the way and manner required! There is something so detestable in this proceeding, that any one might conclude, that Blincoe had been misled in his recollections of the particulars; but so many other sufferers have corroborated his statement, that I can entertain no doubt of the fact. This exhibition took place in August 1799, and eighty boys and girls as parish apprentices, and till they had respectively acquired the age of twenty-one years, were made over, by the churchwardens and overseers of Saint Pancras parish, to Messrs. Lamberts', cotton-spinners, hosiers and lace-men, of St. Mary's parish, Nottingham, the owners of Lowdham Mill. The boys, during the latter part of their time, were to be instructed in the trade of stocking weaving—the girls in lace-making. There was no specification whatever, as to the time their masters were to be allowed to work these poor children, although, at this period, the most abhorrent cruelties were notoriously known to be exercised, by the owners of cotton-mills, upon parish apprentices. According to Blincoe's testimony, so power-fully had the illusions, purposely spread to entrap these poor children, operated, and so completely were their feeble minds excited, by the blandishments held out to them, that they almost lost their wits. They thought and talked of nothing but the scenes of luxury and grandeur, in which they were to move. Nor will the reflecting reader feel surprised at this credulity, however gross, when he considers the poor infants imagined there were no greater personages than the superiors, to whom they were, as paupers, subjected, and that, it was those identical persons, by whom their weak and feeble intellects had thus been imposed upon. Blincoe describes his own conduct to have been marked by peculiar extravagance. Such was his impatience, he could scarcely eat or sleep, so anxiously did he wait the hour of emancipation. The poor deluded young creatures were so inflated with pride and vanity, that they strutted about like so many dwarfish and silly kings and queens, in a mock tragedy. "We began," said Blincoe, "to treat our old nurses with airs of insolence and disdain—refused to associate with children, who, from sickness, or being underage, had not been accepted; they were commanded to keep their distance; told to know their betters; forbidden to mingle in our exalted circle! Our little coterie was a complete epitome of the effects of prosperity in the great world. No sooner were our hearts cheered by a prospect of good fortune, than its influence produced the sad effects recited. The germ of those hateful vices, arrogance, selfishness and ingratitude, began to display themselves even before we had tasted the intoxicating cup. But our illusion soon vanished, and we were suddenly awakened from the flattering dream, which consigned the greater part of us to a fate more severe than that of the West Indian slaves, who have the good fortune to serve humane owners." Such were Blincoe's reflections in May 1822.

It appears that the interval was not long, which filled up the space between their examination, acceptance, and departure from St. Pancras workhouse, upon their way to Nottingham; but short as it was, it left room for dissension. The boys could not agree who should have the *first ride* on their masters' horses, and violent disputes arose amongst the girls, on subjects equally ludicrous. It was afterwards whispered at Lowdham Mill, that the elder girls, previous to leaving Pancras, began to feel scruples, whether their dignity would allow them to drop the usual bob-curtsey to the master or matron of the house, or to the governess by whom they had been instructed to read, or work by the needle. Supposing all these follies to have been displayed to the very letter, the poor children were still objects of pity; the guilt rests upon those by whom they had been so wickedly deceived!

Happy, no doubt, in the thought of transferring the burthen of the future support of fourscore young paupers to other parishes, the churchwardens and overseers distinguished the departure of this juvenile colony by acts of munificence. The children were completely new clothed, and each had two suits, one for their working, the other for their holiday dress—a shilling, in money, was given to each—a new pocket handkerchief—and a large piece of gingerbread. As Blincoe had no relative of whom to take leave, all his anxiety was to get outside the door. According to his own account, he was the first at the gate, one of the foremost who mounted the waggon, and the loudest in his cheering. In how far the parents or relatives of the rest of the children consented to this migration; if they were at all consulted, or even apprised of its being in contemplation, formed no part of Blincoe's communications. All he stated was, that the whole of the party seemed to start in very high spirits. As to his own personal conduct, Blincoe asserts, he strutted along dressed in party-coloured parish clothing, on his way to the waggon, no less filled with vanity than with delusion: he imagined he was free, when he was in fact legally converted into a slave: he exulted in the imaginary possession of personal liberty, when he was in reality a prisoner. The whole convoy were well guarded by the parish beadles on their way to the waggons; but those officers, bearing their staves, the children were taught to consider as a guard of *honour*. In addition to the beadles, there was an active young man or two, appointed to look after the passengers of the two large waggons, in their conveyance to Nottingham. Those vehicles, and very properly too, were so secured, that when once the grated doors were locked, no one could escape. Plenty of clean straw was strewed in the beds, and no sooner were the young fry *safe lodged* within, than they began throwing it over one another and seemed delighted with the commencement of their journey. A few hours progress considerably damped this exultation. The inequality of the road, and the heavy jolts of the waggon, occasioned them many a bruise. Although it was the middle of August, the children felt very uncomfortable. The motion of the heavy, clumsy vehicle, and so many children cooped up in so small a space, produced nausea and other results, such as sometimes occur in Margate hoys. Of the country they passed through, the young travellers saw very little.—Blincoe thinks the children were suffered to come out of the waggon to walk through St. Alban's. After having passed one night in the waggon, many of the children began to repent, and express a wish to return. They were told to have patience, till they arrived at Messrs. Lamberts, when, *no doubt*, those gentlemen would pay every attention to their wishes, and send back to St. Pancras, those who might wish to return. Blincoe, as might have been expected, was not one of those *back-sliders*—he remained steady to his purpose, exulting in the thought, that every step he advanced brought him nearer to the desired spot, where so many enviable enjoyments awaited him, and conveyed him farther and farther from the detested workhouse!

The greater part of the children were much exhausted, and not a few of them seriously indisposed, before they arrived at Nottingham. When the waggons drew up near the dwelling and warehouse of their future master, a crowd collected to see the *live stock* that was just imported from the metropolis, who were pitied, admired, and compared to lambs, led by butchers to slaughter! Care was taken that they should not hear or understand much of this sort of discourse. The boys and girls were distributed, some in the kitchen, others in a large ware-room, washed, combed, and supplied with refreshments; but there was no plum-pudding—no roast beef, no talk of the horses they were to ride, nor of the watches and fine clothing that they had been promised. Many looked very mournful; they had been four days travelling to Nottingham: at a more advanced period of their lives, a travel to the East Indies might not have been estimated as a much more important or hazardous undertaking. After having been well refreshed, the whole of the boys and girls were drawn up in rows, to be *reviewed by their masters,* their friends and neighbours. In Blincoe's estimation, their masters, Messrs. Lamberts', were "stately sort of men." They looked over the children and finding them all right, according to the *invoice,* exhorted them to behave with proper humility and decorum. To pay the most prompt and submissive respect to the orders of those who would be appointed to instruct and superintend them at Lowdham Mill, and to be diligent and careful, each one to execute his or her task, and thereby avoid the punishment and disgrace which awaited idleness, insolence, or disobedience. This harangue, which was delivered in a severe and dictatorial tone, increased their apprehensions, but not one durst open a mouth to complain. The masters and their servants talked of the various sorts of labor to which the children were to apply themselves, and to the consternation and dismay of Blincoe and his associates, not the least allusion was made to the many fine things which had so positively been promised them whilst in London. The conversation which Blincoe heard, seemed to look forward to close, if not to unremitting toil, and the poor boy had been filled with expectations, that he was to work only when it pleased him; to have abundance of money and fine clothes—a watch in his pocket, to feast on roast beef, and plum-pudding, and to ride his masters horses. His hopes, however were, not wholly extinguished, because Nottingham was not Lowdam Mill, but his confidence was greatly reduced, and his tone of exultation much lowered.

The children rested one night at Nottingham in the warehouses of their new masters; the next day they were led out to see the castle, Mortimer-hole and other local curiosities, in the forest of Sherwood, which are so celebrated by bards of ancient times. Many shoes, bonnets, and many other articles of clothing having been lost upon the journey, others were supplied; but withal Blincoe found himself treated as a parish orphan, and he calculated on being received and treated as if he had been a gentleman's son sent on a visit to the house of a friend or relative. By the concurring testimony of other persons who had been entrapped by similar artifices, it appears certain, that the *purveyors* of infant labourers to supply the masters of cotton and silk factories with cheap labourers, adopted this vile, unmanly expedient, in most of their transactions. It will be seen, by the evidence of Sir Robert Peel, Baronet, David Owen, Esq. and other witnesses examined in 1816, that, when children were first wanted to attend machinery in cotton-factories, such was the aversion of parents and guardians to this noxious employment, that scarcely any would submit to consign their offspring to those mills, the owners of which, under the specious pretext of diminishing the burthens occasioned by poor-rates, prevailed on churchwardens and overseers, to put their infant paupers into their hands. Since then, by a gradual progress of poverty and depravity, in the county of Lancashire alone, there are some thousand fathers, mothers, and relatives, who live upon the produce of infant labor, though alloyed by the dreadful certainty, that their gain is acquired by the sacrifice of their children's health and morals, and too frequently of their lives, whereby the fable of Saturn devouring his children, seems realised in modern times.

CHAPTER III.

Lowdham Cotton-Mill, situated near a village of that name, stood ten miles distant from Nottinghan, on the Surhill road: thither Robert Blincoe and his associates were conveyed the next day in carts, and it was rather late when they arrived. The mill, a large and lofty edifice, being surmounted by a cupola, Blincoe, at first, mistook for a church, which raised a laugh at his expense and some jeering remarks, that he would soon know what sort of service was performed there. Another said, he did not doubt but the young cocknies would be very *regular* in their *attendance*. When he came in view of the apprentice-house, which was half a mile distant from the mill, and was told that was *to be his home for fourteen years to come,* he was not greatly delighted, so closely did it resemble a workhouse. There was one source of consolation, however, remaining—it was not surrounded by lofty walls, nor secured by strong gates, as was the case at Pancras. When the first cart, in which was young Blincoe, drove up to the door, a number of villagers flocked round, some of whom exclaimed, "God help the poor wretches."—"Eh!" said another, "what a fine collection of children, little do they know to what a life of slavery they are doomed."—"The Lord have mercy upon them," said a third.—"They'll find little mercy here," said a fourth. The speakers were mostly of the female sex, who, shaking their heads, said,—"Ah! what fine clear complexions!"—"The roses will soon be out of bloom, in this mill." Such were a part of the remarks, which saluted the ears of these children, as they entered the Lowdam mill. In common with his comrades, Blincoe was greatly dismayed, by the gloomy prognostications, which their guardians did all they could to check, or prevent the children from hearing, hurrying them, as rapidly as they could, inside the house.

The young strangers were conducted into a spacious room, fitted up in the style of the dinner-room, in Pancras old workhouse, viz.: with long, narrow deal tables, and wooden benches. Although the rooms seemed tolerably clean, there was a certain rank, oily, smell, which Blincoe did not very much admire. They were ordered to sit down at these tables—the boys and girls apart. The other apprentices had not left work, when this supply of children arrived. The supper set before them consisted of milk-porridge, of a very blue complexion! The bread was partly made of rye—very black, and so soft, they could scarcely swallow it, as it stuck like bird-lime to their teeth. Poor Blincoe stared, recollecting this was not so good a fare as they had been used to at Saint Pancras. Where is our roast beef and plum-pudding, he said to himself. He contrived, with some difficulty, to eat about one half of his allowance. As the young strangers gazed mournfully at each other, the governor and governess, as the master and mistress of the apprentices were styled, kept walking round them and making very coarse remarks. Just as they had passed Blincoe, some of the girls began making faces, and one flung a dab of bread against the wall, where it stuck fast, as if it had been plaister. This caught the eye of the governor— a huge raw-boned man, who had served in the army, and had been a drill serjeant; unexpectedly, he produced a large horse-whip, which he clanged in such a sonorous manner, that it made the house re-echo. In a moment, the face-makers and bread throwers were reduced to solemn silence and abject submission. Even young Blincoe was daunted—he had been one of the ring-leaders, in these seditious proceedings; but so powerful was the shock to his nerves, sustained from the tremendous clang of the horse-whip, it bereft him of all his gaiety, and he sat as demure as a truant-scholar, just previous to his flogging. Yet the master of the house had not uttered a single threat; nor indeed had he occasion; his carbuncled nose—his stern and forbidding aspect and his terrible horse-whip, inspired quite as much terror as was requisite. Knowing, that the apprentices from the mill were coming, this formidable being retired, to the great relief of the young strangers; but so deep an impression had he created, they sat erect and formal, scarcely daring to look beyond the nose. Whilst they were in this subdued and neutralised state, their attention was suddenly and powerfully attracted by the loud shouting of many voices, almost instantly the stone room filled, spacious as it was, with a multitude of young persons of both sexes; from young women down to mere children. Their presence was accompanied by a scent of no very agreeable nature, arising from the grease and dirt acquired in the avocation.

The boys, generally speaking, had nothing on, but a shirt and trowsers. Some few, and but a few, had jackets and hats. Their coarse shirts were entirely open at the neck, and their hair looked, as if a comb had seldom, if ever, been applied! The girls, as well as Blincoe could recollect, were, like the boys, destitute of shoes and stockings. Their locks were pinned up, and they were without caps; very few had on, either jacket or gown; but wore, what, in London, are called, pinafores; in Lancashire, bishops!—that is, long aprons with sleeves, made of coarse linen, that reached from the neck to the heels. Blincoe was no less terrified at the sight of the pale, lean, sallow-looking multitude, than his nostrils were offended by a dense and heavy small of rank oil or grease, that arose at their appearance! By comparison, the new comers appeared like so many ladies and gentlemen. On their first entrance, some of the old apprentices took a view of the strangers; but the great bulk first looked after their supper, which consisted of new potatoes, distributed at a hatch door, that opened into the common room from the kitchen. At a signal given, the apprentices rushed to this door, and each, as he made way, received his portion, and withdrew to his place at the table. Blincoe was startled, seeing the boys pull out the fore-part of their shirts, and holding it up with both hands, received the hot boiled potatoes allotted for their supper. The girls, less indecently, if not less filthily, held up their dirty greasy bishops or aprons, that were saturated with grease and dirt, and having received their allowance, scampered off as hard as they could, to their respective places, where, with a keen appetite, each apprentice devoured her allowance, and seemed anxiously to look about for more. Next, the hungry crew ran to the tables of the new comers, and voraciously devoured every crust of bread and every drop of porridge they had left, and put or answered interrogatories as occasion required.

Thus unfavorable were the impressions produced by the scene that presented itself on his first entrance into a cotton-factory. Blincoe was forcibly struck by the absence of that personal cleanliness which had been so rigidly enforced at St. Pancras. The apprentices were required to wash night and morning; but no soap was allowed, and without it, no dirt could be removed. Their tangled locks covered with cotton flue, hung about their persons in long wreaths, floating with every movement. There was no cloth laid on the tables, to which the new comers had been accustomed in the workhouse—no plates, no knives, nor forks—to be sure the latter utensils were not absolutely necessary with a potato-supper. Instead of salt-cellars, as had been allowed at Pancras, a very stingy allowance of salt was laid on the table, and Blincoe saw no other beverage drunk, by the old hands, than pump water.

The supper being devoured, in the midst of the gossiping that ensued, the bell rang, that gave the signal to go to bed. The grim governor entered to take the charge of the newly arrived boys, and his wife, acting the same part by the girls, appeared every way suitable to so rough and unpolished a mate. She was a large grown, robust woman, remarkable for a rough hoarse voice and ferocious aspect. In a surly, heart-chilling tone, she bade the girls follow her. Tremblingly and despondingly the little creatures obeyed, scarcely daring to cast a look at their fellow travellers, or bid them good night. As Blincoe marked the tears to start in their eyes and silently trickle down their cheeks his heart, responsive sank within him. They separated in mournful silence, scarcely a sigh being heard, nor a word of complaint being uttered.

The room in which Blincoe and several of the boys were deposited, was up two pair of stairs. The bed places were a sort of cribs, built in a double tier, all round the chamber. The apprentices slept two in a bed. The beds were of flock. From the quantity of oil imbibed in the apprentices' clothes, and the impurities that accumulated from the oiled cotton, a most disagreeable odour saluted his nostrils. The governor called the strangers to him and allotted to each his bed-place and bed-fellow, not allowing any two of the newly arrived inmates to sleep together. The boy, with whom Blincoe was to chum, sprang nimbly into his berth, and without saying a prayer, or any thing else, fell asleep before Blincoe could undress himself. So completely was he cowed, he could not restrain his tears. He could not forbear execrating the vile treachery of which he felt himself the victim; but still he declared, it never struck him, at least, not till long afterwards, that the *superiors* of St. Pancras had deceived him. The fault, he thought, lay with Messrs. Lamberts, their new masters. When he crept into bed, the stench of the oily clothes and greasy hide of his sleeping comrade, almost turned his stomach.—What, between grief and dismay, and this nauseous smell, it was dawn of day before Blincoe dropt asleep. Over and over again, the poor child repeated every prayer he had been taught, and strove, by unfeigned piety, to recommend himself to the friend of the friendless, and the father of the fatherless. At last, sleep sealed his weary eye-lids; but short was the repose, he was allowed to enjoy; before five o'clock, he was awakened by his bed-fellow, who springing upright, at the loud tolling of a bell, told Blincoe to dress with all speed, or the governor would flog him and deprive him of his breakfast. Before Blincoe had time to perform this office, the iron door of the chamber, creaking upon its hinges, was opened, and in came the terrific governor, with the horse-whip in his hand, and every boy hastily tumbled out of his crib, and huddled on his clothes with all possible haste! Blincoe and his fellow travellers were the slowest, not being rightly awake. Blincoe said, "Bless me, have you *church-service* so soon?" "Church-service you fool," said one of the larger apprentices, "it is to the mill *service* you are called, and you had better look sharp, or you'll catch it!" Saying this, off he scampered. Blincoe, who was at first amazed at the trepidation, that appeared in the apprentices soon understood the cause. The grim-looking governor, with the carbuncled nose, bearing the emblem of arbitrary rule, a horse-whip, in his hand, made his appearance, and stalking round the chamber, looked in every bed-place: as he passed Blincoe and his young comrades, he bestowed a withering look upon them, which, fully understanding, they hastened below; arrived there, Blincoe saw some of the boys washing themselves at a pump, and was directed to do the same.—The whole mass sat down to breakfast at five o'clock in the morning. The meal consisted of *black bread* and *blue milk-porridge*. Blincoe and his fellow strangers took their places, mingled with the rest of the apprentices, who, marking their dislike of the bread, eagerly seized every opportunity of eating it themselves. Blincoe and his comrades looked wistfully at each other. Consternation sat deeply imprinted on their features; but every tongue was silent; young as they were, they had sense enough to perceive the necessity of submission and the prudence of reserve.

They reached the mill, about half past five. The water was on, from the bottom to the top, in all the floors, in full movement. Blincoe heard the burring sound before he reached the portals and smelt the fumes of the oil with which the axles of twenty thousand wheels and spindles were bathed. The moment he entered the doors, the noise appalled him, and the stench seemed intolerable.

He did not recollect that either of the Messrs. Lamberts were present at the mill, on his first entrance. The newly arrived were received by Mr. Baker, the head manager, and by the overlookers of the respective rooms. They were mustered in the making-up room; the boys and girls in separate divisions. After being looked at, and laughed at, they were dispersed in the various floors of the mill, and set to various tasks. Blincoe was assigned to a room, over which a man named Smith presided. The task first allotted to him was, to pick up the loose cotton, that fell upon the floor. Apparently, nothing could be easier, and he set to with diligence, although much terrified by the whirling motion and noise of the machinery, and not a little affected by the dust and flue with which he was half suffocated. They span coarse numbers; unused to the stench, he soon felt sick, and by constantly stooping, his back ached. Blincoe, therefore, took the liberty to sit down; but this attitude, he soon found, was strictly forbidden, in cotton mills. His task-master (Smith) gave him to understand, he must keep on his legs. He did so, till twelve o'clock, being six hours and a half, without the least intermission.—Blincoe suffered at once by thirst and hunger; the moment, the bell rang, to announce dinner, all were in motion, to get out as expeditiously as possible. Blincoe ran out amongst the crowd, who were allowed to go; never, in his life, before did he know the value of wholesome air so perfectly. He had been sick almost to fainting, and it revived him instantaneously! The cocknies mingled together, as they made progress towards the apprentice-house. Such as were playsome made to each other! and the melancholy seemed to mingle their tears. When they reached the apprentice-room, each of them had a place assigned at the homely board! Blincoe does not remember of what his dinner consisted; but is perfectly sure, that neither roast beef nor plum-pudding made its appearance; and that the provisions, the cookery, and the mode of serving it out, were all very much below the standard of the ordinary fare of the workhouse, in which he had been reared.

During the space of a week or ten days, that Blincoe was kept picking up cotton, he felt at night very great weariness, pains in his back and ancles; and he heard similar complaints from his associates. They might have suffered less had they been taken to the mill at five o'clock, been worked till eight, and then allowed time to eat their breakfast; but six hours confinement, to close work, no matter of what kind, in an atmosphere as foul as that which circulated in a cotton-mill, is certainly injurious to the health and growth of children of tender years. Even in mills worked by water and where the temperature of the air is nearly the same within the mill as without, this is the case; but incomparably more so in mills such as are found in Manchester, where, in many, the average heat is from 70 to 90 degrees of Farenheit's scale. After Blincoe had been employed in the way described, he was *promoted* to the more important employment of a roving winder. Being too short of stature, to reach to his work, standing on the floor, he was placed on a block: but this expedient only remedied a part of the evil; for he was not able by any possible exertion, to keep pace with the machinery. In vain, the poor child declared it was not in his power to move quicker. He was beaten by the overlooker, with great severity, and cursed and reviled from morning till night, till his life became a burthen to him, and his body discoloured by bruises. In common, with his fellow apprentices, Blincoe was wholly dependent upon the mercy of the overlookers, whom he found, generally speaking, a set of brutal, ferocious, illiterate ruffians, alike void of understanding, as of humanity! Blincoe complained to Mr. Baker, the manager, and all he said to him was: —"*do your work well, and you'll not be beaten.*" It was but seldom, either of the masters visited the mill, and when they did, Blincoe found it was useless to complain. The overlooker, who had charge of him, had a certain quantity of work to perform in a given time. If every child did not perform his allotted task, the fault was imputed to this overlooker, and he was discharged: on the other hand, a premium was given, if the full quantity of work was done and not otherwise. If, therefore, Messrs. Lamberts had remonstrated, or had reprimanded the task-masters, by whom the children were thus mercilessly treated, those task-masters could, and most probably would, have said, that if the owners insisted upon so much work being extracted from the apprentices, and a greater quantity of yarn produced, than it was possible to effect by fair and moderate labour, *they must allow them* severity of punishment, to keep the children in a state of continual exertion. Blincoe had not, of course, sense to understand this, the principal, if not the sole cause, of the ferocity of the overlookers; but such was, and is the inhuman policy prevailing in cotton-mills, and whilst that cause remains unchanged, the effect inevitably must be the same. Each of the task-masters, to acquire favor and emolument, urged the poor children to the very utmost!—Such is the driving system, which still holds its course, and which leads to the exhaustion and destruction of annual myriads, and to the most frightful crimes:—and such is the force of avarice, there are plenty of spinners, so depraved, as not only to sacrifice other people's children, but even *their own*. Blincoe was not treated with that sanguinary and muderous ferocity, in this mill, which these pages will soon delineate; but from morning till night, he was continually being beaten, pulled by the hair of his head, kicked or cursed.

It was the custom, in Lowdham Mill, as it is in most water-mills, to make the apprentices work up lost time, by working over hours! a custom, that might not be deemed unreasonable, or found oppressive, if the regular hours were of moderate duration. Blincoe did not say, that this custom was abused in Lowdham Mill, in an equal degree, to what it was in others; but when children of seven years of age, or, by probability, younger, had to work fourteen hours every day in the week, Sundays excepted, any addition was severely felt, and they had to stop at the mill during dinner time, to clean the frames, every other day. Once, in ten days, or a fortnight, the whole of the finer machinery used to be taken to pieces and cleaned, and then they had to remain at the mill from morning till night, and frequently have been unable to find time to get any food from this early breakfast till night, after they had left off, a term frequently extended from fifteen to sixteen hours incessant labour.

As an inducement to the children to volunteer to work, the whole dinner-hour, a premium of a halfpenny was allowed! Small as was the bribe, it induced many, and Blincoe amongst the number! On such occasions, the dinner was brought up in tin cans, and often has Blincoe's allowance stood till night, whilst he was almost famished with hunger, and he has often carried it back, or rather eaten it on the road, cold, nauseous, and covered with flue.

Being half starved, and cruelly treated by his task-masters; being spotted as a leopard with bruises; and still believing his ill-treatment arose from causes beyond the control of the parish officers, by whom he had been disposed of to Messrs. Lamberts, Blincoe resolved to attempt an escape,—to beg his way to London,—to lay his case before the overseers and churchwardens of Saint Pancras, and not only claim redress of injuries, but the fulfilment of the grand promises that had been made to him. "I cannot deny," said Blincoe, "that I feel a glow of pride, when I reflect that, at the age of seven years and a half, I had courage to resent and to resist oppression, and generosity to feel for the sufferings of my helpless associates, not one of whom durst venture to share the peril of the enterprise.—On the other hand," said, he, "I must give them the credit for sincerity; for, if any one had been unguarded or perfidious, who knew of my *intended* expedition, I should have been put under such restraint, as would have effectually prevented a successful attempt to run away! I considered my situation so deplorable, and my state of thraldom so intolerable, that death appeared as a lesser evil. I was not wholly ignorant of the sufferings I might have had to encounter, nor that I might perish on the way, from want of food or shelter, and yet I persevered in an effort, in which, of forty fellow-sufferers, not one had courage to join, although many had parents or relatives, to whom to flee for succour, and I had none! So far, young as I was, I calculated upon difficulty, danger, and sufferings.—In one thing, only, was I deceived; that error consisted in thinking the evils of my then situation intolerable! I had no recollection of calamities so severe, and consequently no standard by which to regulate my judgment. I therefore, rashly determined in my own mind, that my condition admitted of no aggravation,—I was, indeed, soon undeceived! I lived, within the short space of four years, to look back with regret to the comparative degrees of ease, plenty of food, and of all other good things enjoyed at Lowdham Mill!—This sort of knowledge, is, I believe, commonly taught," said Blincoe, "to all the children of misery, as they sink deeper and deeper in woe! The first stage appears the most intolerable; but as they descend, like me, they sink so profoundly in the depths of wretchedness, that in their melancholy progress, those stages and degrees, which, at first, appeared as intolerable, lose all their terrors, in accumulated misery, and the desponding heart, when it takes a retrospective glance at past sufferings, often arraigns its want of patience and fortitude, for murmurings measured by present calamities. Their former condition appeared comfortable! Such was my condition, at a later period, when, to be released from the greater and heavier misery, which I endured at Lowdham, with all its evils, and in the very worst shape, I should have esteemed it as a positive state of happiness." Such was the philosophical reasoning of Robert Blincoe, in 1822. But, to proceed,—steady to his purpose, he embraced the first favourable opportunity of making the projected attempt to escape! He considered his great danger to lie in being retaken on the road between Lowdham and Nottingham; but he knew no other way, and was afraid to make inquiry! When the manager and overlooker of the room he worked in were busy, Blincoe sat off, dressed in his working clothes. His progress began in a sort of canter, looking behind him every fifty yards for the first half-mile, when, finding he had not been seen or pursued, he continued his rapid flight till he reached Buxton, and there, as fate decreed, that flight suddenly terminated; for, as he trotted onwards, a long-shanked, slip-shod tailor, who worked for Lowdham Mill, slid nimbly from his shop-board, which, unfortunately for Blincoe, faced the road, and, placing himself full in the way, with a malicious kind of grin upon his long, lank visage, said, "Oh! young Parson, where art thou running so fast this way?" Saying this, he seized him by the hand, and led him very loath into his cottage, and, giving him a seat in the back part of the room, placed himself between his captive and the door.

Blincoe saw, at one glance, by these precautions, that he was caught. His indignation was so great at first, he would not give any answer; noticing which, his false and artful host said to his wife, "Give the young Parson something to eat and drink,—he is weary, and will be better able to pursue his journey, after he has rested and refreshed himself! The Lord commands us to give food to the hungry, and I dare say," addressing himself to him, "thou art not so full, but thou canst eat a bowl of bread and milk." "I must own, to my shame," said Blincoe, "the carnal man, the man of flesh was caught by the bait! I hungered and I ate, and he gave me so much, and I drank so heartily, that my teeth disabled my legs! To be sure, my fare was not very costly;—it consisted of some oaten bread and buttermilk!"

When this sly fox of a taylor found he could eat no more, still blockading the door, [began] to question Blincoe as to the object of his journey, which the latter frankly explained,—"Aye, I thought so," said the detestable hypocrite, "young parson, I thought so,—I saw Satan behind thee, jabbing his prong into thy ****!—I saw thee running headlong into h—ll, when I stept forth to save thee!" This avowal aroused all Blincoe's indignation, and he was determined to have a scuffle with his perfidious host; but he had swallowed so large a portion of buttermilk, and eaten so much oaten bread, he felt he had lost half his speed! Disdainful, however, of fraud or denial, he again avowed his intention, and its cause. The tailor then commenced an harangue upon the deadly sin of a breach of covenant,—assured Blincoe he was acting under the influence of Satan! that he was liable to be sent to Bridewell, to be flogged, and, when sent back to his work, to be debarred of all liberty, and led to and from the mill with a halter round his neck! Blincoe was neither convinced by this reasoning, nor intimidated by these denunciations; but alas! his gluttonous appetite had disabled him for flight, and being thus disabled, and thus doubly a captive, he made a merit of necessity, and agreed to go back, if his host would be his mediator with Mr. Baker, the manager. This was the precise point to which the jesuitical tailor wished to bring him. Without relinquishing his seat, the treacherous knave doffed his paper cap, and skeins of thread that still hung round his long, shaggy neck,—he combed his black, greasy locks, that hung straight as candles round his lanthorn jaws,—tied a yellow cotton handerkerchief round his neck,—put on a pair of shoes,—took a *crabtree* stick, full of knots, in his right hand, and grasping Blincoe's very tight in his left, he sallied forth on a *work of charity*, as the loathesome hypocrite called his having entrapped and betrayed a poor oppressed orphan child, fleeing from slavery and oppression. "In my heart," said Blincoe, "I detested the wretch with greater bitterness than my task-master; but he held me so tight, I could not escape: and the sight of the bit of crab-tree which he brandished, as he chaunted hymns of thanksgiving, had also no small share of influence in overawing me,—in short, into the counting-house this second Judas led me. After an admonition to beware how again I made an attempt of the kind, the manager gave me a severe but not cruel chastisement." As to the *hospitable* tailor, when he had delivered him up, he slunk away, not waiting to receive Blincoe's thanks. Whether he took the *five shillings,* which Blincoe was afterwards told was the standing reward of those who brought back run-away apprentices, or let it stand till he had five pounds to receive for such services, he cannot ascertain; but he was told, this peeping Tom of Buxton, had rendered many a poor child the same sort of kindness. "In consequence of this scurvy trick," said Blincoe, "I have never been able to conquer the aversion it created against Methodists: although I am bound to believe, the wretch was one of the myriads of *counterfeits,* who flock to their standard from venal and corrupt motives."

After Blincoe had received his punishment, every weal and bruise with which he had started found a fellow. He was handed back to Smith, his task-master, by whom he was laughed at and jeered unmercifully, and worked with an increase of severity. When Blincoe left work, his old associates flocked around him, condoling his misfortune, and offering him half-pence and bits of bread that they had saved! When they heard how the *godly* had caught him, their indignation swelled to such a height, they declared they would drown him in the mill-dam, if ever they had an opportunity. These condolements were grateful to his wounded pride and disappointed hopes. As he retired to his miserable bed, the governor, grinning horribly, made him a low bow in the military style, and gave him a hearty kick on his *seat of honour* at the same instant. In this manner, was he ushered to his bed, laughed at by that portion of the elder apprentices, who had made similar attempts, and had undergone a similar or a more vindictive punishment. Having abandoned all thoughts of escape, Blincoe submitted sullenly and patiently to his fate;—he worked according to his age and stature, as hard as any one in the mill. When his strength failed, and his limbs refused their office, he endured the strap or the stick, the cuff or the kick, with as much resignation as any of his fellow-sufferers. In the faded complexions, and sallow looks of his associates, he could see, as in a mirror, his own altered condition! Many of his comrades had, by this time, been more or less injured by the machinery. Some had the skin scraped off the knuckles, clean to the bone, by the fliers; others a finger crushed, a joint or two nipped off in the cogs of the spinning-frame wheels!—When his turn to suffer came, the fore-finger of his left hand was caught, and almost before he could cry out, off was the first joint—his lamentations excited no manner of emotion in the spectators, except a coarse joke—he clapped the mangled joint, streaming with blood, to the finger, and ran off to Buxton, to the surgeon, who, very composedly put the parts together again, and sent him back to the mill. Though the pain was so intense, he could scarcely help crying out every minute, he was not allowed to leave the frame. He said but little to anyone; but was almost continually bemoaning in secret the cruelty of his fate. Before he was eight years old, Blincoe declared, that many a time he had been tempted to throw himself out of one of the upper windows of the factory; but when he came to look at the leap he purposed taking, his courage failed him— a propensity, he mentioned not as thinking it evinced any commendable feeling, but as an illustration of the natural and unavoidable consequences of working children too hard, and subjecting them to so many severe privations!

About the second year of his servitude, when the whole of the eighty children sent from Pancras Workhouse, had lost their plump and fresh appearance, and acquired the pale and sickly hue which distinguished the factory children from all others, a most deplorable accident happened in Lowdham Mill, and in Blincoe's presence. A girl, named Mary Richards, who was thought remarkably handsome when she left the work-house, and who might be nearly or quite ten years of age, attended a drawing frame, below which, and about a foot from the floor, was a horizontal shaft, by which the frames above were turned. It happened one evening, when most of her comrades had left the mill, and just as she was taking off the weights, her apron was caught by the shaft. In an instant the poor girl was drawn by an irresistible force and dashed on the floor. She uttered the most heart rending shrieks! Blincoe ran towards her, an agonized and helpless beholder of a scene of horror that exceeds the power of my pen to delineate! He saw her whirled round and round with the shaft—he heard the bones of her arms, legs, thighs, &c. successively snap asunder, crushed, seemingly, to atoms, as the machinery whirled her round, and drew tighter and tighter her body within the works, her blood was scattered over the frame and streamed upon the floor, her head appeared dashed to pieces— at last, her mangled body was jammed in so fast, between the shafts and the floor, that the water being low and the wheels off the gear, it stopped the main shaft! When she was extricated, every bone was found broken!—her head dreadfully crushed!—her clothes and mangled flesh were, apparently inextricably mixed together, and she was carried off, as supposed, quite lifeless. "I cannot describe," said Blincoe, "my sensations at this appalling scene. I shouted out aloud for them to stop the wheels! When I saw her blood thrown about like water from a twirled mop, I fainted. But neither the spine of her back was broken, nor were her brains injured, and to the amazement of every one, who beheld her mangled and horrible state, by the skill of the surgeon, and the excellence of her constitution, she was saved!—Saved to what end? the philosopher might ask—to be sent back to the same mill, to pursue her labours upon crutches, made a cripple for life, without a shilling indemnity from the parish, or the owners of the mill! Such was the fate of this poor girl, but, dismal as it was, it will be seen by the succeeding parts of this narrative, that a lot still more horrible awaited many of her fellow-sufferers, whom the parish officers of St. Pancras, pursuant to Acts of Parliament authority, had apprenticed for fourteen years to the masters of Lowdham Cotton Mill. The dreadful spectacle Blincoe had witnessed in the racking of Mary Richards, rendered his employment more odious than ever.

It is already stated, that the food was very ordinary and not very plentiful; the apprentices were so oppressed by hunger that the oldest and most daring sallied out at night and plundered the fields, and frequent complaints were made, and the apprentices got a very bad name, which belonged rather to the masters, in whose parsimony it originated!

When Blincoe had served about three years of his time, an event happened at Lowdham Mill, arising out of the manner in which apprentices were treated, that wrought a complete revolution there, and led to a new era in Blincoe's biography! Among the girls, who were bound apprentices to Messrs. Lamberts of Nottingham and Lowdham, were two sisters, named Fanny and _____Collier, who had a mother residing in London. These young girls finding their health declining from excess of labour, bad provisions, and want of wholesome air and exercise, found means to write a letter to their mother, full of complaints, upon which, the widow undertook a journey to Lowdham, where she resided a fortnight, during which time, she was a reserved and shrewd observer of the condition of her own and of other children, and then returned to the metropolis. As far as Blincoe remembers these circumstances, Mrs. Collier did not make any complaints to Messrs. Lamberts, or to the manager! She reserved such representations for the parish officers of Saint Pancras, which induced them to send down a parochial committee, to inquire into the state and condition of the apprentices. One day, just as the dinner was being served out in the *usual* slovenly manner, without the least notice of the intended visit having been previously given, the Committee arrived, without asking or waiting for permission, they walked into the common room, and tasting the viands upon the table, they found them such as had been described. Whether *conscience* had any concern in the effort to discover and reform abuses in the mill, said Blincoe, I know not; but this I do know, that, if they had had a spark of shame, pity or remorse, the sallow, and sickly appearance of the eighty victims, saying nothing of Mary Richards, who was forever rendered a cripple, ought to have filled them with sorrow and shame, on account of the base and cruel imposition that had been practised in 1799. It is more probable, however, that the atrocious treatment experienced by the thousands and tens of thousands of orphan children, poured forth from our charitable institutions and from parish workhouses, and the dreadful rapidity with which they were consumed in the various cotton-mills, to which they were transported, and the sad spectacle exhibited by most of the survivors, were the real causes, which, in 1802, produced Sir Robert Peel's Bill, for the relief and protection of infant paupers employed in cotton-mills. Hence, the extraordinary liveliness evinced by the overseers and churchwardens of Saint Pancras might have been occasioned by the dreadful scenes of cruelty and oppression developed during the progress of that Bill, which Blincoe never heard of, nor ever saw, till eleven or twelve years after it had passed into a law. It would be difficult to produce a more striking instance of the utter contempt, in which the upstart owners of great establishments treated an act, purposely enacted to restrain their unparallelled cruelty and waste of human life. The act itself declared the masters, owners, or occupiers of every cotton-mill in Great Britain and Wales should have a legible copy of the act, placed in some conspicuous and public part of each mill, and accessible to every one; yet, Blincoe, who was reared in the cotton-mill, never saw or heard of any such law, till eleven or twelve years after it had been enacted! When the committee began their investigation, as to the treatment and condition of the children sent from St. Pancras Workhouse, Blincoe was called up among others and admonished to speak the truth and nothing but the truth! So great however was the terror of the stick and strap, being applied to their persons, after these great dons should be at a great distance, it rendered him, and no doubt the great majority of his fellow sufferers extremely cautious and timid. It is however, likely, that their looks bespoke their sufferings, and told a tale not to be misunderstood. The visitors saw their food, dress, bedding, and they caused, in conjunction with the local magistrates, very great alterations to be made. A new house was ordered to be erected near the mill, for the use of the apprentices, in which there were fewer beds to a given space. The quantity of good and wholesome animal food to be dressed and distributed in a more decent way, was specified. A much more cleanly and decorous mode of cookery and serving up the dinner and other meals was ordered. The apprentices were divided into six classes, and a new set of tin cans, numbered 1, 2, 3, 4, 5, and 6, were made, to be served up to each individual, according to the class to which he or she may belong, to hold the soup or porridge! The old governor was discharged, who had given them all such a fright on their first arrival, and several of the overlookers were dismissed and new ones introduced;—among the latter description of persons was a man, who seemed wholly destitute of humanity—his name was William Woodward—born, I believe, at Crompton Bridge, in Derbyshire. The appearance of this ferocious tyrant at Lowdam Mill proved a much heavier curse, scourge and affliction to Blincoe, than all the grievances which had existed, or were removed! As Woodward's amusement, in tormenting these poor apprentices, will occupy a large space in the next chapter, I shall say little of him in this.

It was the ill fortune of Blincoe and his associates, that, shortly after the reforms specified were introduced, and the hours of labour reduced, so that their situation became every way incomparably more eligible, Lowdam Mill stopped working.

At this period, Blincoe had served about four years of his time, and had learnt to wind rovings, and spin at the throstle, and certainly earned as much money for his master in one week, as would suffice to keep him a month or longer, in meat, drink and clothes; but he had not been instructed in any part of the stocking-trade, nor had he acquired such a degree of knowledge of the cotton-spinning, as might enable him to gain his bread elsewhere.

At this juncture, if justice had been done, the apprentices would have reverted to Saint Pancras parish, and not been abandoned as they were, and turned over to a new master, without any care being taken, that he should, if he took them, abide by the conditions specified in their first indentures, and act up to the regulations introduced at Lowdam Mill.

Blincoe said, he believed the Messrs. Lamberts wrote to the parish officers of Saint Pancras, informing them of the situation of the children, in order that their friends might take back whom they pleased to claim, and if, in this conclusion, Blincoe is right, and these officers neglected to take proper measures for the safety and protection of so large a body of children, as they had

sent to Lowdam Mill, all healthy and straight limbed, they are morally responsible for the unparalleled sufferings to which they were afterwards exposed. When the subject shall again come before Parliament, it will be requisite to have the conduct of the parish officers on this occasion thoroughly investigated, not so much from a wish to have their offences visited with any legal penalty, if such were practicable, as to shew the necessity of abrogating the power invested in them by act of parliament, to place children beyond a given distance from the place of their birth or settlement: and secondly, to deprive them altogether of the power of tearing away children from their parents, and sending them into any manufactories whatever, without the knowledge and consent of their parents, or next of kin. If the parish officers think proper to apprentice them to any of the ordinary and established trades, they ought to have that power independently of their parents. In the mill, where Blincoe was next consigned, the *parish children* were considered, treated, and *consumed as a part of the raw materials;* their strength, their marrow, their lives, were consumed and converted into money! and as their live stock consisting of parish apprentices, diminished, new flocks of victims arrived from various quarters, without the cost of purchase to supply their place!

It is within the compass of probability, that there have been, and are yet, instances, wherein the overseers of the poor, and more especially the *assistant* overseers, who are mere mercenaries, and serve for pay, have been and are, some of them at least, *bribed* by the owners of mills for spinning silk, cotton or woollen yarn, to visit the habitation of the persons receiving parochial aid, and to compel them, when children are wanting, utterly regardless of education, health, or inclination, to deliver up their offspring, or by cutting off the parish allowance, leave them to perish of want!

When Messrs. Lamberts gave up the cotton-yarn establishment, carried on at Lowdam Mill, they permitted all their apprentices who wished to leave their employment in a cotton-mill, to write to their parents and friends, and some few found redeemers; the great bulk were, unhappily left to their fate! Being a foundling, and knowing no soul on earth to whom he could look for succour, Robert Blincoe was one of the unhappy wretches, abandoned to as dismal a destiny as ever befell *a parish apprentice.* It was his evil fortune, with a multitude of fellow sufferers, to be turned over *en masse* to Mr. Ellice Needham, of Highgate Wall, Derbyshire, the master and owner of Litton Mill, near Tideswell.

Before, however, I close this delineation of the character and conduct of the owners of Lowdam Cotton-Mill—Messrs. William, Charles, and Thomas Lambert—it is due to them, if living, whatever may be their fortune, and to their memory, if deceased, to state, that, with the exception of Mary Richards, who

was so dreadfully racked upon a shaft, and her bones mostly broken, not one of the children sent to their mill by St. Pancras parish, were injured as to be made a cripple, nor were they deformed in their knees and ancles. That there were deficiencies as to food and an excess of labour exacted, is clear, by the alterations which were introduced; but still, compared with what they soon afterwards suffered, they were humanely treated.

They were kept decently clad, had a bettermost suit reserved for Sundays and holidays—were occasionally allowed a little time for play, in the open air, and upon Goose *fair-day*, which is, or then was, a great festival at Nottingham— the whole of them were conveyed in carts to that celebrated place, and regaled with furmety, and sixpence in money was allowed to the very youngest! They went pretty regularly to Lowdam Church on Sundays; were not confined within gates and walls, as was the case at most other mills, where parish apprentices were immured! nor were there any iron-bars before the windows! They were *worked hard*; but not so hard as to distort their limbs, nor occasion declines or deaths! Their food latterly was good and cleanly cooked. Their bedding, though coarse, was clean! When they had meat, they were allowed trenchers, knives, forks and spoons. It will presently be seen, when carried away from Lowdam Mill, into what a den of vice, disease and famine, filth and slavery, they were plunged; by what hellions they were worried, and all in defiance of a positive, and recently made law, on purpose for their protection, and in the face of the VISITING MAGISTRATE whose visits were, according to Blincoe's assertion, too frequently directed to the luxurious table of the master, to admit even a chance of justice to the apprentices. May this exposition of crimes and sufferings inflicted upon the friendless, the orphan, the widow's son, induce honest and upright men, senators and legislators, effectually to curb the barbarous propensities of hard-hearted masters, and rescue their nation from a worse stain, than even the African Slave Trade, horrible as was that odious traffic, ever inflicted.

CHAP. IV

The next cotton mill to which poor Blincoe was consigned, together, with those of his companions in tribulation, who had no friend to redeem them from impending misery, belonged to a Mr. Ellice Needham. Like most of his fraternity, his origin was obscure. He is said to have arisen from an abject state of poverty, and had it been by honourable industry, his prosperous fortune had redounded to his credit. Of his primeval state of poverty, it was his weakness to be ashamed. By the profusion of his table, and the splendor and frequency of his entertainments, he seemed to wish to cover and conceal his mean descent.

His house, lawns, equipage, and style of living, completely eclipsed the neighbouring gentry; yet, boundless as was his ostentation, he was in his heart sordidly mean and parsimonious. His cruelty, in wringing from poor friendless orphans, the means of supporting his guilty and unbecoming pomp, sufficiently evinces the baseness of his heart! His mansion, in 1803, and years later, was at Highgate Wall, near Buxton in Derbyshire.

To this arrogant and unfeeling master, Messrs. Lambert made over the unexpired term of years for which the greater part of the parish apprentices had been bound by their respective indentures. What premium was paid, or, if any, I know not. As this master was neither a hosier, nor a lace manufacturer, he had not the power to fulfil the conditions imposed on Messrs. Lamberts, viz. to instruct the girls, during the last year of their time, in lace-knitting, and the boys in stocking-weaving. The consequence was, the poor children lost those important advantages, and those who survived the term of their apprenticeship to Ellice Needham, found themselves without that degree of skill which was requisite to enable them to gain their bread, in almost any other cotton-mill, and could touch none but the very coarsest work.

As Messrs. Lamberts were constrained, by circumstances, to stop their works, it might be, that they had not means to support the apprentices; but were forced to get rid of them with the utmost expedition. There have been instances, where, in case of Bankruptcy, parish apprentices bound to cotton-masters, have been put into carts, driven to the verge of the parish, and there turned adrift without money—without a friend or a place to shelter them. According to Blincoe's account, although Messrs. Lamberts, informed the guardians of the poor of St. Pancras parish, of the necessity they were under of giving up their apprentices, or turning them over to other masters, no steps were taken for the protection of the friendless children, an imputation, the more extraordinary, when the promptitude and decision with which they had acted in the case recited, is considered. It is, therefore, probable, that their activity might be owing to the horrid tales, that had then burst upon the public, descriptive of the cruelty and misery, of which parish children placed out in cotton-mills were the victims. It was, in 1802, that Sir Robert Peel, of Bury, who had the largest number of parish and foundling children, employed in his cotton-mills, of any cotton-master in Great Britain, brought forward his bill for their protection. According to Blincoe's narrative, the committee from St. Pancras arrived at Lowdham Mill, at this juncture, and the reforms introduced at Lowdham Mill, were, therefore, likely to have been owing to the parliamentary agitation of that question; and nothing can be more highly illustrative of the force of public opinion, than this proof of its potent effect on the officers of St. Pancras parish!—Supposing the conjecture to be well founded, at the time the apprentices were removed from Lowdham Mill, this humane act had passed into a law, and had become all but a dead-letter!—It may also have been a reliance upon the effect of that law which induced the parish officers to leave the children to their fate: what *that* fate was will presently appear!

It seems, that Mr. Ellice Needham, the master of Litton Mill, sent to Lowdham, to inspect the condition of the apprentices, who had improved very materially after the introduction of the new regulations. Nothing could be more kind or condescending than Ellice Needham's deportment at Lowdham. To some, he gave money,—to all, he promised most liberal and kind usage: he promised like a Titus: but he performed like a Caligula.

Blincoe could not recollect, with precision, the number of apprentices, male and female, who were removed in carts form Lowdham to Litton Mill. The first day's progress brought them to Cromford, where they halted for the night. The girls were lodged in dwelling-houses; the boys, on straw, in a barn or stable! The next morning, the whole party were marched on foot through the village, as far as Matlock toll-bar, so proud was Woodward (their conductor) of their healthy appearance! Here they again mounted their carts! But this improvement is not imputable to the wholesomeness of cotton-factory employment; but to the effect of the recent modifications introduced at Lowdham Mill, and to their diminished hours of toil.

It was in the gloomy month of November, when this removal took place! On the evening of the second day's journey, the devoted children reached Litton Mill. Its situation, at the bottom of a sequestered glen, and surrounded by rugged rocks, remote from any human habitation, marked a place fitted for the foul crimes of frequent occurrence, which hurried so many of the friendless victims of insatiate avarice, to an untimely grave.

The savage features of the adjacent scenery impressed a general gloom upon the convoy, when Woodward pointed out to them the lonely mill to which they were travelling. As the hands were then at work, all of whom, except the overlookers, were parish children, the conductor of the new comers led them through the mill. The effect of the review filled the mind of Blincoe, and perhaps his unhappy associates, with deep dismay. The pallid, sickly complexions; the meagre, haggard appearance of the Litton Mill apprentices, with their filthy and ragged conditon, gave him a sorrowful foretaste of the dismal fate that apparently awaited him. From the mill, they were escorted to the 'prentice-house, where everything wore a discouraging aspect. Their first meal was water-porridge and oaten cakes: the former thin and ill made—the latter, baked in flat cakes, on iron griddles, about an inch thick; and being piled up in heaps, was liable to heat, ferment and grow mouldy. This was a new and not a very palatable diet. Whilst Blincoe and many of his comrades went supperless to bed, their half-starved comrades, the Litton Mill apprentices, ravenously devoured what the more dainty Lowdham children turned from with loathing, and told them *their stomachs* would come to in a few days, and that they would be glad to pick from a dunghill, the mouldiest pieces, then so disdainfully flung away.

The lodging-room, the bedding, everything was inferior to what it was at Lowdham; and the smell, from oil and filth, incomparably more offensive. Blincoe passed a restless night, bitterly deploring his hard destiny, and trembling at the thought of greater sufferings! Soon after four in the morning, they were summoned to the work, by the ringing of a bell. Blincoe was put to wind rovings. He soon found an immense difference, in his situation, having much more work to perform, and being treated with a brutal severity, hitherto unknown to him.

Blincoe remarked, that few of the apprentices had either knife, fork, or spoon, to use at table, or hats, shoes, or stockings. At Lowdham, particularly during the latter part of their stay there, the children used to wash at the pump, night and day, and were allowed soap! At Litton Mill, they were called out so early, and worked so late, that little or no attention was given to personal cleanliness! On Friday night, the apprentices were washed, combed, and shirted! Blincoe found his companions in a woeful condition: their bodies were literally covered with weals and contusions; their heads full of wounds, and, in many cases, lamentably infested with vermin! The eldest girls had to comb and wash the younger apprentices,—an irksome task, which was carelessly and partially performed. No soap was allowed: a small quantity of meal was given as a substitute; and this from the effects of keen hunger, was generally eaten. The first day's labour in Litton Mill, convinced Blincoe, into what a den of vice and misery he was cast. The overlookers were fierce and brutal, beyond anything he had ever witnessed at Lowdham Mill: to which servitude, terrible as it once appeared, he looked back with regret. In the retrospect of his own conduct, he felt shame and sorrow; for, compared with what he had to perform and to endure, he now considered that he had lived in idleness and luxury at Lowdham. The custom of washing and shifting on Friday night, arose, he said from a notion, that it was more *profitable* to allow those ablutions to be then performed, that the apprentices might be kept to work till *midnight* on Saturday, or even beyond that hour. The apprentices slept about fifty in a room. The governor used to unlock the door of each room when the bell rang:—having unlocked the last room door, he went back to the first, with a switch stick in his hand, and if he found any one in bed, or slowly dressing, he used to lay on without mercy; by which severity, the rooms were soon empty. The apprentices had their breakfast generally of water-porridge, called in this part of Derbyshire "stir-pudding," and oaten cake, which they took in the mill. The breakfast hour was eight o'clock; but the machinery did not stop, and so irregular were their meals, it sometimes did not arrive till ten or eleven o'clock. At other times, the overlookers would not allow the apprentices to eat it, and it stood till it grew cold and covered with flue! Skim-milk, or butter-milk was allowed; but very sparingly, and often in a stinking state, when it was served out. Forty minutes were allowed for dinner; of which time, full one half was absorbed in cleaning the frames. Sometimes the overlookers detained them in the mill the whole dinner-time, on which occasion, a halfpenny was given, or rather promised. On these occasions, they had to work the whole day through, generally *sixteen hours, without rest or food!* These excessive labours, accompanied by comparative starvation, may appear to my reader, as, at first, it did to me, almost *incredible;* but Blincoe's relation, marvellous as it may appear, was afterwards confirmed by individuals, whose narratives *will be given,* and with whom no sort of acquaintance or intercourse had latterly subsisted. Owing to this shamefully protracted time of labour, to the ferocity with which the children were driven by stripes, cuffs, and kicks, and to the insufficiency of food, no less than its bad and unwholesome quality, Blincoe, in common with his fellow-sufferers has often dropped down at the frames, and been so weary, when, at last, he left work, he had given a stronger boy a halfpenny, or a part of his supper, to allow him to lean upon him on his way back to the 'prentice-house.

Bad as was the food, the cookery was still worse. The most inferior sort of Irish-fed bacon was purchased for the consumption of these children, and this boiled with turnips put into the water, I cannot say without washing; but certainly without paring!—Such was the *Sunday* fare of the parish children at Litton Mill. When first Blincoe, and the rest of the children arrived from Lowdham, they noticed many of the other apprentices had neither spoon nor knife: but had to eat as they could, meat, thick-porridge, or broth, nor were the new comers long allowed any such implements. On Sunday, bacon-broth and turnips were served out, which they eat with oaten cake, in dirty wooden bowls. It could not be otherwise, than unpalatable; for the portion of water to be converted into *broth*, was very ample. In this, rusty, half putrid, fish-fed bacon, and unpared turnips were boiled!—A portion of this broth, with coarse oaten cake was served out, as the first course of a frequent Sunday's dinner. Next, the rusty bacon was portioned out with the boiled unpared turnips!—There was generally, a large quantity of broth to spare, which often became very fetid before it was cold. Into this stuff, no better than hog-wash, a few pails more of water were poured and some meal stirred in, and the disgusting mess was served out for supper or the next day's breakfast, as circumstances required. Blincoe declared, that the stench of this broth was often so powerful as to turn his stomach, and yet, bad as it was, keen hunger forced him to eat it. From all these and other sources of sickness and disease, no one will be surprised that contagious fevers arose in the mill; nor that the number of deaths should be such as to require frequent supplies of parish children, to fill up the vacancies. That such numerous draughts made from mills, where there was no increase of building or of machinery, or apparent call for more infant labourers should not have caused parish officers to institute enquiry, as to the fate of their predecessors, goes far toward confirming the worst imputations cast by the surviving sufferers, upon their parochial guardians. The evidence given by Sir Robert Peel and others, before parliamentary committees, will throw still further light on this important subject, and prove how generally the offspring of the poor have been abandoned by their legal guardians, and left at the disposal of greedy and unfeeling sons of traffic. This neglect on the part of parish officers, was the producing cause of many of the avaricous cotton-masters escaping punishment, for offences which richly merited the gallows. Contagious disease, fatal to the apprentices, and dangerous to society, was the degree of magnitude, at which, the independent rich, more, perhaps, from selfish than social feelings, took alarm, and the public prints exposed a part of the existing abuses in cotton-mills, of which parish children were the victims. So horrid were those recitals, and so general and loud the indignation which they excited, that it reached the inmost recesses of the flinty hearts of the great cotton-masters. Their fears taught them mercy, when no longer able to withstand, nor to silence the accusations brought against them by public spirited and disinterested opponents. Some of the greatest delinquents yielded, and even became advocates for the interference of the legislative power, between themselves and their servants. A reference to the appendix will shew, that they were accused by the genuine friends of humanity of aiming, by this concession, to insinuate themselves into the confidence of their opponents, and thereby neutralize and subdue the fine spirit by which they found their grasping, vile, insatiate avarice controlled. Be this as it may, those individuals who took so much pains to obtain the act of 1802, seem to have given themselves no manner of trouble, to see it enforced. Almost before the first year expired, it was considered a dead-letter. Just at this crisis, the cruelties, exercised on apprentices at Litton Mill, were at their height. Excess of toil, of filth, and of hunger, led to the poor children being visited by contagious fevers. This calamity, which often broke, by a premature death, the bands of this vile thraldom, prevailed to such an extent, as to stop the works. At last, such was Blincoe's declaration, he had known forty boys sick at once, being a fourth of the whole number employed in the mill. From the combined testimony of many apprentices, none were considered sick, till it was found impossible, by menaces or by corporeal punishment, to keep them to their work. The medical gentleman, who sometimes attended the sick, aware of the cause of the deaths, used to say, and like a sensible man he spoke:—"It is not drugs, but kitchen physic they want:" and his general prescription was plenty of good bread, beef, soup and mutton broth. When I questioned Blincoe and others, why this medical man did not represent the horrid plight they were in to the magistrates, he said, the surgeon and magistrates were friends and guests of the master and in the frequent habit of feasting with him! Blincoe was among the number of the sick, and remembers pitch, tobacco, &c. being burnt in the chamber, and vinegar sprinkled on their beds and on the floor. Circumstances which sufficiently denote the malignity of the disease, and the serious apprehensions that were entertained. So great has the mortality been, that Mr. Needham felt it advisable to divide the burials, and a part of the dead were buried in Toddington church-yard, although the burial fees were double the charge of those at Tideswell. Notwithstanding this extraordinary degree of sickness and mortality, Blincoe declares that the local magistracy took no manner of notice of these occur-rences!!!

It might be hazardous to trust so far to the memory, the integrity, or the judgment of Blincoe, or to affirm that the conduct of the local magistrates really was thus culpable; but the imputation is corroborated by the total silence of the magistrates of this part of Derbyshire, as to the character and conduct of the owners of Litton Mill, during the parliamentary investigation of 1816,17,18, 19. The concurrent testimony of Blincoe and several of his fellow-sufferrers confirm the fact of contagious fevers having occurred in this mill; of the numerous deaths it occasioned; of the consequent division of the funerals; and of the remarks of the clergyman, by whom the last sad rites were performed; and also, that *once*, there was a Coroner's inquest held! There exists some difference of opinion, as to the material fact, whether the body had not been first deposited in the earth, and afterwards taken up. Not a spark of pity was shown to the sick of either sex: they were worked to the very last moment it was possible for them to work; and when it was no longer possible, if they dropped down, they were put into a wheel-barrow, and wheeled to the 'prentice-house. According to Blincoe's statement, they were left in the common room below, or carried to their berth in the bed-room, and there left to live or die! In this melancholy state, all the change that took place in the diet, was an allowance of some *treacle-tea*, that is, hot water sweetened with treacle. The doctor was seldom called, till the patient was in the agonies of death. Generally speaking, the dying experienced less attention than a sheep or a hog! The owner of Litton Mill was more tender of those animals; because they cost money, and the anxiety of a character like Mr. Needham's could alone be excited by the prospect of a loss of capital! This solicitude was proportioned to the extent of that risk; and as parish children and destitute orphans could be had at a less price than sheep or pigs, to supply the place of those that died, it followed, that they were less thought of. I would not willingly exaggerate the atrocities I am depicting. I would not act so unwisely as to overcharge the picture I am drawing; and it is with some degree of diffidence, I state, in consequence of combined and positive testimony, that no nurses or *nursing* was allowed to the sick, further than what one invalid could do for another! That neither candle nor lamp-light was allowed, nor the least sign of sympathy or regret manifested! These facts, I admit, are so repugnant to every feeling of Christian charity, that they wear the aspect of greatly embellished truths, or, what is but little worse, of malignant fabrications. If they are such, the fault is not mine; for repeatedly, and in the most impressive manner in my power, I admonished Blincoe and his fellow-sufferers, to abstain from falsehood, telling him and them, it would be sure to be detected and lead to their disgrace. What I thought might have more influence with such persons, I also urged the triumph, such baseness on their part, would confer on the cotton master spinners, most distinguished by cruelty and tyranny; yet, still Blincoe and the whole of his former comrades perseveringly and consistently adhered to the truth of the horrid imputations, and declared, if they were called upon, they would at any time confirm their statement. I was bound to given them publicity—if they are founded in truth. If their great features are correctly delineated, no lapse of time ought to be allowed to shelter the delinquents. They should be brought to a public trial; for the imputations extend to too many acts of torture and of wilful deliberate murder; and to the indulgence of propensities, so truly diabolical, as to stagger belief, and yet so well authenticated, as to overpower scepticism. They embrace atrocities exercised upon poor and friendless boys and girls, of a nature no less abominable than the worst of those which apply to that disgrace to womanhood, Elizabeth Brownrig, or more recently, to the unhappy culprit, Governor Wall. There are yet living, perhaps a hundred witnesses who have been partakers of these ferocious inflictions. Many of them, though in the prime of life, are reduced to such a state of decrepitude, as to flash conviction upon the most incredulous, that it could have resulted from nothing but the most unexampled and long continued cruelty. From the continued and relentless exercise of unlimited despotism upon the truly insulated and most friendless of human beings, upon those, for whose especial protection, a law had been then recently enacted, which, had it been enforced, would have efficiently prevented the occurrence of these crimes, and if I were to assert, that it would be difficult, if not impossible, from the record of sufferings inflicted upon Negro slaves, to quote instances of greater atrocity, than what I have, or am about to develope,

I should not exaggerate, nor should I be guilty of bombast, were I to affirm, that the national character had been, and is seriously dishonoured by that system of boundless commercial avarice, in which these detestable crimes originated. It will continue thus shaded, till a full and fair investigation takes place. There never yet was a crisis, when, in the commercial world, the march of avarice was so rapid, or its devastations so extensive upon the morals and well being of society, as within the period embraced by this narrative; a march that seems to acquire celerity in proportion to the increasing spread of its malific *influence*, and to derive *impunity* from the prodigious wealth it accumulates in the hands of a few great and unfeeling capitalists, at the expense of the individual happiness, health, and morals of the millions. This iniquitous system is the prolific parent of that tremendous flood of vice, which has saturated the manufacturing populace, with the most appalling depravity. This has reduced those many hundred thousand weavers, to a state of destitution so extreme, as to render the condition of the most destitute portion, incomparably worse than that of the field-slave in the West India plantations, who has the good fortune to belong to a humane proprietor. This baleful and wide wasting system throws upon the crown the undeserved odium of being the cause or the abettor of these dreadful evils, by which the poor weaver is oppressed; an impression that has neutralized the loyalty of myriads, and fitted them to become, in the hands of unprincipled demagogues, the source of popular commotions, of foul and iniquitous conspiracies, of deep and radical disloyalty. So indurated, so inveterate, is the loathing and aversion cherished towards the executive government, in all its ramifications, by a large portion of weavers, that it has induced multitudes wholly to renouce, to vilify in every practical manner, to degrade christianity! I do not, in this declamation, indulge in light, personal, or selfish motives; for whatever I assert, as positive matter of fact, I hold myself morally responsible, and stand publicly pledged to substantiate my assertion, by adducing, if requisite, not alone the authority on which I make them, but also to *prove* the validity of those authorities.

With this digression, I close the present chapter. In those that follow there will be found a narrative of crimes which cannot fail to excite, in an equal degree, horror and incredulity:—at the recital of acts of wanton, premeditated, gross, and brutal cruelty, scarcely to be equalled in the annals of the Inquisitorial tribunals of Portugal or Spain; yet all those acts of murder and wanton cruelties, have been perpetrated by a solitary master cotton-spinner, who, though perhaps one of the worst of his tribe, did not stand alone; as will be shewn by evidence that cannot be successfully rebutted. Nor was it to be expected that the criminality of that master spinner could fail to produce corresponding depravity amongst the wretched apprentices subjected to his

rude and savage dominion. In the eventful life of W____P____ the depth and
extent of that depravity will be strikingly illustrated!—It will be seen that acts
of felony were committed in the vicinity of Litton Mill, by the parish apprentices, not, if I am rightly informed, from *dishonest intention;* but from a desire
to be transported to Botany Bay; deeming even that alternative preferable to the
endurance of the horrors of the servitude, to which, as parish apprentices, they
had been consigned.

CHAP. V

Recurring to the description, given to me by Robert Bincoe, of the dreadful
state of thraldom, in which, with a multitude of juvenile companions, he was
involved at Litton Mill, I am instructed to say, that as excessive toil, the want
of proper time for rest, and of nourishing wholesome food, gave rise to
contagious diseases, so a liberal supply of good provisions and a cessation from
toil, quickly restored many to health; Instead of taking warning by the results
of these terrible examples, no sooner were the invalids sent back to the mill,
than the system of over-toil, of boundless cruelty, starvation and torture, was
at once resumed. Let it not however be supposed, that any thing in the shape
of dainties had been dispensed to the sick. Wheaten bread, coarse pieces of beef
boiled down in soup, or mutton from broth, with good milk or butter-milk,
sparingly distributed, formed the extent of those indulgences. This diet,
luxurious as it was considered in Litton Mill, did not surpass the ordinary
standard of the daily fare, that Blincoe had enjoyed at St. Pancras workhouse,
and also, during the latter period of his stay at Lowdham Mill.

I have not yet done more than to mention the cuffs, kicks, or scourging, to
which, in common with many other of his unhappy comrades, Blincoe stood
exposed, since, by this account, almost from the first hour in which he entered
the Mill, till he arrived at a state of manhood, it was one continued round of cruel
and arbitrary punishment. Blincoe declared, he was so frequently and immoderately beaten, it became quite familiar; and if its frequency did not extinguish
the sense of feeling, it took away the terror it excited on his first entrance into
this den of ignorance and crime. I asked him if he could state an average number
of times in which he thought he might in safety say, he had suffered corporeal
punishment in a week. His answer invariably was, that his punishments were
so various and so frequent, it was impossible to state with any thing approaching to accuracy. If he is to be credited, during his ten years of hard servitude,
his body was never free from contusions, and from wounds inflicted by the
cruel master whom he served, by his sons, or his brutal and ferocious and
merciless overlookers.

It is already stated, that he was put to the back of a stretching-frame, when he was about eleven years of age, and that often, owing to the idleness, or the absence of the stretcher, he had his master's work, as well as his own to perform. The work being very coarse, the motion was rapid, and he could not keep up to the ends. For this, he was sure to be unmercifully punished, although, they who punished him knew the task assigned was beyond what he could perform. There were different stretchers in the mill: but, according to Blincoe's account, they were all of them base and ferocious ruffians. Robert Woodward, who had escorted the apprentices from Lowdham Mill, was considered the worst of those illiterate vulgar tyrants. If he made a kick at Blincoe, so great was his strength, it commonly lifted him off the floor. If he struck him, even a flat-handed blow, it floored him; If, with a stick, it not only bruised him, but cut his flesh. It was not enough to use his feet or his hands, but a stick, a bobby or a rope's-end. He and others used to throw rollers one after another, at the poor boy, aiming at his head, which, of course was uncovered while at work, and nothing delighted the savages more, than to see Blincoe stagger, and to see the blood gushing out in a stream! So far were such results from deterring the monsters, that long before one wound had healed, similar acts of cruelty produced others, so that, on many occasions, his head was excoriated and bruised to a degree, that rendered him offensive to himself and others, and so intolerably painful, as to deprive him of rest at night, however weary he might be. In consequence of such wounds, his head was over-run by vermin. Being reduced to this deplorable state, some brute of a quack doctor used to apply a pitch cap, or plaister to his head. After it had been on a given time, and when its adhesion was supposed to be complete, the *terrible doctor* used to lay forcibly hold of one corner and tear the whole scalp from off his head at once! This was the common remedy; I should not exaggerate the agonies it occasioned, were I to affirm, that it must be equal to any thing inflicted by the American savages, on helpless prisoners, with their scalping knives and tomahawks.

This same ruffian, (Robert Woodward) who, by the concurrent testimony of many sufferers, stands depicted, as possessing that innate love of cruelty which marked a Nero, a Caligula, or a Robespierre, used when Blincoe could not, or did not keep pace with the machinery, to tie him up by the wrists to a cross beam and keep him suspended over the machinery till his agony was extreme. To avoid the machinery, he had to draw up his legs every time it came out or returned. If he did not lift them up, he was cruelly beaten over the shins, which were bare; nor was he released, till growing black in the face, and his head falling over his shoulder, the wretch thought his victim was near expiring. Then after some gratuitous knocks and cuffs, he was released and instantly driven to his toil, and forced to commence, with every appearance of strength and vigour, though he were so much crippled, as to be scarcely able to stand. To lift the apprentices up by their ears, shake them violently, and then dash them down upon the floor with the utmost fury, was one of the many inhuman sports in Litton Mill, in which the overlookers appeared to take delight. Frequently has Blincoe been thus treated, till he thought his ears were torn from his head, and this for very trivial offences, or omissions. Another of these diabolical amusements consisted in filing the apprentices' teeth! Blincoe was once constrained to open his mouth to receive this punishment, and Robert Woodward applied the file with great vigour! Having punished him as much as he pleased; the brute said with a sneer; "I do this to sharpen thy teeth, that thou may'st eat thy Sunday dinner the better."

Blincoe declared, that he had often been compelled, on a cold winter's day, to work *naked,* except his trowsers, and loaded with two half hundred weights slung behind him, hanging one at each shoulder. Under this cruel torture, he soon sunk; when, to make the sport last the longer, Woodward substituted quarter of hundred weights, and thus loaded, by every painful effort, Blincoe could not lift his arm to the roller. Woodward has forced him to wear these weights for hours together, and still to continue at his work! Sometimes, he has been commanded to pull off his shirt and get into a large square crib, when, the savage, being sure of his mark, and that, not a blow would be lost, used to beat him till he was tired! At other times, Blincoe has been hoisted upon other boys' shoulders, and beaten with sticks till he has been shockingly discoloured and covered with contusions and wounds.

What spinners call a *draw off* at one of those frames at which Blincoe worked, required about forty seconds. Woodward has often insisted upon Blincoe's cleaning all the cotton away under the whole frame, in a single draw, and to go out at the further end, under pain of a severe beating. On one of these occasions, Blincoe had nearly lost his life, being caught between the faller and the head-piece, his head was jammed between them. Both his temples were cut open and the blood poured down each side of his face! It was considered next to a miracle, that he escaped with his life! So far from feeling the least compassion, Woodward beat him cruelly, because he had not made *more haste*! Blincoe says, to the best of his recollection, he was twelve years of age, when this accident happened.

It is a fact, too notorious to be denied, that the most brutal and ferocious of the spinners, stretchers, rovers, &c., have been in the habit, from mere wantonness, of inflicting severe punishments upon piecers, scavengers, frame-tenders, winders, and others of the juvenile class, subjected to their power, compelling them to eat dirty pieces of candle, to lick up tobacco spittle, to open their mouths for the filthy wretches to spit into; all which beastialities have been practised upon the apprentices at Litton Mill! Among the rest, Blincoe has often suffered these indignities. What has a tendency to display human nature in its worst state, is, that most of the overlookers, who acted thus cruelly had arrived in the mill as parish apprentices, and, as such, had undergone all these offensive inflictions!

There was, however, one diversion, which, in all my enquiries as to cotton-mill *amusements* I never found paralleled. Of this Robert Woodward, if I mistake not, has a claim to the honour of being the *original inventor*. It was thus executed.—A tin can or cylinder, about three feet high, to receive the rovings, and about nine or ten inches in diameter, was placed in the midst of the alley or wheel-house, as the space is called, over which the frames travel at every draw, and pretty close to the race. Upon this can or hollow cylinder, Blincoe had to mount; and there to stand upon one foot, holding a long brush extended in the opposite hand, until the frame came out, about three times in two minutes, invariably knocking the can from under him, both fell to the floor. The villain used to place the can so near the race, that there was considerable danger of Blincoe falling on it, and, if so, it would probably have lamed him for life, if it had not killed him on the spot; and he had, with the utmost possible celerity, to throw himself flat upon the floor, that the frame might pass over him! During this short interval, the amateurs, *i.e.*, Robert Woodward, Charnock, Merrick, &c. used to set the can upright again, and it required no small share of ingenuity, in them, to keep time. The frame being returned, poor Blincoe had to leap on his feet, and again to mount nimbly on the hollow column of tin, again to extend his arm, holding the long hair brush, and again sustain a fall, amidst the shouts and yells of these fiends. Thus would the villains continue to persecute and torment him, till they were tired, notwithstanding the *sport* might have been his death. He ran the risk of a broken bone, or the dislocation of a limb, every time he was thus thrown down; and the time the monsters thus wasted, they afterwards made up by additional labour wrung from their wretched victims.

Another of their diversions consisted in tying Blincoe's hands behind him and one of his legs up to his hands. He had then only one leg left free to hop upon, and no use left of his hands to guard him, if he chanced to fall, and if Blincoe did not move with activity, the overlooker would strike him a blow with his clenched fist, or cut his head open by flinging rollers. If he fell, he was liable to have his leg or arm broken or dislocated. Every one conversant with cotton-spinning machinery knows the danger of such *diversions*, and of their cruelty, every one can judge.

There seemed to exist a spirit of emulation, an infernal spirit, it might with justice be designated, among the overlookers of Litton Mill, of inventing and inflicting the most novel and singular punishments. For the sake of being the better able, and more effectually to torment their victims, the overlookers allowed their thumb and fore-finger nails to grow to an extreme length, in order that, when they *pinched their ears*, they might make their nails meet!

Needham himself the owner of the Mill, stands arraigned of having the cruelty to act thus, very frequently, till their blood ran down their necks, and so common was the sport, it was scarcely noticed. As regarded Blincoe, one set of wounds had seldom time to heal, before another set was inflicted; The general remedy that Blincoe applied was, the oil used to keep the machinery in order. The despicable wretches, who thus revelled in acts of lawless oppression, would often, to indulge the whim of a moment, fling a roller at a boy's head, and inflict deep wounds, and this, frequently, without even a shadow of a fault to allege, or even a plausible reason to assign in justification! At another time, if the apprentices stood fair for the infliction of a stripe, with a twig or the whip, the overlookers would apply it, with the utmost vigour, and then, bursting into laughter, call it *a ____ good hit!* Blincoe declared he had, times innumerable been thus assailed, and has had his head cut severely, without daring to complain of the cause. Woodward and others of the overlookers used to beat him with pieces of the thick leathern straps made supple by oil, and having an iron buckle at the end, which drew blood almost every time it was applied, or caused severe contusions.

Among Blincoe's comrades in affliction, was an orphan boy, who came from St. Pancras workhouse, whose proper name was James Nottingham; but better known as *"Blackey,"* a nick-name that was given to him, on account of his black hair, eyes, and complexion. According to Blincoe's testimony, this poor boy suffered even greater cruelties, than fell to his own share! by an innumerable number of blows, chiefly inflicted on his head!—by wounds and contusions, his head swelled enormously, and he became stupid! To use Blincoe's significant expression, "his head was as soft as a boiled turnip." The scalp on the crown, pitting every where on the least compression. This poor boy, being reduced to this most pitiable condition, by unrestrained cruelty, was exposed to innumerable outrages, and was, at last, incapable of work, and often plundered of his food!—melancholy and weeping, he used to creep into holes and corners, to avoid his tormentors. From mere debility, he was afflicted by incontinency of stools and urine! To punish this infirmity, conformably as Blincoe declared, to the will of Ellice Needham, the master, his allowance of broth, butter-milk, porridge, &c. was withheld! During the summer time, he was mercilessly scourged! In winter, stripped quite naked, and he was slung, with a rope tied under his shoulders, into the dam, and dragged to and fro, till he was nearly suffocated. They would then draw him out, and sit him on a stone, under a pump, and pump upon his head, in a copious stream, while some stout fellow was employed to sluice the poor wretch with pails of water, flung with all possible fury into his face. According to the account I received, not alone Blincoe is, but several other of the Litton Mill apprentices, when these horrid inflictions had reduced the poor boy to a state of idiotism,—his wrongs and sufferings,—his dismal condition,—far, from exciting sympathy, but increased the mirth of these vulgar tyrants! His wasted and debilitated frame was seldom, if ever, free from wounds and contusions, and his head covered with running sores and swarming with lice, exhibited a loathsome object! In consequence of this miserable state of filth and disease, poor Nottingham has many times had to endure the excruciating torture of the pitch and scalping cap already named!

Having learnt, in1822, that this forlorn child of misery was then at work in a cotton factory, near Oldfield Lane, I went in search of and found him. At first, he seemed much embarrassed, and when I made enquiries as to his treatment at Litton Mill, to my surprise he told me, "he knew nothing whatever about it." I then, related what Blincoe and others had named to me, of the horrid tortures he endured. "I dare say," said he mildly, "he told you truth, but I have no distinct recollection of anything that happened to me during the greater part of the time I was there! I believe," said he, "my sufferings were most dreadful, and that I nearly lost my senses." From his appearance, I guessed he had not been so severely worked as others of the poor crippled children whom I had seen! As well as I can recollect, his knees were not deformed, or if at all, but very little! He is much below the middle size, as to stature. His countenance round, and his small and regular features, bore the character of former sufferings and present tranquility of mind.

In the course of my enquiries respecting this young man, I was much gratified, by hearing the excellent character given him in the vicinity of his lodging. Several persons spoke of him as being serious and well inclined, and his life and conduct irreproachable.

It might be supposed, that these horrid inflictions had been practised, in this cotton-factory, unknown to the master and proprietor of Litton Mill; but the testimony, not of Blincoe alone, but of many of his former associates, unknown to him, gave similar statements, and like Blincoe, described Ellice Needham the master, as equalling the very worst of his servants in cruelty of heart! So far from having taken any care to stop their career, he used to animate them by his own example to inflict punishment in any and every way they pleased; Mr. Needham stands accused of having been in the habit of knocking down the apprentices with his clenched fists;—kicking them about when down, beating them to excess with sticks, or flogging them with horse-whips; of seizing them by the ears, lifting them from the ground and forcibly dashing them down on the floor, or pinching them till his nails met! Blincoe declares his oppressors used to seize him by the hair of his head and tear it off by a handful at a time, till the crown of his head had become as bald as the back of his hand! John Needham, following the example of his father, and possessing unlimited power over the apprentices, lies under the imputation of crimes of the blackest hue, exercised upon the wretched creatures, from whose laborious toil, the means of supporting the pomp and luxury in which he lived were drawn. To the boys, he was a tyrant and an oppressor! To the girls the same, with the additional odium of treating them with an indecency as disgusting as his cruelty was terrific.

For some trivial offence, Robert Woodward once kicked and beat Robert Blincoe, till his body was covered with wheales and bruises. Being tired, or desirous of affording his young master the luxury of amusing himself on the same subject, he took Blincoe to the counting-house, and accused him of wilfully spoiling his work. Without waiting to hear what Blincoe might have to urge in his defence, young Needham eagerly looked about for a stick; not finding one at hand, he sent Woodward to an adjacent coppice, called the Twitchell, to cut a supply, and laughingly bade Blincoe strip naked, and prepare himself for a good *flanking!* Blincoe obeyed, but to his agreeable surprise, young Needham abstained from giving him the promised flanking. The fact was, the poor boy's body was so dreadfully discoloured and inflamed by contusions, its appearance terrified the young despot, and he spared him, thinking that mortification and death must ensue, if he laid on another "flanking." Hence his unexpected order to Blincoe to put on his things! There was not, at the time, a free spot on which to inflict a blow! His ears were swollen and excoriated; his head, in the most deplorable state imaginable; many of the bruises on his body had suppurated! and so excessive was his soreness, he was forced to sleep on his face, if sleep he could obtain, in so wretched a condition!

Once a week, and generally after sixteen hours of incessant toil, the eldest girls had to comb the boys' heads; an operation, that being alike painful to the sufferer, as disgusting to the girls, was reluctantly endured, and inefficiently performed. Hence arose the frequency of scald-heads, and the terrible scalping remedy! Upon an average, the children were kept to work during a great part, if not all, the time Blincoe was at Litton Mill, sixteen hours in the day. The result of this excessive toil, superadded to hunger and torture, was the death of many of the apprentices, and the entailment of incurable lameness and disease on many others.

The store pigs and the apprentices used to fare pretty much alike; but when the swine were hungry, they used to squeak and grunt so loud, they obtained the wash first, to quiet them. The apprentices could be intimidated, and made to keep still. The fatting pigs fared luxuriously, compared with the apprentices! They were often regaled with meal-balls made into dough, and given in the shape of dumplings! Blincoe and others, who worked in a part of the Mill, whence they could see the swine served, used to say to one another—*"The pigs are served; it will be our turn next."* Blincoe and those who were in the part of the building contiguous to the pigsties, used to keep a sharp eye upon the fatting pigs, and their meal-balls, and, as soon as he saw the swineherd withdraw, he used to slip down stairs, and, stealing slyly towards the trough, plunge his hand in at the loop holes, and steal as many dumplings as he could grasp! The food thus obtained from a pig's trough, and, perhaps, defiled by their filthy chops, was exultingly conveyed to the privy or the duck-hole, and there devoured with a much keener appetite, than it would have been by the pigs; but the pigs, though generally esteemed the most stupid of animals, soon hit upon an expedient, that baffled the hungry boys; for the instant the meal-balls were put into their troughs, they voraciously seized them, threw them into the dirt, out of the reach of the boys! Not this alone; but, made wise by repeated losses, they kept a sharp look out, and the moment they ascertained the approach of the half-famished apprentices, they set up so loud a chorus of snorts and grunts, it was heard in the kitchen, when out rushed the swine-herd, armed with a whip, from which combined means of protection for the swine, this accidental source of obtaining a *good dinner* was soon lost! Such was the contest carried on for a time at Litton Mill, between the half-famished apprentices, and the well-fed swine.

I observed to Blincoe, it was not very rational, to rob the pigs, when they were destined to bleed to supply them with food, as soon as they grew sufficiently fat! "Oh! you're mistaken," said he, "these pigs were fatted for master's own table, or were sold at Buxton! We were fed upon the very worst and cheapest of Irish-fed bacon." There was, it seems, a small dairy at Litton Mill; but the butter was all sent to his house. The butter-milk alone was dispensed, and but very scantily, to the apprentices. About a table-spoonful of meal was distributed once a week to the apprentices, with which to wash themselves, instead of soap; but in nine cases out of ten, it was greedily devoured, and a piece of clay or sand, or some such thing, substituted: such was the dreadful state of hunger in which these poor children were kept in this mill.

To attempt a specific statement, how often Blincoe has been kept to work from five in the morning till midnight, during his period of servitude, would be hazardous! According to his own testimony, supported by that of many others, it was, at times, of common occurrence, more especially on the Saturday! In most mills, the adult spinners left off on that day at *four* in the afternoon, whilst in these, where parish apprentices were employed, it was often continued, not only till midnight; but till six o'clock on the Sunday morning!

Exertion so incessant could not fail to reduce the majority of apprentices to a state of exhaustion and lassitude, so great as nearly to disqualify them to benefit by such instructions as an illiterate clown could afford, who officiated on Sundays as schoolmaster, or by divine worship, when they were allowed to attend. Nothing could be more cheerless, than the aspect of these juvenile sufferers, these helpless outcasts, nor more piteous than the wailings and lamentations of that portion, chiefly of the tenderest years, whom long familiarity with vice and misery had not rendered wholly callous.

A blacksmith, or mechanic, named William Palfry, who resided at Litton, worked in a room under that where Blincoe was employed. He used to be much disturbed by the shrieks and cries of the boys, whom the manager and overlookers were almost continually punishing. According to Blincoe's declaration, and that of others, human blood has often run from an upper to a lower floor, shed by these merciless taskmasters. Unable to bear the shrieks of the children, Palfry used to knock against the floor, so violently, as to force the boards up, and call out "for shame! for shame! are you murdering the children?" He spoke to Mr. Needham, and said, he would not stay in the mill, if such doings were allowed. By this sort of conduct, the humane blacksmith was a check on the cruelty of the brutal overlookers, as long as he continued in his shop; but he went away home at seven o'clock, and as soon as Woodward, Merrick, and Charnock knew that Palfry was gone, they used to pay off the day's score, and to beat and knock the apprentices about without moderation or provocation, giving them black eyes, broken heads; saying, "I'll let you know old Palfry is not here now!" To protract the evil hour, the boys, when they used to go down stairs for rovings, would come back and say—"Palfry and the joiner are going to work all night," and sometimes by this manoeuvre, they have escaped punishment.

It happened one day, when Blincoe was about twelve years old, he went to the counting-house with a cop, such being the custom at every doffing. While Blincoe was there, another apprentice, named Isaac Moss, came in on the same errand. Upon the floor stood the tin treacle can, with about 14 pounds of treacle. The sight arrested the attention of Blincoe, who said softly, "Moss, there is the treacle can come from Tideswell!"—"Eh," Moss exclaimed, "so it is." Blincoe said, "I have no spoon." Moss rejoined, "I have two." Putting his hand to his bosom and pulling out the bowl of an iron spoon and another which he kept for another person, down they sat on the floor opposite to each other, with the can between them and began operations, ladling away as fast as they could! Blincoe had a large sized mouth, and in good condition; but the ruffian, Woodward, having struck Moss a severe blow on the mouth, with a large stick, it had swollen so much, that the poor lad had the mortification of hardly being able to use it, and Blincoe could stow away at least three spoonfuls to Moss's one! While the conscious pair were thus employed, the enemy, unheard and unperceived, stole upon them. It was a dark night; but there was a fire in the counting-house, by the light of which, over some glass above the top of the door, that grim spectre, the terror and the curse of these poor boys, Woodward, saw their diversion! He stood viewing them some time, when suddenly rushing upon them, he seized upon them as a cat pounces upon cheese-eating mice! Blincoe, being most active with his feet, as well as with his spoon, after receiving a few kicks and cuffs, ran off to the factory, leaving Moss in the power, and at the mercy of Woodward.

At ten o'clock, the factory bell rang, and Blincoe went off to the apprentice-house, trembling with apprehension and looking wildly around amongst the apprentices, in hopes of seeing his comrade Moss; but Moss was not to be seen! Presently, an order arrived from Woodward, for the master of the apprentices to bring down Blincoe! Richard Milner, the then governor of the apprentices, a corpulent old man, said, "Parson, what hast thou been doing?"— "Nothing," said the parson; his tremulous voice and shaking limbs contradicting his laconic reply; and away they trudged. When they got to the counting-house, they found Moss stuck erect in a corner, looking very poorly, his mouth and cheeks all over treacle. Woodward, in a gruff voice, said, "So you have been helping to eat this treacle?"—"I have only eaten a little, Sir." Upon which, he hit Blincoe one of his flat-handed slaps, fetching fire from his eyes, and presently another, another, and another, till Blincoe began to vociferate for mercy, promising never to eat forbidden treacle any more! Woodward was full six feet high, with long arms, huge raw bones and immense sized hands, and when he had tired himself with beating Blincoe, he exclaimed: "Damn your bloods, you rascals, if you don't lap up the whole can of treacle, I'll murder you on the spot." This denunciation was music to Blincoe's ears, who had never before received such an invitation. To accommodate the young gentlemen, the governor sent to his own kitchen for two long spoons, and then, with renewed execrations, Woodward bade them set to. Moss then crept softly and silently out of his corner, having been cruelly beaten in Blincoe's absence! Looking ruefully at each other, down the culprits knelt a second time, one on each side of the treacle can! Blincoe had still the best of the sport; for poor Moss's mouth remained deprived of half its external dimensions, and being so excessively sore, he could hardly get in a tea-spoon, where Blincoe could shovel in large table-spoonfuls! Moss kept fumbling at his lame mouth, and looking rather spitefully at Blincoe, as if he thought he would eat all the treacle. Meanwhile

Milner and Woodward sat laughing and chatting by the fire-side, often looking at the treacle-eaters, and anxiously waiting an outcry for quarter! Blincoe ate in a masterly style; but poor Moss could not acquit himself half as well, the treacle trickling down his chin, on both sides of his mouth, seeing which, Woodward suddenly roared out, "Damn you, you villain, if you don't open your mouth wider, I'll open it for you." Poor Moss trembled; but made no reply, and Blincoe being willing to make hay while the sun shone, instead of falling off, seemed, at every mouthful, to acquire fresh vigour! This surprised and mortified Woodward not a little, who, seeing no signs of sickness, hearing no cry for quarter, and being apprehensive of an application for another can, got up to reconnoitre, and, to his amazement, found that the *little Parson*, who was not a vast deal higher than the can, had almost reached the bottom, and displayed no visible loss or diminution of appetite!

Inexpressibly vexed at being thus outwitted before the governor, he roared out in a tremendous voice to Milner, "Why damn their bloods, they'll eat the whole! Halt, you damned rascals, or, I'll kill you on the spot!" In a moment, Blincoe ceased his play, and licked his lips and spoon, to shew how keen his stomach still was! Milner and Woodward then took stock, and found, that, out of fourteen pounds, not three remained; Milner laughed immoderately at Woodward, to think what a luscious mode of punishment he had found out for treacle stealers!—Woodward being extremely exasperated, ordered Samuel Brickman, an overlooker, to fasten Moss and Blincoe together with handcuffs, of which, as well as of *fetters*, there were plenty at Litton Mill, and then forced them to carry the can to the apprentice-house between them. When they arrived at the door, his hand being small, Blincoe contrived to withdraw it from the handcuff, and ran nimbly off into the room amongst the apprentices, leaving the treacle can in Moss's hand. Brickman, unconscious of Blincoe's escape, arrived in the kitchen, where the Governor and his family resided, looked round, and seeing only one prisoner, cried out, "Eh! where's Parson gone." Moss said, he believed he was gone into the apprentice-house. Brickman examined the handcuffs, and finding they were locked, was much puzzled to think how the parson had contrived to get his hand out. The kind and careful Mrs. Milner, knowing that there was money due to Blincoe, for working his dinner-hour, viz. a farthing a day, proposed to have it stopped, to pay for the treacle which Woodward had compelled him to eat, on pain of putting him instantly to death. Such was the law and equity, which prevailed at Litton Mill! That night, in consequence of his sumptuous supper, Blincoe was forbidden to enter his bed, and he laid all night, in the depth of winter, on the hard cold floor.

This part of the subject requires an explanation, as to the equivalent given by the owner to the apprentices, in lieu of their dinner-hour. This hour consisted, in general, of forty minutes, and not always so many. The master, to induce the apprentices to work all day long, promised each three-pence per week, if they worked the whole of the dinner hour, and they had to eat it, *bite and sup*, at their work, without spoon, knife, or fork, and with their dirty, oily fingers! They were thus kept on their feet, from five o'clock in the morning, till nine, ten, and even eleven o'clock at night, and on Saturdays, sometimes till twelve; because Sunday was a *day of rest!* Frequently, though almost famishing, the apprentices could not find time to eat their food at all; but carried it back with them at night, covered with flue and filth. This liberality did not last long. The halfpenny was reduced to a farthing, and this farthing was withheld till it amounted to several shillings, and then, when the master pleased, he would give a shilling or two, and none dare ask for more. Those whom the overlookers pleased to order so to do, had to work their dinner hour for nothing, and their comrades used to fetch their dinners, who, not unfrequently, pilfered a part. The money thus earned, the poor 'prentices used to reserve, to buy wheaten cakes, and red herrings, to them, luxuries of the most delicious kind. Such was the miserable manner in which they were fed, that, when they gave the pence to Palfry (the smith,) to bring the tempting cake of wheaten flour, and the herring, in the morning, they used to say to their comrades, "Old Palfry is to bring me a cake and herring in the morning. Oh! how greedily I shall devour them." They commonly dreamt of these anticipated feasts, and talked of their expected luxuries in their sleep. When Palfry arrived, they would, if they dared, have met him on the stairs, or have followed him to the smithy; but, in an eager whisper, enquired "have you brought my cake and herring?" "Aye, lad," said Palfry, holding out the expected provisions. Eagerly they seized the herring and the cake, and the first full bite generally took off head or tail, as it came first to hand, while the cake was thrust inside their bosom; for they worked with their shirt collar open and generally without jackets. The poor souls, who, having no pence, could have no dainties, would try to snatch a piece slyly, if it were possible, and if that failed, they would try to beg a morsel. If the possessor gave a taste, he held the herring so tight, that only a very small portion could be bitten off, without biting off the ends of the owner's fingers, and their whole feast was quickly finished, without greatly diminishing their appetite. It happened, by some extraordinary stroke of good fortune, that Blincoe became possessed of a shilling, and he determined to have what he termed, a proper blow out; he, therefore, requested Palfry to bring him six penny wheaten cakes, and half a pound of butter. Blincoe was then a stretcher, and had, as such, a better opportunity to receive and to eat his dainties unobserved. The cakes he pulled one by one, from his bosom, and laying them upon the frame, spread the butter on them with a piece of flat iron, and giving his two comrades a small part each, he set to and devoured all the rest; but the unusual quantity and quality nearly made him ill. Blincoe had no appetite for his dinner or supper, and, he, therefore, let another comrade eat it, who engaged to give Blincoe his, when he happened to lose his appetite. Such were the prospective and contingent negotiations carried on by these wretched children, relative to their miserable food.

If Blincoe happened to see any fresh cabbage leaves, potato or turnip pareings, thrown out upon the dunghill, he has run down with a can full of sweepings, as an excuse, and as he threw that dirt on the dunghill, he would eagerly pick the other up, and carry it in his shirt, or in his can, into the mill, wipe the dirt off as well as he could and greedily eat them up. At other times, when they had rice puddings boiled in bags for dinner—the rice being very bad and full of large maggots, Blincoe not being able to endure such food, used to go into one of the woods near the factory, and get what the boys called *bread and cheese*, that is, hips and hipleaves, clover or other vegetable, and filling his bosom, run back to the mill, and eat this trash, instead of foul rice, with which neither butter-milk, milk, treacle, nor even a morsel of salt, was allowed.

Amongst the most singular punishments inflicted upon Blincoe, was that of screwing small hand-vices of a pound weight, more or less, to his nose and ears, one to each part; and these have been kept on, as he worked, for hours together! This was principally done by Robert Woodward, Merrick, and Charnock. Of those petty despots, Merrick was the most unpardonable, as he had been a parish apprentice himself, and ought to have had more compassion. This Merrick was a stretcher, and Blincoe when about 11 or 12 years old, used to stretch for him, while he, Merrick, ate his dinner. Out of kindness, or because he could not eat it himself, Merrick used occasionally to leave a small part of his allowance, and tell Blincoe to go and eat it. On Mondays, it was the custom to give the boys bread and treacle, and turnip *broth* made the day before, which generally stunk to such a degree, that most of the poor creatures could only pick out the oat bread, the broth being loathsome. Whenever Merrick left a bit of bread and treacle in the window, Blincoe used to run eagerly at the prize, and devour it voraciously. One Monday, this overlooker, who was a most inhuman taskmaster, sent Blincoe down to the card-room for a basket of rovings, a descent of four or five stories deep, for this burthen of considerable weight. During the time he was gone, Merrick rubbed tar upon the oat cake, and laid it in the window as usual. When Blincoe returned, the brute said, "go and eat what lies in the window." Blincoe, seeing as he supposed, so much treacle upon the bread, was surprised; for Merrick usually licked it clean off, and to his bitter mortification, found, instead of treacle, it was *tar*. Unable to endure the nauseous mouthful, Blincoe spat it out, whilst Merrick, laughing at him, said,

"What the devil are you spitting it out for." Poor Blincoe, shaking his head, said, "You know, mon," and Blincoe left the remainder of the tarred cake in the window, when his comrade, Bill Fletcher, a poor lad since dead, who came from Peak Forest, took up the bread, and scraping off the tar as clean as he could, ate it up, apparently with a good appetite! To such dreadful straights were they driven by hunger, the apprentices have been known to *pick turnips out of the necessary*, which others, who had stolen them, had thrown there to conceal, and washing them, have devoured the whole, thinking it too extravagant even to waste the peeling.

Palfry, the Smith, had the task of rivetting irons upon any of the apprentices, whom the masters ordered, and those were much like the irons usually put upon felons! Even young women, if suspected of intending to run, had irons riveted on their ancles, and reaching by long links and rings up to the hips, and in these they were compelled to walk to and from the mill to work and to sleep! Blincoe asserts, he has known many girls served in this manner. A handsome-looking girl about the age of twenty years, who came from the neighbourhood of Cromford, whose name was Phebe Rag, being driven to desperation by ill-treatment, took the opportunity, one dinner-time, when she was alone, and when she supposed no one saw her, to take off her shoes and throw herself into the dam, at the end of the bridge, next the apprentice house. Some one passing along, and seeing a pair of shoes, stopped. The poor girl had sunk once, and just as she rose above the water he seized her by the hair! Blincoe thinks it was Thomas Fox, the governor, who succeeded Milner, who rescued her! She was nearly gone, and it was with some difficulty her life was saved! When Mr. Needham heard of this, and *being afraid the example might be contagious*, he ordered James Durant, a journeyman spinner, who had been apprenticed there, to take her away to her relations at Cromford, and thus she escaped!

When Blincoe's time of servitude was near expiring, he and three others, namely, William Haley, Thomas Gully, and John Emery, the overlooker, took a resolution, to go out of the factory at a fixed hour, meaning not to work so many hours: but, according to Blincoe's account, neither he nor his comrades had ever heard up to that time, of any law which regulated the hours of apprentices working in cotton-mills, nor did they know what an act of Parliament meant, so profound was the ignorance in which they had been reared! Blincoe and his mutinous comrades, having left work at the expiration of fourteen hours labour, went off to the apprentice house. Upon this, the manager, William Woodward, sent off an express to the master, (Mr. Needham), at Highgate Wall, a lone and large mansion about four miles distant. Orders came back, to turn all four out of the apprentice-house that night; but not to give them any provisions! Being thus turned out, Blincoe got lodging with Samuel

Brickleton! One or two of his comrades slept in the woods, which luckily was hay time.—Brickleton's hospitality did not include provisions, and having had no feed since twelve o'clock the day before, Blincoe was sorely hungry in the morning, but still he had nought to eat! About nine o'clock, all four, agreeable to the orders they received the night before, went to the counting-house at the mill. Mr. Needham was there in a terrible ill-humour.—As soon as he saw Blincoe come in, he took from his body, his waistcoat and jacket, and fell upon him with his thick walking-stick, which he quickly broke by the heavy blows laid on poor Blincoe's head and shoulders, and he kept on swearing the while, *"I'll run you out, you damned rascal."* As soon as he could escape, Blincoe ran off to his work, when Haley and Emery—who were apprentices, like Blincoe, caught their share of his fury! At noon, Blincoe went eager enough to the apprentice house, having had no food for twenty-four hours. Having in a few minutes, devoured his portion, he ran off at full speed, without hat, jacket, or waistcoat, his head and body greatly bruised, towards the residence of a magistrate, named Thornelly, who resided at Stanton-Hall, a place about six miles beyond Bakewell, and eleven from Litton-Mill! There resided, at this time, at Ashford, about four miles from Litton, a man named Johnny Wild, a stocking-weaver, who had been his (Blincoe's) overlooker, when first he went to Lowdham Mill. Filled with the fond hope of being made at once a gentleman, thither, poor Blincoe, now twenty years of age, directed his course. Johnny Wild was sitting at his frame, weaving stockings, and was surprised to see Blincoe run up to the door like a wild creature, terror in his looks and reeking with perspiration, without hat, coat, or waistcoat. To him, Blincoe told the cruel usage he had met with, and the wounds and bruises he had just received, which were sufficiently visible! Wild and his wife seemed touched with compassion, at the sad plight Blincoe was in, gave him a bowl of bread and milk, lent him a hat, and directed him his way. Thus refreshed, the fugitive set off again, running as fast as he could, looking often behind him. As he passed through Bakewell, Blincoe thought it best to slacken his pace, lest some mercenary wretch, suspecting him to be a Litton Mill apprentice running away, should, in the hope of receiving a reward of a half crown piece, seize him and send him back to prison! As he passed along, many seemed to eye him intently; but no one stopped him. About six o'clock in the evening, being heartily jaded, he arrived at the home of Mr. Thornelly. It happened, that the magistrate was at dinner; but some person, in his employ, understanding that Blincoe came to seek redress for alleged violence, went to the supplicant in the yard, saying, "Who do you want."—"Mr. Thornelly."—"What for?"—"I am an apprentice at Litton Mill, master has beat me cruelly, do look at my shirt?"—"Never mind, never mind," said the person, "you cannot see Mr. Thornelly to-day; he is at dinner; there will be a bench of justices to-morrow, about eleven in the morning, at the sign of the Bull's Head, facing the church at Heam; you must go there." This place lay a few miles from Litton Mill, on the Sheffield road. Finding there was nothing to be done at Stanton-Hall, poor Blincoe began to measure back his weary steps to Litton Mill! He called at Johnny Wild's, as he returned, who allowed him to rest; but, of food, he could not offer any; having a large family, and being but a poor man, he had none to spare! Blincoe gave back his hat, and arrived at the apprentice-house between nine and ten, being then giving-over time! William Woodward, the manager, whose heavy hand had inflicted blows and cuffs beyond calculation on poor Blincoe, was about the first person by whom he was accosted! In a tone, about as gentle as that of a baited-bear, and an aspect much more savage, said, "Where have you been?"—"To Mr. Thornelly,"—"I'll Thornelly you to-morrow," said he, and turned away. Not knowing what the next day might bring forth, Blincoe applied for his mess of water-porridge, which, after a journey of two and twenty miles, tasted highly unsavory, and then he retired to his bed, praying God to end his life, or mitigate its severity—a prayer that was common at Litton Mill!—Sore as he was, he slept; but it was on his face, his back being too much bruised, to lie in that position, or even on his side! In the morning, he rose and went to his stretching frame. Between seven and eight o'clock, Blincoe saw Woodward going to the apprentice-house, from the window of the factory. Seeing this opportunity, without waiting for breakfast, Blincoe again made a start, still without hat, waistcoat or coat, towards Heam, to state to the magistrates the cruel treatment he had received.—The day was fine. The hay was about, and miserable as was poor Blincoe, he could not but feel delighted with the sweet air and romantic scenery. Having been thus expeditious, Blincoe was at Heam, an hour and a half too soon. To amuse himself, he went into the Church-yard. As soon as the magistrates arrived, from whose hands he came to supplicate for justice, Blincoe went to the Bull's Head. The officiating clerk was an attorney named Cheek, who resided at Whetstone-Hall, a mansion situated within half a mile of Tideswell. To this person, Blincoe began unbosoming his grief, and in the earnestness of his harangue, and fearful, lest the attorney did not catch every syllable, the half-naked Blincoe crept nearer and nearer; but Mr. Cheek not relishing the dense, foul scent of oil, grease, and filth, said, "Well, well, I can hear you, you need not come so near; stand back." Poor Blincoe, not a little mortified, obeyed his command, and, by the time Blincoe's piteous tale was ended, the magistrates had mostly arrived, to whom Mr. Cheek, the clerk to the magistrates, read the paper, which Blincoe supposed contained his intended deposition. Blincoe was then sworn. One of the magistrates, Blincoe believes it was a Mr. Middleton, of _____Hall, said, "Where is Mr. Needham?"—

Blincoe replied, "He's gone to-day (Tuesday) to Manchester Market." This prevented their sending a man and horse to fetch him. One of the magistrates then said to Blincoe, "Go strait to the mill, to your work." —"Oh! Sir, he'll leather me," meaning, Mr. Needham would beat him again. "Oh, no! he durst na'-he durst na'," said one of the magistrates in reply. Upon this, some one advised, that a letter should be sent to Mr. Needham, in whose much dreaded presence, Blincoe had no inclination to appear! Blincoe cannot recollect who wrote the letter, but thinks it was Mr. Middleton, who said, "If he leathers you, come to me." This gentleman resided at a distance of about eight miles from Litton Mill. Having this powerful talisman in his possession, Blincoe returned direct to the mill, and, advancing boldly to Woodward, the manager, said, "Here's a letter for Mr. John Needham," the son of the old master, who is now resident in Tideswell! Blincoe informed Woodward, he had been at a justice-meeting at Heam, and as a justice had sent this letter, Woodward did not dare to lay violent hands upon him. This day, poor Blincoe had to fast till night, making a complete round of another twenty-four hours of fasting! On Wednesday, John Needham returned from Manchester market, and appeared, as usual, at Litton Mill.—The letter, from which Blincoe anticipated such beneficial results, was handed to the young Squire, by William Woodward, the manager. He broke the seal, read it through, and ordered Blincoe to be called out of the factory, from his work. Obedient to the summons, and not a little alarmed, he appeared before his young master, whose savage looks shewed, ere he spoke a word, a savage purpose. The first words were, "Take off your shirt, you damned rascal!" Blincoe obeyed, his head and back being still very sore. John Needham instantly began flogging him with a heavy horsewhip, striking him with his utmost force, wherever he could get a blow. It was in vain Blincoe cried for quarter: in vain he promised never again to go to a Magistrate, in any case whatever. John Needham kept on flogging, swearing horribly and threatening furiously, resting between while, till he had fully satisfied his sense of justice! He then unlocked the door, and, saying, "You'll go again, will you?" bade Blincoe put on his shirt, and go to his work. Away went Blincoe, scarcely able to stand , and covered with additional bruises from head to foot. Even this horrid flogging did not deprive Blincoe of his appetite, nor of his determination to seek redress of the Magistrates, and accordingly, the next Sunday night, when some of the time-outs were let out of the prison, Blincoe, availing himself of the darkness of the night, watched the opening of the yard door, and crouching almost on his hands and knees, crept out unseen. Shortly after the order was given to sit down to supper. Every 'prentice, male and female, knew their own places. In about two minutes, two hundred half-famished creatures were seated. Their names were called over, to see that none were missing, when, little parson could not be found. Governor Thomas Fox, on learning of this event, ordered the door warder to be called, who declared most vehemently, he had not let Blincoe out, and further, he had not passed the door; upon this, a general search was made in all the rooms and offices, high and low; but no where was little parson to be found. Meanwhile, as soon as Blincoe found himself outside the hated walls, he set off again up Slack, a very steep hill close to the mill, and made the best of his way to Litton, and going to the house of one Joseph Robinson, a joiner, who worked in Litton Mill, who had known Blincoe at Lowdham Mill, was well acquainted with the horrid cruelties he had suffered, and heartily compassionating Blincoe's miserable state, gave him a good supper, and let him sleep with his sons. In the morning, Robinson, who was really a humane man, and a friend to the poor children, gave Blincoe some bread and meat, and giving him a strict injunction not to own *where* he had slept, Blincoe set off, about six o'clock in the morning, to Mr. Middleton's house. The morning was showery, and Blincoe had neither hat, coat, or waistcoat, and he had about eight miles to go, in search of justice. He arrived at Mr. Middleton's, long before his hour of appearance. At last, Mr. Middleton got up, and Blincoe approaching, crawling like a spaniel dog, said, "Sir, I have come again, Mr. Needham has been beating me worse than ever, as soon as he read your letter over." Seeing the miserable state Blincoe was in, drenched with the rain and half naked, Mr. Middleton said, "go into the kitchen and rest yourself—you should not have come here first; you should have gone to Mr. Cheek, of Whetstone Hall, and he would have given you a summons;" upon this, poor Blincoe said mournfully, "Eh, Sir, he will do nought for me—he is so thick with my master—they are often drinking together." "Pshaw, pshaw," said the Justice, "he's like to listen to you—he must;" but then, as if recollecting himself, he said, "Stop, I'll write you a letter to Mr. Cheek." In the Justice's kitchen, poor Blincoe got some bread and cheese, which was indeed a luxurious food, though unaccompanied with any beer. Blincoe thus refreshed, again set off to Mr. Cheek, a distance of about eleven or twelve miles, bare headed, and dressed only in trowsers and shoes. The rain continuing pouring in torrents. When Blincoe reached Whetstone Hall, one of the first persons he saw, was a woman of the name of Sally Oldfield, her husband, Thomas Oldfield, then dead, had been governor of the 'prentices of Litton Mill. She was then housekeeper to Messrs. Shore and Cheek, at Whetstone Hall. Those gentlemen were amongst the most intimate friends and visitors of Mr. Needham, and Sally Oldfield, who recollected Blincoe, alias parson, said, "Eh, Parson! what do you want here?" "I have a letter from Mr. Middleton to Mr. Cheek." "Eh!" said little old Sally again, "Are you going against your master?" Blincoe told her he was, and how cruelly he had been treated. Sally could not comprehend any right

Blincoe had to complain, and said, "Eh! thou should'st not go against thy master." Saying this, she took him to the kitchen, gave him some bread and cheese, and plenty too, and some good beer, and then said, "Parson, thou mun never go against thy master; what do you have for dinner on Monday?—do you have treacle now?" "No, we have dry bread and broth." "Ah," continued she, *"Treacle is too dear."* Blincoe could scarce refrain from smiling, recollecting the feast of the treacle can; but he said nothing, and not a soul came near him. There Blincoe sat until night, when he began to think the magistrates were hoaxing him, and he thought there was no utility in waiting for justice, or a possibility of obtaining redress! he would never more complain! seven hours sat Blincoe in Lawyer Cheek's kitchen, and not the least notice being taken of him or his letter, he made his solitary way back to the mill, and arrived there just as the mill had loosed, and going direct to Woodward, told him where he had been, and concealing the conviction he felt, that it was not possible to obtain redress; he assured the tyrant, with tears and lamentations, that if he would intercede to prevent his being flogged again, he would never run away more. "On these conditions," said Woodward, "I will, if I can," and from that day Blincoe cannot recollect, that he was either flogged or beaten; but, *still* Blincoe had no knowledge, that there was any Act of Parliament for the protection of poor orphans like himself.—He knew of the magistrates coming to the mill; but he had no distinct idea that they came to *redress grievances!* So great was the terror of the poor ignorant apprentices, no one dared complain, and he cannot recollect that they ever gave themselves any other trouble, than merely going over the mill! Every thing was previously prepared and made ready. The worst of the cripples were put out of the way. The magistrates saw them not. The magistrates could never *find out* any thing wrong, nor hear of a single individual who had any complaint to make!—When Blincoe was about twelve or thirteen years of age, he well remembers an apprentice, almost grown up, who lost his life in an attempt to escape. He had tied several blankets or sheets together, to reach the ground from the chamber window, where he slept, which was three or four stories high. The line broke, he fell to the ground, and he was so much hurt at the fall, he died soon after. Blincoe thinks some surgeon or doctor came to him; but he had not the least recollection of any Coroner's-inquest being held! In addition to the punishments already stated, Robert Woodward and other overlookers have kicked him down a whole flight of stairs; at other times, he has been seized by the hair of his head and dragged up and down the room, tearing off his hair by handsful, till he was almost bald! All the punishments he suffered, were inflicted upon others, and, in some cases, even to a worse degree than on himself. He even considers he came off tolerably well, compared with others, many of whom, he believes, in his conscience, lost their lives, and died at the apprentice-house, from the effects of hard usage, bad and scanty food, and excessive labour.

CHAPTER VI.

Blincoe remained in Litton Mill a year after he had received his indentures, not from inclination; but to get a little money to start with. His wages were only four shillings and sixpence weekly, and this was to have been paid monthly; but, month after month elapsed, and, instead of honest settlement, there was nothing but shuffling! The first money he received was eighteen and sixpence, and being in possession of that sum, he thought himself incalculably rich! He scarcely knew what to do with it! It took away his appetite.—After he was a little composed, he devoted a few shillings to the purchase of some dainties, such as wheaten cakes and herrings! He then worked and lived like others, till his master owed him nearly half a years labour. The pay day came and then he drew nearly thirty shillings, the rest was kept back, so that, Blincoe seeing no prospect before him but perpetual slavery for a merciless master, made up his mind to be off; and on Tideswell May fair, which happens on the fifteenth of May, he put his plan in execution! He knew not where to go; but started the next morning at hazard! When he came to Chapel-a-Frith, he determined to visit a celebrated fortune-teller, called Old Beckka'! She lived in a small back-house, a haggard, black, horrid-looking creature, very old, having a long beard, and dressed like a person who lived in ages past! Her name was very influential all over Derbyshire. So very famous was *old Beckka'*, that people came far and near, and she was reputed to be possessed of land and houses.—She never took a smaller fee than a shilling, even from the very poorest of her votaries. Her name was well known at Litton Mill. If any thing was stolen, Woodward, the manager, or Gully, or some *one* of the overlookers, used to go to Chapel-a-Frith, to consult *old Beckka'*. To this sybil, Blincoe repaired, holding a shilling, between his thumb and finger! Perfectly understanding the object of his visit, she first took the shilling, and then said, "Sit down." He felt really frightened, and, if she had bade him stand upon his head, he declared he should have obeyed! He had been told, that she had really enchanted or bewitched persons, who had endeavoured to cheat or deceive her, or by whom she had been offended, causing them to lose their way, and sent ill fortune in many shapes. Our novice was also told, that ladies and gentlemen of high estate had come in their coaches, all the way from London, to learn their destiny, all which circumstances produced, on his uncultivated mind, the sensations described! No sooner was Robert Blincoe seated, than the witch of Chapel-a-Frith, put a common tea-cup in his hand, containing a little tea grounds, "Shake it well,"

said Beckka. Blincoe obeyed. Then the oracle drained away the water, and
twirling the cup round and round, she affected, with the utmost gravity, to read
his future fortune, in the figures described in the sediment at the bottom.
Assuming a wild stare, and standing erect over him, her eyes apparently ready
to leap from their sockets, she exclaimed, in a hollow sepulchral tone of voice,
"You came from the outside of London, did you not?" "Yea," said the
astonished Blincoe, "I did." "You came down in a waggon, and have been at
a place surrounded with high rocks and great waters, and you have been used
worse than a stumbling stone." Blincoe's mouth, and eyes, and ears, all seemed
to open together, at this oracular speech, as he said, "Yea, yea, it is true." Then
she said,—"Your troubles are at an end.—You shall rise above those, who have
cast you down so low.—You shall see their downfall, and your head shall be
higher than theirs.—Poor lad! terrible have been thy sufferings.—Thou shalt
get up in the world! you'll go to another place, where there'll be a big water,
and so go thy way in peace, and may God prosper thy steps!" Filled with
amazement, mingled with rising hopes of better fortune, Blincoe arose and
departed, making a very low reverence to "*old Beckka*," as he went out, and
impressed with the fullest conviction, that she was truly a sorceress; the
simpleton, forgetting, that his *costume*, his wild and pallid looks, and the *scent*
of his garments, tainted as they were with the perfume of a cotton factory, were
more than sufficient to point out to the fortune-teller, the past and present, from
which she speedily fabricated the future fortune, for her simple visitor! Blincoe
thought he got but a very short story for his shilling! On the other hand, he was
very well contented with its *quality*, since it promised him, and in such positive
terms, that he should rise above his cruel oppressor and become a great man.
Filled with these thoughts, he stepped briskly along, not much encumbered
with luggage; for he carried all his wardrobe on his back. When he arrived at
a spot called "Orange end," where four ways met, he was perplexed which to
take, the oracle of Chapel-a-Frith not having apprised him of this dilemma, nor
which road to take! Being quite in an oracular mood, very happy, that he had
got so far away from Litton, and fully convinced, that, go where he would, and
befall him what would, he could not blunder upon a worse place, nor be
oppressed by a more evil fortune, he tossed up a halfpenny in the air, making
it spin round its own axis, and waiting its course as it rolled, resolved to follow
in that direction. Its course happening to be pointed towards New Mills,
Derbyshire, thither he bent his course, but failed in his application for work.
Blincoe, therefore, walked on, till he came to Mr. Oldknow's Cotton Factory,
at Mellow, and there he crept towards the counting-house, in an humble mood,
and said, in a very meek tone of voice, "If you please, sir, can you give me
work?" The manager, Mr. Clayton, a gentleman by no means deficient in self-

respect, asked sharply: "Where do you come from?" "From Litton Mill, Sir."
"Where are your indentures?" "There they are, Sir," said Blincoe, holding up
the papers. There were two or three gentlemen, in the counting-house, and they
looked earnestly over the indentures and then at Blincoe, one of them saying,
"Did you come from Pancras workhouse?" "Yes, Sir." "Why, we are all come
from thence! we brought many children the other day to this Mill." "Indeed,
Sir," said Blincoe, pitying, in his heart, the poor creatures, and thinking it would
have been merciful to have killed them outright at once, rather than put them
to such a place as Litton Mill had proved to him. Looking at the names of the
subscribing officers and overseers, one of the Pancras parish officers said to Mr.
Clayton: "Some of these officers are dead." Blincoe again exclaimed "Indeed,
Sir,"—recollecting the atrocious lies and cruel deceptions, those men had
practised upon him, in his infant years, by telling him to believe that, in sending
him to a cotton-factory, he was to be made at once a gentleman; to live upon
roast beef and plum-pudding; to ride his master's horses; to have a watch in his
pocket and plenty of money, and nothing whatever to do! Poor Blincoe could
not help thinking to himself;—"Where are the souls of these men gone, who,
knowing the utter falsehood of their seductive tales, betrayed me to a destiny
far more cruel than transportation?" The overseers, looking at the distorted
limbs of this victim of parochial economy, said, "Why, how came you so lame?
you were not so when you left London, were you?" "No, Sir, I was turned over,
with the rest of the unclaimed 'prentices, from Lowdham Mill, to Ellice
Needham, of Litton Mill." "How did they keep you?—what did you live
upon?" "Water porridge—sometimes once, sometimes twice a day—sometimes potatoes and salt for supper: not half enough and very bad food." "How
many hours did you work?" "From five, or occasionally six o'clock in the
morning, till nine, half-past, ten, and sometimes eleven, and, on Saturday
nights, till twelve o'clock." The person wrote these answers down; but made
no comment, nor ever noticed the material facts, that Blincoe had not been
taught the trade he should have learnt, and that the parish officers of Pancras
had utterly neglected him and his miserable comrades, when the Lowdham Mill
factory stopped! The Manager then bade a person shew Blincoe where he
might get lodgings, and bade him come to work in the morning. Blincoe was
too much afraid of giving offence, by asking questions in the counting-house,
to venture to enquire as to his parentage; but, as soon as he had got lodgings,
he strove to make out where the officers were to lodge that night, at Mellow,
to enquire further; but hearing they were just then gone, he was deprived of the
opportunity! This occurrence, filling his mind with melancholy reflections, he
shed many tears in solitude that night! The next morning, he went to his work,
and found it was as hard as at Litton Mill; but of more moderate duration; the

hours being from six in the morning, till seven in the evening. The 'prentices, whom he saw at work, seemed cheerful and contented; looked healthy and well, compared with those at Litton! They were well fed, with good milk-porridge and wheaten bread for breakfast, and all their meals were good and sufficient! They were kept clean, decently dressed, and every Sunday went twice to Marple Church, with Mr. Clayton, their under-master, at their head! On the whole, it struck Blincoe, that the children were in a Paradise, compared with the unfortunate wretches whom he had left at Litton Mill, and he indulged in the humane hope, that the lot of children just then brought down from London, might escape the dreadul sufferings he had had to endure! Unfortunately, the trade, which Blincoe had been fourteen or fifteen years articled to learn, was by no means so good as husbandry labour. The wages, Mr. Oldknow offered him, were *eleven shillings per week*, at the time that a good husbandry labourer could earn from sixteen shillings to a pound! After having been some months in Mr. Oldknow's factory, Blincoe learnt, that, whilst he did as much work, and as well as any man in the factory, which employed several hundred apprentices, Mr. Clayton had fixed his wages at three or four shillings per week less than any other person's. Blincoe could not impute this to any other cause, than an idea, that he was in so crippled a state, he dared not demand the same as another! Such is the mean and sordid spirit, that sways almost the whole of those establishments. When a poor creature has been crippled at one mill, and applies for work at another, instead of commiserating his condition and giving him the easiest and best work and best pay, it is a common custom, to treat them with the utmost contempt, and though they may be able to do their work as well for their masters, though not with the same ease to themselves, as one who has escaped being crippled, the masters generally make it a rule to screw them down to the very lowest point of depression, and, in many cases, give them only half their wages. On this principle was Blincoe dealt with, at Mellor Factory; but, as the wretched diet on which he had been fed at Litton, enabled him to live upon three shillings per week, he saved money each week. Having an independent spirit and not being willing to work for less than his brethren, he took an opportunity one evening, to go to the counting-house and doffing his hat to Mr. Clayton, said, "Sir, if you please, will you be so good to raise my wages?" Turning sharp round, he said, "Raise your wages! why, I took you in upon *charity only!*" "I am sure it was very good of you, Sir," said Blincoe, who well knew that such hands as himself were scarce, and therefore, that his charity began at home.—Hearing Blincoe speak in such humble, yet somewhat ironical terms; for he possessed a rich vein of sarcastic humour, Mr. Clayton said, "Well, go to your work, I'll see." They paid every fortnight at the factory.—The next pay night, Blincoe found himself paid at the rate of thirteen shillings, which was still two shillings under the price of other workmen! This continued a few weeks, when, an old servant, whom they had employed many years, applied for work, and on the Friday night fortnight, Blincoe's wages were sent up to him, with an order *to depart*. This is what is called *getting the bag*. Blincoe being alike surprised and hurt, and knowing he had done his work well and have never lost a minute, set an enquiry on foot, and he was told, from very good authority, it was because he had applied for an advance of wages, and because Mr. Clayton thought it was taking an advantage of him. Curious logic! Mr. Clayton seems totally to forget the advantage he had, in the first instance, taken of poor Blincoe, and feeling very sore, when the young fellow applied for redress, he seized this opportunity, and, in this petty way, to wreak his anger; and as the factory of Mr. Oldknow stood so very high, if compared with that of Ellice Needham of Litton, these blemishes fully prove, how foul and corrupted is the spirit of traffic, since, in its best shape, it could not resist the temptation of taking a mean advantage of the necessities and the misery of a fellow creature.

Although the treatment of parish pauper apprentices was very liberal, compared to what they had endured at Litton Mill, the journeymen were governed by a very tight hand. If they arrived only two or three minutes after the clock had struck, they were locked out; and those, who were within, were all locked in, till dinner time, and not only were the outward doors, below, locked; but every room above, and there was a door-keeper kept, whose duty it was, a few minutes before the respective hours of departure, to unlock the doors, by whom they were again locked, as soon as the work-people arrived! In every door, there was a small aperture, big enough to let a quart can through, so that the food brought by parents and relations could be handed to them within—no one being permitted to go in or out, and, of course, the necessaries, two or three to each room, were within side the room, where the people worked! Such was the rigid order and severe discipline of one of the most *lenient* master cotton-spinners! Mr. Oldknow caused a road to be made from the turnpike to his mill, which saved some length of way, and every stranger, or person not absolutely working in the mill, who used it, had to pay a halfpenny—and, as the road led to New Mills and Mellor, those work-people, in common with all others, had to pay a halfpenny. There was a toll-house erected, and also a toll-bar, and the speculation, if not very neighbourly, is said to have been very profitable.

When Blincoe left this establishment, which seemed to vie with some of the largest factories in Manchester, both in its exterior grandeur, and in magnitude, he had contrived to save the greater part of his wages, and having a few pounds in his pocket, he felt less dismay at this harsh and unexpected

treatment, than if he had acted with less prudence and been destitute. He had
served faithfully and diligently upwards of half-a-year, and a character from so
respectable an employer might be serviceable, he, therefore, made his appearance once more before Mr. Clayton, and doffing his hat, and assuming the most
lowly and respectful attitude, said, in his usual slow and plaintive tone:—"Will
you please, Sir, give me a character?"—"O no! O no!" replied the manager,
"we never give characters here," with an unfriendly aspect! Blincoe thought
it was better to be off and seek his fortune elsewhere, than stop and argue. This
circumstance strongly marks the oppressive character of these establishments.
It is clear, that Mr. Clayton did not chuse to hire Blincoe without a character,
or something equivalent, by requiring to see his indentures; and, after the young
man had served them diligently and honestly, for six months, he surely should
have written to certify, that he had done so, and the denial *might* have prevented
his getting another employer. However the law might stand at present, upon
this point, in any future legislative measure, a clause should be introduced, to
compel every master to give a written character, except where some positive act
of gross misconduct interposed to neutralise the claim!

From Mellor Mill, Blincoe walked to Bollington, in Cheshire, a village not
far from Macclesfield, and about 18 miles distance, having a bundle which,
slung upon a stick, he carried upon his shoulder. He passed several road-side
houses of entertainment, allaying his thirst from the living fountains, and
satisfying his hunger with a penny cake. In this way, he travelled, till he arrived
at Bollington, where he obtained work in a factory, situated on the Macclesfield
road, belonging to a Mr. Lomax. He was placed in the card-room, which is
reckoned the most laborious and unwholesome in the factory, on account of the
great quantity of dirt and dust; but Mr. Lomax promised him a stretching frame,
at the end of a fortnight. The fortnight having expired, Blincoe saw no signs
of being relieved from stripping off the cotton from the cards. He made up his
mind to be off, and march on towards Staley Bridge, in the hope of bettering
his condition! As he was going along some fields, for a short cut, he was met
by a couple of suspicious looking fellows, who, stepping boldy up to Blincoe,
said in a stern voice, "What have you got in that bundle?" "I dunna know,
Mester, but if you'll ask the gentleman on horseback, that is coming on the
horse road, at the other side of the hedge, he'll tell you." Hearing this, and
marking the calm indifference of Blincoe, the interrogators took to their heels,
and never once looked behind them, as he could perceive; and thus the poor
little wanderer outwitted the marauders, and saved his shirt and stockings, and,
by the possibility, the hard-earned treasure he had in his fob. Having thus
adroitly got rid of the thieves, Blincoe made the best of his way to the main road,
and the best use of his legs, till he got in view of some houses, where he thought

himself out of danger. Arrived at Staley Bridge, situated upon a river, which separates Cheshire and Lancashire, and where there are many spinning factories, he applied to a man named William Gamble, who had lived in Yorkshire. This man, twelve or thirteen years before, was one of the overlookers at Lowdham Mill, and very much addicting himself to kicking the apprentices and dragging them about by the hair of the head, up and down the rooms, and then dashing them upon the floor, on account of which propensity, he was reprimanded and removed, when the overseers of Pancras parish arrived. Indeed this man and one Smith, were the terror of the poor children; but Blincoe wanting work and knowing he was an overlooker in Mr. Harrison's factory, which, by way of preeminence, was called *the Bastile*, poor Blincoe had been so many years accustomed to Bastiles, he was not easily daunted. To Gamble he repaired, and who having bestowed so many marks of his *paternal* regard upon Blincoe, he recognized him at once and very kindly got him work at ten shillings per week, which he drew for the *use* of Blincoe, during a few weeks, to whom he acted as *caterer*, and provided him with a bed, so that Blincoe had nothing whatever to do, but his work, which was tolerably moderate, that is, compared with Litton Mill. Notwithstanding its unseemly appellative, the work-people were not locked up in the rooms, as at Mellor.

The master had another method of restraining his work people from going out, and which saved the pay of a door-keeper, namely, by the counting-house being so placed, the people could not go in or out without being seen! There Blincoe worked some months; but not being perfectly satisfied with the conditions in which the stewardship of William Gamble left him, he took the liberty to remove from his hospitable roof, and the result was, he could live upon and lay up one half of his wages. The wages paid at this mill were very low, and the work very laborious, being the stripping of the top cards! The fixed quantum was six pounds per day, which is a severe task. After this, the master went up to Blincoe, and others, as they were at work, and informed them he would have more weight of cotton stripped off the top cards, or turn them away, and Blincoe not feeling inclined to perform more work for that pay, asked for his wages and left the Bastile!

Hence, Blincoe went to Mr. Leech, the owner of another factory, at Staley Bridge, by whom he was engaged at nine shillings a week; but he found the cotton so foul and dirty, and the work so hard, he staid not long; as the owner paid only once in three weeks, it required some privation, before any wages could be got! After three days toil, Blincoe went to his Master and asked him to lend him as much silver as his work came to, and, having obtained it, he took French leave, to the great offence of his employer. Blincoe still remained at Staley Bridge, though unemployed. He next obtained work at the mill of a Mr.

Bailey, whose father had then recently had one of his arms torn off by the blower, and he died in a few hours from the dreadful effects of that accident. Here Blincoe stopped, stripping of cards, for eleven shillings per week, during several months, when, having saved a few pounds, he determined to try his fortune at Manchester, which celebrated town was only seven or eight miles distant. Of London, Blincoe retained only a faint recollection, and he thought Manchester the largest and the grandest place in all the world. He took lodgings in St. George's-road, being attracted by the residence of James Cooper, a parish apprentice from the same workhouse with himself, who had been so cruelly flogged at Litton Mill. By this young man, Blincoe was received in a friendly manner, and he lodged in his house near Shudehill. Blincoe arrived at Manchester at a bad time, just at the return of peace, and he had a difficulty of getting work. His first place was in the factory of Mr. Adam Murray. There the engines worked only four days and a half per week; for which he received no more than seven shillings and a penny. Blincoe suffered much from the heat of the factories at Staley; but in this of Mr. Murray's, he found it almost suffocating, and if there had been as great a heat in the factory at Litton, added to the effects of long hours, and bad and scanty food, it is probably it had cut him off in the first year of his servitude! Blincoe, thinking it was wise to risk the chance of bettering his fortune, left Adam Murray's gigantic factory, at the end of the week, and next went to work in Robinson's factory,* as it is called, which belongs to Mr. Marriet. There he was engaged to strip cards, at half a guinea per week. He worked at this several months, living in a frugal manner, and never going into public-houses, or associating with idle company; but, when he was engaged, by the rule of the overlookers, he was forced to pay a couple of shillings, by way of footing, and then he went to a public-house in Bridge-street, where this silly and mischievous custom, let Blincoe into the first and last act of drunkenness, in which he was ever concerned, and he felt ill several days afterwards. At the same time, many of his comrades, who worked in the same room, and who contributed each so much money, got drunk also. This was spent contrary to Blincoe's wishes, who grieved that he was obliged to drink the ale. If he had refused, he would have been despised, and might have lost his employ; and if a poor fellow had been ever so low and wanted this money for the most essential purpose, it must not be refused. This is a

---

*Whilst Blincoe worked at Robinson's old factory, having, by denying himself even a sufficiency of the cheapest diet, clothed himself more respectably than he had ever been, and having two-pound notes in the pocket, he determined to spend a few shillings, and see the diversions of a horse-race, at Karspool Moor; but not being aware that such beings as pickpockets were in the world, he put his pocket-book in his outside pocket, whence it was stolen by some of the light-fingered gentry, and poor Blincoe had to lament his want of caution.

pernicious custom, and should be abolished. Blincoe continued several months in this factory, living as it were alone in a crowd, and mixing very little with his fellow-work people. From thence Blincoe went to a factory, at Bank Top, called Young's old factory, now occupied by Mr. Ramsbottom, and there, after a time, he was engaged as stoker, or engine man, doing the drudgery for the engineer. Here, he continued three years, sleeping a great part of the time on a flat stone in the fire hole. If it rained in the night he was always drenched! but he had formerly suffered so much by hardships, and the pay was so small, he determined to do his best to save as much money as might suffice to enable him to try to live as a dealer in waste cotton; from which humble state many of the most proud and prosperous of the master cotton-spinners of Manchester have emerged. His employer, liking him, raised his wages to thirteen shillings a week, and, whilst Blincoe was about as black as a chimney-sweeper in full powder, the hope of future independence induced him to bear his sable hue, and his master behaved to him with more humanity, than he had been accustomed to experience. He was however disturbed by some petty artifices of the manager, in the year 1817, and an attempt being made to lower his wages, for which, upon an average, he worked sixteen hours in the day, Blincoe resolved to quit such hard, unremitting and unprofitable servitude, and from that period he commenced dealer and chapman. At the end of the first year, he found his little capital reduced full one-half; but on the other hand, he gained, in experience, more than an equivalent, to what he had lost in money, and, being pretty well initiated into the *mysteries of trade*, and having acquired a competent knowledge of raw or waste cottons, he commenced his second year, in much better style, and, at the end of that year, he had not only regained his lost capital, but added £5 to it.

Blincoe hired a warehouse and lived in lodgings. In the year 1819, on Sunday, the 18th of June, he happened to be, with several other persons, at the christening of a neigbour's child, where several females were present. An acquaintance of Mister Blincoe's (no longer poor Blincoe), a jolly butcher, began to jest and jeer him, as to his living single. There was a particular female friend present, whose years, though not approaching old age, outnumbered Blincoe's, and the guests ran their jokes upon her, and some of the company said, Blincoe, get married to-morrow, and then we'll have a good wedding, as well as a christening, to day. Upon which, Blincoe, leering a little sideways at the lady, said, "Well, if Martha will have me, I'll take her and marry her to-morrow." She, demurely, said "Yes." "Then," said Blincoe, "though taken unawares, now, if you'll stick to your word, I will." She then said, "I'll not run from mine, if you don't." Hearing this, there was a great shout, and when it had subsided, the butcher offered to bet a leg of mutton, that Blincoe would not get

married on Monday, the *19th of June*, and others betted on the same side, when
Blincoe determined to win the bets, and a wife in the bargain. Blincoe said to
his comrades, "Well, that I may not be disappointed, I'll even go to see for a
licence to night." Two of the party went to see all was fair. When Blincoe had
got halfway, being fearful of a *hoax* by Martha, he hit on the device of holding
back, telling her he could not get the license without her presence, and when she
agreed to go, then still more securely to prevent his being laughed at, he said,
"I have not money enough in my pocket, will you, Martha, lend me a couple of
pounds?" In an instant she produced that sum, giving it to Blincoe, and they
proceeded. Blincoe was so bashful he neither took her hand nor saluted her lips;
but, accompanied by two of the persons who had laid wagers, went to the house
direct, of the very celebrated, though not *very reverend, Joshua Brookes*, lately
deceased. The next morning they were married in the old Church! Blincoe won
his bets and his wife! They have lived together with as great a share of conjugal
tranquillity, as falls to the lot of many, who are deemed happy couples, and he
has ever since kept upon the advance in worldly prosperity. He has lived to see
his tyrannical master brought to adverse fortune, to a state of comparative
indigence, and, on his family, the visitation of calamities, so awful, that it
looked as if the avenging power of retributive justice had laid its iron hand on
him and them. In how short a time Blincoe's career will verify the prediction
of the old sybil of Chapel-a-Frith remains to be seen; but it is in the compass
of probability, that he may, in the meridian of his life, be carried as high, by the
wheel of fortune, as in the days of his infancy and youth, he was cast low!

END OF THE MEMOIR OF ROBERT BLINCOE

* * *

CONFIRMATION OF ITS VERACITY

Samuel Davy, a young man, now employed in the Westminster Gas
Works, has called on the Publisher of *Blincoe's Memoir*, and has said, that his
own experience is a confirmation of the general statement in the Memoir.
Samuel Davy, when a child of seven years of age, with thirteen others, about
the year 1805, was sent from the poor-house of the parish of St. George's, in
the Borough of Southwark, to Mr. Watson's mill, at Penny Dam, near Preston,
in Lancashire; and successively turned over to Mr. Birch's mill, at Backborough,
near Castmill, and to Messrs. David and Thomas Ainsworth's mill, near
Preston. The cruelty towards the children increased at each of those places, and,
though not quite so bad as that described by Blincoe, approached very near to

it. One Richard Goodall, he describes, as entirely beaten to death! Irons were used, as with felons in gaols, and these were often fastened on young women, in the most indecent manner, from the ancles to the waist! It was common to punish the children, by keeping them nearly in a state of nudity, in the depth of winter, for several days together. Davy said, that he often thought of stealing, from the desire of getting released from such a wretched condition, by imprisonment or transportation; and, at last, at nineteen years of age, though followed by men on horseback and on foot, he successfully ran away and got to London. For ten years, this child and his brother were kept without knowing anything of their parents, and without the parents knowing where the children were. All applications to the Parish Officers for information were vain. The supposed loss of her children, so preyed upon the mind of Davy's mother, that, with other troubles, it brought on insanity, and she died in a state of madness! No savageness in human nature, that has existed on earth, has been paralleled by that which has been associated with the English Cotton-spinning Mills.

The Turn-Out
Harriet Martineau
(1829)

The 1810s and '20s constituted a difficult and disturbing period in British history, with the latter marking a period of increased production of social protest literature. During this period England seemed to be fighting on a variety of battle fronts: during 1811 and 1812 there was internal strife as the Luddite Rebellion resulted in machine breaking and general violence. Local violence was followed by several years of war: first with the United States and then with France. During the economic depression which followed, rioting again began at home. In 1817 the colliers in Newcastle rioted, followed by strikes in the cotton industry during 1818 and by the weavers in 1819. The culminating event, however, was the Peterloo Massacre in 1819. Adding to the unrest were laws such as the Corn Law of 1815 restricting the importation of foreign wheat and thus raising the prices of flour and bread.

Many blamed trade unions for the violence and for a while such organizations were banned. And while the Combination Act was repealed in 1824, combinations were again restricted in 1825. A surplus of workers, low wages, poor living conditions, and unsafe working conditions all contributed to the workers' unrest. On the other hand, employers and the aristocracy fought against trade unionism, arguing that freedom of contract was purely an individual matter between employer and employee. According to her 1833 Autobiography *it was during this period that Martineau composed two works dealing with combination,* The Rioters *in 1826 and* The Turn-out *the next year: "My* Globe *newspaper readings suggested to me the subject of machine-breaking as a good one,—some recent outrages of that sort having taken place: but I had not the remotest idea that I was meditating writing on Political Economy, the very name of which was then either unknown to me, or conveyed no meaning. I wrote the little story called 'The Rioters' and its success was such that some hosiers and lace-makers of Derby and Nottingham sent me a request to write a tale on the subject of Wages, which I did, calling it 'The Turn-out.'"[1]*

Both The Rioters *and* The Turn-out *are particularly important because of the personal acquaintance George Eliot had with Martineau, and the possible influence of Martineau's work on* Felix Holt.[2]

70

Chapter I.

"I shall pay the wages myself, this afternoon," said Mr. Robert Wallace to his clerk. "I suppose the people mean to renew their demand for an advance?"

"There is something going forward among them, Sir, I am certain. I dare say they will take this opportunity of telling us a bit of their minds. Here comes Henry Gilbert to be paid. He is the spokesman of them all. Now we shall have it."

But Henry Gilbert received his money in silence, and retired while his fellow-workmen were paid their wages. He did not, however, leave the mill; but stood leaning against the wall in an adjoining passage, watching the men, women, and children, as they went to the pay-room. When all had received their money, and Mr. Wallace was locking his desk, Gilbert again approached, backed by all the men who were employed in the mill, and in a respectful but determined manner, demanded an advance of wages.

"On what pretence do you make this demand?" enquired Mr. Wallace.

"Because our labour is not paid as it deserves," replied Gilbert, "and because wages have often been higher, when provisions were cheaper than they now are."

"The state of trade does not warrant an advance of wages," said Mr. Wallace; "and we shall make none."

"You had better give the matter a little more consideration, Sir, before you speak so decidedly. The consequences of your refusal may be very inconvenient to you."

"We made up our minds long ago, as you know, Gilbert; and I told you our reasons last week. If you think that threats will frighten us, you are mistaken."

"I do not threaten any further mischief Sir, than can't be helped, if you go on to deny us what we think we have a right to. We have made up our minds, too; and we will not come any more to work till you give us the wages we demand."

"I am sorry to hear this, Gilbert. The inconvenience to us will be very great; but, depend upon it, you will suffer the most, in the end. You have a right to manage your own affairs as you choose; but I advise you to consider what you are about, before you make use of your influence over these people, to induce them to throw up their means of subsistence. You are a man of sense; and I know you could ill bear to see your fellow-workmen come to want, and to think that you had plunged them into it."

"It is none of my doing, Sir," replied Gilbert; " they have each of them a will of their own. They only asked me to speak for them, not to judge for them. They will tell you so themselves."

"Harris!" said Mr. Wallace, turning to an old workman who stood near him, "is it of your own free will that you throw up your work? Or has any one persuaded you to it?"

"It is of my own will, Sir."

"You have been in our service many years," replied Mr. Wallace, "and I never knew you take any such fancy into your head before. What has made such a change in you?"

"I never understood what our rights are, till lately," replied Harris: "and now I see that it is time to stand out for them."

"You have had some false notions put into your head about your rights," said Mr. Wallace. "I will hear your reasons, if you will listen to mine. I have known you long, and you have been a faithful servant: and I would not spare trouble, if I could prevent your leaving our service in this way."

Harris thanked him, and, after some hesitation, seemed about to speak, when Gilbert interposed, saying that this was not the time and place for explanation; that he had heard all Mr. Wallace could say already, and had repeated it to his companions; and that if the gentleman wished to say any thing more, they should be happy to give him a hearing at their next weekly meeting, of which due notice should be given.

"It is more for your sakes than our own," said Mr. Wallace, "that I wish to point out your mistakes, before it is too late. We shall not advance your wages at present; so you have our answer."

The men bowed and withdrew. The wives and children of some of them waited on the outside, to learn the result of the demand. They were aware that Mr. Robert Wallace and his father were firm, as well as mild, in their conduct to their work-people; and no surprise was therefore felt, when their resistance to the demand was made known.

It was a fine Saturday afternoon, in the month of August. The people did not, as usual, disperse to their homes as soon as the mill was closed. The women seemed to forget their usual preparation for the Sunday; the men did not go into the town to lay out a part of their wages in purchasing necessaries for their families; and the children, who had, by some means, learned that they were not to go to work on the Monday, were in high spirits at the prospect of a holiday. There was little in the appearance of the people which indicated poverty. The place to which they belonged was a large manufacturing town in Yorkshire, which, though exposed, as all manufacturing towns are, to the fluctuations of trade, had enjoyed its full share of prosperity. Trade was, at this time, rather flat, and wages not so high as they had been. There was every prospect of a revival of trade; but the operatives had not patience to wait for the gradual improvement which circumstances would probably bring about, but persuaded themselves, and each other, that their masters could afford and would yield higher wages, if the men had spirit to demand them, and perseverance to stand out for them. The experiment was first tried upon the Messrs. Wallace, who were worsted spinners, and who stood very high in the trade. If they had yielded, all manufacturers in the place would probably have given way also; but, as we have seen, they resisted the demand; and their men, who had anticipated their determination, proceeded, according to a previous agreement, to attend a general meeting of operatives, which was to be held in a field, about a mile from the town. They walked slowly away, in groups, talking earnestly, and expressing in their countenances and gestures the eagerness and firmness with which they intended to maintain their point. Some few loitered behind, as if engaged in conversation, or meaning to retire to their homes; but, in reality, for the purpose of speaking to Mr. Wallace, as soon as they could do so without being observed. These were some of the poorest of the work-people, who were unwilling to give up their only means of subsistence, but not courageous enough to declare publicly their intention of continuing at their work. They gathered round their master, when he appeared, and were encouraged by his assurances that they should not be molested in the discharge of their duty. He was glad, he said, that they were wise enough to earn money while they could; and that as they made their interests the same as his own, he would protect them as well as he could, if protection should be necessary, against the ill-will of their companions.

There was one man, who stood alone in the midst of all this bustle. His arms were folded on his breast, and, though his eyes were fixed on the people before him, he was lost in thought. When they dispersed, and Mr. Wallace approached, as if going to speak to him, he turned away, and walked off. He overtook one of the spinning-girls, who had evidently been waiting for him, and drew her arm within his.

"Mr. Wallace wanted to speak with you, James," said she; "and you walked away as if you did not see him."

"I know it," replied her companion; "but what could I say to him? I can't keep to my work, you know; and he would only tell me what I know already, that it is ruin to me to throw it up."

This man was a younger brother of Henry Gilbert. He had a nearer interest in these events than almost any other person, and was placed in a situation of great difficulty. He had long been attached to a respectable, industrious young woman, who was employed at the same mill. They had saved what they could out of their wages, to enable them to set out in tolerable comfort; and had just agreed that they would marry in a week or two, when James Gilbert was called on by his brother to join in the dispute with their master. James was of an easy, quiet temper, and a rather weak judgment. For his own part, he would have liked to go on working, obtaining what money he could without dispute, even if his intention of marrying had been out of the question. But his brother had always possessed great influence over him, and was much looked up to by him, on account of his superior knowledge and sense; and as he insisted so strongly on the right of the men to obtain higher wages, and on the duty of struggling for them, James had no doubt that it was his place to support his brother, though at a great sacrifice to himself. He bitterly grieved that the contest should take place just at the present time, but dared not think of remaining at his work, in opposition to the opinion and advice of his brother and his fellow-workmen. His perplexity and distress were not lessened when he conversed with Maria Field, the young woman to whom he was attached.

"If it is ruin to us to throw up our work," said she, "why should we do it?"

"Because we shall get great things by it in the end, they say; and it is the duty of the poor to stand by one another."

"I am sure, I had rather go on as we are," replied Maria, "than hope for great things by-and-by, and be ruined in the mean time."

"So had I," replied James; "but you know we must all act together."

"If others choose to bring ruin on themselves, I do not see why you should do the same."

"But it will not be ruin to everybody," replied James, "or, I am sure, I would not join them. Many have nothing to lose; but, I see clearly, that all that we have saved, will be gone presently. They talk very big about the fund that is to be raised; but we can have no help from that while we have a shilling of our own."

Maria sighed.

"We are just as far from marrying as ever we were," continued James; "and after working hard, and saving for so long, we must sit with our hands before us, and see our money waste away faster than we got it."

"But if you must do as the others do," said Maria, "is there any reason why I should not go on with my work?"

"You won't be allowed, if you wish it ever so much," replied her lover. "I heard Gay say to another man, just now, that those who desert the cause deserve to be ducked, and shall be ducked, whether they are men or women. You must not think of running into any such danger, Maria. You know I could not protect you against such a number."

"But suppose I try for a day or two," replied Maria. "You know I could give up at any time, if I found there was any real danger. Hannah Gould works in the same room that I do, and she is going on Monday morning, as usual. I have a great mind to do so too, unless you have any real objection."

"If Henry was here, he would tell you plenty of reasons against it," replied James. "Suppose you go with me to the meeting, and then you will be better able to judge of the matter. Come; this is the way."

"I can't, indeed," replied Maria; "I have a great deal to do at home; and besides, I don't like going to such places. Do you go, and then you can tell me, when it is over, what has been said; and I shall like that better than listening in such a crowd."

"I will come to you, then, as soon as the meeting is over," replied James. "But," continued he, with a melancholy countenance, "I am to give Baylis my answer about the cottage, this evening. Must we give it up, after all?"

"We must, indeed, James," replied Maria, her eyes filling with tears. "We must make up our minds to wait, if you give up your work. But you may hear something at the meeting to change your mind. So don't speak to Baylis till night."

"We shall never meet with a house that will suit us so well again," said James. "I tell you what, Maria; we have waited so long to no purpose, I should not mind running all risks. . ."

"No, no, James, we must not think of it. We should never be happy, if we married with poverty staring us in the face. It is a sad thing that all this has happened just now; but better times will come, and we must wait for them. When every thing else is ready, we shall not have to wait long for a house; so let us give up Baylis's with stout hearts."

They parted, and went their several ways with slow steps and heavy hearts. Maria was far from being convinced that it was her lover's duty to leave his employment, but she supposed that he knew best; and, being aware how painful the sacrifice was to him, she admired his self-denial, and hoped that she should understand the whole matter better when she heard what had passed at the meeting. She busied herself at home, and found some relief to the anxiety of her thoughts in occupation.

When James arrived at the field appointed for the place of meeting, he found a large assemblage of people. The noise and confusion were so great, that it was some time before he could ascertain what was to be done, who was to speak, and from whence. At length, he made his way towards a cart, in which his brother Henry, and a few other persons who meant to address the assembly, had placed themselves. His brother perceived him.

"Come up, James," cried he; "you are the man we wanted. You must second one of our resolutions. Come up, and I'll shew it you."

"Not I, thank you," replied James. "I came to hear, not to speak. I don't half understand or like the matter; and I'll hold my tongue till I do."

"But you shall understand this in a moment," persisted his brother. "Only come up, and you'll see it's as plain as a pikestaff."

But James, for once, was sturdy. "If it is so plain," replied he, "here are hundreds of people that can see it as clearly as I, and that are more willing to speak to it. I'll have nothing to do with it to-night, at any rate."

After some time, a more tractable person was found to fill his place; and the business of the meeting seemed, at length, ready to be brought forward. Henry Gilbert took the chair. He began his speech under some embarrassment; for he was aware that many of his hearers knew little of the purpose of the meeting, and that some disapproved it. Some, on whom he had depended for support, were unaccountably absent; and the sturdiness of his brother had rather disconcerted him. It is true, that none of the masters were there to answer his arguments, or to prevent his having all his own way; but he felt, that if he failed at all, he might fail entirely, the only result of all his exertions being to throw himself out of work, and out of what he loved still better, credit and consequence. He assumed, however, an appearance of confidence which he did not feel; and as he was a fluent speaker, and as he had prepared the substance of his address in his mind, all went well for some time.

"The occasion," said he, "on which you have been called together, is important; and the present time is a critical one. The wisdom and firmness of men are always most tried in the time of a great crisis: such a time is now arrived; and I trust that your wisdom and firmness will not fail. The time is come when the poor man must stand forth to assert the rights on which the rich would trample, to break the chains which tyrants are forging, and to grasp the means of defence which the law of the land affords to those who would resist oppression."

Here a few of Gilbert's supporters began to cheer him; but the crowd did not follow their example, not having yet caught the spirit of the speaker.

"We are told," continued he, "that we ought to bear our hardships, great as they are, with patience. I grant, that patience is a very useful quality, and that the poor man has continual need of it; but there is a limit, beyond which patience itself becomes injurious to ourselves, and to those who are dearer to us even than self. When a man falls sick, when the storms of the sky overwhelm him, when lightning from heaven blasts his hopes, he does right to be patient, because these evils cannot be warded off by human foresight, or removed by human strength; but when his sufferings proceed from men, instead of from Providence, it is his duty to struggle against them to the utmost. A man may patiently behold his children pine in sickness; but shall he stand quietly by, and see the bread which he has earned for them snatched from their very mouths? He may bear the loss of his property by fire; but shall he tamely submit to be stripped of every thing by thieves, while he has strength to struggle, and an arm to strike? No, surely, no! He will punish the robber, he will resist the oppressor, and strain every nerve for the defence of his home and his family. I now call on you, my friends, to exert yourselves to maintain your rights against those who would take them from you. If I prove to you, that the just reward of your labour is kept back from you;—that, as it becomes more difficult to live, less is afforded you to live upon;—that your hardships increase as your families become larger;—I hope you will agree with me, that the sooner we get our grievances redressed, the better; the sooner we begin the struggle, the easier it will be. You all know these things," continued the orator, looking round him. And seeing none but friends, he ventured to add, "Let any one contradict me who can; let any one say that we are not oppressed, and that it is not our duty to resist oppression."

He paused, and repented of his venture, when a plain, quiet-looking young man, who stood beside the cart, leaped into it, and stood waiting to speak, as soon as the cheering, which was now pretty general, should have subsided. With some difficulty he obtained a hearing, when he said, that, according to the request of the chairman, he rose to say that he did not altogether agree with him. Their chairman was certainly right in saying that robbery and oppression of every kind ought to be resisted; but when he went on to say that those who heard him were oppressed, he might, perhaps, be going too far. The picture which had been drawn of the inflictions of Providence and the inflictions of tyrants was very true, if taken by itself; but was the meeting sure that it applied to the present case? If they would take the advice of a plain man, they would remember that there are two sides to every question; and they would pause before they passed any important resolutions, and suspend their judgments if any one attempted to inflame their minds against the masters who had afforded them subsistence for so many years, and who suffered from the badness of the times in the same proportion, though not to the same degree, as their men themselves.

This speech produced a sensible effect, in cooling the ardour of the chairman and the admiration of his hearers. After a few more observations, Gilbert found that the minds of the people were not so far prepared as he expected for the adoption of his measures; and he and his supporters presently agreed that it was better not to propose the resolutions which had been prepared. Gilbert next moved, (adverting to the lateness of the hour, and the absence of many of their companions,) that the meeting should be adjourned till Monday noon.

His former opponent came forward to say that he objected to the time proposed, as it would oblige many workmen to give up either their work or the advantage of attending the meeting. To his knowledge, many of the operatives intended to go to their work as usual on Monday morning; and as they were precisely the people who most needed to be convinced by the arguments of the chairman and his friends, he hoped that, out of consideration to them, the meeting would be held after working-hours. No fair discussion could take place, where all who looked at one side of the question were at liberty to be present, and all their opponents unavoidably absent.

Gilbert declared, that the only object of these meetings was to encourage fair discussion; and that he had reason to believe, from the absence of many whom he expected to see, that the evening was not the best time for assembling. The sense of the meeting was, however, against him, and he gave way.

He was far from being satisfied with the proceedings. He had deprived himself of the opportunity of finishing his speech, which he had prepared with great care, and which he intended should be very impressive. The resolutions he had prepared were not passed, and he feared that some formidable opposition might take place at the next meeting. He strongly urged upon his supporters the necessity of exerting their influence to the utmost, during the two intervening days, and of gaining over as many as they could to befriend their cause.

His brother's feelings were the very opposite of his own. James' spirits were raised, by the intimation which had been given that many intended to continue their work. He sought out the person who had said so, and asked him if he was sure of the fact.

"Quite sure," replied the man; "and if you are wise, you will do the same."

"But if the poor do not stand by one another," observed James, "how are they to redress their grievances? If we give way now, the masters will be all the stronger for the opposition we have made."

"So they will," replied the man; "and that's the reason I think it a pity that the turn-out has been set a-going at all. But it is better to give way now than later."

"But why give way at all?" enquired James, who was anxious to obtain as many opinions as he could to form his own by.

"Because, if we consider only on which side the power lies, the masters can hold out the longest; and because I am not at all sure that the masters are in the wrong in this case. If trade had been brisk all this time, and the masters had lowered our wages, while they were putting large profits into their own pockets, we should have been quite right to stand out against the injustice. But I think, that, in this case, the distress has not been owing to them, and that they can't help us if they would."

"Who is to help us, then? and what is the distress owing to?" enquired

James.

"I have no time to tell you all I think now," replied the man: "but come to the meeting on Monday, and then you may, perhaps, hear something on both sides of the question. In the mean time, if you'll take a friend's advice, you will not throw yourself out of work, till you know why."

James went to Maria, to tell her that he was determined not to give up his work, unless his brother should urge some very strong reasons to make him change his mind.

"If he gives you real reasons," replied Maria, gently, "you can't help being convinced; but don't give way to any thing but reason."

"Certainly not," replied James, decidedly, while, at the same time, he felt a secret dread of his brother's influence.

"And what kind of a chairman did Henry make?" enquired Maria.

"He spoke very well; but he was unlike any other chairman that ever I saw, for one thing. He wanted to carry every thing his own way, instead of giving equal favour to all parties."

"I hope they will appoint another chairman next time," said Maria; "and then Henry can say all he likes, without its being improper."

"Well, now," said James, "I want to know, whether we really must give up this cottage of Baylis's? Things seem brightening up again!"

"Indeed, I think, we must not venture to take it till we see our way a little clearer. If Baylis will give us another week to consider of it, it is all very well."

"He won't do that," said James; "for there's another person ready to take it, if I don't."

But this other person was circumstanced very much as James was, and determined to wait the result of the turn-out, before he took the cottage; so, to James's great joy, Baylis granted him another week, to make up his mind. He went home with a lightened heart, to deposit his weekly earnings; and Maria, after having cleaned her room, and made all ready for the next day, sat down to mend her clothes, and to think over what had passed, and what was next to be done.

Chapter II.

James saw but little of his brother the next day. There was much bustle in the town; so much, that a stranger arriving in the place would almost have forgotten that it was Sunday. The people stood in groups about the streets; and the manufacturers themselves were busy, going to each other's houses, to consult what measures should be taken, to put a stop to disagreements so injurious to the interests of the masters, so fatal to those of the men. James quietly looked on, assuring himself that his part was taken, for the present at least. No one troubled him with arguments or persuasions during the day; and in the evening he and Maria walked together. They were very glad to get out of the crowd and bustle, which they were not fond of at any time, and which was particularly disagreeable on a Sunday. They much preferred the quiet of the fields, where there was nothing to disturb them as they talked over their affairs, and tried to encourage their hopes and forget their cares.

It was nearly dark when they returned; but they found time to make a little circuit, which brought them in front of the cottage which they had hoped, before this time, to have secured for their own. It was a pretty place, and in every respect suitable to their wants. It consisted of two rooms on the ground-floor, and one above; a good-sized garden lay behind it; and the situation was airy and pleasant, being a little way out of the town.

"How pretty it will look when it is furnished!" exclaimed James. "What a pity it seems, when we have actually money enough to begin with, that we can't come to it at once. I made no doubt, a little time since, that we might be in it by this day fortnight. Who knows but we may, after all?"

"Hush!" said Maria; "there is Mr. Wallace."

Mr. Robert Wallace was accustomed to interest himself in the concerns of the most deserving of his work-people: he was acquainted with James's attachment, and could feel for the difficulty in which he was now placed. He enquired, whether James had taken the house, and expressed his hope that in another week he might without imprudence engage it. He was glad to hear that both of them intended to go to the mill the next morning, and advised them to begin their work half an hour earlier than usual, as he feared they might meet with opposition on the way. He hoped they would not be discouraged by the jeers or threats of their companions, but keep steadily to their business as long as they believed it to be their duty to work. Maria trembled when she heard this. She feared little for herself, but she knew that her lover's resolution was not proof against either jeers or threats, and she dreaded lest, in this case, his indecision should be his ruin. While they were talking, they heard the noise of an approaching crowd, and were presently surprised by the sight of an immense multitude of people, who were entering the town for the purpose of parading the streets. They walked in ranks, in a very orderly manner, carrying placards and banners, on which were inscribed various mottos, some very ingenious, and all indicating preparation. A band of music headed the procession, and struck up a lively tune at the entrance of the town. Five men walked a-breast, immediately behind the band, Henry Gilbert being in the middle. As soon as he saw Mr. Wallace, he bowed, and was passing on, when that gentleman stepped forward to speak to him. "Halt!" cried Gilbert, and the word was echoed through the whole line of the procession. The music stopped.

"I am surprised," said Mr. Wallace, addressing himself to Gilbert, but speaking so distinctly that many more might hear, "I am surprised that you should choose Sunday evening for this display. If you must have your procession and your band, if you must parade the streets, to-morrow will do as well, and then you will not disturb quiet and serious people, who pay a greater regard to this day than you seem to do."

"That would be all very well, Sir, if to-morrow would suit our purpose: but, if it be true, as I am told," and here he looked full at his brother, "that some of our people intend to go to work to-morrow, in spite of warning, there is no time left but this evening, to shew our numbers, and give notice of the general meeting which is to be held at eight o'clock to-morrow evening, in the Mill-field, and at which, Sir, your company is requested."

"I shall certainly be there," replied Mr. Wallace, "and then, whatever I may think of all this parade, I shall find no fault with it. But I protest against such a disturbance on a Sunday evening: and so far from its being necessary to give further notice of your meeting, I am persuaded that there is not a person within five miles, who does not know where it is to be held, and at what hour."

"So much the better for the truth, on whichever side it lies," replied Gilbert; and, as Mr. Wallace retired, he bowed, and made a signal to the band to strike up. The procession again moved forwards, and James, who had encountered looks which he did not like from many of his old companions, was heartily glad when they were all out of sight.

"Did you know nothing of all this?" enquired Mr. Wallace.

"Not I, Sir, or I am sure I should have kept out of the way."

"Your brother seems to make sure of your obedience, whether he lets you into his plans or not," observed Mr. Wallace, laughing.

"Then he reckons without his host," replied James, whose spirit was roused. "But, I dare say, this show was all got up in a hurry."

"No, no," said his master; "those banners and placards were not made in a minute. Well, I shall see you at your work in the morning; in the mean time, and at all times, stick to the right, and be at no man's bidding."

When James arrived at his own house, after seeing Maria safe home, he went straight to bed, being rather afraid of meeting his brother. He did not apprehend a quarrel, for they had never quarrelled since they were boys; but he feared lest his mind should be unsettled, and his resolution hardened, on the first occasion on which he had ever determined to act for himself in direct opposition to his brother's will. If he had been quite certain on which side the right lay, he would have had more courage and firmness; but while he felt that he could scarcely be wrong in pursuing his employment till he had the means of forming a judgment, he was quite inclined to believe that his brother had good reasons for what he did, and was sure of his ground. So, as he did not wish to be convinced just at present, he determined to avoid his brother for this one night. He had been in bed an hour before Henry came home. He heard the door open; he heard Henry apply to a neighbour for a light; he heard the enquiry, "Is not James come home yet?" and the reply, "O yes, an hour ago, or more."

Henry softly opened the door of his room, and came, with the light in his hand, to the bedside: but James pretended to be asleep; and, somewhat disappointed, the enterprising brother retired to get his supper, drawing a comparison in his own mind between himself and James, the conclusion of which was gratifying to his self-complacency.

"Here am I," thought he, "with my head so full of the concerns of hundreds of people, that it will be a wonder if I get any sleep for a week to come; while he lies snoring there, easy while he can get his daily bread, and never caring how the world wags. Well, these lazy people will know in time how much they owe us. I don't know that I'm quite just in thinking so of James either. There's one person that he's more bound to care for, than for all the world besides; and perhaps if I were just going to be married, I should be anxious to get money while I could. It's a pity, to be sure, that he wasn't married last week, and they he might have turned out with us, and been maintained out of the fund, and have kept his little stock, in the shape of furniture. But it can't be helped; and for his own good, as well as the cause, he must be kept from his work. I heard him turn in his bed: I will see whether he is awake now."

But James was, to all appearance, as fast asleep as ever; so Henry, after fastening the door and window, betook himself to his bed, which was in the same room with his brother's.

In the morning, James lay awake a long time before he rose, planning how he could dress and leave the house without disturbing Henry. But he might have spared his planning; for Henry was on the watch, and, as soon as he began to stir, accosted him with, "I say, James: no hurry up this morning, you know. What are you stirring so early for? The day's your own."

"Yours may be, but not mine," replied James. "I promised to be up early."

"O! you're going to walk with Maria, I warrant?"

"Yes, I am," replied James. But he did not think himself bound to say in which direction they were going.

"Then an hour hence will do as well. It's early yet, and she has no more to do than you have to-day."

"True; but I engaged to be with her by a quarter past five."

"It's as late as that already," said Henry.

"Then I must make the more haste." And James bustled about to finish dressing.

"Why, you're in as great a hurry as if you were too late for your work," observed Henry, catching his brother's eye with so knowing a glance, that James burst out a-laughing.

"Why, that's the truth of it," said he; "and you knew it all the time. I know you have fifty reasons to give why I should stay at home; but I can't stop to hear them now."

"You can hear some of them," replied Henry. "You have half an hour yet. The gates don't open till six, and it's now a quarter past five: and it will take you only a quarter of an hour to walk. Just listen, and I will tell you enough to convince you that it would be a kindness to lock you into your room, rather than let you go to work."

James made towards the door.

"Why, man, I'm not really going to lock the door. I don't want to use any force but argument; and I'm sure that's strong enough for any body that is not a fool."

"I'm not a fool," replied James; "so to-night you may try the force of argument upon me, if you like. As to any other kind of force, we are about a match for each other; so you need not think it was what you said about the door, that made me open it. I'm in a hurry, that's all; so good bye, and a pleasant holiday to you."

"I wonder what has given the lad such a will of his own, all in a hurry!" thought Henry, after his brother was gone. "I suppose Maria has put this spirit into him. In such a case as this, one may always make sure that a woman is at the bottom of it. Well, she is right, according to her way of thinking; and I must take the more pains to bring them all round to-night, that's all."

James and Maria found all quiet when they reached the mill. The precaution of opening the gates half an hour earlier than usual answered its purpose; for when a few idle people collected, a little before six, to tease the workmen who did not choose to join them, they found the work of the mill going on, and no one left on the outside to afford an object for their mirth. They then determined to return at breakfast-time; but here too they were baffled: for the work-people had brought their meals with them, and did not leave the mill till night. Then, indeed, jeers and abusive words were bandied about pretty freely, but no stones were thrown; and Maria declared, that if nothing worse was attempted, she should not mind, and should persevere with her work.

James made the best of his way to the Mill Field, in the hopes of having all his doubts cleared up, and his irresolution overcome, one way or the other. But he was destined to be disappointed. Mr. Robert Wallace, who had intended to be at the meeting, and to take a considerable share in the discussion, was prevented, by an unfortunate accident, from attending. During his afternoon ride, he had been thrown from his horse, and had sprained his ankle. It was very vexatious, and could not have happened at a worse time; for he was the only one of the masters who united the courage, the ability, and inclination, to mix with the men, to aid their discussions, and counteract their proceedings. He was now to be confined to the house for three weeks at least, and by that time it would be too late to do any good, if the men should persevere in their turn-out. He did not, however, feel the less interest in the meeting because he was disabled from attending it; and he sent a note to James, (who would, he knew, be an attentive listener and an intelligent reporter,) to request him to call and give an account of the proceedings, as soon as they should be over.

James obeyed the request, and carried what he thought very wonderful news; but it was no more than Mr. Wallace was prepared for.

When he arrived at the house, he was shewn into the parlour. It was the first time that he had ever been in the drawing-room of a gentleman's house; and he stopped at the door, rather abashed, when he saw that his master was not alone. Mr. Robert Wallace was lying on the sofa, his father was reading to him, and his sister was at work beside him. The old gentleman laid down his book, and beckoned to James to approach. He did so, and, with some hesitation, sat down on a chair to which his master pointed. When his respectful enquiries about the effects of the accident had been answered, he was called upon to reply to various questions about the meeting.

"You had a large attendance, I suppose, James?"

"Very large, indeed, Sir. The Mill-Field is almost as bare as if no grass had ever grown there."

"And plenty of flags and music, I dare say, to make a fine sight of it?"

"O yes, Sir: I was quite surprised. I should think they must have been preparing for it this month past. The procession made such a show, I was frightened to think where the money was to come from. But they have got that ready, too; I am sure I can't think how."

"There has been a great deal going forward just under your nose, that you never found out," said his master, laughing. "So, they don't tell you where they got the money?"

"No, Sir. There's a committee appointed to sit once a week, at the Blue Boy, and they are to manage the money matters. They have a good deal in hand, and there's ever so much more likely to come in. And those that throw up their work are to have enough allowed them to live upon as long as the turn-out lasts."

"With the exception of those who have funds of their own, I suppose?" said his master.

James assented, with a sigh.

"Their money will soon be exhausted, if the turn-out continues pretty general," said Mr. Wallace.

"They say not, Sir; and they have appointed two deputies to travel about. And when somebody objected to the expence of the journey, they said, they could make it answer very well."

"And what are the deputies to do? and where are they going?"

"One of them (my brother Henry) is to go to Nottingham, and Derby, and Leicester; and the other is to go all through Yorkshire and Lancashire; and my brother is to learn all he can from the stocking-weavers, about how they manage against the masters. They say, that the people he is going to see, turn out very often."

"They do, indeed," said Mr. Wallace. "I am glad your brother is going there; he may see enough to make him tremble for the consequences of what he is doing here. But the fund must be a large one, if it will bear these travelling-expences in addition to the other calls upon it."

"But I forgot to say, Sir, that the chief purpose of the journey is to collect money. They say, that there are funds in many places, for the purpose of supporting a turn-out, and that we shall get help now; and then, when we have got high wages again, we are to subscribe to support those who help us now, if they should have to turn out."

"You seem to think, that a turn-out is likely to become a very common thing?"

"They said so to-night, Sir. They say, that a spirit has been roused up among the operatives, all over the kingdom, and that they begin to understand their rights; and that if they now make a vigorous struggle, they will set themselves on an equal footing with the masters, at once, and for ever."

"They had better learn first what they have to struggle against," said Mr. Wallace, "or they may chance to pull down ruin on their own heads, as well as their masters. I suppose, they lay all the blame of the present low wages on the masters?"

"Yes, Sir, they do."

"And do they think it is the masters' doing, that trade is flat at present?"

"No, Sir. They know that the manufacturers would be as glad as any body of a brisk trade; but they say, when trade falls off, the masters can best bear the loss, instead of putting it on the poor."

"I should say, James, that the fairest way is to share the loss, as we do at the present time. The poor share our gains in good times, and it is surely unreasonable in them to expect to go on gaining, while we are losing. If we go on paying our men high wages, while we sell our goods low, we shall lose money by every sale; in a little while it will all be gone; we must turn off all our hands, and shut up our mill. Do not you see this?"

"To be sure, Sir. But if you did not choose to sell your goods so low?"

"Then they might lie by in our warehouses; we should soon have all stock, and no money to pay our men with; while our neighbours, who choose to sell at the market-price, keep on all their hands at lower wages."

"But if all the masters were to agree not to sell under a certain price, the market-price would be always the same, and then the rate of wages would not vary. But I am making too bold, Sir, to talk in this way to you."

"Not at all, James. I have wished all along that the men should have a little talk with the masters, that they may learn to understand one another better about this affair.—You think we might all agree to keep up the price of our goods. Now it is certain, that if any set of manufacturers may venture to dictate to the public, we may; for we stand at the head of this branch of our trade. Well, suppose all the manufacturers of this place fix a certain price upon their goods, and promise their men a certain high rate of wages. For a little while, the public is obliged to come up to their price; but buyers soon begin to complain, and say, 'There is no reason for these goods being so dear. Wool is low-priced, and every thing is favourable to the trade. We have no notion of putting so much money into the manufacturers' pockets, without some good reason. We will make cotton or silk goods answer our purpose.' Some enterprising person hears these complaints: he sets up a manufactory, and says, 'I will let you have worsted goods at a cheaper rate.' The public are very willing to buy of him. His profits are small, but he has a fine trade; his success encourages others to set up in the same line. Our customers leave us; we cannot sell our stock, and are obliged to turn off our hands. But, rather than be turned off, they beg us to lower our prices. 'But we cannot, unless we lower your wages.' 'Well, then, reduce our wages; only let us get our trade back, if we can.'"

"But, Sir, a new manufacturer can't make such prime goods as we can: we should still have the advantage in the quality."

"True, James; for a little while: but 'practice makes perfect,' you know; and in the mean time the difference in quality would be more than made up for by the difference in price. Then our men would take fright when they say that we should not long be able to employ them, and would offer themselves to the new manufacturers, at moderate wages, rather than wait to take the chance of high wages, or nothing."

"But, Sir, would not the new manufacturers be glad to enter into an agreement with you to keep up the high prices? They might, perhaps, do as much business as ever, and put more money into their pockets."

"I think not. They would say, 'It is best to "let well alone."' We have a very good trade, and are satisfied; and if we raise our prices, others will undersell us, as we have undersold you.'—Besides, James, if every manufacturer in our line, in the whole world, was to enter into the agreement, it would answer no purpose. The public are under no obligation to buy worsted goods. Our stock might lie by for the moths to eat, while silk and cotton would be universally worn."

Miss Wallace smiled, and said, "I can answer for the ladies, at least. Every lady would rather wear silk than bombazeen, if she could get it at the same price, or cheaper."

"I see such an agreement is out of the question, Sir," said James. "And I see how the rate of wages depends on the demand for goods. But have the masters nothing to do with the demand? Can't they vary their manufacture so as to please people's taste, any how?"

"You do not seem to be aware," said Mr. Wallace, smiling, "that the public are as much our masters, as we are yours. We make to their orders, and cannot dictate to them what they must like, and what they must wear."

"Then what is it, Sir, that makes the demand so variable?"

"There are many reasons for it. The changes of fashion affect our trade very much. Sometimes, bombazeen and stuff dresses are the fashion for ladies; and then, rather than not be in the fashion, they will pay higher than usual for them."

"I can fancy that very well, Sir. But what is the reason (if I may ask) that there are such changes in the sale of goods that are never out of fashion; such as stockings? I never heard of any fashion in the common kinds of stockings."

"There are several reasons for that, too, James. There is great variation, you know, in the price of cotton and silk, so that the stockings which are made from them can be sold cheaper at one time than another, and more people be tempted to buy. And, then, goods are taken to new places in the countries abroad, and if they please the foreigners, a demand is created there. And if they happen, at any time, to be particularly cheap, the people at home lay by stocks, knowing that they will be sure to come into use. This makes a demand for a little time; but while people are wearing out their stocks, trade is dull; and when people want new stockings, trade revives again: and so on. From one cause or another, there are continual changes."

"But it's a sad thing, Sir, to be always liable to these changes. When times were good, every body said our prosperity would last; but we have been going down in the world, lately: and I shall not believe, another time, that trade will continue good. But it is hard for a poor man to be tossed up and down in such a way."

"There is no reason to suppose that the time will ever come when there will not be fluctuations in trade," said Mr. Wallace; "but these fluctuations are productive of much good to some classes of society, and the evil which they bring with them may be, in a great degree, obviated by prudence on the part of the poor. If work-people like you, James, understood their own interest, they might put their means of subsistence beyond the reach of common chances and changes: and, whatever happened, they might almost make sure of their daily bread."

"I suppose you mean, Sir, by saving up money, while their wages are high?"

"That is one way of placing themselves above want. A man who has a little fund in a savings-bank, has less reason to fear bad times than one who spends all his wages every Saturday night."

"I used to think so, Sir; but I declare I don't know now what to say about it. I have been laying by my earnings, for two years, in the savings-bank; and now I shall have to see it waste away, week after week, when I might just as well have spent it as I got it, and be living now on the fund, as the others are going to do."

"Why should you consume either the public or private fund, while you can go on earning? You have the full use of your limbs and your senses, and you have the strongest possible inducements to work. We have plenty of employment for you: and what reason on earth can there by for your refusing it?"

James shook his head. "When a man is pulled two ways, Sir, as I am, it's hard to know what to do."

"Not at all, I think, James. Go straight on, in your own way, as long as you think it the right one; and if you are firm, not all the world can pull you out of it. I can easily believe, that your brother and his companions will be very glad to have you among them, especially as you will be no expence to them for some time to come; but, unless you approve of their measures, you are not obliged to countenance them. If you do, it's another matter."

"The truth is, Sir, I am not sure, either way; but I will make up my mind as soon as I can."

"In the mean time," said Miss Wallace, "it is a great comfort to know that you have a little fund of your own to depend on. I have seen a poor woman to-day, who repents most bitterly that she and her husband did not lay by a part of their earnings while they might. They and their three children as now so reduced, that there is little better than starvation before them. They are to have a weekly allowance from the fund; but it is so small, that it will barely find them bread."

"They have joined the turn-out, then?" said Mr. Wallace.

"They have," she replied. "It is Hannah Gould I am speaking of."

"Hannah Gould!" exclaimed James; "I thought she meant to go on with her work."

"So she did, but her husband will not allow her," replied Miss Wallace. "He has been threatened, and he left his work to-day, and obliges his wife to give up hers also. She came to me, to entreat me to employ her in washing, or cleaning, or in any way I could. I told her I was surprised that she should ask me to assist her, when she was using her employers so ill; but she cried so that it made my heart ache, while she said that she would give the world to be able to go on with her work."

"Do you think any plan can be a good one, which is upheld by such tyranny as this?" said Mr. Wallace to James.

"I fear not, Sir: and I think the men have no right to complain of their masters, while they are so tyrannical themselves."

"I asked the woman," continued Miss Wallace, "whether her children are not able to earn something: but it happens, most unfortunately, that they are employed in our mill also, and have been obliged to turn out; so all the resources of the family are cut off at once."

"That puts me in mind," said her brother, "of what I was going to say before. Another way in which the poor may guard against want, is by bringing up their families to different occupations. I have tried again and again to impress this upon the minds of our men, when I have seen them bring one child after another to our mill, to be set to work. It is certainly a great temptation to a poor man to place his children at an employment, where, at seven years of age, they may earn half-a-crown a week, and get more as they grow older: but he should remember, that, when bad times come, they come upon all at once; when one is out of work, all are idle. It is very true, that a boy who is brought up to be a shoemaker or a carpenter, does not begin earning so soon, and does not, for a long time, earn so much as a spinner; but it is surely a great comfort to a man, when he is out of work himself, to have two or three sons at different trades, who are able to contribute to the support of the family."

"I was talking over this matter with Hannah Gould this afternoon," observed Miss Wallace. "She told me, that, some years ago, when they were very well off in the world, a good opportunity occurred for apprenticing their eldest boy to a shoemaker; and both the boy and she wished it: but her husband said, he had much better be earning five shillings a week at our mill, than learn a trade which would bring in nothing for years to come. So the lad added his portion to the earnings of the family, which was actually not wanted, and was always spent as it came in; and now, when he might have been well established as a shoemaker, he cannot earn a farthing, and adds to the distress of his family, instead of helping to support them."

"They must have earned a great deal formerly," observed her brother.

"Upwards of forty-five shillings a week, at one time," replied Miss Wallace; "and yet they laid by nothing."

James had been so much interested by what had passed, that he never thought how late it was growing. It was now just dark, and Miss Wallace rang for the candles. James started up, and begged pardon for having intruded so long. His master spoke kindly to him, and saying that he was likely to be confined to the house for some time, desired James to call, if he had any thing to communicate about the turn-out, or wished for any information on the important questions now at issue between the masters and men. James bowed low, and thought to himself what a happy thing it would be, if all masters were as free with their people, and as anxious about their interests.

The streets were full of people, who stood talking over the important affairs which filled every mind; and James met many acquaintances, who invited him into public-houses for a little chat. But, irresolute as he sometimes was in matters of opinion, his habits of temperance and regularity were fixed; and, feeling that he had no time for further talk this night, and no money to spend at a public-house, he made his way steadily through the bustle of the streets, and soon arrived at his own home.

Chapter III.

Henry Gilbert was fully engaged, all this evening, in making arrangements for the business which was to be transacted during his absence. He assembled the committee, who were to meet weekly at the Blue Boy, and put them in the way to manage their affairs; he promised to write once a week, and to transmit supplies of money, as he should receive them; he wrote letters to the committees of operatives of various manufacturing towns, and sent a handbill to the printer's, which he had composed in the course of the day, and resolved to circulate, if the meeting should go off well. The absence of Mr. Wallace was an unexpected piece of good fortune; and all wore so favourable an aspect, that, when he returned home, after midnight, he forgot his fatigues, in the hope that the masters would soon give way, and wages be as high as ever. He found his brother awake, and anxious to see him, and ascertain his purpose about his journey.

"I am to be off in six hours from this time," said Henry.

"And how long will you be gone?"

"A month or more, I dare say. I shall write to you, James, by the parcels I shall send to the committee. So you may enquire at the Blue Boy for letters from me. I hope to send you flourishing news."

"I wish you may," replied James; "but, as far as I can learn, matters are any thing but flourishing, in the places you are going to."

"They can't be worse than they were before the turn-out," replied Henry; "and they are likely to be better soon, if the people persevere in their demands. I wish, before I go, James, that I could make you see what a mean-spirited thing it is of you to go on taking your work, while we are running all the risk of trying to get higher wages for you."

"For yourselves, you had better say, Henry. It's my belief, that better wages will come all the sooner for our waiting patiently."

"Then you think quite wrong, James, as I have proved to you again and again. I will argue the matter with you once more, now, tired as I am. Just listen."

"I know all you have to say, thank you, brother; so there's no occasion; and it's time you were asleep, if you are to be off so early in the morning."

"Well, but it's very provoking," persisted Henry. "I declare I'm ashamed, while I'm so forward in the cause, that my own brother should slink away from me. I heard ever so many people say, to-night, that it is very shabby to let them push and struggle as they do, while you take your money as long as you can get it. I warrant, you will be as ready as any to take better wages, when the masters give way."

James sighed, and was silent.

"It's for your own good, for your own credit, that I care so much," continued Henry. "It signifies little to me, on my own account; but I don't like to hear people talk of you as they do. Now, promise me, before I go, that you will do as others do."

"I can't promise that," replied James: "but I will think the matter over again: and yet I've thought about it till I'm tired and sick of it."

His brother could get no more from him. They walked together to the coach, in the morning, where they found a party of operatives assembled to see their leader depart on his travels. When James had shaken his brother by the hand, and watched the coach till it turned the corner at the end of the street, he quitted the group of idlers, and pursued his way to the mill. They gave three cheers, on the departure of their deputy; and James sighed, as he heard them, and thought how strange it was that he, who liked the security of belonging to a party, and was more disposed to shelter himself behind others, than to court observation, should now be left standing alone in an affair of great importance; exposed to the displeasure of his excellent master on one hand, and to that of his brother, and to the sneers and taunts of his companions, on the other. The necessity of decision increased every hour, but the difficulty increased also. He had a kind of persuasion that ruin would be the end of the matter, either way;

but this persuasion, instead of inspiring courage, contributed to his irresolution. He usually ended by going to Maria for comfort, while his conscience was, all the time, whispering to him the uncomfortable truth, that Maria's difficulties were the very same as his own, and that it was therefore his duty to support her, instead of being dependent on her stronger mind.

Henry Gilbert was well satisfied with his station on the top of the coach, for it happened that he was as happily placed for an argument on his favourite subject, as if he had been declaiming in the Mill-Field, or holding forth at the Blue Boy. He sat next to a gentleman who seemed quite disposed for conversation, and whose attention was so attracted by the group of persons who cheered Gilbert on his departure, that he asked the meaning of their attendance. Henry was proud of his office, and did not care if all the world knew where he was going, and for what purpose; and supposing, by the gentleman's question, that he was a stranger in Yorkshire, he gave him a full account of the turn-out and its attendant circumstances. The gentleman made many inquiries, and accounted for his interest in the narrative by saying that he was a hosier, and lived at Derby; that there was at present a turn-out in that place, and that there had been several since he set up in business; so that he had had a good deal of experience in such things.

"And do you think they are likely to stand out long, Sir?" enquired Gilbert.

"Probably not," replied the gentleman, "for they are reduced to the lowest degrees of poverty."

"Why, Sir, they can hardly be worse off than they were before the strike, as far as I can learn."

"You are mistaken," replied the gentleman. "It is true that their wages were low; but it is surely better to earn eight or ten shillings a week, than nothing at all."

"I think it is worth while giving up ten shillings a week, for a time, if they can get sixteen or twenty by it, for a continuance."

"But they will do no such thing; the state of trade does not allow of it," said the gentleman.

"They had twenty shillings a week, ten years ago," observed Gilbert, "and they have had less and less every year since; and is it to be expected that they will allow themselves to be ground down in that manner?"

"You are right in your fact, it is true that wages have been lower every year for ten years; but that is no fault of the masters, nor can they remedy the evil."

"What is to be done then, Sir?"

"To find a remedy for an evil, we must first ascertain its cause. I do not know how it may be in your branch of trade, but in ours it is undoubtedly true, that the supply of labour exceeds the demand: the supply of workmen exceeds the demand of work to be done. I have been in business many years, and have watched the growth of the evil, and I can therefore speak with certainty on the subject. When I first went into partnership with my father, ours was not so large a trade as it is at present, though a very good one. Labour of every kind was well paid at that time; agricultural labour better than any: so that, instead of operatives coming in crowds to ask for work; as they do now-a-days, we were obliged to ask them to do our work, and to pay them high wages to induce them to do so. We sold our goods at a great profit, and gradually extended our trade; but, by degrees, many other hosiers set up in our neighbourhood, paid their people the same wages that we did, and had, for a time, an equally good trade; but the demand did not increase in proportion to the quantity of goods manufactured; so that the market was overstocked. We suffered by the depreciation of our stocks, for we were now compelled to sell our goods low, though we had paid high for the materials and labour we had employed. We were obliged to leave off manufacturing for a little time; and, when we began again, to lower our wages. This occasioned much discontent among the people: for it unfortunately happened that their numbers had increased as our trade had been going down. Those who had been able to marry on their high wages, had, by this time, families growing up who wanted employment. Many of their neighbours too, seeing their prosperity, brought up their children to be frame-work knitters, or became so themselves; so that there was nearly double the number of hands, while our trade had not increased in nearly the same proportion. Well; when we began to manufacture again, there were so many who wished to be employed, that we set on a great number of hands, and got a great deal of work done, though we paid away no more in wages than we had done at first. The natural effect of this was to make those who had quitted their trades to become frame-work knitters, return to their old occupations again; and then wages rose a little."

"And I suppose, Sir," said Gilbert, "that your people did not bring up their children to their own business, as there were too many hands already?"

"They would have been wise not to have done so," replied the gentleman: "but they did not look far enough to see their own interest. I did all in my power to shew them the advantage of bringing up their children to different trades, that, when one fails, there may be others to depend on; but I did little good. The fact is, that children of thirteen and upwards can earn almost as much as their parents at our business; and this temptation is so strong, that the consequences are overlooked. These consequences are evident enough now, however; the number of hands has multiplied so far beyond the demand, that I do not believe that class of people can enjoy any permanent prosperity, till they bring up their children to other occupations, so that the number of operatives may be considerably lessened."

"How did matters stand at the conclusion of the war, Sir? I should have thought that the numbers of workpeople in your trade would have been suddenly increased, as I am told was the case with all trades; and yet wages were higher then than they are now."

"The rate of wages was very high that year and the next; but that is accounted for, by the great demand of goods which was created by our intercourse with the Continent. And it is an additional proof how much too rapidly the supply of operatives has increased, that, notwithstanding the new markets which have been opened to us on the Continent, wages have been lower and lower every year, since the first flush of business which was occasioned by the peace. Now, it seems to be strange, that, when the poverty of the operatives so evidently proceeds from causes over which their masters have no power, these masters, who, I am sure, are as kindly disposed as possible towards their people, should bear the whole blame."

"I can't help thinking, the masters might prevent or remedy a great deal of the evil, if they chose," replied Gilbert.

"In what manner? I am sure it would be a most acceptable secret for them to learn; for their interests are the same as those of their men."

"The same as their men, Sir!" exclaimed Gilbert. "Do you mean that it is no advantage to the masters to pay low wages, while they are putting large profits into their own pockets? And if it is no disadvantage to them to fix a rate of wages, and keep to it, why don't they do it?"

"What I mean is, that it is always well for the masters to be able to give their men good wages; and that, when wages are very low, it is a sure sign that the interests of the masters are suffering. As for their paying low wages while their profits are high, it's no more possible for them to go on doing so, than to pay high wages while they make no profits."

"Why, Sir? I have heard them complained of for doing it, many a time: and it is one of the great things we have to find fault with."

"Then I think you find fault on insufficient grounds. It is not in the nature of things that the manufacturers should do so."

"Please to tell me, Sir, what you mean by 'the nature of things;' for those words don't make me see the matter clear."

"Well, then, I will explain my meaning. You and I both agree that manufacturers of every kind wish to keep wages as low as they can; but I am of the opinion that they cannot, if they would, reduce them, permanently, below a just level. When the demand for goods is very brisk, the manufacturer employs as many hands as he can obtain. So do other masters in the same branch of trade. But if there be not men enough to supply them all, one who cannot get the number he wants, raises his wages, so that the operatives are glad to work for him. His neighbours find that their men are inclined to leave them, and are obliged to raise their wages also, and to continue them at the same rate as long as the demand lasts. When prices fall, and their profits are diminished, wages are lowered again, of course."

"But, Sir," said Gilbert, "your case only supposed that there are not hands enough to do all the work: you were saying, a little time ago, that there are too many."

"While there are too many, the masters do not make large profits, for the very evident reason, that there are plenty of goods in the market, and the prices are therefore low. It is only while the demand exceeds the production, that large profits can be made; and then wages are high. So now you see what I mean by saying, that the interests of the masters and men are the same, whether they will or no."

"Then, Sir, it would be for the good of both to have a fixed rate of wages; for I am sure it is for the interests of the men."

"I thought you must have known," said the gentleman, "that the experiment has been tried, and failed. In the year 1819, there was a turn-out among our people. Wages were then as low as had ever been known, though not so depressed as they have been since. The masters were very sorry for the condition of the poor; and, though they foresaw the consequences, consented, at the request of their men, to establish an advanced list of prices. The demand declined, hands were discharged, prices fell, and as wages could not fall, only a very few of the best hands were employed, and the majority of the people were in a state of actual starvation. They came to the masters, to beg that the agreement might be broken, and that many hands might be employed on low wages, rather than a few at the fixed rate. In the mean time, the masters had suffered so much from the depreciation of their stocks, that their means of employing operatives were very much cramped: and though the agreement was thus soon annulled, the men felt its consequences for a long time, in the decline of their masters' trade. Depend upon it, no good will ever be done by thus interfering with the natural course of things."

"You will hardly persuade starving people to let things take their natural course, if they think any change will be for the better," said Gilbert.

"They will best mend their condition by conforming to the natural course of things, instead of trying to control events which are beyond the power of any one set of men. Commerce will be regulated by the events of kingdoms; trade will be brisk or flat, prices will rise and fall, and masters and men may struggle and strive, and help or oppose one another to the end of their days, without producing any permanent effect on the general state of commercial affairs: but if they cannot make trade suit their purposes, they must learn to make their purposes suit the state of trade. They will never be able to stretch their gains so as to maintain any number of people they choose; but they may ascertain how many labourers can be supported by any particular branch of manufacture, and, if they are wise, will proportion the supply of labour to the demand."

"But, Sir," said Gilbert, "if you think the over-proportion of hands the great evil of all, I wonder you disapprove of a turn-out; because it withdraws a great number of hands from the trade."

"True," replied the gentleman; "and this one consequence of a turn-out is beneficial as far as it goes. But the advantage is only slight and temporary; and the inconvenience, distress, and mischief produced, are very great. It is evident, that if all hands are withdrawn from the trade for a month, it is nearly the same as if a twelfth part of the number of operatives was withdrawn for a year."

"Quite the same, surely, Sir."

"Not quite; for we are to consider that the trade of the masters suffers in the mean time; for they are unable to execute their orders, which are, in consequence, transferred to their competitors in other places. If the turn-out continues for two months, it is nearly the same thing as a sixth part of the hands being withdrawn for a twelve-month; and as this occasions a sale of stocks, and a temporary advance in the price of goods, while the people are maintained independently of their masters, it is in some degree beneficial. But if a turn-out lasts long enough to injure trade materially, its evil effects more than counterbalance the temporary advantage gained: and we must also consider the poverty the people endure in the mean time, the bad effects of idleness, of contention with their employers, and of dependence on the bounty of the public:—evils which it can never be worth while to incur for so transient an advantage as I have described; and that advantage, too, not the one the people have in view when they turn out. If they obtain their object—an advanced list of prices—the consequences are unmixed evil, as I have already told you."

"I was not satisfied though, Sir, with what you told me. If times are bad, it comes much to the same thing, whether a few are well paid, or many badly paid. Indeed, it seems to me better that the father of a family should be well paid in bad times, and his children be able to turn their hands to other things, than that they should all work, and only bring in the wages of one. If times are good, it seems right that the masters should be obliged to pay high wages while they can afford it."

"When trade is good, wages will be high, with or without an agreement: when it is bad, manufacturers who have capital will rather keep out of the markets for a time, than pay higher wages than their profits will afford: and those who have little capital, and are therefore obliged to make and sell, will send their work to be done at some place out of the limits of their agreement."

"What a pity," exclaimed Gilbert, "that the agreement cannot extend over the whole country!"

"In that case," replied the gentleman, "trade would fly out of the kingdom, instead of from one county into the next. The agreement is a bad thing in itself, depend upon it; and the more it is extended, the worse will be the results.—All experience shews it to be so. Parliament has now and then regulated the rate of wages: but it has invariably been found that such regulations and a good trade could not subsist together. Either trade has stood still, or the regulations have been broken. So it has ever been, and so it will ever be."

Gilbert made no reply, and the gentleman continued.—"I have only spoken of a turn-out as it affects trade. Of the extent and pressure of domestic misery which it occasions, I think you cannot be aware, or you would not be so ready as you are to encourage your townsmen in their proceedings. You will see enough, where you are going, to shake your confidence, and to sicken your heart; and I wish, when you return home, that you may not find those very men who cheered you on your departure, ready to call you to account, ay, and even to curse you, for having persuaded them to snatch the bread from their children's mouths, and to plunge themselves into such misery as years and years of toil cannot retrieve."

Gilbert was startled: it was but three days since he had told his townsmen that their masters wished "to snatch the bread from their children's mouths," and now it seemed that the same accusation might possibly be brought against himself. The apprehension that the whole system of opinions, on which he had been acting so vigorously, might be wrong, crossed him from time to time, in the course of the preceding conversation; and he now sat, lost in thought, with gloom on his countenance and sadness in his heart, while the gentleman conversed with a passenger on the other side. In a short time the coach stopped at the gate of a pretty country house; and the gentleman, turning to Gilbert, said, "I am going to alight here, so I wish you good morning. I shall be at Derby before you reach the place; and, if you wish for any further conversation, I hope you will call on me there. My name is ____; but stay, I will give you my card, and then you will not forget where to find me."

He gave his address to Gilbert, who thanked him, but did not choose to commit himself by promising to call. He was pleased by the gentleman's kind and easy manner; but he did not like the opinions he had heard, well supported as they were, and had no wish to be convinced that his own were wrong: so, as soon as he had made his parting bow to his travelling companion, he began to run over in his mind all the arguments on his side of the question, and worked up his imagination by thinking of the speeches he had made and meant to make, the arrangements he had formed, the compliments he had enjoyed and the thanks he anticipated, till the new impressions he had just received lost much of their force, and he steadied his wavering mind by applying to its support all the old prejudices, which had been nearly over-thrown by fair argument. If Gilbert had been merely a factious and ambitious man, he would not have been thus troubled: he would have pursued his own ends, without caring for reason or argument; and the sufferings of others would have been of small account with him. But his ambition was mixed with better motives: it was a sincere belief that he could benefit his townsmen, which made him first come forward in the present cause; and if a love of power and applause led him on, he never long forgot that it was not for his own sake alone that he sought them. If he had once been thoroughly convinced that his cause was a bad one, he would have forsaken it, though at the sacrifice of his plans of ambition; but he had not the means of obtaining so sudden a conviction; and against a more gradual one, his mind was barred by his prejudices and interests. He was made uneasy by doubt, for a while, and was sorry that any thing could be said on the opposite side of the question; but, like most other people, he suffered his judgment to be biased by his interests, and not only recurred to his old opinions, but half determined that he would avoid argument in future, for fear he should again be troubled with doubts. He soon convinced himself, that he could have said much more than he did, to prove himself right;—he determined not to be taken by surprise another time, but to have his arguments more ready;—he remembered, that it was the interest of the masters to talk as the gentleman had done;—and, having thus satisfied himself, he began to look about him more than he had yet found time to do, to admire the country, and to talk about the harvest with the other passengers on the coach.

Chapter IV.

Henry Gilbert intended to take up his abode, while he remained at Leicester, with a relation, who was a frame-work knitter in that place. He had, once before, paid a visit to this cousin George, who was then in comfortable circumstances, and living in great respectability; and, as he had been very lately married, and had written in high spirits to announce the event, Henry expected to enjoy his visit very much: and, on his arrival at Leicester, he lost no time in making his way to the house where George formerly lived, and where he expected to find him now. But the house was shut up, and, on enquiry, he learned that his cousin had removed, about three weeks before, to another part of the town. He had great difficulty in finding the alley to which he was directed; and, when a neighbour led him up a steep flight of stairs, to the garret of an old and almost ruinous house, he felt convinced that there was some mistake, and that he had not yet succeeded in finding his cousin's abode. This conviction was strengthened by the appearance of the room, when the door was opened. A young woman was sitting on a bed, which was laid on the floor, and was the only article of furniture in the room except a clothes-chest. She was employed in mending the tattered gown she had on; and her appearance was slatternly in the extreme. Her cap, dirty and ragged, had slipped back on her head, and her hair was hanging about her ears: she was thin and haggard; and the few clothes she wore did not fit her, and were so worn, that it seemed as if no mending would make them long hold together. She looked up, as Henry opened the door, and, in a hoarse voice, asked what he wanted. Henry said he was sorry he had disturbed her, and that he had mistaken the room;—he was in search of a person named George Gilbert, and he supposed he had best enquire at the next house.

"George Gilbert lives here," said the young woman; "but he is not at home at present."

Henry was shocked. "And are you his wife?" he enquired.

"Yes, I am; and who are you, if I may ask?"

"You may have heard George speak of his cousin Henry?"

"O, yes: but if you are Henry Gilbert, I am afraid my husband will not like to see you. Times are changed with us, and he will be ashamed to meet you."

"No need to be ashamed of poverty, where all are poor; and especially if it is owing to a struggle to get back the poor man's rights," said Henry. But, though he spoke thus, he was so overcome with this sight of wretchedness, that he would gladly have taken a seat. There was no chair in the room; but he sank down on the chest, though he saw that the young woman felt no wish that he should remain with her.

"When will your husband return?" he enquired.

She shook her head, but did not reply.

"Perhaps, if you could tell me where to find him, I might go and speak to him, instead of meeting him here first. He might like that better."

"He is sometimes with the committee, at the White Lion, down the street yonder: but I don't know whether you'll find him there now."

Henry left here, and proceeded to the place. He was sick at heart; and the sounds of drunken mirth, which issued from the public-house, disgusted him. "Our committee shall be conducted in a more orderly way," thought he: "this noise is quite discreditable to the managers." The noise increased. Three or four men, some drunk, some sober, but all ragged and wretched-looking, came out of the door of the White Lion. One of them reeled on the pavement, and staggered against Henry, who caught hold of him, to save him from falling. It was his cousin George. This was too much for Henry. He turned from George, leaned his head against the wall, and burst into tears. One of the bystanders observed him, and addressed him thus: "If you are a relation of this man, it would be the greatest kindness you could do him, to prevent his attending the committee. I have seen him for some time past, spend his whole weekly allowance in liquor, as soon as the money is put into his hands. He has a wife, starving at home; and the woman who keeps the house knows that, as well as I do, and it's a shame that she supplies him with liquor as often as he asks for it."

The landlady, who stood at the door, heard this, and instantly retorted, "It is no business of yours how the man spends his money. As long as he pays for his liquor, he shall have it; and nobody has a right to prevent it."

"It must be prevented, however," said the man: "I am on the committee, and I shall look to it. Our funds are intended to supply the people with bread, and not to encourage them in drunkenness. George Gilbert had better go to the workhouse at once, than starve six days in the week, and get drunk on the seventh. "Come," said he to Henry, "help me to get him home."

"What will his poor wife say?" said Henry.

"O, it's no new thing to her: it was just the same this day week," replied the man.

She was not surprised, but evidently much grieved that Henry should have seen her husband in this state. Henry laid him on his miserable bed, and, slipping a small sum of money into the wife's hand, he left the house, saying, that he would call early in the morning, that he might see his cousin before he went out for the day. Henry was very conscientious about the disposal of the public money with which he was entrusted: he knew that it was his duty to collect funds, instead of giving any thing away; but the scene of want which he had just beheld affected him so deeply, that he could not resist attempting to relieve it, determining to go to bed supperless himself, as the money which he had bestowed was not his own.

As the committee was now sitting, he returned to the White Lion, and introduced himself, and announced his business. He spent the rest of the day in going over various parts of the town, to ascertain the state of the operatives; and, in the evening, he sat down to pen his first report to the committee at home. He informed them that the condition of the people was worse than they had anticipated, as the funds of the turn-out were failing; that, so far from being able to induce the committee to furnish him with a supply, they had entreated their Yorkshire brethren to assist them in holding out a little longer: this, however, was out of the question; and it was therefore much to be feared, that, in this place, the masters must gain another triumph. The time was not yet come, however, and something might yet turn up, which would help them to prolong the struggle. He hoped to be able to send a more encouraging report from the next place he should visit; and, in the mean time, begged leave to urge that the spirit of the operatives should be kept up by all possible means; and that no time should be lost in applying, by letter, to the operatives of Norwich, Kidderminster, and other places, to solicit their support and co-operation. He concluded by requesting them to put the inclosed letter into his brother James's hands.

This last-mentioned letter was to be written after his interview with his cousin, the next morning. Henry was disappointed at not being accommodated without expence at George's house, as he had calculated. The scenes he had witnessed impressed him with the necessity of the utmost frugality, and he therefore sought out the cheapest lodging he could procure. After a restless night, he rose early to refresh himself by a walk, and then proceeded to George's garret. He found him ill in health, and wounded in spirits; stung with shame at having been seen by his cousin, the day before, in so degraded a state, and dreading to meet him. Henry's kindness, however, soon induced him to open his heart; and the poor young man felt relieved when he had confided to his cousin all his misery, and his repentance for various acts of imprudence of which he had been guilty. Henry blamed him frankly for much misconduct, especially for his weakness in giving way to the temptation to drown his cares in liquor; but he held out hopes of better times, and soothed him by his kind sympathy. Having done what he could to encourage him to break through his bad habits, and to bear up for the present, he bade him farewell, grieved that it was not in his power to bestow more substantial kindness. He wrote to his brother, dispatched his packet, and then took his departure, much disappointed that nothing more remained to be done in this place. His letter was as follows

"Dear James,

I did not intend to have written to you yet, but I have a piece of advice which I cannot refrain from giving you as soon as possible. Whatever you do, don't marry while the turn-out lasts. No matter whether you go on with your work or not, (which I hope you have given up by this time, or soon will,) such times as these are not times for marrying; and though I know you and Maria have waited long, and though I am sorry you must still wait, I am sure you will be glad in the end that you have had patience. I dare say you agree with me, as it is; I am sure you would, if you had seen our poor cousin George and his wife. He married just before the turn-out began, and in full prospect of it, which was very foolish, as he owns now, poor fellow. But they thought they should be no poorer together than separate; or, as I should rather say, they were tired of waiting. Nothing can repair the mischief now, in my opinion. If times should be ever so good, henceforth, they will never love one another as they would have done, if they had been more prudent. He could not bear to see her all dirt and rags, and to come home to nothing but a poor empty garret; so he began to like the public-house, and spent what little money he got there, instead of bringing it home to her; so it was not to be wondered at that her temper is rather soured; and I am afraid that no prosperity will make them very happy in their own minds, or with each other. I should be very sorry to see Maria reduced to the condition of George's wife, or either of you suffer in your tempers; so I thought I had better write at once, and give you the warning, which I hope you will take as it is meant.

If you feel any interest in the affairs of the turn-out, (which I cannot doubt, especially if you are by this time one of us,) you can learn from the committee what I have been doing in the way of business. I have no time to say more than that I am, with regards to all friends,

Your affectionate brother,
Henry Gilbert."

The reports which the committee continued to receive from Gilbert were not so satisfactory as he or they could have wished. As his journey lay through those parts where poverty at present prevailed, and where a turn-out was a common event, he failed in obtaining supplies of money; but he learned better how to obtain money from places which were not so impoverished. He was surprised to witness the boldness and importunity with which the operatives appealed to the public for support; and he was equally surprised to see how readily the public answered the appeal. In spite of all the representations the masters could make, in spite of the warnings of experience, the rich and middle classes continued to give money almost as often as they were asked. They knew that by thus supporting the turn-out they were materially injuring the interests of trade, while they could administer no permanent relief to the operatives, but there was something in the wretched plight of the men, which moved the compassion of all who saw them, and prompted the effort to relieve their present distress, whatever the consequences might be. The masters themselves did not cease to feel for the distresses of their men, though convinced of the badness of the cause, and suffering from its effects. Scarcely one of them knew how to keep his money in his pocket, when he saw the wan faces and tattered clothing of the men whom he had known industrious and prosperous. Scarcely one but would turn out of his way, when the distant drum announced the approach of a procession; not because he feared to meet his men, but because the sight of so much misery, which he could not relieve, was distressing. Many people wondered that, while actually wanting bread, the operatives should choose to have their processions ornamented with flags, and preceded by a band of music; but their policy was good, and they gained by it. The sights and sounds attracted attention; and the contrast between the gaiety of the trappings, and the squalid appearance of those who bore them,—between the liveliness of their tunes, and the gloomy countenances of those who marched to them,—was so forcible and so sad, that the sympathies of the beholders were powerfully wrought upon, and money flowed in on every side. Gilbert was an acute observer, and thought to himself, as he followed one of these processions through the streets of Derby, "We began too soon with our flags and music. We paid a great deal for them, and made nothing by them; our men looked as if they wanted for nothing. By the time they look like these poor creatures, (if that time must come,) the novelty of the processions will be over. Well, if the gentlefolks don't send money out to us, as we pass their houses we must go from door to door, as they do here."

Though Gilbert was not able to do much by his own exertions for the benefit of the fund, he put his brother deputy in the way of better success. He wrote to him, to beg that he would lose nothing for want of asking; and assured him that he would find the public mind in favour of their cause, if he was but bold enough in claiming assistance. He urged the same thing on the committee, and with great success. In a short time, supplies flowed in from every quarter. The weavers of Norwich sent a remittance from time to time, attended by many assurances of sympathy and support. Though they had never gone through the process of a regular turn-out, they knew something of the nature of disputes about wages, and had now and then had a struggle with their masters, in the course of which they had impaired the dignity of their cause, and tried the tempers of their employers, by petty acts of violence. Brickbats and stones were not the best arguments they could use to shew the justice of their claims; nor were the attention and consideration of the masters so easily secured by breaking their windows, as they might have been in other ways. Their leaders, however, their deputies, and the members of their committee, tried to substitute fair argument for threats and tumult, and expressed their warm approbation of the conduct of the Yorkshire operatives, however mistaken in principle, were almost uniformly quiet and peaceable in their behaviour. The operatives of Kidderminster and many other places contributed their aid to the struggle: and when Henry Gilbert returned, after a month's absence, he found the affairs of the turn-out in a more flourishing state than he had ventured to hope. When he reckoned up the funds in hand, he thought over what his first travelling companion had said to him about the group of followers who had cheered his departure. "Nobody seems inclined to call me to account, much less to curse me," thought he. "Some of the people, to be sure, are not quite so warm in the cause as they were at first; but others are; and there are no signs of such poverty as there is in other places. I hope we may avoid such distress as that, because we were not so reduced when we began: and, indeed, I think the masters will soon be tired of telling their correspondents that they cannot execute their orders. They will soon be glad to take us on our own terms."

But his tone was not so triumphant when he had met his brother James, and had called to see Maria. *They* did not call him to account, or shew by word or look that they blamed him, or doubted the wisdom of his measures. The time for remonstrance was past; all were now involved together, and together they must make the best of their lot; but the gentleman's warning came across Henry's mind, whenever his feelings were touched by his brother's distress: and this happened every day, and many times in a day. James and Maria had encountered so much opposition and ill-will by continuing their work, and were at length so alarmed by threats, that they had, at the end of a fortnight from Henry's departure, relinquished their employment. The cottage in which they had hoped, ere this, to have been comfortably settled, was occupied by others, and their prospect of marrying was more distant and uncertain than ever. Their endeavours to obtain employment of another kind were in vain; for those who had turned out before them, engrossed all that was to be had. They were allowed nothing from the fund, while they had any of their own money left; so they were obliged to go to the savings-bank, to draw out a weekly sum for their support. Though they barely allowed themselves necessaries, they foresaw that their little hoard would soon be gone; and when Henry exulted in the flourishing state of the fund, they lamented in secret over every remittance which assisted to prolong the struggle, and to keep them in idleness. Maria strove to employ herself, in order to relieve her mind; but when she had mended her clothes, and done every thing she could think of to make her room tidy and clean, nothing remained to be done. She tried to help her neighbours, but they were most of them as idle as herself, and many were parting by degrees with their furniture and clothes, as the allowance they received from the fund would not suffice to maintain their families. The days appeared very long and tedious. Maria was able to read, and her lover took her on long walks with him: but she could not read all day; and, from being unused to the amusement, she could not enjoy it for a long time together. As for the walks, they soon became listless and melancholy: they were not enjoyed as such pleasures are when preceded by hard labour. They were little relished, because they had not been earned. Besides, James and Maria had little that was pleasant to talk about. They had nothing to say of the labours of the past day, or of that which was coming; no intercourse with their master, no cheerful chat with their companions; nothing to look forward to, but a change for the worse in their condition; nothing to relate but the increasing distress of their neighbours, or some new prognostication that the turn-out would last for many months yet, or that, if it did, the trade of the place would be gone for ever.

Though they loved one another as much as ever, and each would have made any sacrifice for the other's good, their intercourse was not what it had been. They were dull and silent when they were together; and as they might be together every day, and all day long, their intercourse was not prized as it had been, when they parted for a day of toil, and met for an hour of refreshment. Maria grew thin, and James looked gloomy; and when he expressed his fear that she did not allow herself comforts enough, and begged her to take care of her health, and not be afraid of spending money while she had it, she declared that it was not food nor rest, but work that she wanted.

"It *is* hard, I declare," said James, "that people may not work when they wish it, and when there's plenty for them to do."

"Have you told your brother," asked Maria, "that you have changed your mind about the goodness of the cause?"

"No," he replied, "I am not sure yet about the matter."

"I thought that last conversation with Mr. Wallace convinced you quite?"

"So I thought at the time, and after each of the three conversations I have had with him. But, somehow, there's a great deal to be said on both sides: and there's no occasion to decide; because, you know, it is plain enough how I must act, whatever I may think. And I do not want to argue it all over again with Henry, for I am tired of hearing so much about it."

"I wish I could see you look as brisk and cheerful as your brother does," said Maria.

"I wonder sometimes how it is that he keeps up so well," said James; "for, if he makes us pinch, he lives as low as any of us; and I suppose he has more cares, having so many to care for. He does not spare himself, that I must say for him; and what he does is for the public good, whether he be right or wrong."

"He does not know what it is to be idle," observed Maria; "he is as busy now as in his hardest working days; and it is an easier thing to live low, when one has not time to think about it. Henry cares a good deal, too, about what people think of him; and he must be anxious sometimes, when he remembers that he is answerable for so much; but this kind of care is a very different thing from ours: I sometimes think that his troubles will come when ours are over."

"No, no," said James; "when Henry has once taken up an opinion, he keeps it, whatever happens. If he were to see us all in the workhouse, or dying of starvation, he would still insist upon it that he is in the right, and that the next generation will think so, if we don't."

It occurred to Maria, if the brothers had been able to temper each other's character, how much sorrow might have been avoided. Though she looked on her lover in the most favourable light, she could not help being aware that he was deficient in resolution and firmness. Henry was as much in the other extreme: if he could have imparted some of his decision to his brother, and have received in return a disposition open to conviction, their opinions and conduct would have been more correct, and their happiness more secure.

At the time when the affairs of the turn-out were in the most prosperous state, a deputation was sent from the committee to each of the masters, to inform them how distant was the prospect of their men returning to work at the old prices, and to invite them to yield the point at once, that the interests of trade might no longer suffer. Though this proceeding wore some appearance of bravado, it was not so intended. The present was thought a good opportunity for putting an end to the long-disputed question, which the operatives now believed must at length be decided in their favour. But the masters looked forward to the time when the supplies, which now poured in, must fail; and, though dispirited at the prospect of a long continuance of the struggle, they remained firm.

"You had my answer long ago," said Mr. Wallace, in reply to the deputation.

"We hoped you might have changed your mind; Sir, in consequence of the news we brought."

"Your intelligence makes no difference in my opinion of the event," he replied. "You live upon casual supplies; we, upon our capital. The question is, which can hold out the longest? Though you are injuring your own interests as much as ours, by compelling us to consume our capital, the alternative is better than that of driving away our trade for ever, by raising the price of wages and of goods higher than the demand will justify. Of two great evils which you force upon us, we choose the least, and abide by our choice. Our capital may grow again; but our trade, once gone, is gone for ever."

"But the time is come, Sir, when some change must be made. We cannot live on the wages you offer us."

"If that be the case," replied Mr. Wallace, "I am very sorry. I know times are worse with you than they have been; and so they are with us. But you apply in the wrong place for a remedy; and the means by which you seek a cure, will only hasten your ruin. Your support depends on the capital of your employers, and in proportion as that capital wastes away, your ruin approaches. But perhaps you have not leisure or inclination to listen to argument just now: nor is this the time when it will make the most impression."

"Our public meetings are open to you, Sir. We shall be happy to hear you there, and hoped to have seen you among us before this time."

"I shall probably come, when I can hope to be of any use; at present, you are too full of your imaginary success, to give due weight to argument. In a little time, perhaps, your experience may verify my observations, and then I will state my opinions. In the mean while you have my answer."

"This gentleman is a match for us all, in spirit," said Henry Gilbert, as the deputation left the house.

"And yet," observed another man, "he is not so high as some people are. He is always ready to give his reasons, and to hear ours, as if he acted from his own judgment, without party-feeling, or pride, or interest."

"It is curious," observed another, "to go from house to house, and see how differently the masters behave. The one we went to first, this morning, frowned and thumped upon the table, and spoke very positively, but I do believe he was afraid of us all the time. He said the same thing over and over again, as if he had planned it all beforehand, and had got his reasons by heart from some body else."

"And did you see the young ladies all huddled together, and peeping from the top of the stairs?"

"O yes, and the servants too; as if they thought we were so many monsters."

"And Mr. D_____ was quite as odd in a different way. He seems to think we are so many machines, that stood still just when he wanted them to go. He talks about getting the constables to us, just as he would send for the carpenter to mend one of his mills."

"And he's very much surprised," added Gilbert, "to find there is such a thing as a machine that *won't* be mended."

"With all his blustering, he won't stand out so long as Mr. Wallace, you'll see," said one of the men.

"Mr. L_____ will be the first to give way," observed Gilbert; "but it will do us little good, for he is not to be depended on for a day. He always agrees with the last speaker. Why could not he speak decidedly this morning? He must have had time to make up his mind on this subject, one would think. But there he stood, twirling a key on his finger, and promising to consider of it, and consult his friends; and as soon as we had left the house, he sent his son out to say he could not act against the other masters. Why could not he tell us so to our faces?"

"Mr. Wallace thinks that the masters should act in concert," observed another of his companions, "but then he makes sure first that he thinks them in the right. It is something better than party-feeling, or fear of being left alone, that makes him so firm. I dare say Mr. D_____ is fully convinced, too; but he might treat us a little more like men, that can think, and feel, and act from their own reason."

"We are sure of being well treated where we are going," said Gilbert; "so I am glad we have left this call to the last. We must make haste, or it will be past the gentleman's dinner-time."

Chapter V.

Time rolled on, and no accommodation of their differences took place between the manufacturers and their men. The operatives declared that they had still no intention of yielding; but some quick-sighted people observed an ominous change in their circumstances and proceedings. No more boasting of the amount of their funds was heard; the operations of the committee became more mysterious; Gilbert was observed to be sometimes out of spirits,—though this was not to be wondered at, for it was enough to make any one's heart ache to see the extreme of misery to which the greater part of the poor population of the place was now reduced. Winter was approaching; it had, indeed, almost arrived; for the month of November had set in, dreary, cold, and foggy. How were the poor creatures, who had found it difficult to subsist during the summer on their scanty allowance, to endure the hardships of winter without increased resources? It could not be, as all shrewd people said; though Gilbert observed that no one but themselves could judge what their resources were. He was as active as ever, flitting about among the people; encouraging some, explaining matters to others, and exhorting all to persevere for this once, at whatever sacrifice. But his task was not so easy a one as it had been.

"It's all very well to talk so," said one, "but you must shew us how to stand out without starving. My wife has sold all her clothes: the only gown she has left is dropping to pieces; and how is she to get another? Our allowance barely finds us bread."

"I dare say you are very right," observed another; "but my case is a hard one, and I must give way. My poor child has been ill this month, and gets worse every day: and I can't get either physic or proper food for it. You can't expect me to sacrifice my child."

"Look at my old mother," said a third, "and ask me to stand out if you can. There she sits shivering with cold, and I can give her no firing; she has the rheumatism, and yet I was obliged to sell my last blanket this morning, to get her a loaf of bread. I could sacrifice any thing myself, and I am sure I wish as well to the cause as any one; but no duty on earth can come in the way of my duty to my mother."

Gilbert began to be very unhappy. Words were all that he had to give, in return for these complaints. If he could have afforded clothes to one, medicine and food to another, and firing to a third, he could with more confidence have urged his arguments; but no such things were at his command. The struggle between his intense desire to carry a point which he believed to be so important to the interests of the operatives, and his compassion for their sufferings, was painful, was agonizing. Day after day, he wore out his strength of mind and body by labour, anxiety, and deprivation, (for he barely allowed himself food enough to sustain him.) Night after night, he sought in vain for refreshment and repose. Cold, hungry, and miserable, he arose more wearied than he had lain down, to witness new scenes of distress, and to undergo new struggles. He looked so ill, that his companions were sure, that, however invincible his resolution, his bodily strength would not hold out much longer.

"We had better give up," said the committee to him; "you have done your part, and you cannot work impossibilities. The struggle is too hard for us, and the event is certain."

"No, no; it is not certain," said Gilbert. "Who knows what help may be at hand? Never mind me; I had rather die than give up; and it is not for myself that I care. Let us hold out to a man, till the meeting on Monday; then we will make a great effort, and see what can be done."

"Promise us then, that if no help comes by that time, the people shall be allowed to do as they choose."

"I will promise no such thing," he replied. "I will not bind myself in any way."

"Then beware of the consequences," said they. "The destruction of the people will be on your head."

"It might be," he replied, "if I had used force. My influence over them has been by argument only: they all have the free use of their reason and their will. I have given them advice, and they chose to take it. I am not responsible for the consequences, as they had their choice whether to follow me or not."

"But you promised them success in return for their struggle. The promise has failed, and the least you can do is to let them get out of their misery as fast as they can."

"I only promised them success if they persevered, and I will venture to promise the same still. If they choose to lose their point by giving way, the fault is theirs, not mine."

"The choice is no longer in their power, as you know; and we therefore entreat you to give your countenance to their yielding. It is the only way to preserve your popularity."

"I will never sacrifice principle to popularity," exclaimed Gilbert, whose judgment was not cool enough, just now, to distinguish between an obstinate adherence to his own will, and that firmness which should lead him to sacrifice all to a sense of duty. He was at this time actuated by mixed motives. He undoubtedly believed that his conduct and opinions had hitherto been right; but he also knew that it was now impossible to gain his end, and that the misery of the people would be much increased by further delay; but he could not bring himself to yield: and while he assured himself that he was only exercising a well-principled firmness, a closer examination into his feelings would have told him, that he was unwilling to relinquish his power, to fall into the ranks instead of holding a command, and to acknowledge that plans so long laid and so vigorously pursued as his, could fail.

The argument in the committee became warm: Gilbert found that all were against him, and that, unless he yielded in part, he should lose every thing. He therefore reluctantly promised, that, unless the appearance of things brightened before Monday, the question of yielding or standing out should be discussed at the meeting; and the people should be allowed to decide the matter for themselves.

Gilbert hurried away from the committee-room in a troubled state of mind. In a narrow street, through which he was passing, he saw Maria, on the opposite side of the way, walking with her head bent down, and with a slow, listless step. She did not perceive him, and he was, at first, inclined to pass on without speaking to her; but he remembered that he had not seen her for some days, and it was not in his nature to be unkind; so he crossed over, and followed her. Before he reached her, however, she turned into a shop,—a small, dark, dismal-looking, pawnbroker's shop. He entered it, and laid his hand on her arm. She looked up, and Henry was grieved to see how much she was altered. Her cheeks were thin and pale, and her eyes were swelled with crying. The tears started again, when Gilbert asked her what could have brought her to this place. She pointed to a bundle of clothes which she carried under her shawl.

"Come, take my arm," said he, "and let us take a turn in the street, and have a little chat before you settle your business, unless you are in a hurry. I will carry your bundle for you."

Maria did as he requested; but, instead of speaking, she wiped away the tears which fell faster and faster.

"How is this?" enquired Gilbert. "Are these your own clothes you were going to sell, or pawn? I know you will not think me impertinent for asking, for I am all the same as a brother to you, you know."Maria thanked him for his kindness, and said that she was indeed going, for the first time, to sell some of the things she could best spare."Then is the money you had in the savings-bank all gone?"

"Here is the last shilling, which I took out yesterday," replied she.

"Dear, dear! I had no notion it was so nearly gone. Well, it *is* a sad thing, after you had worked so hard, and saved so carefully. I would have sacrificed any thing of my own, rather than you should have done it; but you know, Maria, the effort we have made was for the public benefit, and unless all joined in it, no good could have been done."

Maria was silent, restraining her inclination to ask what good had been done.

"I am glad I happened to see you just now," continued Henry. "I must prevent your selling your clothes, indeed. There is no occasion for you to do that, as long as any of the fund is left. I am sure you have as good a right as any body to assistance from it; for you have not applied for a farthing, ever since the turn-out began. The rule is, to give no help to those who have *money* of their own: we say nothing about furniture or clothes. I wonder James did not explain this to you."

"I knew it all," answered Maria; "but I did not wish James to know that all my savings are gone; and I beg you will not tell him."

"I will do as you wish, certainly, Maria; but he will be sure to ask: and, indeed, I think it is your duty to him and yourself, to take what you can get from the fund, instead of stripping yourself of every thing. You may as well keep clothes to your back, at any rate, as long as you can."

"James and I determined, long ago," said Maria, "to take nothing from the fund, as long as we could keep life within us by any other means."

"Well, now, I did not think either of you had been so proud. You speak as if I wanted you to go into the workhouse. I wonder you don't see the difference!"

"I *do* see the difference, Henry; and if I were forced to do one or the other, I think I had rather take parish relief. It is not pride, I assure you, that makes us feel as we do."

"What is it, then?"

"We don't approve of the turn-out, and we did not turn out of our own free will; so we don't choose to be maintained by your fund, as if we thought and acted in agreement with you."

"You may speak for yourself, Maria; but I know, from James's own lips, that he does approve of the turn-out, and that he thinks my view of the case a right one."

"He did think so once," replied Maria, "but he has changed his mind."

"O, but he told me so twice, at different times; and only the other day, I was talking about it, and he made no objections; so I supposed he was agreeing with me all the time."

Maria blushed for her lover's want of spirit, but she replied, "He is so tired of the subject, that I dare say he was glad to escape arguing it all over again."

"People should never be tired of arguing where truth is in question," replied Henry. "But, as I was going to say, if you don't choose to take any thing from the fund, I must beg you to accept of my little allowance for this one week;

by the next, some great change may take place."

Maria steadily refused this. She did not wish to be under such an obligation to any one; and her sense of propriety told her, that the brother of her lover was the last person from whom she should accept it. She thanked Henry for his kindness, but declined it.

"Well, then, it can be done in this way. I can get a week's allowance from the committee, without saying who it is for. I have influence enough to do that very easily."

"Thank you," said Maria: "but if it would be mean to take money openly from a fund, and for a purpose I do not approve; it would be much more so, to apply for, or accept it secretly. I cannot consent to it, indeed."

"Why, you won't let me help you in any way," said Henry. "I can give you this bit of comfort, at any rate, if you will promise to tell it to no one but James. It is very likely that you will be able to return to your work, next week. The meeting on Monday may be the breaking up of the turn-out. Ay, you look very glad, as I thought you would. You know that is a feeling I can't join in, holding the principles I do: but if I am obliged to give way at last, it will be a consolation to me to see you and James look happy again."

"And hundreds more," said Maria; "for hundreds are worse off than we are."

This news inspired her with hope and courage. She thought she could bear any thing for this one week, if it was to be the last of the struggle. She carried home her bundle, and determined to sell nothing but her best gown, which was too good for her present circumstances, and the least necessary part of her wardrobe. It was intended for a wedding-gown, and it cost her a sigh to part with it; but she knew she must not think of being married for a very long time, and it was better to make money of it, to supply her pressing wants, than let it lie by unworn. While she went into the town to buy her candle, her few potatoes, and her loaf of bread, Henry, who had been struck by her firmness in refusing assistance from himself and from the fund, was thinking what he could do to serve her, and to alleviate the distress she had fallen into through his means. He opportunely met Mr. Wallace; and, with a respectful bow, begged a few minutes' attention from him.

"If you want to say any thing new," said Mr. Wallace; "but you know there is no use in urging your old demands."

"It is quite a different kind of thing, Sir, that I want to say. It seems strange for me to be asking a favour of you, Sir, but it is not for myself. It is for people who would have been very glad to have been working for you all this time."

"Of whom there are many," said Mr. Wallace.

"May be so, Sir; but those I am speaking of, have steadily refused taking any allowance from the fund, because they thought the cause a bad one. Now, though, of course, I don't agree with them, it seems no more than just that I should try to get them work before any body else, because it is owing to me that they gave it up. It is my brother James and Maria Field that I mean. They went to the mill as long as they were allowed; and, since that time, they have lived entirely upon their savings, and are now selling their clothes, rather than have any thing to do with the fund. So, I hope, Sir, if we should be obliged to give up in the end, (which I am still very uncertain about,) they will be some of the first that you will give work to."

"Certainly," replied Mr. Wallace. "They have a claim before all others: but it grieves me to think how many who will ask for work, must be denied. This turn-out has done such irreparable injury to our trade, that we cannot set on half the number of hands that are now idle. The distress this winter will be dreadful; and I hope, Gilbert, the pain you will suffer in witnessing it, will be a warning to you how you head a turn-out another time."

"I shall be sorry, Sir, and God knows I am sorry for the distress; but I cannot blame myself in any way. I still think the principle is right, and if we could hold out to the end. . ."

"If you could hold out, matters would be worse than they are. It is well for you that you cannot. But we have said all this before. I will employ your brother and Maria, as you request. Have you any thing more to say?"

"Nothing, Sir, except that I am very much obliged to you for your promise."

"The request comes well from you, Gilbert, who differ so widely from them; and I am glad you made it. But it is only granted because your brother has the first right to employment; and I do not expect to hear intercessions from you in favour of any body else."

"I am not apt to ask many favours, Sir," said Henry, proudly; "and I only asked this, because justice required it."

Gilbert's anxiety increased as each day of this important week passed away. On the Wednesday and Thursday nothing occurred to inspire the hope that prospects were brightening.

The committee made so sure that Monday would end the business, that, in spite of Gilbert's arguments, authority, and entreaty, they expended some of the little fund still remaining, in relieving a few of the most urgent cases of distress which were brought before them. In vain he declared that they had no right to dispose of their money in so irregular a way; that it was taking from the many, to give to a few who had no prior claim; and that, till the Monday, they were bound by their agreement to respect his authority. It would not do: his day of power was nearly gone by; and, sick at heart, and indignant, he left the committee to do as they would, and reserved his strength for the last effort, which he determined should be a vigorous one. He resolved to keep quiet till the meeting, and then to try whether he had not yet power enough over the people, to induce them to defer their submission for yet another week. On Friday he walked backwards and forwards before the Blue Boy, watching the poor wretches who went to petition for relief, grieved to see the small remains of the fund distributed in a way which could not further the common cause, but refraining from interfering with the proceedings of the committee. On Saturday, while he was thus pacing the pavement, the postman brought a letter addressed to the committee. Henry seized it, and tore it open. It was from the weavers' committee of Norwich, and contained a five-pound note. "All is not over yet," thought he; and he carried the letter to the committee-room in triumph. Its contents were not received with the usual avidity; and it was evident that Henry was the only one who welcomed this supply, more seasonable, in his opinion, than any that had ever been transmitted on a similar occasion.

"What are five pounds among so many?" exclaimed one of his companions.

"Enough to warrant our saying that our prospects are brightening, and enough to release me from my promise about Monday's meeting," replied Gilbert.

"No, no," said another, "you are not released from your promise, till we have enough to pay a week's allowance all round."

"Which we might have had," retorted Henry, "if you had not paid away money as if we had hundreds at command. My part is taken: a remittance has come in, and more may follow; so I shall say and do what I please on Monday."

His hopes were again raised by the arrival of another letter, the next day, conaining an inclosure of five pounds, from some friends in Lancashire. He published the fact of the arrival of the letters, though not of the amount of their inclosures. He went from house to house, to animate the spirits of the people, to exhort them to attend the next day's meeting, and to endeavour to form an imposing procession; that, by the display of their numbers, the timid might be inspired with courage, and the desponding with hope. He impressed on them the necessity of being exact to the time and place of meeting, and of going with minds well-disposed to the common cause, and guarded against the arts of some who, he feared, would, after all, prove traitors. But, with all his precaution, he was unaware of the danger of opposition from one who, instead of being a traitor to the cause, had always been its declared enemy.

Mr. Robert Wallace had, for some time, been aware that the grand crisis was approaching; and he believed that the day was now come when he might do good, by taking part in the discussions of the public meeting. He was the only one of the masters who felt any inclination to do so. Some were too high; others too timid: some were convinced that matters would come round better without their interference; others left it to Mr. Wallace, who was beloved and respected by the men, and possessed great influence over them.

Chapter VI.

Never did Gilbert wish more earnestly for fine weather, than on this day. His wish was gratified: the sun shone brightly, and the day was mild and clear. The meetings were now held in the mornings, as the evenings were dark and cold; and, where all were idle, one time of day was as convenient as another. The procession was to be formed in a field at the outskirts of the town, to start at ten o'clock precisely, to pass through all the principal streets, and thence along the road to the usual place of meeting, the Mill-Field.

Gilbert was the first at his post. He was soon followed by a few stragglers; and while he was giving them directions concerning their march, the band of music arrived, accompanied by two or three men with banners. After this, there was a long pause. Gilbert looked at his watch; it was half-past nine. He observed on the folly of being late on such an occasion; but as the minutes passed away, their numbers increased but little. One poor wretch slowly climbed a stile; another crept through the hedge; a few lagged along the pathway. There was no life nor spirit in them. They were shivering with cold, pinched with hunger, and broken-spirited.

"Come, make haste, my good fellow," said Gilbert; "you look as if you were going to be hanged."

"I should not mind if I were," replied he.

"Why, victory is better than hanging, man! We are going to get a great victory to-day, you know."

"If we do," said the man, "it will be our last. We shall hardly live to get another next week."

"O, but you will, though; trust me for it. If you are so cold," said he, addressing another, "you had better walk a little faster. Exercise is better than firing, at any time."

"For those that have strength," replied the poor creature; "but I am ill, and my legs fail me. I had better go home again."

"You will be sorry to miss the meeting," replied Gilbert. "The walk will do you good, depend upon it; and the music will cheer up your heart."

"I thought," continued he, to another new-comer, "that I had made you understand how necessary it is to be in good time on an occasion like this. It is now past ten, and not a quarter of your number is come. Did you see any on the road?"

"None coming this way," replied the man, "but many standing about in the streets."

"O, then, they mean to join us nearer the town, I suppose," said Gilbert; "but they might have taken the trouble to come here, as they promised, and then we might have made a better figure. We must be off; there is no time to lose."

He put his forlorn troop into the best order he could; and the music striking up, they began their march. A few stragglers joined them on their way; but so few, that their leader was ashamed to march them through the principal streets. They made a circuit through some bye streets, and reached the Mill-Field, glad to hide their insignificance by mixing with the crowd there assembled. The concourse was immense; and it soothed Henry's mortification to perceive this. Perceiving Mr. Wallace, he was a little startled; but he respectfully bade him welcome to the meeting, and offered him the best seat on the waggon which served as hustings. Then collecting round him the friends who had promised to support him, he was prepared to open the meeting. But the people did not appear equally prepared to listen. It was impossible to obtain silence. The voices mingled, till the sound resembled the roaring of the ocean: here and there persons were seen speaking vehemently, using earnest gestures, and evidently producing a strong effect on their hearers, and prepossessing their minds, one way or the other, before the business of the meeting began. Many women were present with their children, who, terrified by the noise and pressure, added their cries to the general discord. Very few looked towards the hustings, or seemed to remember for what purpose they were assembled; and it was impossible to make them hear, by any exertion of voice. Gilbert attempted it, but in vain. He ordered the music to strike up, hoping, by this means, to gain their eyes, at any rate: but the din only rose louder. Gilbert ordered the music to stop.

"The appearance of the people is very tumultuous," observed Mr. Wallace.

"They know the meeting to be a very important one, Sir, and they are eager about it. But they are not disposed for violence: no fear of that. Harris! (I can't make him hear.) Harris! reach me the largest of those flags. I will try what this will do."

He swept the large flag over the heads of those who stood within a few yards of the waggon, and who naturally turned round to see from whence this call on their attention proceeded. This attracted the notice of those beyond them; and by degrees the motion spread through the whole mass of the assembled multitude. Every face was turned in one direction. How various were the countenances thus offered to the eye of the observer! One expression, indeed, was common to all; all told of anxiety and want. But of these wan faces, some were clouded with gloom, some with despondency and despair; some few were lighted up with hope; some were full of eagerness; some listless and indifferent. In a little time the murmur of a multitude of voices was hushed: the people addressed themselves to listen; the mothers stilled their children's cries, and Gilbert's voice was heard to the furthest corner of the field.

"From the unusual difficulty," said he, "which I have found in obtaining your attention, I am induced to begin my address by requesting you to remember that this meeting is one of very great importance; and that, in proportion to the importance of the subjects to be discussed, should be the quietness of your demeanour in listening, and the seriousness of your thoughts in reflecting and deciding. I am happy to be able to say, (and it is greatly to your honour that I am able to say,) that you have needed no exhortations from your leaders to keep the peace. No breach of the peace has been committed, from the first day of our independence to the present moment: no unmanly threats have been used, no windows have been broken, no property destroyed; not a single act has been committed, of which the law can take hold to your disadvantage. Your masters themselves can bear witness to the excellence of your conduct in this respect: and, trust me, they respect you for it. It proves to them that our opposition to their views does not proceed from a spirit of faction, from a love of frolic and mischief, or an inclination to thwart and provoke them. It proves to them that our measures have been taken deliberately; that our purposes are formed on principle; and that we are prepared to assert our rights peaceably, though firmly; and that while we undergo suffering for the sake of duty, that sense of duty enables us to resist every temptation to relieve our wants by a breach of the laws. As your conduct has hitherto been thus honourably distinguished, I doubt not that it will be so still; that those who are about to address you, will be favoured with your undivided attention, and that, whatever may be the result of the discussions of this day, whether favourable to your opinions and wishes, or no, (and where there is so great a variety of opinions, some will be gratified and others disappointed,) you will keep the command of your tempers, and remember the respect which is due to your masters from their superior station, and the consideration and kindness we all owe to one another. You will avoid all tumult and all angry contention: you will temperately make use of your privilege of sanctioning or opposing the measures which are about to be submitted to you; and the matter once decided, you will quietly disperse to your homes. One of the most respected of our masters is now present; and it is my wish that he should see us as we are, and that he should know, from his own observation, what is the temper and spirit of these meetings. By this means, he will be most favourably impressed concerning our cause; and by this means may the differences which have so long subsisted be brought to a glorious and happy termination."

"The purpose of this meeting is to decide on a point which, though not in itself new, demands a new effort of determination on your part. There are some among you, (I would hope they are but few,) there are some also among your leaders, (I would hope fewer still,) who think that the time has arrived when we must yield the point which has been so long, so earnestly, so nobly, contested. I have for some time heard whispers of such a change; I have seen here and there a gloomy face, and heard murmurs of discontent; and, on enquiry, have found that some factious person had been dropping poison into the ears of those, who, if they had been able to see into his mind, would have spurned his base suggestions, and defied his unworthy arts. I became afraid that faction would spread, if you, my friends, were left unwarned of your danger; and I have therefore called you together, that you may hear the truth, and judge for yourselves. I have conversed with such of these tempters as came in my way, with the view of discovering what reasons they can urge for their new opinions; but, truly, they seem to me to have nothing to urge, but what would have come as well from them three months ago: nothing but what your discernment will at once perceive to be fallacious; nothing but what your feelings will at once spurn, as being mean, cowardly, and treacherous to our cause. Listen to me, while I relate and reply to their arguments: and I call upon every principle of honour, pride, and conscience, within you, to reject them with the indignation they deserve."

He paused for a moment, in the hope of being applauded. A few faint cheers were raised, not entirely unmingled with hisses. But the perfect silence with which he had been heard being presently restored, he proceeded to relate the reasons which had been urged for submission: such as the increasing distress of the people, the superior power of the masters, the injury which trade was sustaining, &c. To these he replied with all the earnestness and eloquence he could command, and artfully gave to a few facts the colouring which would best suit his purpose. He allowed that the distress of the people was great; but urged that it was not unexpected, nor likely to be durable. He reminded them of their heroism in voluntarily incurring their present distress for the sake of their children's rights; he spoke of the respect with which they were regarded by their brethren in all parts of the kingdom, for the greatness of the sacrifices; and implored them not to forfeit, by a weak and untimely submission, the honour they had gained. That their submission would be weak and untimely, he proceeded to shew, by saying that *all* the masters could not hold out long; that however big those might talk who had large capital, those who had small must give way; and that when one had submitted, all the others would follow. As to what had been said about the emptiness of their treasury, he could prove that it was not true. Remittances had been received up to that very day, accompanied by the most animating assurances of support. If any further proof were needed that their resources were not exhausted, it was found in the fact that an extra allowance had been made of late to such families of the union as had suffered most from the pressure of the times. Was it conceivable that an irregular issue of money should have been made by the committee, unless the funds were able to bear such an additional charge? He hoped he had said enough to convince them that there was no *necessity* for yielding. Those who said there was, proved themselves tyrants; for all knew the proverb, "Necessity is the tyrant's plea." "They have no better plea to urge," he continued. "They cannot say that our cause is a bad one; they cannot say that our principle is a wrong one; they cannot say that it was an error to assert our rights; they cannot say that it was an error to persevere thus far; and if they say that it will be an error to stand out yet longer, what argument do they bring to support their words? None but the plea which proves them to be tyrants. Yes! they tyrannize over your rights, by obliging you to relinquish them; they tyrannize over your children, by depriving them of the privileges which their fathers have struggled to obtain for them; they tyrannize over your leaders; over those who have watched, and laboured, and sacrificed every thing for your sakes. I can testify this, for I have been called on to resist their tyranny. They demanded submission from me; they demanded it, my friends, in your name; but I refused to yield. I knew that it was not, that it never could be, your wish, that all my cares and labours should end in base submission; that all I have done and suffered for you should be in vain. (Loud applause.) When I refused to yield, I was told that your destruction was inevitable, and that your ruin would be on my head. This also I refused to believe. The threat of destruction is an idle threat, and falsely is it said that I am answerable for what befals you. I boast no such power over you, as has been attributed to me. Are you my slaves, ready to crouch or to rise at my bidding? You spurn the thought. Are you like a flock of sheep, which I can drive hither and thither as I will? No! you are men: with reason and a will of your own; subject to no man's authority, the slaves of no man's caprice. I am your servant, not you master: my service has been faithful; though, God knows, far from easy. For you I have undergone days of labour and nights of watchfulness; for you I have denied myself food, and rest, and recreation; for your sakes have I familiarized myself with sights of sorrow and sounds of discontent; for your sakes have I borne the displeasure of our masters, and the contempt and blame of my companions. Thus have I served you: and what do I ask in reward of my service! Only, to be allowed to serve you effectually, as well as faithfully; only to be allowed to continue my sacrifices and struggles till I have brought you through; till your sacred rights are for ever secured to yourselves and your children. Such are my motives, and such is my aim. (Loud applause.) But to obtain this end, your support, your cordial and continued support is necessary. One arm is too weak to break the rod of oppression; one voice is not powerful enough to overawe the clamour of tyrants: the courage of one heart may fail, the strength of one soul may sink before the frown of despots: I feel as if *my* courage were strong, and *my* resolution firm, and yet I will not answer for myself. I dare not promise never to flinch or quail, unless I have the support of those for whom I willingly sacrifice all, of those to whose approbation I look for my reward. Give me that support, and I will engage never to yield but with life. That support shall be as a weapon and a shield to me, and the struggle shall last, till victory be secured. (Cheers.) These shouts inspire me with hope, with the certainty, that your support is pledged to me. I thank you; from my soul I thank you. If you wish for the recompence of your sufferings, persevere; if you wish for the respect of your masters, persevere; if you wish for the prosperity of your country, for honour and esteem from your countrymen, for the gratitude of your children, and the approbation of your own consciences, persevere. The claims of your children are strong. When they look up in your faces, it is as if they besought you not to sacrifice their rights: and if, in their ignorance of your wants, they ask you for bread which you have not to give, console yourselves with the thought, that they will hereafter honour you for your virtuous poverty; that if, moved by their complaints, you go to your masters, and sell their rights for bread, every mouthful will at length be repaid with curses; but if you can put forth your strength in proper season, to deny the cravings of their weakness, you will be rewarded by their future prosperity and your own. Judge by your present distress what theirs will be, in after years, when the power of the rich will have been strengthened by indulgence, and when the means of resistance which you now enjoy will be yours no longer. Imagine them pining in distress and want, the grave opening before them, and they longing to cast themselves into it. Could you bear to hear them say, 'It would have been better to have died in the struggle that our fathers made, than to live in distress like this. But we should not have died, we could have been sustained, if they had not yielded. A little more firmness would have secured our rights; our present misery is their work.' Could you bear to hear this? Oh, no! Then protect their interests, secure their blessings, and BE FIRM."

The shouts of applause which followed this speech were so prolonged and so often renewed, that the speaker who next presented himself, seemed to have little chance of obtaining a hearing. He was one of Gilbert's opponents in the committee; a plain man, who could only state plain facts in the plainest way. When he was at length favoured with the attention of the meeting, his discouraging facts were so unpalatable, after Gilbert's very exciting address, that he was assailed with groans and hisses. Mr. Wallace saw that some better kind of effort must be made to counteract the effect of what had been already said; and, pulling the speaker by the sleeve, he advised him to retire, saying, "Give me your facts, and I will bring them in: the people will listen to me, I know." The man retired, as he was requested, and Mr. Wallace took his place. Gilbert waved his hat, as a signal to the people to cheer, which they did; some because they were really glad to see him among them, others because they did not wish to be less gracious than their companions, and the majority because Gilbert set them the example.

"I have come among you, my good friends," said he, as soon as silence was restored, "in the hope that, by mutual explanation, a mutual good understanding might be established between the two classes whose interests have been the subject of a long and obstinate contention. If you practise the candour you profess, you will listen to me without interruption; if your aim be, as you declare, to follow truth, you will give your best attention to what I have to say. It will not be in my power to rivet your attention, as your leader has done; for, instead of allowing myself to appeal to your feelings, I must confine myself to arguments and facts. I must conclude that the arguments and facts on your side of the question have been frequently and satisfactorily discussed, as I have heard no allusion to them to-day; but as I now address you for the first time, I must begin by establishing my ground, instead of asserting that I am right, and then working up your feelings, as if I were certain that you agreed with me. I will first tell you how far I agree with you. I agree with you all in thinking that the speech we have just heard, does and ought to produce a great effect on the feelings of every person present. I fully believe that the speaker means all he says; that you are all actuated by good intentions in pursuing your present line of conduct; and that the interests of your companions and your children are the object of your great sacrifices. I agree with you, that no sacrifice can be too great, where the rights of your offspring are in question; that you entitle yourselves to their future gratitude, by undergoing distress for their sakes; and that any sacrifice is preferable to that of the approbation of your own consciences. As to these important points, our judgment and feelings agree; and hence arises my hope, that when a full explanation has taken place, we may arrive at a closer agreement on the subjects which still remain for dispute. When I see how great is your distress, when I remember the extent of your sacrifices, when I admire your patience, and applaud the peaceableness of your conduct, I regret, from the bottom of my heart, that so much virtue should be, as I think, misapplied; that so much fortitude should be exercised in multiplying, instead of counteracting evils. When I reflect on the advantages which would result from your patience, your firmness, and your self-denial, if rightly directed, I feel a strong desire to shew you where, in my opinion, you are in error, and to offer a helping hand, in the hope that you will not reject it, to extricate you from your difficulties. You will at least give me credit for being sincere and earnest in my wish to assist you, and actuated by principle in the opposition I have hitherto made to your demands." (Cheers.)

"You are aware that the wealth, the capital, of a country, consists of land and its fruits, the produce of manufactures, houses, money, and whatever is possessed for the purposes of use and enjoyment, by the inhabitants of that country. Some possess more of this capital, and some less: some are enriched by the labours of their fathers, others by their own. The unequal division of this property occasions inequality of ranks. From the king down to the little farmer or shopkeeper, all have a portion, greater or smaller, of this capital. There is a large class, however, who do not, when they set out in life, possess anything: that class is the labouring population. Now, it is clear, that some mutual accommodation must take place between these different classes; for the rich man cannot live on gold or horses, nor the poor man on air. The rich man cannot cultivate all his grounds, repair his houses, or manufacture his clothes himself; and he is therefore willing to accept the services of the poor man, who says, 'I will work for you, if you will maintain me.' When all the personal wants of the capitalist are supplied, he finds that he has still a great deal of wealth remaining; he sees that if he employs a part of it in purchasing materials, and the rest in paying labourers, a large quantity of some commodity may be produced, which, when sold, will return him his capital, accompanied by a profit. If he is a farmer, he buys horses, ploughs, manure, and seed, for his fields, and hires a certain number of men, who cultivate his farm, in return for the maintenance he affords them; and if he manages his affairs prudently, he finds, after his crops are sold, that he has got back his capital, and a profit besides. If the capitalist chooses to employ his money in trade, he buys a quantity of raw material of some kind, gives wages to operatives, and sends into the market a manufacture, which he hopes will sell for more than was spent in its production. Unless it does, he gives up his trade, as profit is his object. If he gains a small profit, it will be only sufficient to supply his wants and those of his family; and his capital will be the same as it was before he set up in trade. If his profits are large, he takes a part to live upon, and adds the rest to his capital. As his capital increases, he can manufacture a greater quantity of goods, and employ more workpeople; but if, from any cause, his capital is lessened, he is obliged to contract his trade, and maintain fewer labourers: if he loses the whole of his wealth, he turns off all his hands. Thus the labouring population subsists on the capital of the rich; it is their only dependence; and in proportion to the quantity of capital afloat in any country or town, is the number of people who can gain a maintenance by their labour. It is as much the interest of the poor as the rich, that capital should grow, and, above all, that it should not be laid by. A chest of gold is worth no more than a chest of old clothes, unless it is intended to be unlocked, and its contents brought into use. While it is locked up, it is of no use in the world to any body; but if circulated, it may maintain hundreds and thousands of labourers, and yet be continually increasing its own amount. Now, if the capital employed in trade invariably brought a good profit to its possessor, there would be a certainty of a comfortable maintenance to a continually increasing number of labourers: but in our world of change this is not the case. From causes too numerous to be mentioned here, there are continual fluctuations in trade. In one year, the manufacturer may make no profit at all; in which case he is obliged to consume a part of his capital, and to employ fewer workmen. In another year he may increase his capital, by unusually large gains; and then the poorer class is sure to partake of the advantage, for he increases his demand for their labour. Generally speaking, the fortunes of masters and men rise and fall together, and their interests are eventually the same. When times are bad, it is for the good of both that they should try, by all possible means, to keep the capital of the masters entire; or, if they cannot do that, to consume as little of it as possible. Both should retrench, both should live upon the smallest possible sum which will maintain their place in society, that, when trade revives, there may be capital ready to employ, to supply the former means of subsistence to labourers. It is manifestly unjust, that capitalists should indulge in the luxury and waste of property, while they lower the wages of their men, on pretence of preserving as much of their capital as they can; and it is no less unjust, or eventually ruinous to the labouring classes themselves to pay them higher wages than the rate of profit will afford. If they encroach on the capital of their employers, they may enjoy their wages for a while, but the time will surely come when their masters will say, 'You had more than your share of subsistence while our property lasted: it is now all gone, and we can maintain you no longer. Let times improve as they will, we can never rise again, for you have deprived us of the means of carrying on our trade.' Happily, matters never arrive at such an extremity as this; because the two classes, masters and men, are a check upon each other: but that there is danger of such an event, I will shew you, by applying all this reasoning to the case we are met to discuss."

"I am aware," continued he, "that I am addressing you in a manner to which you have been little accustomed; in a manner very unusual at public meetings; but as this is the only means of explaining my views to you as a body, I wish to do it fully, though at the risk of wearying you with argument. I thank you for the attention which you have given to the first division of my address, and

I hope that when I speak of affairs which more immediately regard your interests, I shall not be heard with less patience and candour."

"It is necessary to repeat, what we all know too well, that the trade of our town has long been declining. The causes of this decline are, evidently, only temporary. We are only subject to the fluctuations to which every branch of manufacture is liable, and there is every reason to hope that prosperity will in time revisit us, when the causes of the present depression have ceased to operate. It is my opinion, that a great revival would already have taken place, if we had been in a condition to profit by it; and that our dissensions alone prolong our season of adversity. You are aware that the markets to which we send our goods have been overstocked; the goods, which were manufactured at the average cost, sold for far less than the average profit, then for no profit at all, and, latterly, at a considerable loss. Those manufacturers who have large capitals prefer keeping their goods on hand till prices rise, to selling them at a great loss. In either case, a certain portion of capital is consumed, but less by keeping out of the market, than by selling at the lower prices. Manufactures who have but little capital are obliged to incur the greatest loss, as their business depends on the quick return of their capital. They must keep their money afloat, at all events, and they therefore continue to manufacture; and, when their old stock is sold off, they get materials and labour so cheap, that perhaps they contrive to make a very small profit, or, at any rate, not to lose. It is well for the poor that the little manufacturers continue their trade, because low wages are better than no wages at all. Some months ago, as you know, very few of you could obtain employment, except at the lowest rate of wages that was even known in this place. But after a while the market-price rose, we began to sell our stocks, and there was every prospect of an increased demand, and, consequently, of a rise of wages. Just at this time, however, your patience failed you: you imagined, I believe, that your masters were making great profits, which they did not intend you to share. This was quite a mistake, for we were, at that very time, living on our capital. Some of you thought that you had a right to live on our substance, as long as we had any; but how it can be proved that you possess this right, or that, if exercised, it would not hasten your ruin, I own I cannot see. Whatever, or however various, your reasons might be, you demanded an advance of wages, before the rate of our profits admitted of such as advance without injury to ourselves, and ultimately to you. Suppose, now, that trade had so far improved, that, at the low price of materials and wages, our capital was returned to use at the end of the year, with a profit of three hundred pounds. These profits are consumed by the maintenance of our family, and perhaps it is only by sacrificing some of our usual comforts that our capital remains entire. It is evident that it has only remained entire by keeping our wages low; if they had been high, a part of our capital would have been consumed, and we should not have been able to employ so many hands the next year. But supposing the men to understand their true interest, and to have patience to wait the natural rise of prices, the event will answer their expectations. The demand increases when the markets are cleared; prices rise, our profits increase; we can afford higher wages without consuming our capital, or lessening our number of hands. To this improved state our trade was tending, when you turned out. You required us to bestow our capital upon you; that is, to maintain you comfortably now, while we were losing money, at the certainty of being able to afford you less, or nothing, by and by, when trade would be flourishing, if we had but a capital to carry it on with. I repeat, that your interests and ours are the same; that when we make good profits, you get high wages; and that, by insisting on high wages when trade does not afford them, you bring your masters to poverty, and yourselves to destruction."

"The consequences of the turn-out have been, a continuance of the depression of our trade much beyond its natural period, and permanent injury to the manufacturing interests of this place. We have lost many good customers, who could not wait for your return to your work. Many a large order has been sent to some place where other masters and wiser men smile at your folly in throwing away your means of subsistence. By this time a large portion of our capital might have returned, with a profit which would have enabled us to raise your wages higher than they can now be for many months. By this time we might have extended our trade at home and abroad, instead of letting what we already possessed slip through our fingers. By this time you might have congratulated one another on the improvement in your prospects, instead of grieving that, if you were to yield to-day, your masters cannot employ the half of your number. By this time, you might have had warm clothes on your backs, fires in your houses, bread in your cupboards, and each, perhaps, a little sum in the savings-bank, as a resource against a change of times. And now—but I need not describe your present state. You have felt the pinchings of cold, and the cravings of hunger; you need but look on your companions, on your wives and children; you need but think on your own wasted powers, to be aware of the extent of the misery which your fatal mistake has brought upon you. I mean not to insult you with the mention of your distress; do not think that I am insensible to your sufferings. It is because I feel deep compassion and strong interest for you, that I thus refer to your sacrifices; your well-meant, but useless and injurious sacrifices. I make use of them to conjure you to better your fortunes, as fast as you can. The mischief done is irreparable: when, therefore, it has served the purpose of a warning, let it be mentioned no more. It can never be forgotten; but, instead of taunting one another with it, let us seek for a path which will lead us out of the mire into which we have plunged ourselves, happily not so deeply but that we may still be extricated. This path lies open before you. Return to your employments, and accept the maintenance which your labour may even yet obtain. If your return be not speedy, the way will be closed against you for ever. Your masters will never yield; they will refuse, as much for your sake as their own. If *they* yield, the ruin of both parties is inevitable; if *you* yield, the welfare of both is secured, as far as it is in human power to compass so great an end. Return, I conjure you, if you would escape destruction; return, if the lives of your children are dear to you: if you prefer plenty to starvation, smiles to tears, cheerfulness to gloom, comfort to destitution, return while you yet may. I warn you, that a part only of your number can at present obtain employment; but, yet a little while, and all may apply in vain. This speedy return is your only hope, for, if the truth were told, only ten pounds remain in your treasury, and, out of this small sum, the expences of this meeting, its music and decorations, are to be defrayed. I love the music of cheerful voices better than that which is hired to intoxicate your spirits, or drown your complaints: let this music be once more heard in your houses; it will awaken you to enjoyment, instead of mocking your distress. Make use of the means which yet remain to amend your condition, and restore your former comforts. Reproach no one for what you have already endured; look on it as a past misfortune, and a future warning. Continue to respect your leaders for the integrity of their motives, but decide for yourselves concerning the correctness of their views. This is the course which your masters will pursue towards you. They think you have committed an error, but they feel for you sorrow unmixed with anger, and would willingly relieve your misery at any personal sacrifice. They will receive you with kindness; they will respect your feelings, they will regard your wants, they will protect your interests as their own. They already respect you for your patience, and the peaceableness of your conduct; thus much I can truly say, in the name of them all. For myself, it only remains to thank you for the favourable disposition with which you have heard me, and to express my best wishes, and pledge my best exertions, for your welfare and prosperity."

Mr. Wallace had been but little applauded during his address, for the attention of his hearers had been so completely fixed, that they thought only of listening. A long pause succeeded the conclusion of his speech, and then a universal shout arose. It was renewed again and again. The applause was continued, till Gilbert was assured that all was lost. He had become a good deal agitated towards the conclusion of the address, and made one attempt to speak in reply to it; but he saw that the public mind was against him; and, overcome by his feelings, he retired to the back of the cart, and, sinking down, hid his face in his hands. The disappearance of their leader was interpreted by the people as a sign that the matter was decided. No other speaker came forward, and the meeting was therefore dissolved.

It is not to be supposed that Mr. Wallace would have obtained such influence over the minds of his hearers, if their wishes had not, at any previous time, been on his side.

Henry Gilbert's speech had, for a little time, excited their feelings, and renewed their old impressions concerning the common cause; but an inclination to yield had long been gathering strength with each day of want and misery, and the majority had gone to the meeting with a determination to withdraw their allegiance from their leader, if he was not already disposed to bid them do as they pleased. His oratory put their intentions out of their heads for a time, but Mr. Wallace gave them new strength. Their resolution was declared by their lengthened shouts, and they crowded round their master, to announce to him that the turn-out was at an end.

The houses of the masters were besieged, during the remainder of this day, by applicants for employment at the old prices. The few who could obtain it returned with gladdened countenances to tell their children that they would no longer want bread. The many who were refused, retired to their cold and cheerless homes, to regret, not that the turn-out was at an end, but that it had even taken place.

As James and Maria were returning from the Mill-Field, they were overtaken by Henry, who, laying his hand on his brother's shoulder, said, "I have Mr. Wallace's promise that you shall both be supplied with work immediately; so your minds may be at ease."

"Thank God!" they both exclaimed; "then our worst days are over! But did you get this promise for us, Henry?"

"Yes: but it was no more than I owed to you, because it was through me that you lost your employment. It will be a comfort to me to see you able to marry:—the only comfort I have left, I think." And he left them abruptly.

"Poor fellow!" exlaimed James. "So this is the end of all his labour and management! This it is to have an ambitious, sturdy temper! But he means so well, it is a great pity he should have failed so completely."

"I think," said Maria, "that his error has been in having acted with too much confidence in his own knowledge. If he had understood what he was about perfectly, he would have been right to be firm; but he undertook the matter without understanding it."

"Yes," replied James, "but I had no idea how far wrong he was, till I heard Mr. Wallace's speech. Well, thanks to him, our way is not straight before us!"

"We must be content with our wages, and wait patiently for better times," said Maria.

"O, but I am tired of waiting," replied her lover. "We have waited and waited, these two years, and Mr. Wallace and many others have held us up as an example of prudence, and have bid people observe how happy we should be after we married, in a nice house, with good clothes and furniture, and pleased with ourselves and each other, for being patient. And now, what has it all come to? We have not a farthing in the world, and no more prospect of marrying than we had two years ago. I wish we had married—we could not have been worse off."

"O yes, James, we might. Remember your cousin George; remember, too, that it is by no fault of our own that we are now so poor. If we wait two years more, I hope all that Mr. Wallace said of us will come true; for surely there will never be another turn-out in this place. Our money will never be taken from us in the same way again."

"One turn-out in a lifetime is enough for any poor man, I should think," replied James. "But, two years, Maria!—that is a dreadful long time to wait!"

"Well," replied she, "times may mend, and we may save money faster than we have done. But we had better not think much about it; we ought to be glad that we can get bread once more, instead of being anxious about the future. I wish we were sure of as much for your brother."

"He is such a good workman," replied James, "that he is sure of employment: but he must be uneasy in his mind for a long time to come. Whenever he sees us look grave, whenever he sees a poor ragged child, or a drunken man, or a starved-looking woman, he will think, 'Perhaps the turn-out is the cause of this.' And when he hears that manufactures are flourishing in other places, while half the people here are out of work, he will remember that the turn-out drove away our trade. Whatever he may think now, depend upon it, Maria, he will soon be as well convinced as we are, that, though it is a hardship to have low wages, any thing is better than a TURN-OUT."

Notes

[1]See Harriet Martineau, *Autobiography*, vol. 1 (Boston: Osgood, 1877), p. 103.

[2]See Joseph Kestner, *Protest & Reform: The British Social Narrative by Women, 1827-1867* (Madison: Wisconsin UP, 1984), p. 33.

The Seamstress
John Galt
(1833)

The seamstress first appeared in Victorian fiction in 1833 when Tait's Edinburgh Magazine *published John Galt's "The Seamstress." The story centers around a minister's widow, Miss Peggy Pingle, who is an example of Scottish "eydency," a positive form of feminine industry. During the Victorian era the seamstress became a popular literary figure, appearing in over two dozen works.*

The popularity of the seamstress occurred for a variety of reasons. First, she was popular because of universality: in Victorian England all women were taught to sew, regardless of social class. Thus people reading about a woman sewing could identify with the character, either as women who sewed or as men whose mothers, wives, and sisters sewed. She was also a product of the industrial revolution: the industrialization of the textile industry lowered the price of fabric and made it possible for middle-class women, as well as those in the aristocracy, to follow the whims of fashion. And, finally, the plight of the seamstress was an issue which could be taken up equally by interventionists and advocates of a laissez faire approach to industry, thus receiving twice the attention. And because she did not work in the factory, the seamstress escaped the stigma of being a factory worker, who was often associated with low moral standards.

Actual conditions in the dress trade, however, were often quite harsh. As early as 1747 the London Tradesman *published an article cautioning parents not to place their daughters in dressmaking unless they are able to set them up after their apprenticeship, stating that in spite of "'vast profits' the milliners 'yet give but poor, mean Wages to every Person they employ under them: Though a young Woman can work neatly in all manner of Needle-Work, yet she cannot earn more than Five or Six Shillings a Week, out of which she is to find herself in Board and Lodging.'"[1] And in the 1833 Parliamentary discussions concerning factory legislation, it was pointed out that cotton mill workers were found to be healthier than milliners.*

Galt's interest in the seamstress is an illustration of "a genuine case of

129

industry free from labour," and apparently results from ignorance concerning the hardships endured by these working women, rather than intentional oversight. Although Miss Pingle is forced to practice "the frugalest economy," her greatest hardship is the sameness of her days. And it is the patient acceptance of this existence which illustrates the character trait Galt wishes to portray.

Galt has been called "the founder of the Scottish realistic novel," ² and this story is considered to be one of his best. Of particular note in "The Seamstress" are his attention to detail and his ability to create a sense of universality in character.

* * *

Besides the beautiful inflexions which help to make the idiomatic differences between the languages of Scotland and England, the former possesses many words which have a particular signification of their own, as well as what may be called the local meaning which they derive from the juxta-position in which they may happen to be placed with respect to others. Owing to this peculiarity, the nation has produced, among the lower classes, several poets, who, in the delicate use of phraseology, equal the most refined students of other countries. Indeed, it is the boast of Scotland, that in the ploughman Burns, she has produced one who, in energy of passion and appropriate expression, has had no superior. No doubt something may be due to the fortunate circumstance of the Scotch possessing the whole range of the English language, as well as their own, by which they enjoy an uncommonly rich vocabulary, and, perhaps, the peculiarity to which we are alluding may have originated in this cause. For example, the English have but the word "industry," to denote that constant patience of labour which belongs equally to rough and moderate tasks; but the Scots have also "eydency," with its derivatives, descriptive of the same constancy and patience, in employments of a feminine and sedentary kind. We never say a ditcher or a drudger is eydent; but the spinster at her wheel, or the seamstress at her sewing, are eydent; and to illustrate a genuine case of industry free from labour, as we conceive eydency to be, we have recourse to a reminiscence of our youth, in itself at once simple, interesting, and pathetic.

THE TALE.

Miss Peggy Pingle lived by herself, on the same flat or floor of an old-fashioned, respectable house, in the royal borough of Stourie. A minister's widow, who had but Sir Harry's fund* for her jointure, occupied the domicile on the other side of the common stair.

Miss Peggy's apartments consisted of a small back chamber, her own room, and a front kitchen, as it must be called from the character of the furniture, though, for the uncarpeted tidiness, it might have been compared to any parlour. The only thing for which it was remarkable was a hospitable-looking roastingjack, which for many years had been in a state of widowhood, not being called to perform the purposes of its creation for a long period. There was also a dresser, which aspired to the rank of a side-board; but, like all vulgar things, its original condition could not be disguised by its assumed gentility. It was ornamented with various articles of porcelain, so arranged that handleless pouries endeavored to conceal the defects of spoutless tea-pots with nippleless lids.

Miss Peggy herself was rather on the go, with small piercing eyes of a light-grey colour; not particular generous in her attitudes, being habitually inclined to draw her elbows close to her sides—speaking with her lips so drawn together that her dainty words were squeezed into a lisp. She had been in her youth the daughter of a respectable gauger, who had but his pay to live on, and who dying young, left Miss Peggy and her mother in very straitened circumstances, insomuch that the meek and illess maiden had to make the needle her breadwinner, and her mother the spinning-wheel serve all the purpose of a pacing-horse, as the song sings in "My Jo Janet."

In the course of nature, old Mrs. Pingle, who had long been in a peaking and pining way, went out of the world; and Miss Peggy's great eydency to convert her time into a livelihood, began to be observed by her neighbours. Those stirring and full-handed matrons among them, who saw she worked with a smaller candle, and rose earlier after her mother's death, naturally concluded that she had suffered, by the event, some new stinting in her narrow means; and, by a kind-hearted hypocrisy, often invited her to take tea with them, saying, "It need na be a breach in your eydency, so be sure and bring your seam;" and their ramplor children were not less kind to slipping Miss Peggy, whom one of the audacious boys used to call her, and described her as speaking always with a corriander sweetie in her mouth, or the end of the thread with which she had last punctured the eye of her needle.

Day after day was with Miss Pingle as the to-day is like the yesterday—twins could not more resemble each other. The only difference perceptible in her condition was produced by the season. She had heard from her father that, on the 10th of October, fires were lit for the winter in the Excise-office, and

---

*The late excellent and Reverend Sir Harry Moncrieff, who for so many years made the hearts of ministers' widows glad by his judicious superintendence of their pensions.

extinguished there, for the summer, on the 5th of April, without consulting the weather; and the routine of office was as faithfully observed by the frugal Seamstress, as if it had been ordained, and as unavoidable as the four-and-twenty hours are separated into day and night.

In the coldest days, after the 5th of April, Miss Peggy was seen plying her needle with a blue beak and a pellucid jewel at it; and on the warmest, after the 10th of October, her meagre arms were swaddled with the wonted-black worsted mittens. The only irregularity in the pure flow of her rill of life, was from the lengthening and shortening of the days; but she attained at last to such precision on this subject, that she could foretell on what distant day, hour, and minute, candles should be lighted with the least waste of what she called the convience.

It, therefore, does not require any argument to prove that Miss Peggy was a creature ordained for eydency—not one of those rough and bustling individuals who belong to the industrious class; and the whole trickling current of her obscure sequestered life illustrates this truth.

Her father, as we have mentioned, being restricted to a narrow income, his regular salary, her mother was obliged by all expedient means to make the guinea gild as large a surface as possible. Accordingly, Miss Peggy was brought up in the frugalest economy of pinched gentility; and as her father died young, she was obliged, along with her mother, to maintain as it were the same station with contracted means, or, more properly, with no other means than the most commendable assiduity, namely, the matron constantly at her weary wheel, and our heroine with her unwearied needle.

We make this important distinction between the wheel and needle, because, although we have often overheard malcontent murmurings against the former, yet we do not recollect, in any one instance, the latter spoken of either with complaint or disparagement.

Miss Peggy Pingle being thus obliged, by what statesmen call the exigences of her position, to be as sedentary as a judge, without a *dies non*, except Sunday, was necessarily not exposed to the temptations of life. She never had leisure for gallanting with persons of her own age. The garish damsels with whom, in her youth, she might have been expected to associate, were all to her as innocent as daffodils in a parterre; and the young men as the inaccessible rose-trees, that are best and least dangerous when seen afar off. In consequence, she reached nearly the years of discretion unobserved by the male sex—a time of life that all the ladies of our acquaintance, under thirty, say is the years between thirty and forty; we once, however, heard a dowager of four-score-and-six confess that rule was not universal, as she had not then reached the happy period. However, without attempting to determine this uncertain point, it came to pass that Miss Peggy reached her thirty-sixth year and upwards. She was, in fact, what they call in the west of Scotland, where they cultivate a peculiar vernacular, a Dumbarton youth, before she had any reason to suspect that she was not in the kingdom of Heaven, or the kirkgate of Irvine, where there is neither marrying nor giving in marriage.

At that period Dominie Loofie found himself in want of a spouse, and having heard it said that, no doubt, Miss Peggy had a sparing, went to her, and declared his ardent passion, one Saturday afternoon. She intreated him, with many endeavours to appear languishing, that he would spare her blushes till Monday night, that she might have time to consult her friends, whether she ought to marry at all, assuring him if they advised her to change her life, there was not another of the male speshy on whom she would so cordially bestow her hand.

One sees in this transaction all the delicacy of one marked out by destiny to give the world an example of eydency. There was an assurance to the Dominie that, as far as Miss Peggy was herself concerned, there could be no doubt that his suit was highly acceptable; the only thing suspicious lay in the application for the opinion of friends, which was not alarming; who having ever heard that any friend dissuaded a lady rather long kept from endeavouring to fulfil the essential purposes of her creation.

It happened, however, that in this case a difficulty arose, which was not foreseen, and which proved fatal: all Miss Peggy's kith and kin highly approved of the match, and no obstacle was visible, only the minister of the parish being afar off, a cousin advised her to see that "all the law papers anent the matrimony were clear; for at your time of life," said he, "matrimony, Miss Peggy, must be a matter of money; and, therefore, I advise you to look well to number one."

Miss Peggy, accordingly, at the time appointed, communicated the unanimous opinion of her friends to the schoolmaster, who was delighted at the bliss in prospect, and quoted to her a passage from Ovid's Art of Love, in Latin, which the lady justly remarked was most pretty to those who knew the signification. But when she spoke of the settlement, the corners of his mouth fell down, and taking up his hat, he went away, saying, very dryly, that he never could endure a woman who, in such a tender crisis, could think of such a sordid topic. The marriage was accordingly broken off; and Miss Peggy resolved on a life of single-blessedness, often declaring an admonishment to young widows, overly anxious to make themselves agreeable, that the masculine gender were perjured wretches, and no woman, but from a sense of duty, would countenance above one in her lifetime.

After the perjury of Dominie Loofie, Miss Peggy Pingle was the most exemplary of her sex. At first she deemed it advisable, being so crossed in love, to take to her bed; but, even in the most dolorous posture, her eydency was conspicuous. When any of the neighbours came in to solace her, and to speak of the great trial she had come through, she could only mope in a melancholy manner patching her discourse with appropriate texts of Scripture; but, when left alone, the time sometimes hung heavy on her hands, and, to lighten the wings of its flight, she had a seam at the end of her pillow, next the wall, with which she amused herself, as young ladies of quality are said to do, by playing sentimental airs on lute or harp, when they have cause to be in the same disconsolate condition; which, to be sure, is not often, especially if they have plenty of money.

When a decorous space of time had elapsed, Miss Peggy resumed her seat and seam at the window, and although she had met with, as she confessed to many occasional visitors, what would stick to her heart for the term of her life, it was not required that she should go about, making a moan of widowhood, though the needle was really ordained to be her bread-winner.

It is true, that corrupt human nature sometimes got the better of resignation; and Miss Peggy, in her endeavours to forget the false-hearted Dominie, began, as she grew older, to accept invitations to share the ploys and pastimes of young parties; but, at them all, she ever plied her thrift, which had grown into habitude, for she remembered on such occasions, as she often said herself, the day when she was not always such a staid woman as she then appeared, or had ever seemed since the time of her purloined affections—remarks which she frequently made when she had hardened the ends of her thread in the candle, to make it go through the needle-eye with more agility.

At last Miss Peggy became well stricken in years, and her legs rheumatized, by which she was obliged to remain at home, especially in the cold, or wet nights of winter; but her eydency suffered no abatement. In consequence, however, of being necessarily much alone, she acquired a competent knowledge of the phenomena of nature, as they were developed around her. She could tell the character of the weather without, by the dim, bright, or blazy aspect of the spark in her grate, that serve to make the cold more sensible; and could read the omens which made her penurious candle oracular, in the burning "tow-wicks, dipped in the fat of Pharoah's lean kine," as the huxter, who supplied her, used to say, with a wink, and the special orders of Miss Peggy Pingle.

Sometimes we thought her singularly interesting, and her prognostications from the combustion visible to the naked eye in her grate, were highly so; but her boding candle often displayed more signs of dread advents about to ensue than make the dismal lights mystical that enhance the glory about the cenotaphs of dead kings.

"Do you see that spangle upon the wick," Miss Peggy has said, "burning as clear as the eye of a lighthouse?—that betokens a letter from a far friend; if it kithes bright to you, like the morning star, there will be blithe tidings; but if red and grim, like a collegener's bowit in a kirk yard, down on your knees and make your shrift to *The Maker*." If your neglected snuff were become as mushroom-like as the Premier's wicks at a cabinet dinner, Miss Peggy was sure that a come-to-pass was not far off; and a curl of the grease, as it was turned out or in, was a winding-sheet that foretold the exit of a friend or a foe.

But pyrology was her most especially science: she could divine, when embers were red and yellow, that sailors' wives, with close-drawn hoods, would restless walk the shore; when bright, that cold-rife lovers would cuddle together; and, when flame broke lambent from the coal that kechling gossips were with secret.

But Miss Peggy was then waxing old;
"When the sunset of life gives its mystical lore,
And coming events cast their shadows before;"
and, though her needle seemed untired in its speed, she sometimes caught with it the skin of her finger instead of the linen; and her seams, instead of the spotlessness of former years, were often stained with blood—emblems of coffin-nails and burial sugar biscuits, and of the fulness of time when it was appointed she should be gathered to her fathers; but, even then, the considerate spirit of eydence was seen.

Well do we recollect the making of her testament; indeed, though then only in our teens, we were much in the confidence of Miss Peggy, and acted as her chamber council on that occasion.

She had the table set out; and we attended by appointment. Besides materials for writing, she had prepared divers pieces of paper, of different sizes, to represent the different legacies she intended to bequeath; and, having seated herself opposite to us, she gathered them towards her, and began. But, as the making of a will is a very solemn undertaking, before she commenced the dictation her heart filled full, and the tears, for some time, flowed from her eyes; at last, becoming more composed, she began.

After the usual preamble, which we executed in the most approved fashion, being then a sharp lad in a lawyer's office, she proceeded; and having, in due course of law, forgiven all her enemies, which, indeed, was soon done, for I never heard she had one; and, having directed her just debts to be all paid, for she did not owe a farthing, she gave the most particular orders about her funeral; then, she had recourse to the bits of papers, and from them drew the remembrance of those legacies and testimonies of regard on which she had long meditated. Among them, she bequeathed to us a double bottle with two necks, which she recollected we had admired in her cupboard when a boy.

At the conclusion of the ceremonial, and when all the papers were exhausted, she gave a deep sigh, and said that it behoved her to make a clau' respecting the residuary legatee; and she appointed Dominie Loofie, as she said tenderly, "for auld lang syne." I did not doubt, as the other bequests were not extravagant, that she had left him a good penny; and, after the interment, he certainly got well on to two pounds.

When the will was made, she placed her domicile in order; and, soon after, took to bed, and departed this life, as she had lived, in the most methodical and quiet manner, her dead clothes being found in one corner of her drawers tied up together, with the will, which we had assisted in framing, pinned in such a manner to the parcel that it could not be missed. The minister himself said at the dirgie, that he did not think that a more prejinct creature had been in the world since the days of Martha mentioned in scripture.

Notes

[1]See Ivy Pinchbeck, *Women Workers and the Industrial Revolution, 1750-1850* (London: Routledge, 1930), p. 289.

[2]See Bradford Allen Booth, editor, *The Gathering of the West* (Baltimore: Johns Hopkins, 1939), p. 1.

The Curse of the Factory System

John Fielden
(1836)

John Fielden, the Radical master cotton spinner, began publicly working for factory reform as early as 1816 when he and his brothers petitioned Parliament on behalf of the Manchester factory movement. And it was Fielden who, in 1847, introduced into Parliament the bill which became the Ten Hours Act.

The Curse of the Factory System clearly speaks of Fielden's concerns about harsh conditions while it foreshadows his objection to the introduction of the New Poor Law, particularly the attempt to transfer labor from the agricultural South to the industrial North. To Fielden, such policy came from unscrupulous employers attempting to gain cheap labor, and would have a terrible effect on wages. Fielden seeks to demonstrate that such policy is actually contrary to the manufacturers' general interests since it would undercut the purchasing power of the people.

But The Curse of the Factory System is, primarily, an argument for the legislative restriction of the hours of labor of all workers, adults as well as children. Although by this time Fielden had already decided that the Ten Hours Bill was the most that could be hoped for from Parliament, he nevertheless continued to argue that a ten-hour work day was inhumane.

Throughout the pamphlet, Fielden draws lightly on his own experiences as a child factory laborer and mill owner, but he grounds his argument on a wide variety of case studies and eyewitness accounts. He uses few statistical reports, and then only to further document the findings of a case study. Because of the emphasis on the human element, rather than numbers, Fielden's approach might appear somewhat subjective; but the fact that the vast majority of reporting comes from documented sources rather than from Fielden himself leaves the reader with the impression of objectivity. Fielden's choice of language, which carries little emotional force, reinforces the sense of objective reporting. And although he relies heavily on stylistics, typography such as italization and capitalization would not be viewed as elements of subjectivity but as elements of effective rhetorical style derived from Thomas Carlyle.

Fielden's experience as a child factory worker and as a factory owner present him with a unique opportunity to view the problems concerning factory conditions from both sides and present a solution based on understanding and mutual benefits.

* * *

(In previous sections, Fielden has presented evidence on the deleterious effects of long working hours on both children and adults, his information drawn from The Memoir of Robert Blincoe *as well as government reports, pamphlets, articles and letters. In the following section, he offers an argument based on economics.)*

Is it, then, our *interests* that require us to work these children into deformity and the grave? I fear your answer will be *"yes,"* and, with unfeigned sickness of heart that I should be compelled to appeal to you to desist from this practice of maiming and killing, *because* maiming and killing are *not your interest*, I will, since I must, show you that we get nothing by this over-working; while, as a nation, we lose by it. The dream of our day is, that England is to be the *workshop of the world*, and the dread is, lest this should be prevented by *"foreign competition."* It is a fallacy; a bugbear; but let us examine it.

If to destroy foreign competition means any thing, it means that we should prevent any other people from producing or manufacturing any thing produced or manufactured in the factories in England. If I am told that this is not contended for, nor expected; but that that which is necessary to be done, is, that we should manufacture in England so *cheaply* that no people engaged in like pursuits can *undersell* us in any market in the world; my answer is, that the customers in those markets will take good care that we do this; and therefore we need have no concern on that score. But what is meant by *cheap*, as applied here? If barter, or the *exhange of* one commodity for another commodity, without the intervention of money in the transaction, were the prevailing practice, there would then be no difficulty in defining the word cheap; for, in that case, every one will admit that the American, for instance, who exports cotton to France, Switzerland, and England, would demand, and have, too, the same number of knives, of piece-goods, or any other articles in exchange for his cotton in one country as another, where the same articles are produced in all, or he would refrain from supplying cotton to any country refusing to give him the same number of those articles, or something else that he wants, until the stock of cotton in that country became so scarce that it would command the same quantity of those things which it did in the other countries to which he took it. Here, then, we have the principle which nations, trading with one another, always have recognised and ever must recognise. Any attempt to defeat this principle by the intervention of what passes for money, to measure the value of these things, in either one country or another, may serve to perplex, and involve in difficulties, those coming under its operation; but it never can give the parties doing so any permanent advantage. Therefore, the manufacturers of England, France, and America, meeting each other with similar manufactured goods in Mexico, for instance, must sell these manufactures to the Mexicans at the same price, or not sell at all. They always have done so, and they must continue to do so, whatever be the money price of these things in the respective countries where these men have manufactured them.

Then, how do the manufacturers of England, France, and America, sustain the apparent dearness of their mode of manufacture which one or more of them may have to sustain over the other? What these manufacturers take in return from Mexico, must be sold at such a price in their respective countries, as will enable them to go on manufacturing. And thus, the apparent dearness of manufacturing in one country, as compared with another, falls on the consumers in that country, and is paid in the price charged on the returns that the manufacturer brings back. If payments be made in Mexico, to these three competing rivals, and one or more of them would be unable to get a remunerating return for his manufactures by taking the specie home, owing to the law regulating the currency or value of specie in his country, which has stamped a fixed price on it, such rival converts his specie into something else, either in Mexico, or by taking it, or the value of it, to other parts; and purchasing those things which the law of his country does not affix any price to; and thus, he effects his object of charging upon the consumer of his own country the disadvantages he labours under from manufacturing at what is called a *dearer price*. And, by these means, he continues to export trade to Mexico with advantage, and ought to do so without any dread of foreign competition. My experience in the export trade to Mexico (and many other places) convinces me of the truth of this fact; for, I find that the Americans and French, with their goods, have met the goods which I have sent to these different markets, and sold them on terms similar to my own; and that they have continued to do this over a succession of years, during which period their manufactures have been increased in a proportion equal to the increase in England, while, at the same time, the cost of manufacturing has been much greater, as I am now going to show. To go into detail on the operations by which their higher cost of production is thrown upon the consumers in their own country, is foreign to my object here, and would require an explanation of their protecting tariff-duties and navigation-laws which would take up more space than I am willing to devote to it; my object being merely to show, that there never is such a competition in meeting foreign manufacturers in the markets of the world as the English manufacturers appear to dread, and that there would not be such a competition, even were the English manufacturers placed in a position more disadvantageous than any that they can ever be in. For, our geographical position, our climate, our mines and minerals, and the dexterity and persever-ance of our workpeople, to say nothing of the superiority of our machinery, give to England advantages which she always has and always must possess over any other manufacturing nation in the world, unless, indeed, the political philoso-phers of our day should break down the spirit of the people by requiring them to work themselves to death, which has nearly been done already, by denying the Ten-hour Bill that has now been sought for these twenty years and upwards.

The political economists in England, who everlastingly bellow out "for-eign competition," and who, during these ten years, have been receiving *three* pieces of the English manufactured goods in return for their fixed incomes, where they ought to have received *one* piece only; these gentlemen, I have no doubt, know their watch-word to be a fallacy; and their anxiety to keep up the delusion among the manufacturers, is a convincing proof of it. A Dr. Ure is, it seems, now amongst the most conspicuous of the agents of these philoso-phers, and is trying, not to get the manufacturers down to *ten* hours' labour a day, but to lengthen the period to *fifteen* or *sixteen* hours a day, by telling us that some of our competitors work that long time. These oppressors of mankind sometimes overshoot their mark, by prevailing on their dupes to push their recommendations to an extent that frustrates their designs. Now, in showing what I am about to do, we may, perhaps, perceive whether they are not in that position at the present time.

* * * * *

To prove, then, the increase of manufactures in France and America, and the position we are in, I will here insert, a statement that I had prepared from returns the best and most authentic I could get, which I intended to submit to the Members of Parliament, who met the short-time delegates in Manchester, in December last. But, as that meeting required all the time for the delegates to give the information they desired to give, and a motion was carried to get a meeting of the manufacturers themselves, in order that they might state what were their objections to comply with the wishes of the delegates, and to assist them to get a Ten-Hour Bill, I have kept back this statement then, hoping that I should have a more fitting opportunity to introduce it at the manufacturers' meeting; but, I regret to say, that that meeting could not be obtained.

STATEMENT.

The consumption of cotton in Europe and America, is 1,500,000 bales, annually, averaging about 300 lbs. each:

Of which 940,000 bales, nearly two-thirds, are consumed

in Great Britain.
280,000 bales, fully one-fifth, are consumed in France.
216,000 bales, nearly one-seventh, are consumed in America.
64,000 bales, nearly one twenty-fourth, are consumed in other
parts.
From reports we have the following stated as facts:—
Additional cost of French cotton goods above those of England, average
30 to 40 per cent.
Inferiority of French machinery, 25 per cent
Ditto, ditto, labour, 20 per cent

Dr. Bowring.

In summer, spinner and weavers in France turn to agricultural pursuits for
relaxation. A duty of 40 per cent. on English yarns would not save French
spinners from being ruined by their admission.

Delegates from Lisle and Lyons in
1834

Coals in France cost ten times as much as in England. Iron is also very dear.

Sanson Davillier, 1834

English yarns 45 to 75 per cent. cheaper than French.

Chamber of Commerce, Lyons

.

A duty of 40 per cent. on English yarns would not save French spinners
from being ruined by their admission.

Le Marchand, *of Rouen, and others*
from Lisle and Alsace

The cotton manufacture in France was established under the continental
system of Napoleon. The consumption of cotton in 1810 was 25,000,000 of
pounds. And yet, notwithstanding the great disadvantages it labours under, the
consumption had been augmented in 1832 to 81,738,900, an increase of 224 per
cent.

Then, as regards America, our next rival competitor, we have it in
evidence,—

That the manufacturers pay 14*s*. 11*d*. wages for the work that is done in
England for 10*s* .6*d*.; or, more by 42 per cent.

That machinery in America costs double what it does in England.

That fuel in America is also much dearer than in England, and the interest of money much higher.

That the factory workers in America leave the factories two or three months a year, and go to their parents.

And yet, notwithstanding these difficulties, the Americans, who consumed only 103,483 bales of cotton in 1826; in 1834 consumed 216,888 bales, making an increase, in the last nine years, of 109 per cent.

I would ask any one, after he is in possession of these facts, whether it is not vain to think of destroying these competitors, if such be the object of those who advocate long hours of work; and whether it would not be much more wise to seek for a different and a better remedy to protect the manufacture of cotton, and the immense number of persons in Great Britain dependent upon it for employment. It would be well, too, to look to the effect that has been produced on all classes by the course we have been and are still pursuing, to overcome this competition of foreign rivals. If we will investigate this question in the manner it deserves, we shall find that we are ruining ourselves by giving away our labour to foreigners. In support of this assertion, I will give the following facts.

The Americans, during a period of eighteen years prior to 1833, could purchase in England, with the proceeds of 300 lbs. of Upland cotton, on an average of these years, only 24 pieces of 74-cloth; but, in 1833, they could purchase, with the proceeds of the same quantity of cotton, 30 pieces. And, in like manner, they could purchase 29 pieces in 1834, and 32 pieces in 1835. An increase of 33 1/3 per cent.

During the eighteen years prior to 1833, the Americans could, with the proceeds of 300 lbs. of cotton, purchase only 131 lbs. of 30 hanks water twist: in 1833, 177 lbs.: in 1834, 178 lbs., and in 1835, 190 lbs. An increase of 45 per cent.

During the eighteen years prior to 1833, the Americans, with the proceeds of 300lbs of cotton could only purchase 86lbs. of half-ell velveteens. In 1835, they could, for the same, purchase 136obs. An increase of 58 per cent.

During the eighteen years prior to 1833, the Americans, with the proceeds of 300 lbs. of cotton, could purchase only 15 2/3 pieces of 28-inch 72 power-loom cloth. The average this year has been 24 pieces for the same. An increase of 53 per cent.

In the years 1826 and 7, the Americans, with the proceeds of 300 lbs. of cotton, could purchase only 344 yards of domestic, or stout cloth.

In 1828-9 . . . 365 yards, an increase of 6 per cent.

     1830-1 . . . 388 12   ”

     1832-3 . . . 464 34   ”

1834-5 . . . 564 64   "

The quality of the cotton and the cloth being the same throughout these years in every one of these different articles of manufacture.

The five articles here selected are what are called leading articles, into which a very great proportion of the cotton imported into England is worked up; and they constitute a fair criterion of the general state of the manufacture. Now, if these facts do not prove a rapid and appalling decline, as to foreign trade, in our manufacturing pursuits, notwithstanding the reiterated boasts of the prosperity of our manufactures put forth through the press, it appears to me impossible to say what would be an indication of such decline. Had the manufacturers and the cotton-growers come in close contact with each other, and exchanged and taken away each of them their commodities in *bulk*, the eyes of the British manufacturers would long ago have been opened, and a stop would have been put to the losing game we have pursued. The Englishman would have said to the foreigner: "Our manufactures are too plentiful, for you will not give us the same quantity of cotton for them that you were wont to do; but we will reduce the hours of work in our factories, as our workpeople have long desired us to do, and then you will be glad to give us as much cotton for our manufacutres as you formerly did." This is what the English manufacturer would have said long ago if his dealings had been carried on by bartering, instead of being carried on by selling for money; and it is what he ought now to say.

While we have been thus profuse towards *foreigners*, we have latterly been raising the price of all these articles to the home consumers, and competing with each other in our manufactories who could screw the greatest quantity of labour out of those we employ. Is it not time that this system should be changed? We shall not have to wait long before spinners will be as anxious for a short-time bill as the operatives. Dr. Kay, of Manchester, whose pamphlet of 1832 I have quoted above, tells us, in his first Report to the Poor-law Commissioners, dated 22nd July, 1835, that there are now erecting in the cotton district of Lancashire and its immediate vicinity, factories which will bring into operation 7500 horse-power above what is in work now; that is, about one-sixth more; and if we are destined to see this realized, my opinion is, that we shall then see *the beginning of the end!* We have nothing to fear from foreign competition. It is the greatest humbug that Englishmen were ever made to believe in; but from competition amongst ourselves we have every thing to fear; and if we do not restrain ourselves in time, or the Legislature do not restrain us, we shall very soon destroy ourselves.

How ought this change to be made? By doing justice to our working people, and immediately adopting the Ten-hour Bill. What would be its effects? It would make our yarn and goods cheaper to *home* consumers, and restore to us the quantity of foreign produce which we formerly had in exchange for our exports. We are arrived at a new era in manufactures, and if the crop of cotton in America be not abundant (which I believe it is), we shall be sensible of this fact before we get over the year 1836; but we are *not* pursuing a system which we never did before; we are making our goods cheap to foreigners and dear to home consumers.

I think there is abundant proof in the foregoing statement that the economists have overshot the mark; they have pushed out their principle of exacting the greatest possible quantity of labour for the lowest possible remuneration to those performing it, until they have turned the tables against themselves; and if they will continue to despise the entreaties of the ill-treated factory hands, and still insist on their being worked from twelve to fifteen hours a day, results may at no distant time arrive, that shall alarm the masters and the public, as much as they were alarmed by the fevers in 1796, and again by the cholera in 1832. They may see immense numbers of people in the manufacturing districts thrown out of work, and all the horrible suffering and danger consequent upon such a state.

The advance of the price of cotton that has been going on in this country during the last three years, has had three causes: partly, a diminished stock; partly, that quick consumption, owing to our long hours of work, which makes us tread so closely on the heels of the cotton-growers; and, partly, by speculations in cotton, caused by an increase in the circulating medium. These causes have raised the price of our manufacture to home consumers, at least from 15 to 20 per cent.; while, concurrent with these effects, the cotton-growers have gained an advantage in exchanging cotton for goods, to the extent of 50 per cent., as shown in the foregoing statement; and since that statement was written the cotton-grower has derived much greater advantages in the exchange of cotton for goods. If the present hours of work be continued, the people will have to pass through a fiery ordeal to bring back again 300 lbs. of cotton for 16 pieces of 72 power-loom cloth, instead of giving 24, the number we gave last year. And this must be done, before the cotton manufacture again is what it ought to be with regard to the exchange of our manufactures for foreign productions. There are two ways of effecting this: the one is by rich and powerful men continuing to work the same hours they now do, while their weaker brethren, unable to bear up against the losses consequent upon their attempt to do so, will break down under their difficulties, and their people be thrown out of employ. The other is, by an immediate general reduction of the hours of labour to *ten* in the day, which would be more beneficial to all.

No one who reflects, can be otherwise than alarmed at the prospect that this state of things presents. If what Dr. Kay says be true, namely, that *one-sixth* additional power will be in operation in the cotton manufacturing districts in Lancashire in 1837, then this, if the present hours of work be continued, must require an increased quantity of cotton to about the same extent. Where is it to come from? Recollect that the growers of cotton cannot increase their slaves to cultivate this plant with the same facility that we are increasing our steam-engines and our machinery. This is a natural impediment that we cannot overcome; and, therefore, I say that the economists have overshot their mark, and that, if the manufacturers will still be their dupes, and neglect all the entreaties made by their workpeople to reduce the hours of work, a visitation may come upon them such as I have described.

I have made minute calculations, bearing on the probable supply and consumption of cotton in 1838. I assume that Dr. Kay's statement is correct, that within two years from July 1835, we shall have an increase of *one-sixth* in the power employed in the manufacture of cotton, in "Lancashire and its immediate vicinity," independent of Scotland and other parts where cotton is manufactured. To keep all the factories now in being, and those that Dr. Kay says will be, in motion, and, working the present hours and present sort of work, it will require an increase of *one-sixth* in the quantity of cotton imported. Now, taking the average of the annual increase of cotton imported for the last fourteen years, and assuming that it will be same for the next two years, I do not see how the factories, taken collectively, can work more than *ten* hours a day during the year 1838. To lessen the consumption of cotton by one-sixth, would cause the price of cotton to fall, and would secure us 300 lbs. again in exchange for 16 pieces of goods instead of 24 pieces; and this reduction in the price of cotton would enable the manufacturer to sell his manufactures at a lower price than he does now, after receiving the same sum that he had in 1835 for himself, and his workpeople, for labour, and for interest of "capital." This diminution of consumption by one-sixth, would also admit of the increase of manufacturing establishments, beyond those now in preparation, where there would be employment for more hands (perhaps for the unfortunate hand-loom weavers), and an investment for more "capital" quite as rapidly as the growth of cotton can be increased; and also with a much fairer prospect to the manufacturers, of having a profitable business, and the consumers at home, manufactured goods at a lower price. For, to continue the present hours of work, will only benefit the growers of raw material imported into this country, and speculators who dabble in it, while it will be injurious to those who work up these raw materials, and to the consumers of manufactured articles generally.

I have thus endeavoured to show my brother manufacturers that their own *interest*, apart from those motives of humanity which ought to have a tenfold preponderance, suggests the immediate adoption of a Ten-hour Bill, and I implore them to petition the Legislature for it forthwith. But, though I have confined my inquiry to the cotton business, in which I am engaged myself, I am convinced that the same reasoning applies to all other manufactures, not even excepting that, which, from some cause or other is Mr. Rickards's favourite, the woollen. The over-working prevails in all; the law ought to be applied to all, and all manufacturers ought, at once, to acknowledge the fact, and petition for the remedy. (*Here Fielden inserts parts of Dr. Kay's report, commenting on how long working hours contribute to injury and vice among the workers.*)

* * * * * *

I have mentioned Dr. Ure above, a gentleman who, it appears, has found out in his travels, that, in foreign countries, the people work longer hours than we do, and who concludes that we must follow their example, to avoid the ill effects of this other species of "foreign competition." I draw different conclusions from the facts that I know. I know that it was proved before Mr. Sadler's Committee by an overseer, that some of his class of workmen had been sent for to go to Rouen, and other places in France, there to introduce the English sytem; that they first had to resist the workpeople in quitting their work for recreation, which they have been accustomed to do when they required it; that the French looked upon this as an arbitrary thing, and resisted it at Rouen; that—but I will quote his words from page 244. "I was acquainted with a man who went to Rouen to superintend a factory there, and, in consequence of his *endeavouring to establish the English system*, the workmen turned out, to the amount of 4000 or 5000; *the military were called in*, and *several lives were lost. The military were kept in the town a great length of time.*" This, I suppose, our political economists would call "free labour!" Labour not in any way to be interfered with!

* * * * * *

I ask, for what the workpeople, and the good men of all parties, have for many years been petitioning the Legislature to grant, an *effective Ten-Hour Bill*. I ask for what the late Sir Robert Peel asked the House to grant in 1815; since which time the consumption of cotton has been increased from 6000 to 18,000 bags per week, and the labour of both children and adults very much increased in intensity and depreciated in value. I ask for this, because it is all they ask for. For I think that our factory-system will not be what it ought to be, until the time of all be reduced to eight hours a day, with two hours for training and instruction, such as I recommended to the Regeneration Society in 1833; on which occasion I published my opinions in reply to a letter I had from Mr. Fitton, a worthy and intelligent constituent of mine, which letter was published with mine. A Ten-Hour Bill for *all*, then, I ask for, because I know that the adults require it for their protection equally with the children. I ask for it, too, because I know that this country is in a position to grant it, and without doing wrong to any individual. Will the memorialists and my brother manufacturers persevere in their efforts to prevent it? And will the Legislature yield to the suggestions of the oppressors, and deny the prayers of the oppressed? If they will, then the responsibility be upon their head, and not on mine.

In conclusion, however, I hope that my constituents, the memorialists, will think that I did right in declining to urge their prayer upon the President of the Board of Trade, and, as a brother manufacturer, I call on them to assist me in obtaining that mere justice for our work-people which I have shown in the preceding pages to be so wanting. I beg them to believe that it is not without reluctance that I spread abroad the knowledge of what English manufacturers have done; that it is not without shame, as an Englishman, that I show England to be much more boastful of her justice and humanity than prompt and vigilant in securing them to her laborious people; and that I do it, not so much to rake up past enormities, as to prevent them in future. If they will look calmly into the short narrative that I have given, I am sure they will be convinced that the origin of our cruelties was as I have stated; that their progress has been also as I have stated, and that the results are to be seen in the wretchedness, the vice, the soured temper and degeneracy, so ably shown forth by Dr. Kay, Mr. Greg, and the Inspector Rickards. They will also, I hope, agree with me and those gentlemen, that no measure has ever passed the Legislature efficient for the purpose of staying this curse, as mighty as the machine which has caused it. And I hope, if they cast an eye to their own and their country's *interest*, that they will ponder on it well; for I feel strongly assured that they will then arrive at the conclusion that I have come to, that our interest does not stand in the way of that justice and humanity which our workpeople ask for. If it did, no man would be sooner a sufferer than myself, and they know well to what an extent; for I believe that no manufacturer in England is more largely engaged than myself in that precise manufacture in which the Americans in particular are attempting a competition. I beg them, therefore, to despise the fears, whether pretended or real, of the political economists, who have pretty clearly shown us, that, while they would make England the "workshop of the world," they would not scruple to make her also the slaughter-house of Mammon.

The Orphan Milliners
A Story of the West End
Miss Camilla Toulmin
(1844)

The publication of Thomas Hood's poem "The Song of the Shirt," in the December 1843 issue of Punch, *captured the imagination of the public and focused attention on the plight of needlewomen. For social-protest writers focusing on needleworkers, such as Toulmin, of primary concern were the background, working conditions, and final ramifications of the women forced to earn a living sewing. Thus, a major issue was the long hours needlewomen had to work, especially during the social seasons, particularly the main one which ran from March through July, but also the smaller one which occurred during November and December. Toulmin, like many authors, used Hood's poem to gain reader interest: the refrain is the epigraph to her novel.*

Toulmin uses other sources within the novel, as well. When Toulmin describes her seamstresses as "pale and thin," with "weak eyes," and "distortions of the spine" she is echoing information recorded in The Report of the Second Children's Employment Commission *(1843). Nor is death by consumption a dramatic exaggeration, but, rather, realism based on sources such as Edwin Chadwick's* Report on the Sanitary Condition of the Labouring Population of Great Britain (1842):

Deaths from Disease of Milliners and Dressmakers, in the Metropolitan Unions during the year 1839, as shown by the Mortuary Registers[1]

Age	Number of deaths	Average age	Number of deaths from consumption	Average age	Number of deaths from other lung diseases	Average age
Under 20	6	17	4	18	—	—
20 Under 30	24	24	17	23	1	23
30 Under 40	11	34	6	34	1	33
40 Under 50	2	45	—	—	1	40
50 Under 60	4	54	1	58	2	55
60 Under 70	5	64	—	—	—	—
Total	52	32	28	26	5	41

*[Note:] Out of 52 deaths in the year, 41 of the deceased attained an age of
25. The average age of the 33 who died of lung diseases was 28.*

*A final concern for many of the early novelists, particularly women, was
the role other women played in the working conditions of seamstresses, and
what role women could play in changing conditions. Although Toulmin does
acknowledge the role of the thoughtless client in the suffering of needlewomen,
unlike many of her contemporaries, she focuses her attention on the owners of
millinery establishments. They are the ones who actually make the decisions
as to the amount of work done, the hours kept, and the conditions under which
the young women must live. Of particular interest is the model Toulmin
establishes at the end: Henrietta is shown to be a model employer, especially
when contrasted with the earlier unfavorable portrayal of Madame Dobière.*

* * *

*"Work—work—work!
Till the brain begins to swim!
Work—work—work!
Till the eyes are heavy and dim!"—Hood.*

There is a certain spot in one of the midland counties, which, for the sake
of preserving its incognito, I will call Willowdale. It is really but three of four
miles from a market town, yet lying away from the high road, and being still
further removed from any railroad, it is about as secluded a place as the
imagination can picture. Yet beautiful exceedingly is its rich meadowland; and
pleasant to view the varied beauty of its flowering, fruitful orchards; and pure
the health-giving breezes that come from the neighbouring hills. Above all, to
my heart has it the exquisite charm of silence,—that profound silence which is
felt as a delicious sensation! The few cottages which are scattered over about
a quarter of a mile of the Dale, are called—by the dwellers therein—a village;
though by malicious detractors they have been said to comprise only—a
hamlet. Narrow the distinction, I grant; but measure two little persons together,
and see if they do not stand upright, to say nothing of getting on tiptoe if they
dare.

In one of the prettiest of these cottages lived for some years a widow and
her two daughters. A small life annuity secured to Mrs. Sandford, was their
only dependence; and Willowdale had been chosen as a residence, because
house rent was low, and the little income would go farther in such a neighbourhood than elsewhere. It does not seem to have occurred to the mother, that
it was possible to *add* to their narrow means by any exertions of her own, and
so provide against casualties. No; she was one of those characters in whom

feminine softness borders very decidedly on feminine weakness. Of placid, unaspiring temper, she thought little of the future, and was easily contented with the present. The little she did think for the future was, that of course her daughters would marry, and thus be provided for, and protected. Too many mothers, who think little, think thus; and so neglect to cherish in those they love a spirit of self-reliance, or to place within their reach the means of self-dependence. Woe to the helpless in this struggling world!

The even thread of poor Mrs. Sandford's life was snapped suddenly at last. She was under fifty, and a week before her death had appeared in as robust health as ever. I wonder how many hundred evenings she had sat in the garden long after the heavy dew had risen; and yet at last to take cold that fine autumn night! To be sure, she was rather stout and plethoric, as became so "easy" a character,—and we know inflammation of the lungs sometimes goes hard with such persons. Mrs. Sandford dead! It came as a severe shock to all the kind-hearted neighbors, who crowded the pretty little cottage, as they eagerly pressed forward with offers of assistance. The medical man who had been called in—a new comer to the neighbourhood—looked sad and sympathising as he pressed the hands of the bereaved and weeping girls. "It was a most distressing case—so very sudden—pity he had not been called in earlier," &c.&c. Well, he did not take the second fee Henrietta offered him, but put it back, and closed his own over her little hand, with a "No,no!—God bless you, my poor child." There was really a heart in his breast, beneath that rusty black waistcoat and snuff-besmeared frill.

The funeral was over, with its dull formalities, that seem so cold and are so heart-rending. Henrietta—or Etty, as she was generally called—was nineteen, and Annie five years her junior. Of course responsibility devolved on the elder sister—though, if in the multitude of counselors there is always wisdom, they must have been sagely advised. Every member of the little community of Willowdale was a friend—though, alas with very limited power. The *catalogue raisonnée* of these might be as follows:—Two elderly maiden sisters, who had lived in the county nearly all their lives—who had once seen the sea, but would have thought crossing it a tempting of Providence; the widow of an army surgeon, who knew, as one would judge from her lively reminiscences, a good deal of Indian life, but of no other; a half-pay captain, with health impaired, and carrying a bullet he received in "the Peninsula." But enough,—the list would be tedious, and would wear a strong family likeness. Much goodness of heart was there in the little band; but a small, very small share of that practical knowledge of the world, which would have been highly valuable in directing the desolate orphans. However, in one opinion they were unanimous, namely, that Henrietta should write to a wealthy cousin in the

North—the only relative she could claim,—and ask his advice and assistance. He expressed much regret at their bereavement, and enclosed a trifling present to assist in the purchase of mourning,—expressing a wish to be informed if Henrietta's acquirements were of a sort to qualify her for a governess. Timid and humble, she had no hesitation in answering "No,"—and she was right; for though she loved reading, and had an active inquiring intellect, little food for the mind had been placed within her reach; and Mrs. Sandford's easy disposition had contented itself with imparting to her children the few "acquirements" she herself possessed. The wealthy relative then proposed that the girls should be apprenticed to a London dressmaker,—kindly considering it would be a satisfaction not to separate them, and generously offering to provide the requisite money.

The girls, though hardly yet recovered from the shock of their mother's death, still entered into the project with much of the eagerness and enthusiasm of youth: nor was there anything in the manner and opinions of their surrounding friends to chill their hopes of happiness and independence. The widow of the army surgeon very well remembered that a milliner in Calcutta had returned "home," after five years of business, with a handsome fortune. The old maids were sure dressmakers must grow rich, they charged so enormously; and what was rather more to the present purpose, someone else knew somebody whose wife's sister-in-law's second cousin actually was a milliner in London, and who became a person of considerable importance, volunteering to make inquiries, and procure an introduction in that quarter. But I must hurry over the progress and detail of preparation. It is enough that inquiries were made and arrangements completed; and a letter, the joint production of the sisters, was written to their rich relation, whom they had never seen, and towards whom, notwithstanding his kindness, they felt a mysterious awe mingled with their gratitude. Mrs. Sandford was not a person to have saved anything from her little income; quite the contrary—she was rather "behind-hand;" so that when the furniture of the cottage was sold to pay rent, and trifling debts, and travelling expenses were calculated, Henrietta found she would have about five pounds, with which to begin the world. Yet if good will, and, in many instances, some self-sacrifice, were taken into account, the poor orphans were very rich in keepsakes and parting offerings, presented to them by the Willowdale community.

They were to reside in the establishment of Madame Dobière; such an arrangement having been taken into account in the premium paid. It was night when, after a wearying journey, they arrived at the mansion in ____Street, Hanover Square, which was to be henceforth their home. They were almost awed at its grandeur, the brilliantly lit show-room, and the noble entrance; but something the opposite of this was felt when they were ushered, after a frugal meal, into the dingy, cold, uncomfortable garret, crowded with beds, not destined to be pressed, for hours to come, by the toil-worn band our orphans were about to join. Poor girls! had they been less ignorant of the world and its ways, that night would have been yet more sorrowful than it proved. The morsel of candle with which they had been entrusted warned them to hurry their unpacking; but it was a moon-lit night, and long after they had wept in each other's arms—they scarcely knew why—and endeavoured to sleep, the bright light which streamed through the curtainless windows, seemed to come as if with a message to keep them from repose. That very moonlight, which had for so many years fallen on their neat white bed, casting in the summer, when they needed no other curtain, the quivering shadow of a trained laburnum!

Annie was the first to sleep; but after the clocks from the neighbouring steeples had tolled one, the door was opened, and Henrietta saw a pale thin girl of twenty enter. There was nothing remarkable in her appearance; there are hundreds of such who rise and toil everyday, and wither and die every year, in the great metropolis. She attempted to undress, but sleep overpowered her, and she threw herself on a bed without even removing her gown. Again the church clocks struck, telling that another hour belonged to the past. Soon afterwards two apprentices were heard upon the creaking stairs; and when they had entered, and Henrietta had had time to notice them, she felt surprised that they, up an hour later, were evidently less fatigued than their companion; but the mystery was soon solved.

"Poor Bessy!" said one, alluding to the girl who lay dressed upon the bed; "two nights has she been up: I thought she would have fallen asleep over that fancy ball dress. Well, I suppose our turn will come before the week is out; for though it is not the season, and I call it a shame to have such 'long hours,' she won't have 'day hands' for this country order, so what is to be done?"

"Oh, don't talk," said the other; "I am so tired, and my eyes so prickle, let us get to bed when we can."

And to bed they hurried, without bending the knee to ONE. Let us hope that some murmured prayer to guide and bless, mounted to HIS throne!

From sheer bodily weariness Henrietta Sandford fell asleep before three other occupants of that gloomy attic entered singly and softly.

Madame Dobière piqued herself on the method of her irregularities. Indeed, she talked about it as if it were a system for the strict performance of the cardinal virtues. From frequently hearing the same precepts inculcated, it is possible that the more impressible minds among her young workwomen half believed that they were in one of the best conducted establishments in London. Madame was a little sharp-featured woman of forty, who usually dressed in black silk, or brown merino, without tuck or trimming; because ladies do not like to see their milliners themselves adopt the mode they recommend. But on Sundays, and on the frequent holidays she gave herself—why Cinderella's fairy change could not have been more striking than hers. It was even said she had *once been found out,* in borrowing from her show-room a bonnet destined for a countess. Yet I am afraid she would have been shocked at the mere accusation, for Madame Dobière stickled much for propriety. For instance, she would not suffer a brother to visit one of her resident apprentices—it was not proper where there were so many young women, whom she felt herself bound to protect; but at midnight, her "day hands" might traverse the streets alone on their way to their wretched lodgings! Madame Dobière was also one of that class, who, like the monkey in the fable, always find a "paw" to win for them the object of their desires. She could not have cut out and fitted a dress herself, if she might have had a hundred dresses to have made for the doing it. But to hear her angry blame at failure, and matter-of-course treatment of success in others, who could ever have guessed her own inability to excel! Not at first any of those by whom she was surrounded; for the corps of dressmakers is commonly recruited from unsophisticated country girls. And thus would she harangue on the subject of her admirable arrangements—how "in the season she had so many extra hands, that few were kept up more than one night a week,—how at other times of the year, they often worked only twelve hours a day—though, of course, they must take their chance, if work should come in. After all, what was a night's rest to a young person—she should not care for it a bit, were it not that her mind required repose—she worked harder than they— the whole weight of the business was on her;" and then she would wind up with a sigh, or throw herself back in her chair apparently exhausted. In conclusion, Mr. Dobière (his real name was Dobs; but Madame, having travelled as lady's maid in her youth, and having thus picked up a few French phrases, thought it expedient to Frenchify that plebeian monosyllable,) was a peaceable individual, whose occupation, whatever it was, called him "into the City" every morning. He was punctual as clock-work always returning at six; when, if he did not take Madame to the play, and they had not a few friends to drink tea, or had not some such engagement, he usually assisted his wife in arranging her accounts.

Who, then, did manage the business of this pleasure-loving lady? Her factotum—a woman who received a high salary, for which she certainly worked indefatigably. But Miss Smith was a greater tyrant than Madame; and was one of those hard, passionless, yet scolding women, who receive unanimously the title of shrews. To *this* had she been moulded by the ordeal passed by a milliner's apprentice. Yet as heat, which hardens one substance, may dissolve another; so did the busy party gathered in Madame Dobière's workroom present, in varied development of character, a most fruitful theme for philosophic inquiry.

But our country girls were no philosophers. They did not attempt to trace cause and effect, or even to wonder how it was that one of their companions was silent, and selfish, and morose; why another was irritable and angry one hour, and the next winning love by her exalted generosity. Yea exalted, perhaps, in taking on herself some mutual blame, or relieving with her more nimble fingers the slow or dull. What little kindnesses become great ones to the wretched and oppressed! Nor did they seek to know why they all were pale and thin; or how it was that many had weak eyes, and not a few suffered from distortion of the spine. Yet, by degrees, Henrietta perceived how different must be their existence to that which their inexperience had painted. But they had good constitutions in their favour, and Etty bore up bravely for a while against the sedentary life—the poor living—the want of sleep—and want of relaxation; while *her* character was developed by intense application to acquire skill in the business; and so great was her progress, that in an incredibly short space of time she became one of the most efficient "hands" in Madame Dobière's establishment. Yet this very concentration of her energies, perhaps, prevented her from perceiving the gradual but melancholy change that was taking place in Annie; though dearly she loved her, with an affection more protecting than is generally that of a sister; and so blended did it seem with her own life, that the most powerful motive she had felt to exertion was the hope that dear Annie's opening youth might be passed more brightly than her own could be.

Thus passed the winter; and now the "busy season" was come.

"Etty," said the child to her sister, one day, speaking in a high-pitched tone across the room—"Etty, I am so giddy—so ill;" and before Etty could fling down her work and reach her side, Annie had fainted—saved only from a serious fall by some nearer companion.

"Throw some water over her," said Miss Smith, without relinquishing for a moment her own cutting out—"she'll soon come to again;—why, one would think you had never seen a girl faint before!"

But the water did not restore her, and Henrietta and another carried her from the close and crowded room. The fresh air was more curative, and before they had reached their dormitory she had recovered her senses.

"Oh! stay with me, Etty," said the sufferer,—"do not leave me."

"I will stay, darling—be composed." And Henrietta pillowed her sister's head upon her bosom, while hot tears coursed down both their cheeks; those of the elder girl flowing partly from a sort of self-reproach that she had not before noticed the hollow eyes and pallid countenance of her dear Annie.

"You are ill, my sister," she continued—"you must have advice—they will surely send for a doctor. Let me go, dearest, just to ask this—I will be back directly."

"No, no, there is no need," returned the other; "I think—I am almost sure, that I am only faint for want of food. I did not tell you, dear,—what use would it have been?—But I could not eat that coarse dry bread and cheese last night—and then, to-day again, that horrid fat cold mutton. Oh! Etty, is it wrong of me to be so dainty?"

"Dainty, indeed!" murmured the girl who had assisted to carry her up stairs—"dainty, indeed! we are all sick to death of the hard Dutch cheese, and the everlasting mutton. But Madame contracts with her butcher—and the nastier it is, the less we eat. It is a shame, that it is—and I am sure you girls are the worst off of all, for you have no friends to go to on a Sunday, and so don't get a dinner even once a week."

There was a quick step upon the creaking stairs, and in a moment Miss Smith threw open the door.

"Come, Sandford," said she, "you don't suppose you can waste half an hour of daylight, dawdling up here, do you? Besides, that white satin dress is promised for to-night, and——" Miss Smith corrected herself; she was going to say, "no one understands that *papillon* trimming so well as yourself;" but she thought it more expedient to change the phrase for "I cannot spare any one to help you."

Henrietta looked up, but neither spoke nor moved. "Say you'll come in a minute or two," murmured the other girl, certainly without turning her head, almost without moving her lips. "Get rid of her," she continued; "I want to speak to you."

"I will come in a few moments," said Henrietta, obeying the advice mechanically. And Miss Smith bounced out of the room.

"Have you got any money?" asked the girl, whom everybody called Jane.

"Yes, one sovereign," replied Henrietta; "but that is all; for we were to have no salary for the first six months."

"Pity to change it," said her interrogator quickly; "money flies when once it is changed; I will lend you a shilling, and coax one of the servants to get her something hot and nice—that will do her more good than all the doctors."

The kind-hearted Jane was quite right; it was food the poor child wanted, although there is no exact record of what "hot and nice" thing it was one shilling purchased.

Strange it was, but true, that from that hour every thing in the establishment of Madame Dobière wore a different aspect to Henrietta's eyes. In common parlance, "the veil had dropped from them;" and though such phrases are very trite, I think we most of us know the difference between understanding their meaning and feeling their truth. The latter was now Etty's case: she felt instinctively, how thick had been the "veil" through which she had hitherto looked, though woven perhaps by her own over-anxiety to excel,—and so find the road to independence—which had half-deadened every other faculty. But now her intelligent mind, quickened by keen feeling, perceived the truth; and called into the show-room by Madame on her way downstairs from leaving Annie, she listened to what was going on with quite different feelings from those she had hitherto experienced.

"At a word, Madame Dobière," said a fashionable looking personage,— "at a word, will you, or will you not, promise me the dress by six o'clock to-morrow?"

"Really," exclaimed Madame in a hesitating manner, "really—I don't know—the time is so very short—if I had only had it yesterday——"

"Oh! very well," returned the lady—"I would not be disappointed on any account. And I have no doubt Mrs. P—— can make it up for me; in fact, I have been very particularly recommended to try her."

"Well, ma'am," interrupted Madame Dobière, dreading that her rival would take away a customer, "to oblige *you*, ma'am, I will undertake it—but I assure you we must work half the night."

"Oh! nonsense, you always say that; I am sure I have often had a dress made up in less than four and twenty hours."

Probably she had; and probably it never occured to the thoughtless woman, as she rolled away in her carriage, enervated by worldly prosperity, and made selfish by perpetual luxury, that she had on such occasions done her part in wearing out not only silks and satins, but youth, health, and life. And for what? To minister to what a powerful writer calls "the disgusting foolery of idiotic vanities," the arrangements for which must be delayed till the last moment, because the pampered dame cannot decide between blue and pink; or because she must wait for a letter from Paris, to tell her, from headquarters, the prevailing mode; or—which is not at all unlikely—because she has outrun her pin-money, and is some days screwing her courage to ask husband or father for "only ten pounds." In nineteen cases out of twenty, the hurry at last proceeds from some such contemptible cause; so that when the mere fashionist hears by chance the wrongs of the poor apprentices canvassed, it were at least wise of her not to throw a stone at the mistresses, whom she so often drives, certainly, to one sort of tyranny. Yet what is so monstrous as a woman with a hard heart— and well do I believe that many who seem cruel, are only—thoughtless. Alas! I fear that those among us who judge ourselves the most considerate, have sins of this kind, both of omission and commission, for which we must answer.

Nor was this all. A shudder ran through Henrietta's veins, as now she remembered that even in six months two of their young companions had been snatched away by death; one actually breathing her last in the house, and tidings of the death of the other having reached them in less than a month after her removal. Another circumstance, too, would dwell in her mind—aye, and in a different form from that it had borne yesterday. Within the last few weeks, the girl before mentioned, with hasty temper and stong feelings, but yet whom everybody loved, had ceased to be among them. She was not dead. Nay, her fine constitution had so battled with the trials which she had encountered, that they had scarcely dimmed her radiant beauty; besides, this orphan girl had been but a few months exposed to their evil influence. What then? She had parted from them suddenly, though, as it afterwards proved, she must have made her preparations for days. And now there were vague rumours of ease—nay, splendour and luxury—but that she was an outcast, a thing to be shunned and abhorred! And with all the horror with which innocence does and *should* look upon vice, had Henrietta regarded her, even though an incident only the day before had changed scorn into something very like gratitude in more hearts than one.

Nicely timed, arriving at the hour when Madame Dobière and Miss Smith were almost always in the show-room, was delivered a huge packet, addressed to one of the apprentices, who had been the chief favourite of the erring sister. It was found to contain several pounds of tea, with these words roughly scrawled in pencil:—

"From Fanny, for all of you;—more when this is used; but you had better not say who from."

Now tea was the one great luxury; the best thing in the world for the "dreadful headaches" from which they all, more or less, suffered. And yet, as a wretchedly small quantity was allowed to them, if they indulged in anything which deserved the name one day, they paid the penalty of it the next by going entirely without. The feelings with which the present of the outcast was therefore received, may be easily understood. Yet though the deed were one to be registered in heaven's chancery, it had all the hurtful influence which good, proceeding through evil, almost ever acquired; even as clear water passes not over mud, without growing impure. It is, surely, much to be desired and rejoiced at, that the wise and thoughtful of the gentler sex, who are removed by station from insult, and by holy affections from temptation, should look sometimes upon the fallen with sorrow and compassion, and not justify the poet's words that—

> "Every woe a tear can claim,
> Except an erring sister's shame."

But among those who, so far from being protected from temptation, are exposed to it on every side, the case is wholly different. To such hearts, pity, or a yearning affection for its object, is a dangerous guest,—one that may stealthily destroy the finer perceptions of the moral sense, till, in the confusion of right or wrong, little else than chaos remains. Perhaps Madame Dobière's poor apprentices had better have continued to drink "slop," or milk and water, than, by the force of circumstances, to have thought of the fallen Fanny with gratitude, and to have spoken of her among themselves with a lingering kindness, a strange curiosity, and a pleasant surprise, that she was *not* a monster—*not* devoid of human sympathies. Alas! Henrietta Sandford, the comparatively recent comer, the country girl brought up with strictest principles, but taught by suffering, was beginning to understand and make allowances for temptation;—a dangerous knowledge—a perilous frame of mind.

Some months passed away, Annie growing worse and worse, being not unfrequently confined to her bed; and Henrietta improving wonderfully in her business, sustained in her exertions only by a hope she had nursed almost into realization. With the shrewdness she had now acquired, she was quite aware of the value of her own services; and now that their salaries had begun, her hope was that she should induce Madame Dobière somewhat to increase them, on condition that they lived out of the house. There was not much difficulty in coming to this arrangement; for, in the first place, a sickly child like Annie was a frequent trouble; and, in the next, Madame Dobière, who used a large proportion of her house for show-rooms, was extremely glad to have accommodation for two more apprentices. How the poor girls revelled in the idea of their humble lodging, which would be *home* to them! and Annie was sure she "should do quite as much work,—for even if she were too ill to come out, Etty could always bring home plenty for her." And so it was. And at first, in their lowly dwelling, they found something, comparatively speaking, like comfort: yet was it a new phase of life, with new dangers as well as new pleasures.

Of course their pittance was as little as would support life, though, fortunately for their appearance, they possessed a tolerably good wardrobe, which had hitherto required but little replenishing. I cannot tell how it was—I only relate the fact—that they did somehow or other make acquaintances; and on the Sundays, after their late rising, (for toil-wearied, and worn out for want of proper rest, they seldom left their bed in time for church) they often spent the remainder of the summer Sabbath in some excursion with one or two of their fellow apprentices and their companions. Apparently this was the only avenue for acquaintanceship of any sort; yet so much did the thing extend, that their Sunday parties—generally to some favourite suburban spot—were very seldom omitted. Doubtless, air and exercise once a week were very beneficial to them; and at all events, Annie's failing health was Henrietta's best excuse for granting themselves the indulgence. Besides, it cost them little or nothing; for these parties always consisted of friends of both sexes, and the "gentler sex" never paid. Alas! for the fact that it was so; for the right pride—no matter how lowly the station—true feminine dignity, is surely one of the brightest jewels in the crown of Womanhood!

Yet it could scarcely have been as the companion of milliners' apprentices and of shopmen, that Henrietta Sandford first met one, whom she knew only by the name of Charles Morton. How did they meet? Was it the civility of offering half an umbrella one rainy night? (one has heard of such things;) or was he interested in Annie's appearance, when he chanced, one Sunday, in the Park, to seat himself on a bench beside her? and being in the medical profession, did he offer advice and attendance? I think I have heard a rumour of some such origin of their acquaintance. Yet not how it began, but how it progressed, is the question. Annie gradually became worse; for she was in a decline, and beyond the reach of human aid—and this sufficient excuse for their ceasing to join in the Sunday excursions. But had not this been the case, all inclination to cultivate such pleasures was gone from the heart of Henrietta. Although not accomplished, not well educated, she inherited, from her father, some natural refinement of mind; and the power of early association was strong; so that the conversation of Charles Morton, and his kindly sympathy, seemed to bring back early days, and with them—almost happiness. But it is vain to indulge in tedious details; she loved with all the strength and fervour of a first and deep attachment. And he?—It had "begun in folly;" he had broken no code of man's moralities; for long intended no harm; and when dark selfish thoughts crept into his heart, he neither rebuked their presence, nor greatly encouraged their stay: he determined to let things take their course, and to trust to the "blind chance" of which fools talk, but which does not exist in the world. The effect to which these causes had led, was simply and naturally that Henrietta Sandford stood on a precipice, ready to leap into the gulf of ruin! Her position known by these tokens: —First, and chiefly, that she listened with a trusting, hopeful love to words of passion, from one whom she knew had no thought of making her his wife; and that she listened calmly, half approvingly, to the poor sophistries woven to mislead such hearts as hers; secondly, that she thought of her sometime companion, the Fanny before mentioned, with more sympathy than was maidenly; and thirdly, that when the whisperings of conscience, growing fainter and fainter, would yet at times be heard—she answered them with the self deception of promised "comfort and ease for Annie, dear Annie."

It was at such a height of peril as this that Madame Dobière's business occasioned Henrietta to call on a certain youthful customer, to receive orders concerning wedding dresses. It was early in the day, and she was shown into a small drawing-room,—one of a magnificent suite,—and desired to wait there a few minutes. A half-closed folding door communicated with the next apartment; and without the power of retreating, and too timid to make her presence known, she could not avoid hearing many fragments of a low-toned conversation held in the adjoining room. They were lovers who were there— the pair so soon to be wed. Breathing of deep heart love was many a sentence; yet what was it that pointed the difference between these lovers and her love? Not, reader, the difference of their station—that had nothing to do with it. What was it that, when the graceful girl—perhaps Henrietta's junior—entered the room, made her feel that she was in the presence of a purer being? And when afterwards she took her quiet instructions about the dresses, and saw her remove a miniature she wore (as if proud of the right of wearing it,) from her neck to try one on,—and when she heard her allude to her marriage with modest dignity,—what was it that made the tears start to poor Etty's eyes, and her heart whisper, "*My* love is not like this?" Oh! it was not a blind chance which prepared her mind, by the reception of such thoughts, for the events of the day.

On her return to Madame Dobière's, she had no sooner repeated the instructions she had received, than she was informed a card had been left for her in her absence; it bore the name of her wealthy relative—the benefactor who had placed her in the establishment, and was indeed left there by his son. To such a visitor Madame had been extremely courteous, and had promised him a meeting with Henrietta that afternoon; and, moreover, that it should be at her humble lodging,—an arrangement which he seemed much to prefer.

With a heart full of grateful recollections, yet trembling with a vague anxiety as to the purport of her relative's visit, Henrietta returned home at the appointed hour. She inquired of the people of the house if anyone had asked for her, and was told, "only the doctor, who was upstairs with her sister." The doctor, I need scarcely repeat, was Charles Morton; but this was a most unusual hour for a visit,—and Etty was so overpowered by her emotions—half surprise and half joy—that she paused for something like composure, ere she entered the room. The first object she beheld was Annie, half reclining, as she had left her, on a sofa (by night converted into a bed), yet busily plying the needle. It was some black garment she was making; and truly her pallid countenance, her hollow eyes, and attenuated features—and yet more, the long thin fingers— conveyed such an impression of disease and death, that one might have fancied she was preparing a mourning garb for some loved one, who would sorrow at her death. By her side sat Charles Morton, but with a face so changed and haggard, that Henrietta could not refrain from uttering an ejaculation of horror and surprise.

"Do I look ill?" he said: "it is nothing—it will soon pass away." But when he took her hand, Henrietta observed that he relinquished it quickly, throwing it from him as something almost to be rejected. Stunned by his coldness, she answered some questions he put to her, clearly and distinctly—till in the doing so, she mentioned the expected visit of her cousin.

"I am your cousin!" said he, sinking his head upon his hand, and speaking quickly; "My name is not Morton—but I knew not of our relationship till today. Henrietta, I am speaking to you now as your relative—I am doing my father's bidding. I scarcely knew that we had relations of your name; and had it not been that my father was anxious about you, he would never have mentioned to me that he had interested himself for you. But, as far as I can understand, he has had some communication with your Willowdale friends; who, perhaps, from your letters, suspect your many trials, and assuredly are aware of poor Annie's illness. At all events, he commissions me to make every inquiry connected with your position; and desires me to use my own discretion in rendering you assistance." He paused a moment, ere he said, in a trembling voice, "You will trust to my discretion—my *cousin*?" He laid an emphasis on the last word, that seemed again to stun, but really strengthened Henrietta.

"Oh, yes," was all she murmured.

"My plan then is, that this hateful apprenticeship should cease;—money, you know, can break such bonds,—and there needs be no scruple; my father is a rich man, and your *nearest relation;*—I then propose that you should be established in business for yourself;—would you not like it to be in the town of L————, near your Willowdale friends? With your London experience, you would certainly make a hit—and better, a fortune—in the country." He tried to speak in a tone of gaiety, but it would not do. Annie, who had dropped her work to listen to these, to her, most joyful tidings, yet broke the silence by exclaiming, with something like a sigh, "Shall we never see you again?"

The eyes of Henrietta and her cousin met—revealing the soul of each; and despite the presence of Annie, who was frightened at the scene which followed, he caught Henrietta for a moment in his arms, and imprinted a kiss upon her forehead—exclaiming, "We know the truth—the very truth—'tis best we part—you cannot be my wife. *I have never thought of you as my wife.*"

Henrietta shrank—slipped from his arms. "Saved—saved!" she murmured, in a choking voice; "Oh God, I thank Thee!"

"Amen!" responded her cousin.

My simple story is almost done. Simple I may well call it; for such heroines as mine measure life by the inner world of the feelings, not by moving accidents of romantic adventures. Henrietta has been three years in business, is considered the favourite milliner of L————, and is noted for her extreme indulgence to the young people in her employ,—regulating their hours of work, and making her arrangements with every regard to their health and happiness. On one point, however, she is very particular;—she insists on knowing precisely with whom and how every Sunday and holiday is spent. They regard her with grateful affection, which, standing alone in the world as she does, I am sure she must prize. For, alas! the pure country air, and proper food, and freedom from life-wearing toil, came too late to save poor Annie. In the nearest churchyard to Willowdale is she buried; and her memory is enshrined in many a warm heart besides that of poor Etty. Henrietta herself has never quite recovered her former healthful, youthful beauty, and she looks somewhat older than she is. Yet she has many suitors in her own station of life, and "they say" she has a preference. I hope it may be so; I am certain she will never give her hand without giving her heart: second love is sometimes a *better* love than first. I doubt not she would make an excellent wife.

Notes

[1]See Edwin Chadwick, *Report on the Sanitary Conditions of the Labouring Population of Great Britain*, ed. M.W. Flinn. (Edinburgh: University Press, 1965), p. 176.

The Mysteries of London

G.W.M. Reynolds

(1850)

The 1840s and 1850s witnessed a dramatic rise in the number of social protest novels written by the middle class. Perhaps the most radical of these authors was G.W.M. Reynolds who made a career of social protest literature for the middle and working classes. Reynolds, a lifelong Republican and a Chartist, rose to prominence with his massive dissection of social ills, The Mysteries of London. *Patterned after Eugene Sue's* The Mysteries of Paris, The Mysteries of London *ran from 1845 to 1855, beginning in* The London Journal *and later being published in book form by George Vickers and John Dicks. The series united Newgate crime novels and sensational fiction with social protest and was so immensely popular that it sold more than a million copies and was translated into several languages.*

The Mysteries of London *follows the adventures of twin brothers, one of whom journeys through the higher realms of society and the other through the lower regions, effectively contrasting the rich and the poor. Interspersed in the primary plot are chapters that concentrate on the denizens of criminal and poverty-stricken districts, these sections serving as vehicles for Reynolds' arguments about various social problems.*

Reynolds makes heavy use of parliamentary reports as he fulminates against social wrongs. The section of The Mysteries of London *that is most clearly derived from Blue Books is "The Rattlesnake's History" for which the 1842 Report of the Children's Employment Commission is the source. Working conditions in coal mines were among the worst industrial excesses, especially relating to women and children. Children as young as four years old worked in mines, and women and girls transported enormous weights on their backs or in heavy trams. Miners were often paid in goods from a tommyshop, and the prices were inflated so the workers could not get out of debt. Essentially, miners were slaves and the working conditions were extremely brutal. In "The Rattlesnake's History," Reynolds details these conditions, adding a further dimension in his indictment of the immorality forced upon the workers by such adverse conditions. The same parliamentary sources were*

163

used by Disraeli in Sybil *and by Charlotte Elizabeth Tonna in* Wrongs of
Woman, *among others.*

*Parliamentary reports also provide data for "Crankey Jem's History" in
which Reynolds criticizes the system of transporting prisoners to Australia.
Reformation of the penal system was one of Reynolds' causes, and with a rising
demand for reform of the most notorious penal colonies, Reynolds was
prompted to present information on the inhumane treatment of prisoners in
Australia. The most likely source for "Crankey Jim's History" is the 1837*
Report from the Select Committee on Transportation, *though Parliamentary
committees had been investigating the system of transportation since 1810.
Conditions were so terrible that some criminals chose to be hanged rather than
be transported. The Parliamentary committees investigated several areas of
abuse including severe punishments, poor food, excessively hard labor, pros-
titution among convicts and abuses of the ticket of leave system.[1] Reynolds
charged that the system of transportation and the brutal treatment of prisoners
was not only physically but morally corrupting, and in other sections of* The
Mysteries of London, *he offered his ideas on penal reform, which primarily
consisted of more humane treatment and both religious and secular education
for convicts. Apparently criticism of the system of transportation was effective
because in 1846 transportation to Van Diemen's Land and New South Wales
was abolished and the entire system of transportation ended in 1869.*

Chapter CXVI.
The Rattlesnake's History*

    I was born in a coal-mine in Staffordshire. My father was a married man,
with five or six children by his wife: my mother was a single woman, who
worked for him in the pit. I was, therefore, illegitimate; but this circumstance
was neither considered disgraceful to my mother nor to myself, morality being
on so low a scale amongst the mining population generally, as almost to amount
to promiscuous intercourse. My mother was only eighteen when I was born.
She worked in the pit to the very hour of my birth; and when she found the
labour-pains coming on, she threw off the belt and chain with which she had
been dragging a heavy corf (or wicker basket), full of coal, up a slanting road,—

*In case the reader should doubt the accuracy of any of the statements relative to the employment
of the youth of both sexes in the English coal-mines, which he may find in this chapter, we beg
to refer him to the "Report and Appendix to the Report, of the Children's Employment Commission,
presented to Both Houses of Parliament by command of Her Majesty, in 1842."

retired to a damp cave in a narrow passage leading to the foot of the shaft, and there gave birth to her child. That child was myself. She wrapped me up in her petticoat, which was all the clothing she had on at the time, and crawled with me, along the passage, which was about two feet and a half high, to the bottom of the shaft. There she got into the basket, and was drawn up a height of about two hundred and thirty feet—holding the rope with her right hand, and supporting me on her left arm. She often told me those particulars and said how she thought she should faint as she was ascending in the rickety vehicle, and how difficult she found it to maintain her hold of the rope, weak and enfeebled as she was. She, however, reached the top in safety, and hastened home to her miserable hovel—for she was an orphan, and lived by herself. In a week she was up again, and back to her work in the pit; and she hired a bit of a girl, about seven or eight years old, to take care of me.

How my infancy was passed I, of course, can only form an idea by the mode of treatment generally adopted towards babies in the mining districts, and under such circumstances as those connected with my birth. My mother would, perhaps, come up from the pit once, in the middle of the day, to give me my natural nourishment; and when I screamed during her absence, the little girl, who acted as my nurse, most probably thrust a teaspoonful of some strong opiate down my throat to make me sleep and keep me quiet. Many children are killed by this treatment; but the reason of death, in such cases, is seldom known, because the Coroner's assistance is seldom required in the mining districts.

When I was seven years old, my mother one day told me that it was now high time for me to go down with her into the pit, and earn some money by my own labour. My father, who now and then called to see me of a Sunday, and brought me a cake or a toy, also declared that I was old enough to help my mother. So it was decided that I should go down into the pit. I remember that I was very much frightened at the idea, and cried very bitterly when the dreaded day came. It was a cold winter's morning—I recollect that well, and the snow was very thick upon the ground. I shivered with chilliness and terror as my mother led me to the pit. She gave me a good scolding because I whimpered; and then a good beating because I cried lustily, but everything combined to make me afraid. It was as early as five in that cold wintry morning that I was proceeding to a scene of labour which I knew to be far, far under the earth. The dense darkness of the hour was not even relieved by the white snow upon the ground; but over the country were seen blazing fires on every side,—fires which appeared to me to be issuing from the very bowels of the earth, but which were in reality burning upon the surface, for the purpose of converting coal into coke; there were also blazing fields of bituminous shale; and all the tall chimneys of the great towers of the iron furnaces vomited forth flames,—the whole scene thus forming a picture well calculated to appal and startle an infant mind.

I remember at this moment what my feelings were then—as well as if the incident I am relating had only occurred yesterday. During the daylight I had seen the lofty chimneys giving vent to columns of dense smoke, the furnaces putting forth torrents of lurid flame, and the coke fires burning upon the ground: but that was the first time I had ever beheld those meteors blazing amidst utter darkness; and I was afraid—I was afraid.

The shaft was perfectly round, and not more than four feet in diameter. The mode of ascent and descent was precisely that of a well, with this difference—that, instead of a bucket there was a stout iron bar about three feet long attached in the middle, and suspended horizontally, to the end of the rope. From each end of this bar hung chains with hooks, to draw up the baskets of coal. This apparatus was called the *clatch-harness*. Two people ascended or descended at a time by these means. They had to sit cross-legged, as it were, upon the transverse bar, and cling to the rope. Thus, the person who got on first sate upon the bar, and the other person sat a-straddle on the first one's thighs. An old woman presided at the wheel which wound up or lowered the rope sustaining the clatch-harness; and as she was by no means averse to a dram, the lives of the persons employed in the mine were constantly at the mercy of that old drunken harridan. Moreover, there seemed to me to be great danger in the way in which the miners got on and off the clatch-harness. One moment's giddiness—a missing of the hold of the rope—and down to the bottom of the shaft headlong! When the clatch-harness was drawn up to the top, the old woman made the handle fast by a bolt drawn out from the upright post, and then, grasping a hand of both persons on the harness at the same time, brought them by main force to land. A false step on the part of that old woman,—the failure of the bolt which stopped the rotatory motion of the roller on which the rope was wound,—or the slipping of the hands which she grasped in hers,—and a terrible accident must have ensued!

But to return to my first descent into the pit. My mother, who was dressed in a loose jacket, open in front, and trousers (which, besides her shoes, were the only articles of clothing on her, she wearing neither shift nor stockings), leapt upon the clatch-iron as nimbly as a sailor in the rigging of his ship. She then received me from the outstretched arm of the old woman, and made me sit in the easiest and safest posture she could imagine. But when I found myself being gradually lowered down into a depth as black as night, I felt too terrorstruck even to cry out; and had not my mother held me tight with one hand, I should have fallen precipitately into that hideous dark profundity.

At length we reached the bottom, where my mother lifted me, half dead with giddiness and fright, from the clatch-iron. I felt the soil—cold, damp, and muddy—under my feet. A lamp was burning in a shade suspended in a little recess in the side of the shaft; and my mother lighted a bit of candle which she had brought with her, and which she stuck into a piece of clay to hold it by. Then I perceived a long dark passage, about two feet and a half high, branching off from the foot of the shaft. My mother went on her hands and knees, and told me to creep along with her. The passage was nearly six feet wide; and thus there was plenty of room for me to keep abreast of her. Had not this been the case, I am sure that I never should have had the courage either to precede, or follow her; for nothing could be more hideous to my infantine imagination than that low, yawning, black-mouthed cavern, running into the very bowels of the earth, and leading I knew not whither. Indeed, as I walked in a painfully stooping posture along by my mother's side, my fancy conjured up all kinds of horrors. I trembled lest some invisible hand should suddenly push forth from the side of the passage, and clutch me in its grasp: I dreaded lest every step I took might precipitate me into some tremendous abyss or deep well: I thought that the echoes which I heard afar off, and which were the sounds of the miner's pickaxe or the rolling corves on the rails, were terrific warnings that the earth was falling in, and would bury us alive: then, when the light of my mother's candle suddenly fell upon some human being groping his or her way along in darkness, I shuddered at the idea of encountering some ferocious monster or hideous spectre:—in a word, my feelings, as I toiled along that subterranean passage, were of so terrific a nature that they produced upon my memory an impression which never can be effaced, and which makes me turn cold all over as I contemplate those feelings now!

You must remember that I had been reared in a complete state of mental darkness; and that no enlightened instruction had dispelled the clouds of superstition which naturally obscure the juvenile mind. I could not read: I had not even been taught my alphabet. I had not heard of such a name as Jesus Christ; and all the mention of God that had ever met my ears, was in the curses and execrations which fell from the lips of my father, my mother, her acquaintances, and even the little girl who had nursed me. You cannot wonder, then, if I was so appalled, when I first found myself in that strange and terrific place.

At length we reached the end of that passage, and struck into another, which echoed with the noise of pickaxes. In a few moments I saw the *undergoers* (or miners) lying on their sides, and with their pickaxes breaking away the coal. They did not work to a greater height than two feet, for fear, as I subsequently learnt, that they should endanger the security of the roof of the passages, the seam of coal not being a thick one. I well remember my infantine alarm and horror when I perceived that these men were naked—stark naked. But my mother did not seem to be the least abashed or dismayed: on the contrary, she laughed and exchanged a joke with each one as we passed. In fact, I afterwards discovered that Bet Flathers was a great favourite with the miners.

Well, we went on, until we suddenly came upon a scene that astonished me not a little. The passage abruptly opened into a large room,—an immense cave, hollowed out of the coal in a seam that I since learnt to be twenty feet in thickness. This cave was lighted by a great number of candles; and at a table sate about twenty individuals—men, women, and children—all at breakfast. There they were, as black as negroes—eating, laughing, chattering, and drinking. But, to my surprise and disgust, I saw that the women and young girls were all naked from the waist upwards, and many of the men completely so. And yet there was no shame—no embarrassment! But the language that soon met my ears!—I could not comprehend half of it, but what I *did* understand, made me afraid!

My mother caught me by the hand, and led me to the table, where I found my father. He gave us some breakfast; and in a short time, the party broke up— the men, women, and children separating to their respective places of labour. My mother and myself accompanied one of the men, for my mother had ceased to work for my father, since she had borne a child to him, as his wife had insisted upon their separating in respect to labour in the mine.

The name of the man for whom my mother worked was Phil Blossom. He was married, but had no children. His wife was a cripple, having met with some accident in the mine, and could not work. He was therefore obliged to employ someone to carry his coal from the place where he worked, to the cart that conveyed it to the foot of the shaft. Until I went down into the mine, my mother had carried the coal for him, and also *hurried* (or dragged) the cart; but she now made me fill one cart while she hurried another. Thus, at seven years old, I had to carry about fifty-six pounds of coal in a wooden *bucket*. When the passage was high enough I carried it on my back; but when it was too low, I had to drag or push it along as best I could. Some parts of the passages were only twenty-two inches in height; this was where the workings were in very narrow seams; and the difficulty of dragging such a weight, at such an age, can be better understood than explained. I can well recollect that when I commenced that terrible labour, the perspiration, commingling with my tears, poured down my face.

Phil Blossom worked in a complete state of nudity; and my mother stripped herself to the waist to perform her task. She had to drag a cart holding seven hundred weight, a distance of at least two hundred yards—for ours was a very extensive pit, and had numerous workings and cuttings running a considerable way underground. The person who does this duty is called a *hurrier*; the process itself is termed *tramming*; and the cart is denominated a *skip*. The work was certainly harder than that of slaves in the West Indies, or convicts in Norfolk Island. My mother had a girdle round her waist; and to that girdle was fastened a chain, which passed between her legs and was attached to the skip. She then had to go down on her hands and knees, with a candle fastened to a strap on her forehead, and drag the skip through the low passages, or else to maintain a curved or stooping posture in the high ones.

Phil Blossom was what was called a *getter*. He first made a long straight cut with a pickaxe underneath the part of the seam where he was working: this was called *holing*; and as it was commenced low down, the getter was obliged to lie flat on his back or on his side, and work for a long time in that uneasy manner.

I did as well as I could with the labour allotted to me; but it was dreadful work. I was constantly knocking my head against the low roofs of the passages or against the rough places of the sides: at other times I fell flat on my face, with the masses of coal upon me; or else I got knocked down by a cart, or by some collier in the dark, as I toiled along the passages, my eyes blinded with my tears or with the dust of the mine.

Many—many weeks passed away; and at length I grew quite hardened in respect to those sights and that language which had at first disgusted me. I became familiar with the constant presence of naked men and half-naked women; and the most terrible oaths and filthy expressions ceased to startle me. I walked boldly into the great cavern which I have before described, and which served as a place of meeting for those who took their meals in the mine. I associated with the boys and girls that worked in the pit, and learnt to laugh at an obscene joke, or to practise petty thefts of candles, food, or even drink, which the colliers left in the cavern or at their places of work. The mere fact of the boys and girls in mines all meeting together, without any control,—without anyone to look after them,—is calculated to corrupt all those who may be well disposed.

I remained as a carrier of coal along the passages till I was ten years old. I was then ordered to convey my load, which by this time amounted to a hundred weight on each occasion, up a ladder to a passage over where I had hitherto worked. This load was strapped by a leather round my forehead; and, as the ladder was very rudely formed, and the steps were nearly two feet apart, it was with great difficulty that I could keep my balance. I have seen terrible accidents happen to young girls working in that way. Sometimes the strap, or tagg, round one person's forehead has broken, and the whole load has fallen on the girl climbing up behind. Then the latter has been precipitated to the bottom of the dyke, the great masses of coal falling on the top of her. On other occasions I have seen the girls lose their balance, and fall off the ladder—their burden of coals, as in the other case, showering upon them or their companions behind. The work was indeed most horrible: a slave-ship could not have been worse.

If I did not do exactly as Phil Blossom told me, the treatment I received from him was horrible; and my mother did not dare interfere, or he would serve her in the same manner. He thrashed me with his fist or with a stick, until I was bruised all over. My flesh was often marked with deep weals for weeks together. One day he nipped me with his nails until he actually cut quite through my ear. He often pulled my hair till it literally gave way in his hand; and sometimes he would pelt me with coals. He thought nothing of giving me a kick that would send me with great violence across the passage, or dash me against the opposite side. On one occasion he was in such a rage, because I accidentally put out the candle which he had to light him at his work, that he struck a random blow at me with his pickaxe in the dark, and cut a great gash in my head. All the miners in pits *baste* and *bray*—that is, beat and flog—their helpers.

You would be surprised if I was to tell you how many people in the pit were either killed or severely injured, by accidents, every year. But there are so many dangers to which the poor miners are exposed! Falling down the shaft,—the rope sustaining the clatch-harness breaking,—being drawn over the roller,—the fall of coals out of the corves in their ascent,—drowning in the mines from the sudden breaking in of water from old workings,—explosion of gas,—choke-damp,*—falling in of the roofs of passages,—the breaking of ladders or well-staircases,—being run over by the tram-wagons, or carts dragged by horses,—the explosion of coal,—and several other minor accidents, are all perpetually menacing the life or limbs of those poor creatures who supply the mineral that cheers so many thousands of firesides!

Deaths from accidents of this nature were seldom, if ever, brought under the notice of the coroner: indeed, to save time, it was usual to bury the poor victims within twenty-four or thirty-six hours after their decease.

I earned three shillings a week when I was ten years old, and my mother eleven. You may imagine, then, that we ought to have been pretty comfortable; but our household was just as wretched as any other in the mining districts. Filth and poverty are the characteristics of the collier population. Nothing can be more wretched—nothing more miserable than their dwellings. The huts in which they live are generally from ten to twelve feet square, each consisting only of one room. I have seen a man and his wife and eight or ten children all

*Explosions of carbonated hydrogen gas, which is usually called by the miners "sulphur," sometimes prove very destructive, not only by scorching to death, but by the suffocation of foul air after the explosion is over, and also by the violence by which persons are driven before it, or are smothered by the ruins thrown down upon them—*Appendix to First Report*

huddling together in that one room; and yet they might have earned, by their joint labour, thirty-shillings or more a week. Perhaps a pig, a jackass, or fowls form part of the family. And then the furniture!—not a comfort—scarcely a necessary! And yet this absence of even such articles as bedsteads, is upon principle: the colliers do not like to be encumbered with household goods, because they are often obliged to *flit* —that is, to leave one place of work and seek for another. Such a thing as drainage is almost completely unknown in these districts; and all the filth is permitted to accumulate before the door. The colliers are a dirty set of people; but, poor creatures! how can they well be otherwise? They descend into the mine at a very early hours in the morning: they return home at a very late hour in the evening, and they are then too tired to attend to habits of cleanliness. Besides, it is so natural for them to say, *"Why should we wash ourselves tonight, since tomorrow we must become black and dirty again?"* or *"Why should we wash ourselves just for the sake of sleeping with a clean skin?"* As for the boys and girls, they are often so worn out—so thoroughly exhausted, that they go to rest without their suppers. They cannot keep themselves awake when they get home. I know that this was often and often my case; and I have preferred—indeed, I have been compelled by sheer fatigue, to go to bed before my mother could prepare anything to eat.

Again, how can the collier's home possibly be comfortable? He makes his wife and children toil with him in the mine: he married a woman from the mine; and neither she nor her daughters know anything of housekeeping? How can disorder be prevented from creeping into the collier's dwelling, when no one is there in the daytime to attend to it? Then all the money which they can save from the *Tommy-shop*, (of which I shall speak presently) goes for whiskey. Husband and wife, sons and daughters all look after the whiskey. The habits of the colliers are hereditarily depraved: they are perpetuated from father to son, from mother to daughter; none is better nor worse than his parents were before him. Rags and filth—squalor and dissipation—crushing toil and hideous want—ignorance and immorality; these are the features of the collier's home, and the characteristics of the collier's life.

Our home was not a whit better than that of any of our fellow-labourers; nor was my mother less attached to whiskey than her neighbors.

But the chief source of poverty and frequent want—amounting at times almost to starvation—amongst persons earning a sufficiency of wages, is the truck system. This atrociously oppressive method consists of paying the colliers' wages in goods, or partly in goods, through the medium of the tommy-shop. The proprietor of a tommy-shop has an understanding with the owners of the mines in his district; and the owners agree to pay the person in their employment once a month, or once a fortnight. The consequence is that the miners require credit during the interval; and they are compelled to go to the tommy-shop, where they can obtain their bread, bacon, cheese, meat, groceries, potatoes, chandlery, and even clothes. The proprietor of the tommy-shop sends his book to the clerk of the owner of the mine the day before the wages are paid; and thus the clerk knows how much to stop from the wages of each individual, for the benefit of the shopkeeper. If the miners and their wives do not go to the tommy-shop for their domestic articles, they instantly lose their employment in the mine, in consequence of the understanding between their employer and the shopkeeper. Perhaps this would not be so bad if the tommy-shops were honest; because it is very handy for the collier to go to a store which contains every article that he may require. But the tommy-shop charges twenty-five or thirty percent dearer than any other tradesman; so that if a collier and his family can earn between them thirty shillings a week, he loses seven or eight shillings out of that amount. In the course of a year about twenty pounds out of his seventy-five go to the tommy-shop for nothing but interest in the credit afforded! That interest is divided between the tommy-shop-keeper and the coal-mine proprietor.

In the district where my mother and I lived there was no such thing at all as payment of wages in the current money of the kingdom. The tommy-shop-keeper paid the wages for the proprietors once a month: and how do you think he settled them? In ticket-money! This coinage consisted of pewter medals, or markers, with the sum that they represented, and the name of the tommy-shop on them. Thus, there were half-crowns, shillings, sixpences, and half-pence. But this money could only be passed at the tommy-shop from which it was issued; and there it must be taken out in goods. So, you see, that what with the truck-system and the tommy-shop, the poor miners are regularly swindled out of at least one fourth part of their fair earnings.

The wages, in my time, were subject to great change: I have known men earn twenty-five shillings a week at one time, and twelve or fifteen at another. And out of that they were obliged to supply their own candles and grease for the wheels of the carts or *trams*. The cost of this was about three-pence a day. Then, again, the fines were frequent and vexatious: it was calculated that they amounted to a penny a day per head. These sums all went into the coffers of the coal-owners.

Such was the state of superstitious ignorance which prevailed in the mines, that everyone believed in ghosts and spirits. Even old men were often afraid to work in isolated places; and the spots where deaths from accidents arose were particularly avoided. It was stated that the spectres of the deceased haunted the scenes of their violent departures from this world.

By the time I was twelve years old I was as wild a young she-devil as any in the mines. Like the other females, I worked with only a pair of trousers on. But I would not consent to hurry the trams and skips. I saw that my mother had got a great bald place on her head, where she pushed the tram forward up sloping passages; and as I was told that even amidst the black and filth with which I was encrusted, I was a good-looking wench, I determined not to injure my hair. I may as well observe that a stranger visiting a mine, and seeing the boys and girls all huddling together, half-naked, in the caves or obscure nooks, could not possibly tell one sex from the other. I must say that I think, with regard to bad language and licentious conduct, the girls were far—far worse than the boys. It is true that in the neighbourhood of the pits Sunday-schools were established; but very few parents availed themselves of these means of obtaining a gratuitous education for their children. When I was twelve years old, I did not know how to read or write: I was unaware that there was such a book as the Bible; and all I knew of God and Jesus Christ was through the oaths and imprecations of the miners.

It was at that period—I mean when I was twelve years old—that I determined to abandon the horrible life to which my mother had devoted me. I had up to that point preserved my health, and had escaped those maladies and cutaneous eruptions to which miners are liable; but I knew that my turn must come, sooner or later, to undergo all those afflictions. I saw nine out of ten of my fellow-labourers pining away. Some were covered with disgusting boils, caused by the constant dripping of the water upon their naked flesh in the pits. I saw young persons of my own age literally growing old in their early youth,— stooping, asthmatic, consumptive, and enfeebled. When they were washed on Sundays, they were the pictures of ill-health and premature decay. Many actually grew deformed in stature; and all were of stunted growth. It is true that their muscles were singularly developed; but they were otherwise skin and bone.* The young children were for the most part of contracted features, which, added to their wasted forms, gave them a strange appearance of ghastliness, when cleansed from the filth of the mine. The holers, or excavators, were bow-legged and crooked; the hurriers and trammers knock-kneed and high-shoul-dered. Many—very many of the miners were affected with diseases of the heart. Then, whoever saw a person, employed in the pits, live to an advanced age? A miner of fifty-five was a curiosity: the poor creatures generally drooped at five-and-thirty, and died off by forty. They invariably seemed oppressed with care and anxiety: jollity was unknown amongst them. I have seen jolly-looking butchers, blacksmiths, carpenters, ploughmen, porters, and so on: but

---

*Amongst the children and young persons I remarked that some of the muscles were developed to a degree amounting to a deformity; for example, the muscles of the back and loins stood from the body, and appeared almost like a rope passing under the skin—*Report*

I never beheld a jolly-looking miner. The entire population that labours in the pits appears to belong to a race that is accursed!

I pondered seriously upon all this; and every circumstance that occurred, and every scene around me, tended to strengthen my resolution to quit an employment worse than that of a galley-slave. I saw my mother wasting all her best energies in that terrible labour, and yet remaining poor—beggared! Scarcely enough for the present—not a hope for the future! Sometimes I wept when I contemplated her, although she had but little claim on my sympathy or affection; nevertheless, when I saw her bald head—her scalp thickened, inflamed, and sometimes so swollen, that it was like a bulb filled with spongy matter, and so painful that she could not bear to touch it,—when I heard her complain of the dreadful labour of pushing the heavy corves and trams with her sore head,—when I perceived her spine actually distorted with severe work; her stomach growing so weak that she frequently vomited her food almost as soon as it was eaten; her heart so seriously affected that the intervals of violent palpitation frequently made her faint; her lungs performing their functions with difficulty; her chest torn with a sharp hacking cough, accompanied by the expectoration of a large quantity of the *black-spit:* —when I saw her thus overwhelmed with a complication of maladies—dying before my eyes, at the age of thirty-three!—when I looked around, and beheld nine out of ten of all the persons employed in the pits, whether male or female, similarly affected,—I shuddered at the bare idea of devoting my youth to that horrible toil, and then passing to the grave while yet in the prime of life!

I thought of running away, and seeking my fortune elsewhere. I knew that it was no use to acquaint my mother with my distaste for the life to which she had devoted me: she would only have answered my objections by means of blows. But while I was still wavering what course to pursue, a circumstance occurred which I must not forget to relate.

One morning my candle had accidentally gone out, and I was creeping along the dark passage to the spot where Phil Blossom was working, to obtain a light from his candle, when I heard him and my mother conversing together in a low tone, but with great earnestness of manner. Curiosity prompted me to stop and listen. "Are you sure that is the case?" said Phil.—"Certain," replied my mother. "I shall be confined in about five months."—"Well," observed Phil, "I don't know what's to be done. My old woman will kick up the devil's delight when she hears of it. I wish she was out of the way: I would marry you if she was."—Then there was a profound silence for some minutes. It was broken by the man, who said, "Yes, if the old woman was out of the way you and I might get married, and then we should live so comfortable together. I'm sure no man can be cursed with a wife of worse temper than mine."—"Yes," returned my mother, "she is horrible for that."—"Do you think there would be much harm in pushing her down a shaft, or shoving her head under the wheel of your tram, Bet?" asked Phil, after another pause.—"There would be no harm," said my mother, "if so be we weren't found out."—"That's exactly what I mean," observed Phil.—"But then," continued my mother, "if she didn't happen to die at once, she might peach, and get us both into a scrape."—"So she might," said Phil.—"I'll tell you what we might do," exclaimed my mother in a joyful tone: "doesn't your wife come down at one to bring you your dinner?"—"Yes," replied Phil Blossom: "That's all the old cripple is good for."—"Well, then," pursued my mother, "I'll tell you how we can manage this business."—Then they began to whisper, and I could not gather another word that fell from their lips.

I was so frightened at what I had heard that I crept quickly but cautiously back again to my place of labour, and sate down on the lower steps of the ladder, in the dark—determined to wait till someone should come, rather than go and ask Phil Blossom for a light. I had suddenly acquired a perfect horror of that man. I had understood that my mother was with child by him; and I had heard them coolly plotting the death of the woman who was an obstacle to their marriage. At my age, such an idea was calculated to inspire me with terror. I think I sate for nearly an hour in the dark, my mind filled with thoughts of a nature which may be well understood. At length a young woman, bearing a corf, came with a light; and I was no longer left in obscurity. I then plucked up my courage, took my basket, and went to Phil Blossom for a load of coal. My mother was not there; and he was working with his pickaxe as coolly as possible. He asked me what had made me so long in returning for a load; and I told him I had fallen down a few steps of the ladder and hurt myself. He said no more on the subject; and I was delighted to escape without a braying or basting. While I was loading my corf, he asked me if I should like to have him for a father-in-law. I said "Yes" through fear, for I was always afraid of his *nieves*, as the colliers call their clenched fists. He seemed pleased; and, after a pause, said that if ever he was my father-in-law, I should always take my *bait* (or meals) with him in the cavern. I thanked him, and went on with my work; but I pretty well comprehended that the removal of Phil's wife by some means or another had been resolved on.

Shortly before one o'clock that same day my mother came to the place where I was carrying the coals, and gave me a *butter-cake* (as we called bread and butter), telling me that she was going up out of the mine, as she must pay a visit to the tommy-shop for some candles and grease for herself, and some tobacco for Phil Blossom. I did not dare utter a word expressive of the suspicions which I entertained; but I felt convinced that the proceeding was in some way connected with the subject of the conversation which I had over-heard. A strange presentiment induced me to leave my place of work, and creep along the passage to the foot of the shaft, in order to see whether Phil's wife would come down at the usual time with his bait. Several *half-marrows* and *foals* (as we called the young lads who pushed the trams) were at the end of the passage just at the foot of the shaft; and we got into conversation. It is a very curious thing to look up a shaft from the very bottom; the top seems no bigger than a sugar-basin. Well, the boys and I were chattering together about different things, when the click of the clatch-harness at the top of the shaft fell upon my ears. I peeped up and saw someone get on the clatch: then the creaking of the wheel and roller was heard. "Here comes someone's bait, I dare say," observed one of the half-marrows.—"I wish it was mine," said another; "but I never get anything to eat from breakfast-time till I go home at night."—Scarcely were these words spoken when a piercing scream alarmed us: there was a rushing sound—the chains of the harness clanked fearfully—and down came a woman with tremendous violence to the bottom of the pit, the clatch rattling down immediately after her. A cry of horror burst from us all; the poor creature had fallen at our very feet. We rushed forward; but she never moved. The back part of her head was smashed against a piece of hard mineral at the bottom of the shaft. But her countenance had escaped injury; and as I cast a hasty glance upon it, I recognised the well-known face of Phil Blossom's crippled wife!

One of the boys instantly hastened to acquaint him with the accident. He came to the spot where his wife lay a mangled heap, stone dead; and he began to bewail his loss in terms which would have been moving had I not been aware of their hypocrisy. The half-marrows were, however, deceived by that well-feigned grief, and did all they could to console him. I said nothing: I was confounded!

In due time the cause of the *accident* was ascertained. It appeared that my mother had gone up the shaft, but when she got to the top she struck her foot so forcibly against the upright post of the machinery, that she lamed herself for the time. The old woman who presided over the machinery (as I have before said) very kindly offered to go to the tommy-shop for her, on condition that she would remain there to work the handle for people coming up or going down. This was agreed to. The very first person who wanted to go down was Mrs. Blossom; and my mother alleged that the handle unfortunately slipped out of her hand as she was unwinding the rope. This explanation satisfied the overseer of the mine: the intervention of the coroner was not deemed necessary;—my mother appeared much afflicted at the *accident:* Phil Blossom mourned the death of his wife with admirable hypocrisy;—the corpse was interred within forty-eight hours;—and thus was Phil's wife was removed without a suspicion being excited!

I was now more than ever determined to leave the mine. I saw that my mother was capable of anything; and I trembled lest she should take it into her head to rid herself of me. One day she told me that she was going to be married to Phil Blossom: I made a remark upon the singularity of her being united to the very man whose wife had died by her means;—she darted at me a look of dark suspicion and terrible ferocity; and, in the next moment, struck me to the ground. From that instant I felt convinced that I was not safe. Accordingly, one Sunday, when I was washed quite clean, and had on a tolerably decent frock, I left the hovel which my mother occupied, and set out on my wanderings.

I had not a penny in my pocket, nor a friend on the face of the earth to whom I could apply for advice, protection, or assistance. All that stood between me and starvation, that I could see, was a piece of bread and some cheese, which I had taken with me when I left home. I walked as far as I could without stopping, and must have been about six miles from the pit where I had worked, when evening came on. It was November, and the weather was very chilly. I looked round me, almost in despair, to see if I could discover an asylum for the night. Far behind me the tremendous chimneys and furnaces vomited forth flames and volumes of smoke; and the horizon shone as if a whole city was on fire: but in the spot where I then found myself, all was drear, dark, and lonely. I walked a little farther, and, to my joy, espied a light. I advanced towards it, and soon perceived that it emanated from a fire burning in a species of cave overhung by a high and rugged embankment of earth belonging to a pit that had most probably ceased to be worked. Crouching over this fire was a lad of about fifteen, clothed in rags, dirty, emaciated, and with starvation written upon his countenance. I advanced towards him, and begged to be allowed to warm myself by his fire. He answered me in a kind and touching manner; and we soon made confidants of each other. I told him my history, only suppressing my knowledge that the death of Phil Blossom's wife arose from premeditation, instead of accident, as I did not wish to get my mother into a scrape, although I had no reason to have any regard for her. The lad then acquainted me with his sad tale. He was an orphan; and his earliest remembrance was experienced in a workhouse, of which, it appeared, he had become an inmate shortly after his birth, his parents having been killed at the same time by the explosion of a fire-damp in the pit in which they had worked. When the lad was eight years old, the parish authorities apprenticed him to a miner, who gave him the name of *Skilligalee*, in consequence of his excessive leanness. This man treated him very badly; but the poor boy endured all for a period of seven years, because he had no other asylum than that afforded him by his master. "At length," said the boy, "a few weeks ago, master got hurt upon the head by the falling in of some coal where he was working; and from that moment he acted more like a madman than a human being. He used to seize me by the hair, and dash me against the side of the pit; sometimes he flogged me with a strap till my flesh was all raw. I could stand it no longer; so, about three weeks ago, I ran away. Ever since then I have been living, I can scarcely tell how. I have slept in the deserted cabins on the pits' bank, or in the old pits that have done working: I have got what I could to eat, and have even been glad to devour the bits of candles that the colliers had left in the pits. All this is as true as I am here.* Yesterday I found some matches in a pit; and that is how I have this good fire here now. But I am starving!"

The poor fellow then began to cry. I divided with him my bread and cheese; and, when we had eaten our morsel, we began to converse upon our miserable condition. He had as much abhorrence of the mine as I had; he declared that he would sooner kill himself at once than return to labour in a pit; and I shared in his resolution. In less than an hour Skilligalee and myself became intimate friends. Varied and many were the plans which we proposed to earn a livelihood; but all proved hopeless when we remembered our penniless condition, and he exclaimed in despair, "There is nothing left to do but to rob!"—"I am afraid that this is our only resource," was my reply.—"Do you mean it?" he demanded.—"Yes!" I said boldly; and we exchanged glances full of meaning.

"Come with me," said Skilligalee. I did not ask any questions, but followed him. He led the way in silence for upwards of half an hour, and at length lights suddenly shone between a grove of trees. Skilligalee leapt over a low fence, and then helped me to climb it. We were then in a meadow planted with trees—a sort of park, which we traversed, guided by the lights, towards a large house. We next came to a garden; and, having passed through this enclosure, we reached the back part of the premises. Skilligalee went straight up to a particular window, which he opened. He then crept through, and told me to wait outside. In a few minutes he returned to the window, and handed me out a large bundle, wrapped up in a table cloth. He then crept forth, and closed the window. We beat a retreat from the scene of our plunder; and returned to the cave. The fire was still blazing, and Skilligalee fed it with more fuel, which he obtained by breaking away the wood from an old ruined cabin close by.

We next proceeded to open the bundle, which I found to contain a quantity of food, six silver forks, and six spoons. Skilligalee then told me that the mansion which we had just robbed was the dwelling of the owner of the mine

*See *Report*, page 43, section 194.

wherein he had worked for seven years, and where he had been so cruelly treated by the pit-man to whom he had been sent with messages to the proprietor, from the overseer in the mine, and that the servants on those occasions had taken him into the kitchen and given him some food. He had thus obtained a knowledge of the premises. "Last night," he added, "I was reduced by hunger to desperation, and I went with the intention of breaking into the pantry. To my surprise I found the window open, the springbolt being broken. My courage, however, failed me; and I returned to this cave to suffer all the pangs of hunger. Tonight you came: companionship gave me resolution; and we have got wherewith to obtain the means of doing something for an honest livelihood."

We then partook of some of the cold meat and fine white bread which the pantry had furnished; and, while we thus regaled ourselves, we debated what we should do with the silver forks and spoons. I said before that I was decently dressed; but my companion was in rags. It was accordingly agreed that I should go to the nearest town in the morning, dispose of the plate, purchase some clothes for Skilligalee, and then rejoin him at the cave. This matter being decided upon, we laid down and went to sleep.

Next morning I washed myself at a neighbouring stream, made myself look as decent as I could and set off. Skilligalee had told me how to proceed. In an hour I reached the town, and went to a pawnbroker's shop. I said that I was servant to a lady who was in a temporary difficulty and required a loan. The pawnbroker questioned me so closely that I began to prevaricate: he called in a constable, and gave me into custody. I was taken before the magistrate; but I refused to answer a single question, being determined not to betray my accomplice. The magistrate remanded me for a week; and I was sent to prison. There I herded with juvenile thieves and prostitutes; and I cared little for my incarceration, because I was tolerably, and at all events, regularly fed. When I was had up again, the owner of the mansion which I had helped to rob, was there to identify his property. I, however, still persisted in my refusal to answer any questions: I was resolved not to incriminate Skilligalee; and I also felt desirous of being sent back to gaol, as I was certain of there obtaining a bed and a meal. In vain did the magistrate impress upon me the necessity of giving an explanation of the manner in which the plate came into my possession, for both he and the owner of the property were inclined to believe that I was only a tool, and not the original thief;—I remained dumb, and was remanded for another week.

At the expiration of that period, I was again placed before the magistrate; and, to my surprise, I found Skilligalee in the court. He was still clothed in his rags, and looked more wretched and famished than when I first saw him. I gave him a look, and made a sign to assure him that I would not betray him; but the moment the case was called, he stood forward and declared that he alone was guilty,—that he had robbed the house, and that I was merely an instrument of whom he had made use to dispose of the proceeds of the burglary. I was overcome by this generosity on his part; and both the magistrate and the owner of the property were struck by the avowal. The latter declared that he did not wish to prosecute: the former accordingly inflicted a summary sentence of imprisonment for a few weeks upon Skilligalee. He then questioned me about my own condition; and I told him that I had worked in a mine, but that I had been compelled to run away from home in consequence of the ill treatment I received at the hands of my mother. I expressed my determination to put an end to my life sooner than return to her; and the gentleman, whose house had been robbed, offered to provide for me at his own expense, if the magistrate would release me. This he agreed to do; and the gentleman placed me as a boarder in a school kept in the town by two elderly widows.

This school was founded for the purpose of furnishing education to the children of pitmen who were prudent and well disposed enough to pay a small stipend for that purpose, that stipend being fixed at a very low rate, as the deficiency in the amount required to maintain the establishment was supplied by voluntary contributions. There were only a few boarders—and they were all girls: the great majority of the pupils consisted of day-scholars. At this school I stayed until I was sixteen, when the gentleman who had placed me there took me into his service as housemaid.

During the whole of that period I had never heard of my mother, or Phil Blossom. I now felt some curiosity to discover what had become of them; so, one day, having obtained a holiday for the purpose, I went over to the pit where I had myself passed so many miserable years. The same old woman, who had presided at the handle of the roller that raised or lowered the clatch-harness, during the period of my never-to-be-forgotten apprenticeship, was there still. She did not recognise me—I was so altered for the better. Clean, neatly dressed, stout, and tall, I could not possibly be identified with the dirty, ragged, thin, and miserable-looking creature who had once toiled in that subterranean hell. I accosted the old woman, and asked her if a woman named Betsy Flathers or Blossom worked in the mine. "Bet Blossom!" ejaculated the old woman: "why, she's been dead a year!"—"Dead!" I echoed. "And how did she die?"—"By falling down the shaft, to be sure," answered the old woman.—Although I entertained little affection for my mother, absence and a knowledge of her character having destroyed all feelings of that kind, I could not hear this intelligence without experiencing a severe shock.—"Yes," continued the old woman, "it was a sort of judgment on her I suppose, for she herself let a poor creature fall down some four or five years ago, when she took my place at the handle here for a few minutes while I went to the tommy-shop for her. She married the husband of the woman who was killed by the fall; and everybody knew well enough afterwards that there wasn't quite so much neglect in the affair as she had pretended at the time, but something more serious still. However, there was no proof; and so the thing was soon forgot. Well, one day, about a year ago, as I said just now, Phil Blossom came up to me and asked me to run to the tommy-shop to fetch him some candles. I told him to mind the wheel, and he said he would. It seems that a few minutes after I had left on his errand, his wife came up the clatch; and, according to what a lad, who looked up the shaft at the time, says, she had just reached the top, when she fell, harness and all, the whole pit echoing with her horrible screams. She died the moment she touched the bottom. Phil Blossom was very much cut up about it; but he swore that the handle slipped out out of his hand, and then went whirling round and round with such force that he couldn't catch it again. I own people did say that Phil and his second wife led a precious dog and cat kind of a life; but the overseer thought there the matter ended."—"And what has become of Phil Blossom?" I inquired.—The old woman pointed down the shaft as much as to say that he was still working in the mine.—"Did they have any children?' I asked. —"Bet had one, I believe," said the old woman; "but it died a few days after it was born, through having too large a dose of Godfrey's Cordial administered to make it sleep."—I gave the old woman a shilling, and turned away from the place, by no means anxious to encounter Phil Blossom, who, I clearly perceived, had rid himself of my mother by the same means which she had adopted to dispose of his first wife.

As I was returning to my master's house, I had to cross a narrow bridge over a little stream. I was so occupied with the news I had just heard, I did not perceive that there was another person advancing from the opposite side, until I was suddenly caught in the arms of a young man in the very middle of the bridge. I gave a dreadful scream; but he burst out into a loud laugh, and exclaimed, "Well, you needn't be so frightened at a mere joke." I knew that voice directly; and glancing at the young man, who was tolerably well dressed, I immediately recognised my old friend Skilligalee. It was then my turn to laugh, which I did very heartily, because he had not the least notion who I was. I, however, soon told him; and he was quite delighted to meet me. We walked together to the very identical cave where we had first met when boy and girl. Now he was a tall young man, and had improved wonderfully. He told me that he had become acquainted with some excellent fellows when he was in prison. And that he had profited so well by their advice and example, that he led a jovial life, did no work, and always had plenty of money. I asked him how he managed; and he told me, after some hesitation, that he had turned house-breaker. There was scarcely a gentleman's house within twelve miles round, that he had not visited in that quality. He then proposed that I should meet him on the following Sunday evening, and take a walk together. I agreed, and we separated.

I did not neglect my appointment. Skilligalee was delighted to see me again; and he proposed that I should leave service, and live with him. I consented; and. . . ." Here the Rattlesnake abruptly broke off.

(At this point, Reynolds returns to the criminal activities of the Rattlesnake, Skilligalee and the Resurrection Man.)

Chapter CXCL
Crankey Jem's History

My father's name was Robert Cuffin. At the death of *his* father he succeeded to a good business as grocer and tea-dealer; but he was very extravagant, and soon became bankrupt. He obtained his certificate, and then embarked as a wine merchant. At the expiration of three years he failed again, and once more appeared in the *Gazette*. This time he was refused his certificate. He, however, set up in business a third time, and became a coal merchant. His extravagances continued: so did his misfortunes. He failed, was thrown into prison, and took the benefit of the Insolvents' Act—but not without a long remand. On his release from gaol, he turned dry-salter. This new trade lasted a short time, and ended as all the others had done. Another residence in prison—another application to the Insolvents' Court—and another remand, ensued.

My father was now about forty years of age, and completely ruined. He had no credit—no resources—no means of commencing business again. He was, however, provided with a wife and seven children—all requiring mainte-nance, and he having nothing to maintain them on. I was not as yet born. It appears that my father sat down one evening in a very doleful humour, and in a very miserable garret, to meditate upon his circumstances. He revolved a thousand schemes in his head; but all required some little credit or capital wherewith to make a commencement; and he had neither. At length he started up, slapped his hand briskly upon the table, and exclaimed, "By heavens, I've got it!"—"Got what?" demanded his wife.—"A call!" replied my father.—"A call!" ejaculated his better half, in astonishment.—"Yes; a call," repeated my father; "a call from above to preach the blessed Gospel and cleanse the unsavoury vessels of earth from their sinfulness."—His wife began to cry, for she thought that distress had turned his brain; but he soon convinced her that he was never more in earnest in his life. He desired her to make the room look as neat as possible, and get a neighbour to take care of the children for an hour or two in the evening, when he should return with a few friends. He then went out, and his wife obeyed his instructions. Sure enough, in the evening, back came my father with a huge Bible under one arm and a Prayer-Book under the other, and followed by half-a-dozen demure-looking ladies and gentlemen, who had a curious knack of keeping their eyes incessantly fixed upwards—or heaven-ward, as my father used to express it.

Well, the visitors sat down; and my father whose countenance had assumed a most wonderful gravity of expression since the morning, opened the prayer-meeting with a psalm. He then read passages from the two sacred books he had brought with him; and he wound up the service by an extemporaneous discourse, which drew tears from the eyes of his audience.

The prayer-meeting being over, an elderly lady felt herself so [struck by] my father's convincing eloquence that a considerate old gentleman sent for a bottle of gin; and thus my father's "call" was duly celebrated.

To be brief—so well did my father play his cards, that he soon gathered about him a numerous congregation; a chapel was hired somewhere in Goodman's Fields; and he was now a popular minister. His flock placed unbounded confidence in him—nay almost worshipped him; so that, thanks to their liberality, he was soon provided with a nicely-furnished house in the immediate vicinity of the chapel. Next door to him there dwelt a poor widow, named Ashford, and who had a very pretty daughter called Ruth. These families were amongst the most devoted of my father's flock; and in their eyes the reverend preacher was the pattern of virtue and holiness. The widow was compelled to take a little gin at times "for the stomach's sake!" but one day she imbibed too much, fell down in a fit, and died. My father preached a funeral sermon, in which he eulogised her as a saint; and he afforded an asylum to the orphan girl. Ruth accordingly became an inmate of my father's house.

And now commences the most extraordinary portion of the history of my father's life. You will admit that the suddenness of his "call" was remarkable enough; but this was nothing to the marvellous nature of a vision which one night appeared to him. Its import was duly communicated to Miss Ashford next day; and the young lady piously resigned herself to the fate which my father assured her was the will of heaven. In a few months the consequences of the vision developed themselves; for Miss Ashford was discovered to be in the family way. My father's lawful wife raised a storm which for some time seemed beyond the possibility of mitigation; the deacons of the chapel called, and the elders of the congregation came to investigate the matter. My father received them with a countenance expressive of more than ordinary demureness and solemnity. A conclave was held—explanations were demanded of my father. Then was it that the author of my being rose, and, in a most impressive manner, acquainted the assembly with the nature of his vision. "The angel of the Lord," he said, "appeared to me one night, and ordered me to raise up seed of righteousness, so that when the Lord calls me unto himself, fitting heirs to carry on the good work which I have commenced, may not fail. I appealed to the angel in behalf of my own lawfully begotten offspring; but the angel's command brooked not remonstrances, and willed that I should raise up seed of Ruth Ashford: for she is blessed, in that her name is Ruth."—This explanation was deemed perfectly satisfactory: and, when the deacons and elders had departed, my father succeeded somehow or another not only in pacifying his wife, but also in reconciling her to the amour which he still carried on with Miss Ashford.*

Thus my father preserved both his mistress and his sanctity—at least for some considerable time longer. The fruit of that amour was myself; and my name is consequently Ashford—James Ashford—although my father insisted upon calling me Cuffin. Time wore on; but by degrees the jealousies which my father had at first succeeded in appeasing, developed themselves in an alarming manner between the wife and the mistress. Scenes of violence occurred at the house of his Reverence; and the neighbours began to think that their minister's amour was not quite so holy in its nature as he had represented it. The congregation fell off; and my father's reputation for sanctity was rapidly wearing out. Still he would not part with my mother and me; and the result was that his lawful wife left the house with all her own children. My father refused to support them; the parish officers interfered; and the scandal was grievously aggravated. Death arrived at this juncture to carry away the principal bone of contention. My mother became dangerously ill, and after languishing in a hopeless condition for a few weeks, breathed her last.

Having thus stated the particulars of my birth, it will not be necessary to dwell on this portion of my narrative. I will only just observe that, at the death of Miss Ashford, a reconciliation was effected between my father and his wife; and that the former contrived to maintain his post as minister of the chapel—though with a diminished flock, and consequently with a decreased revenue. Nevertheless, I obtained a smattering of education at the school belonging to the chapel, and was treated with kindness by my father, although with great

*This episode is founded on fact. The newspapers of 1840, or 1841, will in this instance furnish the type of Mr. Robert Cuffin in the person of a certain Reverend who obtained much notoriety at Rickmansworth.

harshness by his wife. Thus continued matters until I was fifteen, when my father died; and I was immediately thrust out of doors to shift for myself.

I was totally friendless. Vainly did I call upon the deacons and elders of the congregation; even those who had adhered to my father to the very last, had their eyes opened now that he was no longer present to reason with them. They spurned me from their doors; and I was left to beg or steal. I chose the former; but one night I was taken up by a watchman (there were no police in those times) because I was found wandering about without being able to give a satisfactory account of myself. You may look astonished; but I can assure you that when a poor devil says, *"I am starving—houseless—friendless—pennyless,"* it is supposed to mean that he can't give a satisfactory account of himself! In the morning I was taken before the magistrate, and committed to the House of Correction as a rogue and vagabond.

In prison I became acquainted with a number of young thieves and pickpockets; and, so desperate was my condition, that when the day of emancipation arrived, I was easily persuaded to join them. Then commenced a career which I would gladly recall—but cannot! Amongst my new companions I obtained the nickname of *"Crankey,"* because I was subject to fits of deep despondency and remorse, so that they fancied I was not right in my head. In time I became the most expert housebreaker in London—Tom the Cracksman alone excepted. My exploits grew more and more daring; and on three occasions I got into trouble. The first and second times I was sent to the hulks. I remember that on my second trial a pal of mine was acquitted through a flaw in the indictment. He was charged with having broken into and burglariously entered a jeweller's shop. It was, however, proved by one of the prosecutor's own witnesses that the shop door had been accidentally left unlocked and unbolted, and that consequently he had entered without any violence at all. Thanks to the laws, he escaped on that ground, although judge and jury were both convinced of his guilt. Time wore on; and I formed new acquaintances in the line to which I was devoted. These were Tom the Cracksman, Bill Bolter, Dick Flairer, the Buffer, and the Resurrection Man. With them I accomplished many successful burglaries; but at length I got into trouble a third time, and a stop was put to my career in London. It was in the year 1835 that the Resurrection Man and I broke into a jeweller's shop in Princes Street, Soho. We got off with a good booty. The Resurrection Man went over to the Mint; I let Dick Flairer into the secret, gave him a part of my share in the plunder, and then took to a hiding place which there is in Chick Lane, Smithfield. Now I knew that Dick was staunch to the backbone; and so he proved himself—for he brought me my food as regularly as possible; and at the end of a week, the storm had blown over enough to enable me to leave my hiding place. I hastened to join the Resurrection Man in the Mint, where I stayed two or three days. Then the miscreant sold me, in order to save himself; and we were both committed to Newgate. Tidkins turned King's Evidence; and I was sentenced to transportation for life. The Resurrection Man was discharged at the termination of the business of the sessions.

Myself and several other convicts, who were sentenced at the same session, were removed from Newgate to the Penitentiary at Millbank. Amongst the number were two persons whose names you may have heard before, because their case made a great noise at the time. These were Robert Stephens and Hugh MacChizzle, who were the principal parties concerned in a conspiracy to pass a certain Eliza Sydney off as a young man, and defraud the Earl of Warrington out of a considerable property. We remained about a fortnight in the Penitentiary, and were then transferred to the convict ship at Woolwich. But before we left Millbank, we were clothed in new suits of grey, or pepper-and-salt, as we called the colour; and were also ironed. The convict ship was well arranged for its miserable purpose. On each side of the between-decks were two rows of sleeping berths, one above the other; each berth was about six feet square, and was calculated to hold four convicts, eighteen inches space to sleep being considered ample room for each individual. The hospital was in the fore-part of the vessel, and was separated from the prison by means of a bulkhead, in which partition there were two strong doors, forming a means of communication between the two compartments. The fore and main hatchways, between decks, were fitted up with strong wooden stanchions round them; and in each of those stanchions there was a door with three padlocks, to let the convicts in and out, and secure them effectually at night. In each hatchway a ladder was placed, for us to go up and down by; and these ladders were always pulled on deck after dusk. Scuttle-holes, or small ports to open and shut for the admission of air, were cut along the vessel's sides; and in the partition between the prison and the hospital was fixed a large stove, with a funnel, which warmed and ventilated both compartments at the same time. When we were placed on board the convict ship, we had each a pair of shoes, two pairs of trousers, four shirts, and other warm clothing, besides a bed, bolster, and blanket. Of Bibles, Testaments, and Prayer-Books, there were also plenty.

The moment the surgeon came on board, he arranged the mess-berths and mess-tables. All the clothing, linen, bedding, and other articles were marked with consecutive numerals in black paint, from No. 1 up to the highest number of convicts embarked. Thus, we messed and slept along the prison-deck in regular numerical progression. In food we were not stinted: each man had three-quarters of a pound of biscuit daily; and every day too, we sat down to beef, pork, or pease-soup. Gruel and cocoa were served out for breakfast and supper. Every week we received a certain quantity of vinegar, lime-juice, and sugar, which were taken as preventatives for scurvy. Each mess selected a head, or chairman, who saw the provision weighed out, and that justice was done in this particular to each individual at his table.

The surgeon selected six of the most fitting amongst the convicts to act the part of petty officers, whose duty it was to see his orders punctually executed, and to report instances of misconduct. Four of these remained in the prison; and the other two were stationed on deck, to watch those convicts who came up in their turns for airing. The *Captains of the Deck,* as the officers were called, had some little extra allowance for their trouble, and were moreover allowed a certain quantity of tobacco.

It was in January, 1836, that we sailed for Sydney. Although I had no wife,—no children,—and, I may almost say, no friend that I cared about,—still my heart sank within me, when, from the deck of the convict-ship, I caught a last glimpse of the white cliffs of Old England. Tears came into my eyes; and I, who had not wept since childhood, wept then. But here were several of my companions who had left wives and children, or parents, behind them; and I could read on their countenances the anguish which filled their inmost souls!

The surgeon was a kind and humane man. The moment we were out of sight of land, he ordered our chains to be taken off; and he allowed us to enjoy as much air upon deck as we could possibly require. The guard, under the command of a commissioned officer, consisted of thirty-one men, and did duty on the quarter-deck in three alternate watches. A sentry, with a drawn cutlass, stood at each hatchway; and the soldiers on watch always had their firearms loaded.

When we had been to sea a little time, most of the convicts relapsed into their old habits of swearing, lying, and obscene conversation. They also gambled at pitch and toss, the stakes being their rations. Thieving prevailed to a very great extent; for the convict who lost his dinner by gambling, was sure to get one by stealing. They would often make wagers amongst themselves as to who was the most expert thief; and when the point was put to a practical test, dreadful quarrels would arise, the loser of the wager, perhaps, discovering that he himself was the victim of the trial of skill, and that his hoard of lime-juice, sugar, tobacco, or biscuit had disappeared. Stephens, who was at the same mess with myself, did all he could to discourage these practices; but the others pronounced him "a false magician," and even his friend, MacChizzle, turned against him. So at last he gave up the idea of introducing a reformation amongst his brethren in bondage. The fact is, that any convict who attempts to humbug the others by pretensions to honesty, or who expresses some superior delicacy of sentiment, which, of course, in many instances is actually experienced, had better hang himself at once. The equality of the convict ship is a frightful equality,—the equality of crime,—the levelling influence of villainy,—the abolition of all social distinctions by the hideous free-masonry of turpitude and its consequent penalities! And yet there *is* an aristocracy even in the prison of the convict-ship,—an aristocracy consisting of the oldest thieves, in contra-distinction to the youngest; and of *townies* (Londoners,) in opposition to *yokels* (countrymen). The deference paid by the younger thieves to the elder ones is astonishing; and that man who, in relating his own history, can enumerate the greatest number of atrocities, is a king amongst convicts. Some of the best informed of the convicts wrote slang journals during the passage, and read them once a week to the rest. They generally referred to the sprees of the night, and contained some such entries as this: —*"A peter cracked and frisked, while the cobbles dorsed; Sawbones came and found the glim doused; fadded the dobbins in a yokel's crib, while he blew the conkey-horn; Sawbones lipped a snitch; togs leered in yokel's downy; yokel screwed with the darbies."* The exact meaning of this is: —"A chest broken open and robbed while the convicts slept: surgeon came in and found the lamp put out; the thief thrust the clothes which he had stolen into a countryman's berth, while he was snoring fast asleep; the surgeon ordered a general search; the clothes were found in the countryman's bed; and the countryman was put into irons."

I must observe, that while the ship was still in the Thames, none of the convicts would admit that they deserved their fate. They all proclaimed themselves much-injured individuals, and declared that the Home Secretary was certain to order a commutation of their sentence. The usual declarations were these: —"I am sure never to see New South Wales. The prejudice of the judge against me at the trial was evident to all present in the court. The jury were totally misled by his summing-up. My friends are doing every thing they can for me; and I am sure to get off." —Out of a hundred and ten convicts, at least a hundred spoke in this manner. But the ship sailed,—England was far behind,—and not one single convict had his hopes of a commuted sentence gratified. Then, when those hopes had disappeared, they all opened their budget of gossip most freely, and related their exploits in so frank a manner, that it was very easy to perceive the justice of the verdicts which had condemned them.

The voyage out was, on the whole, a tolerably fine one. It lasted four months and a half; and it was, consequently, in the middle of May that we arrived in sight of Sydney. But, when thus at the point of destination, the sea became so rough, and the wind blew such "great guns," that the captain declared there was some mischief at hand. The convicts were all ordered into the prison, the ports of which were closed; and the heat was stifling. The tempest came with appalling violence. Crash went every loose thing on board, —the timbers creaked as if they would start from their settings,—the ropes rattled,—and the wind whistled horribly through the rigging. The ship was lifted to an immense height, and then by the fall of the mountain wave, was plunged into the depths of the trough of the sea;—at one moment dipping the studding-sail boom into the water,—and the next lying nearly on its beam-ends on the opposite side. I afterwards learnt from a sailor, that the waves were forty feet high, twenty below the ordinary level of the sea, and twenty above it. Thus when we were in the trough, they were forty feet above our heads! Towards evening the storm subsided; and early next morning Sydney broke more clearly upon our view.

Sydney is beautifully situated. It possesses a fine ascent from a noble harbour; and its bays, its coves, it gardens, its gentlemen's seats, form a pleasing spectacle. Then its forests of masts—the Government-house, with its beautiful domain—the numerous wharfs—the thousands of boats upon the glassy water—and Wooloomooloo, with its charming villas and its wind-mills,—all these combine to enhance the interest of the scene. The town itself is far more handsome than I had expected to find it. The shops are very fine— particularly the silversmiths', the haberdashers', and confectioners', which would not disgrace the West end of London. They are mostly lighted with gas, and in the evening have a brilliant appearance. There is an astonishing number of grog-shops—nearly two hundred and fifty, for a population of 30,000 souls. George Street and Pitt Street are the principal thoroughfares: and the rents are so high that they average from three to five hundred pounds a year. There are no common sewers in Sydney; and, although the greater portion of the town stands upon a height, yet many of the principal streets are perfectly level, and the want of a vent for the foul water and other impurities is sadly felt. I may add, that the first appearance of Sydney and its inhabitants does not impress a stranger with the idea of being in a country so far away from Europe; the language, the manners, and the dress of the people being so closely similar to those of England. But wait a little while, and a closer observation produces a different effect. Presently you will see the government gangs of convicts, marching backwards and forwards from their work in single military file,— solitary ones straggling here and there, with their white woolen Paramatta frocks and trousers, or grey or yellow jackets with duck overalls, all daubed over with broad arrows and initial letters to denote the establishment to which they belong,—and then the gaol-gang, moving sulkily along with their jingling leg-chains,—all these sad spectacles telling a tale of crime and its effects, and proclaiming trumpet-tongued the narrative of human degradation!

The ship entered the harbour; our irons had already been put on again some days previously; and we were all landed under the care of the guard. We were marched to the gaol-yard; and there our clothes were all daubed over with broad arrows and the initials P.B.—meaning *"Prisoners Barracks,"* to which establishment we were conducted as soon as the ceremony of painting our garments was completed. This barrack had several large day-rooms and numerous sleeping wards, the bedsteads being arranged in two tiers, or large platforms, but without separation. In every room there was a man in charge who was answerable for the conduct of the rest; but no one ever thought of complaining of the misbehaviour of his companions. A tread-mill was attached to the building: there were moreover several solitary cells—a species of punishment the horrors of which no tongue can describe.

In the course of a few days we were all divided into sections, according to the degrees of punishment which we were to undergo. Stephens and MacChizzle were kept at Sydney: I was sent with some thirty others to Port Macquarie— a place about two hundred and sixty miles, as the crow flies, to the north of Sydney.

The scenery is magnificent in the neighbourhood of Macquarie Harbour: but the life of the convict—oh! that is fearful in the extreme! I know that I was a great criminal—I know that my deeds demanded a severe punishment; but death had been preferable to a doom like that! compelled to endure every kind of privation,—shut out from the rest of the world,—restricted to a very limited quantity of food, which never included fresh meat,—kept in chains and under a military guard with fixed bayonets and loaded fire-arms,—with no indulgence for good conduct, but severe penalities, even flogging or solitary confinement, for the smallest offences,—constantly toiling in the wet, at felling timber and rolling it to the water,—forced to support without murmuring the most terrible hardships,—how did I curse the day when I rendered myself liable to the disciplines of this hell upon earth! I will give you an idea of the horrors of that place:—during the six months that I remained there, nineteen deaths occurred amongst two hundred and twenty convicts; and of those *nineteen,* only five were from natural causes. Two were drowned, four were killed by the falling of trees, three were shot by the military, and five were murdered by their comrades! And why were those murders perpetrated? Because the assassins were tired of life, but had not the courage to commit suicide; and therefore they accomplished crimes which were sure to be visited by death upon the scaffold!

The chain-gang to which I belonged was stationed at Philip's Creek; and our business was to supply timber for the ship-builders on Sarah's Island. We were lodged in huts of the most miserable description, and though our toils were so long and arduous, our rations were scarcely sufficient to keep body and soul together. The timber we cut was principally Huon pine; no beasts of burden were allowed; and we had to roll the trunks of trees to an immense distance. What with the humid climate, the want of fresh meat, and the severity of the labour, no man who fell ill ever entertained a hope of recovery. Talk of the civilised notions of the English—talk of the humane principles of her penal laws,—why, the Inquisition itself could not have been more horrible than the doom of the convict at Macquarie Harbour! Again I say, it was true that we were great criminals; but surely some adequate mode of punishment—some mode involving the means of *reformation*—might have been devised without the application of so much real physical torture! I have heard or read that when the Inquisition put its victims to the rack, it afterwards remanded them to their dungeons, and allowed them leisure to recover and be cured;—but in the penal settlement of Port Macquarie those tortures were renewed daily—and they killed the miserable sufferers by inches!

Our rations consisted daily of one pound and a half of flour, from which twelve percent of bran had been subtracted, one pound and a half of salt meat, and half an ounce of soap. No tea—no vegetables. The flour was made into cakes called *damper,* cooked in a frying-pan; and this wasteful mode of preparing it greatly diminished its quantity. Besides, divide those rations into three parts, and you will find that the three meals are little enough for men toiling hard from sunrise to sunset. The convict who did not keep a good lookout on his provisions was certain to be robbed by his comrades; and some men have been plundered to such an extent as actually to have been on the very verge of starvation.

I had not been at Macquarie Harbour more than five months, when Stephens and MacChizzle arrived, and were added to our chain-gang. This punishment they had incurred for having endeavoured to escape from Sydney, where they had been treated with some indulgence, in consequence of their station in life previous to their sentence in England. So miserable was I, with hard work and scanty food, that I resolved to leave the place, or perish in the attempt. I communicated by design to Stephens and MacChizzle; and they agreed to accompany me. Escape from Macquarie was known to be a most difficult undertaking; and few convicts who essayed it were ever able to reach the settlements in other parts of the Colony. They were either murdered by their comrades for a supply of food, or perished in the bush. Formidable forests had to be traversed; and the chance of catching kangaroos was the only prospect of obtaining the means of existence. Nevertheless, I resolved to dare all those horrors and fearful risks, rather than remain at Philip's Creek. Five or six others, in addition to Stephens and MacChizzle, agreed to adopt this desperate venture with me; and one night we stole away—to the number of ten—from the huts.

Yes—we thus set out on this tremendous undertaking, each individual possessing no more food than was sufficient for a single meal. And ere the sun rose all our store was consumed; and we found ourselves in the middle of a vast forest—without a guide—without victuals—almost without a hope! Convicts are not the men to cheer each other: misfortunes have made them selfish, brutal, and sulky. We toiled on in comparative silence. One of my companions, who had been ten years at Macquarie Harbour, was well acquainted with the mode in which the natives search for traces of the opossum, and, when hunger began to press upon us, he examined every tree with a hollow limb, and also the adjacent trees for marks of the opossum's claws. For, I must tell you, that this animal is so sagacious that it usually runs up a neighbouring tree and thence jumps to the one wherein its retreat is, in order to avoid being traced. The convict to whom I have alluded, and whose name was Blackley at length discovered the trail of an opossum, and clambered up the tree in which its hole was found, by means of successive notches in the bark, big enough to place the great toe in. Having reached the hole, he probed it with a long stick, and found that there actually was an opossum within. Thrusting in his hand, he seized the animal by the tail, pulled it out, and killed it by a swinging dash against the trunk of a tree. But this was little enough among so many. We, however, made a fire, cooked it and thus contrived just to mitigate the terrible cravings of hunger. The flesh of the opossum is like that of a rabbit, and is therefore too delicate to enable a hearty appetite to make a good meal on a tenth portion of so small an animal.

On the following day Blackley managed to kill a kangaroo, weighing about sixty pounds; and thus we were supplied with food for three or four days, acting economically. The flesh of the kangaroo is much like venison, and is very fine eating. We continued our way amidst the forest, which appeared endless; and in due time the kangaroo's flesh was consumed. Blackley was unwearied in his exertions to provide more food; and, so much time was wasted in these endeavours, that we made but little progress in our journey. And now, to our terror, Blackley could find no more opossums—could kill no more kangaroos. We grew desperate: starvation was before us. Moody—sulky—glaring on each other with a horribly significant ferocity, we dragged ourselves along. Four days elapsed—and not a mouthful of food had we touched. On the fifth night we made a fire, and sat round it at considerable distances from each other. We all endeavoured to remain awake: we trembled at the approach of drowsiness— *for we knew the consequences of sleep in our desperate condition.* There we sat—none uttering a word,—with cracked and bloody lips—parched throats— eyes glowing with cannibal fires,—our minds a prey to the most appalling thoughts. At length MacChizzle, the lawyer, fell back in a sound slumber, having no doubt found it impossible to bear up against the weariness which was creeping over him. Then Blackley rose, and went farther into the wood. It required no ghost to tell us that he had gone to cut a club for a horrible purpose. The most breathless silence prevailed. At length there was a strange rustling amongst the trees at a little distance; and then cries of indescribable agony fell upon our ears. These tokens of distress were in the voice of Blackley, who called us by name, one after another. A vague idea of the real truth rivetted us to the spot; and in a short time the cries ceased altogether. Oh! what a night of horror was that! An hour had elapsed since Blackley's disappearance; and we had ceased to trouble ourselves concerning his fate:—our own intolerable cravings for food were the sole objects of our thoughts. Nor was MacChizzle doomed to escape death. A convict named Felton determined to execute the purpose which Blackley had entertained—though in a different manner. Afraid to venture away from the party to cut a bludgeon, he drew a large clasp-knife from his pocket, and plunged the long sharp blade into the breast of the sleeper. A cry of horror burst from Stephens and myself; and we rushed forward—now that it was unfortunately too late—to save the victim. We were well aware of the man's intentions when he approached his victim; but it was not until the blow was struck that we had the courage to interfere. It was, however, as I have said—too late! MacChizzle expired without a groan.

I cannot dwell upon this scene: depraved—wicked—criminal as I was in many respects, my soul revolted from the idea of cannibalism, now that the opportunity of appeasing my hunger by such horrible means was within my reach. Stephens and I retired a little from the rest, and turned our backs upon the frightful work that was in progress. Again I say—oh! the horrors of that night! I was starving—and food was near. But what food? The flesh of a fellow-creature! In imagination I followed the entire process that was in operation so close behind me; and presently the hissing of the flesh upon the embers, and the odour of the awful cookery, convinced me that the meal would soon be served up. Then how did I wrestle with my own inclinations! And Stephens, I could well perceive was also engaged in a terrific warfare with the promptings of hunger. But we resisted the temptation: yes—we resisted it;—and our companions did not trouble themselves to invite us to their repast.

At length the morning dawned upon that awful and never-to-be-forgotten night. The fire was now extinguished; but near the ashes lay the entrails and the head of the murdered man. The cannibals had completely anatomised the corpse, and had wrapped up in their shirts (which they took off for the purpose) all that they chose to carry away with them. Not a word was spoken amongst us. The last frail links of sympathy—if any really had existed—seemed to have been broken by the incidents of the preceding night. Six men had partaken of the horrible repast; and they evidently looked on each other with loathing, and on Stephens and myself with suspicion. We all with one accord cut thick sticks, and advanced in the direction whence Blackley's cries had proceeded a few hours previously. His fate was that which we had suspected: an enormous snake was coiled around the wretch's corpse—licking it with its long tongue, to cover it with saliva for the purpose of deglutition. We attacked the monstrous reptile, and killed it. Its huge coils had actually squeezed our unfortunate comrade to death! Then—for the first time for many, many years—did a religious sentiment steal into my soul; and I murmured to myself: *"Surely this was the judgment of God upon a man who had meditated murder."*

That same day Stephens and myself gave our companions the slip, and struck into another direction together. We were fortunate enough to kill a kangaroo; and we made a hearty meal upon a portion of its flesh. Then how did we rejoice that we had withstood the temptation of the cannibal banquet! Stephens fell upon his knees and prayed aloud: I imitated his example—I joined in his thanksgiving. We husbanded our resources as much as possible; and God was merciful to us. We succeeded in killing another kangaroo, even before the first was entirely consumed; and this new supply enabled us to reach a settlement without further experiencing the pangs of hunger. Prudence now compelled us to separate; for though we had rid ourselves of our chains, we were still in our convict garb; and it was evident that two persons so clad were more likely to attract unpleasant notice, than one individual skulking about by himself. We accordingly parted; and from that moment I have never heard of Stephens. Whether he succeeded in escaping from the colony altogether, or whether he took to the bush again and perished, I know not:—that he was not retaken I am sure, because, were he captured, he would have been sent to Norfolk Island; and that he did not visit that most horrible of all the penal settlements—at least during a period of eighteen months after our escape from Macquarie—I am well aware, for reasons which I shall soon explain.

In fact, I was not long at large after I separated with Stephens. My convict-dress betrayed me to a party of soldiers: I was arrested, taken to Sydney, tried, and sentenced to transportation to Norfolk Island. Before I left England in 1836, and since my return towards the end of 1839, I have heard a great many persons talk about Norfolk Island; but no one seemed to know much about it. I will therefore tell you something concerning it now.

A thousand miles to the eastward of Sydney there are three islands close together. As you advance towards them in a ship from Sydney, Philip Island, which is very high land, and has a bold peak to the south, comes in view: close beyond it the lower hills of Norfolk Island, crowned with lofty pines, appear in sight; and between those two islands is a small and sterile speck called Nepean Island. Norfolk Island is six miles and a half long, and four broad—a miserable dot in the ocean compared to the vast tract of Australia. The soil is chiefly basaltic, and rises into hills covered with grass and forest. Mount Pitt—the loftiest eminence in the island—is twelve hundred feet above the level of the sea. The Norfolk Island pine shoots to a height of a hundred feet,—sometimes growing in clumps, elsewhere singly, on the grassy parts of the island, even to the very verge of the shore, where its roots are washed by the sea at high water. The apple-fruited guava, the lemon, grapes, figs, coffee, olives, pomegranates, strawberries, and melons have been introduced, and are cultivated success-fully. The island is everywhere inaccessible, save at an opening in a low reef fronting the little bay; and that is the point where the settlement is situated. The Prisoners' Barracks are pretty much upon the same plan as those at Sydney, and which I described to you just now. There is a room, called the Court-House, where the Protestant prisoners meet on Sunday to hear prayers; and there is another, called the Lumber-Yard room, for the Roman Catholics. The prayers in both places are read by prisoners. The principal buildings in the settlement are the Commandant's Residence, the military Barracks, the Penitentiary, the Gaol, and the Hospital. The convicts are principally employed in quarrying stone; and as no gunpowder is used in blasting the rocks, and the stone is raised by means of levers, the labour is even more crushing than that of wood-felling at Port Macquarie. The prisoners, morever, have to work in *irons;* and the food is not only insufficient, but bad—consisting only of dry maize bread and hard salt meat. Were it not for the supply of wild fruits in the island, the scurvy would rage like a pestilence. Between Macquarie Harbour and Norfolk Island I can only draw this distinction— the former is *Purgatory* and the latter *Hell!*

There is no attempt to reform the prisoners in Norfolk Island, beyond prayer-reading—and this is of scarcely any benefit. The convicts are too depraved to be amended by mere moral lessons: they want *education;* they require to be *treated like human beings,* instead of brute beasts, criminal though they are; they need *a sufficiency of wholesome food,* to enable them to toil with something approaching a good will; they ought to be *protected against the tyranny of overseers,* who send them to gaol for the most trivial offences, or on the slightest suspicions; they should not be *forced to labour in chains which gall their ankles almost to the bone,* when a guard with loaded muskets is ever near, and seeing that shackles on the legs would not prevent violence with the hands were they inclined to have recourse to it; nor should they be *constantly treated as if they were merely wild beasts whom it is impossible to tame save by means of privation, heart-breaking toil, and the constant sense of utter degradation.* How can men be redeemed—reclaimed—reformed by such treatment as this? Let punishment be terrible—not horrible. It is monstrous to endeavour to render the criminal more obstinate—to make the dangerous one more ferocious—to crush in the soul every inducement to amend— to convert vice into hardened recklessness. The tortures of semi-starvation and overwhelming toil, and the system of retaining men's minds in a state of moral abasement and degradation in their own eyes, will never lead to reform. When at Macquarie Harbour, or at Norfolk Island, I have often thought how comparatively easy it would be to reclaim even the very worst among the convicts. Teach them *practically* that while there is life there is hope,—that *it is never too late to repent*,—that man can show mercy to the greatest sinner, even as God does,— that the most degraded mind may rise from the depths of its abasement,—that society seeks reformation and prevention in respect to crime, and not vengeance,—that the Christian religion, in a word, exists in the heart as well as in a book. But what sentiments do the convicts entertain? They are taught, by oppressive treatment, to lose sight of their own turpitude, and therefore to consider that all mankind is bent on inflicting a demoniac vengeance upon them;—they look upon the authorities as their persecutors;—they begin to fancy that they are worms which are justified in turning on those who tread them underfoot;—they swear, and blaspheme, and talk obscenely, *merely because there is no earthly solace left them save in hardening their own hearts against all kindly sympathies and emotions;*—they receive the Word of God with suspicion, because man does not practically help them to a belief in the divine assurance relative to the efficacy of repentance;—they are compelled by terrific and unceasing hardships to look upon the tears of a contrite heart as the proofs of moral weakness:—and, in a word, they study how to avoid reflections which can lead, so far as they can see, to no beneficial end. They therefore welcome hardness of heart, obstinacy, and recklessness of disposition as an actual means of escape from thoughts which would, under favourable circumstances, lead to moral amendment and reformation.

You may be surprised to hear such ideas from my lips; but I have pondered much and often upon this subject. And if ever these words which I am now uttering to you, Henry Holford, should find their way into print,—if ever my narrative, with its various reflections, should go forth to the world,—be you well assured that these ideas will set people thinking on the grand point— *whether society punishes to prevent crime and to reclaim the offender, or merely to avenge itself upon him?*

My own prospects were gloomy enough. My life was to be passed in exile, misery, and torture. I loathed my associates. They took all possible pains to tease and annoy each other. They converted a beautiful spot—one of the loveliest islands in the world—into a perfect hell upon earth;— and seemed determined to supply any deficiency which the authorities had left in the sum of our unhappiness. They concocted various schemes of mischief, and then the most hardened would betray their comrades merely for the pleasure of seeing them flogged! I shall never forget a convict saying to me one day, "I doubt the existence of a God; but I wish, if there is one, that he would take away my life, for I am so very miserable. I have only six years more to serve; and I am determined either to escape, or to murder someone and get hanged for it." — This man's name was Anson; and from that moment he and I had frequent conversations together relative to an escape from the Island. But how few were our hopes? Surrounded by the ocean—pent up in so narrow a space, as it were—so distant from all other lands—fearful to confide in our companions—and unable to carry our scheme into effect without assistance, we were frequently induced to give it up in despair.

Not very far from the Commandant's house was a singular little cave, hollowed in the rugged limestone that forms two low hills,—the flat and the reef on the south of the island. This cave was near a lime-kiln, and was concealed by a stone drawn over its mouth. I had been nearly eighteen months on the island, (during which time, as I before said, Stephens was not sent to join the gangs; and therefore I concluded that he either perished in Australia, or effected his escape to Europe,)—eighteen months, I say, had elapsed, when Anson and I were one day at work in the lime-kiln, with a small gang. When the midday meal-time came, he and I strolled apart from the rest; and none of the sentries took any notice of us, because escape from that point in the broad day light was impossible. As were were walking along and conversing, we discovered the cave. This circumstance gave a new impulse to our ideas, and to our hopes of an escape; and a few days afterwards, we put our plan into execution. We enlisted two other convicts in the scheme,—two men in whom we imagined that more confidence was to be placed than in any of the rest. By their aid we contrived to purloin at dusk a sack of biscuits; and this we conveyed to the cave. On the next night one of our new accomplices contrived to rob a small house of entertainment for seamen, of three suits of sailors' clothes; and these were conveyed to the cave. Our plans were now all matured. A small decked yacht, cutter-rigged, and belonging to the Commandant, lay close by the shore; and we knew that there were only a man and a boy on board at that time. Our project was a desperate one; but the risk was worth running, seeing the result to be gained—namely, our freedom. When our arrangements were completed, we all four one evening absconded as we were returning home from the day's toils, and took refuge in the cave. No time was to be lost. About midnight, Anson and I swam off to the yacht, contrived to get on board, seized each a windlass-bar, and, descending to the cabin, mastered the man and the boy. We bound them in such a way that they could not leave their hammocks; and then we fastened down the hatchway to drown their cries in case they should shout for assistance. We next lowered the little skiff, and returned to land. Our companions joined us, with the bag of biscuit and the clothes, at a point previously agreed upon; and we all succeeded in reaching the cutter in safety. Then we set sail; and, favoured by the darkness of the night, got clear away without having excited on shore a suspicion that the yacht had moved from its moorings.

As we had conjectured, there was very little provision on board, for the Commandant never used the yacht for more than a few hours' trip at a time. We had therefore done wisely to provide the biscuit; but there was not two days' supply of meat on board. We accordingly steered for the back of Philip Island, which we knew to abound in pigs and goats, and to be uninhabited by man. Anson and another of our companions went on shore with firearms, which we had found in the cutter; and within two hours after daylight they shot four pigs and thirteen goats. Myself and the other convict who remained on board to take care of the vessel and guard the seaman and the boy, caught several kingfish and rock cod. We were thus well provisioned; and another trip to the shore filled our water casks. We next proposed to the seaman and boy either to join us, or to take the skiff and return to Norfolk Island as best they might. They preferred the latter offer; and we accordingly suffered them to depart, after compelling the sailor to exhange his clothes for one of our convict suits; so that we had now a proper garb each. In their presence we had talked of running for New Caledonia—an Island to the north of Norfolk Island; but the moment they were gone, we set sail for New Zealand, which is precisely in a contrary direction—being to the south of Norfolk Island. Our craft was but little better than a cockle-boat: it was, however, decked; fine weather prevailed; and moreover, it was better to die by drowning than perish by the gradual tortures of a penal settlement.

We were in sight of New Zealand, when a fearful storm came on suddenly at an early hour on the thirteenth morning after we had quitted Norfolk Island. A tremendous sea broke over our little craft, and washed poor Anson overboard. The other two convicts and myself did all we could to save the vessel, and run her into a bay which we now descried in the distance; but our inexperience in nautical matters was put to a severe test. When our condition was apparently hopeless, and we expected that the sea would swallow us up, a large bark hove in sight. We made signals of distress; and the vessel steered towards us. But a mountainous wave struck the stern of the cutter, and stove in her timbers. She immediately began to fill. We cut away the boom, and clung to it as to a last hope. The vessel went down; and, small as it was, it formed a vortex which for a few moments sucked us under, spar and all. But we rose again to the surface, clinging desperately to the boom. Suddenly one of my comrades uttered a fearful cry—a cry of such wild agony that it rings in my ears every time I think of that horrible incident. I glanced towards him: the water was for an instant tinged with blood—a shark had bitten off one of the wretched man's legs! Oh! what an agony of fear I experienced then. The poor creature continued to shriek in an appalling manner for a few seconds: then he loosened his hold upon the spar, and disappeared in the raging element. My only surviving companion and myself exchanged looks of unutterable horror.

We were drifting rapidly in the direction of the bark, which on its side was advancing towards us. When within hail, it lowered a boat. But I was destined to be the only survivor of the four convicts who had escaped from Norfolk Island. When only a few yards from the boat, my companion suddenly relaxed his hold upon the spar, and sank with a loud cry—to rise no more. The water was not tinged with blood—and therefore I do not suppose that he was attacked by a shark: most probably a sudden cramp seized him;—but, whatever the cause, he perished! I was dragged in an exhausted state into the boat, and was speedily safe on board the bark.

The vessel was a trading one, and bound for Hobart Town, whence it was to sail for England. I gave so plausible an account of the shipwrecked cutter, that the real truth was not suspected, especially as I was attired on a sailor's dress; and as the bark was not to remain many days at Hobart Town, where, moreover, I was not known, I entertained the most sanguine hopes of being able to ensure my safe return to England. In three weeks,—after encountering much bad weather—we entered the Derwent; and, taking in a pilot, were carried safe up to Sullivan's Cove.

Hobart Town is the capital of Van Diemen's Land, and is beautifully placed on the banks of an estuary called the Derwent. The streets are spacious: the houses are built of brick; and the roofs, covered with shingles, have the appearance of being slated. Mount Wellington rises behind the town to the height of 4000 feet, and is almost entirely clothed with forests. There is in Hobart Town a spacious House of Correction for females: it is called the Factory, and contained at that time about two hundred and fifty prisoners. They were employed in picking and spinning wool, and in washing for the Hospital, Orphan-School, and other institutions. The women were dressed in a prison garb, and had their hair cut close, which they naturally considered a grievous infliction of tyranny. When they misbehaved themselves, they were put into solitary confinement; and I heard that many of them had gone raving mad while enduring that horrible mental torture. I saw a chain-gang of a hundred and ten convicts, employed in raising a causeway across a muddy flat in the Derwent: they looked miserably unhealthy, pale, and emaciated, being half-starved, over-worked, and compelled to drink very bad water. The Government House is a fine building, on the banks of the Derwent, and about a mile from the town. The Penitentiary at Hobart Town contains about six hundred prisoners, and is the principal receptacle for newly-arrived convicts. They are sent out in gangs, under overseers and guards, to work on the roads, or as carpenters, builders, sawyers, or masons, in the various departments.

After remaining almost a fortnight at Hobart Town, the bark sailed for England, by way of Cape Horn; and I was now relieved from all fears of detection—at least for the present. As I have spoken of the condition of the female convicts in Hobart Town, I may as well give you some account of how transportation affects women; for you may be sure that I heard enough of that subject both at Sydney and at Macquarie Harbour. A female-convict ship is fitted up on precisely the same plan as that of the men, with the addition of shelves whereon to stow away the tea crockery. The women's rations are the same as the men's, with the extra comforts of tea and sugar. This they have for breakfast, and oatmeal for supper. No guard of soldiers is required on board: nor is there a bulkhead across the upper deck in mid-ships. Instead of *captains of the vessel,* there are matrons appointed by the surgeon to take care of the *morals* of the rest; and these matrons are usually old brothel keepers or procuresses, who know how to feign a sanctity which produces a favourable impression in their behalf. Women convicts are dreadfully quarrelsome; and their language is said to be more disgusting and filthy than that of the men. However vigilant the surgeon may be, it is impossible altogether to prevent intercourse between the females and the sailors; and it often happens that some of the *fair ones,* on their arrival in the colony, are in a way to increase the Australian population. Perhaps the surgeon himself may take a fancy to one or two of the best looking; and these are sure to obtain great indulgences—such as being appointed nurses to the sick, or being permitted to remain on the sick list through out the voyage, which is an excuse for allowing them wine and other little comforts. The women always speak *to* and *of* each other as ladies; and the old procuresses, when chosen as matrons, are treated with the respectful *Mrs.* Thus it is always, *"Ladies,* come for'ard for your pork," or *"Ladies,* come up for your biscuit," or *"Ladies,* the puddings are cooked." Of an evening they dance or sing,—and as often quarrel and fight. This cannot be wondered at, when it is remembered that there is no attempt at classification; and women who may have been chaste in person, though criminal in other respects, are compelled to herd with prostitutes of all degrees, from the lowest trull that skulks in the courts leading out of Fleet Street to the fashionable nymph who displays her charms at the theatre. The very chastity of a woman who has been sentenced perhaps for robbing furnished lodgings, or plundering her master in her capacity of servant, or for committing a forgery, is made a reproach to her by the prostitutes and old procuresses; and her life is miserable. Moreover, it is next to impossible that she can escape a contamination which prepares her for a life of profligacy when she reaches the colony.

Before the female convict-ship leaves the Thames, numbers of old procuresses and brothel-keepers go on board to take leave of the girls with whom they are acquainted. These hags, dressed out in their gayest garb, and pretending to be overwhelmed with grief (while they really are with gin), represent themselves to be the mothers or aunts of the *"poor dear creatures"* who have got into trouble, and assure the surgeon that their so-called daughters or nieces were most excellent girls and bore exemplary characters previous to their present *"misfortune."* The surgeon—if a novice, or a humane man—believes the tale, and is sure to treat with kindness the "poor creatures" thus recommended to him. About twenty years ago a Religious Society in London sent out in an emigrant ship, twelve *"reclaimed unfortunate girls,"* with the hope that they might form good matrimonial connections among the free settlers in the colony; there always having been—especially at first—a great dearth of European females in Australia. These girls were called the *Twelve Apostles;* and all England rang with the good work which had been accomplished by the Religious Society. But on the arrival of the Twelve Apostles at Sydney, seven of them were found to be in the family way by the sailors; and the others immediately entered on a course of unbounded licentiousness.*

A few days before the female convict-vessel arrives at Sydney, the women—old and young—busy themselves in getting ready their finery for landing. The debarkation of female convicts always takes place with great effect. The prostitutes appear in their most flaunting attire; and many of them have gold ornaments about them. They are then sent to the Paramatta Factory. This establishment cannot be looked on as a place of punishment—nor as a place of reformation. The inmates are well fed, and are put to no labour. There is an extensive garden, in which they can walk at pleasure. Some of them are allotted to free settlers requiring servants; but the grand hope of the female convict is to marry. This prospect is materially aided by the fact that both free settlers and ticket-of-leave convicts are allowed to seek for help-mates in the Factory. When they call for that purpose, the fair penitents are drawn up in a row; and the wife-seeking individual inspects them as a general does his army, or a butcher the sheep in Smithfield Market. If he fancies one of the candidates, he beckons her from the rank, and they retire to a distance to converse. Should a matrimonial arrangement be made, the business is soon finished by the aid of a clergyman; but if no amicable understanding is come to, the nymph returns

*Fact.

to the rank, and the swain chooses another—and so on, until the object of his visit is accomplished. So anxious are the unmarried free settlers or the ticket-of-leave convicts to change their single state of blessedness, and so ready are the fair sex to meet their wishes, that few women whose husbands die remain widows a couple of days, some not more than four-and-twenty hours. A few years before I was in the colony, an old settler saw a convict-girl performing penance on a market-day, with her gown-tail drawn over her head, for drunkenness and disorderly conduct in the Factory. He walked straight up to her—regardless of the hootings of the crowd—and proposed marriage. She was candid enough to confess to him that she was five months gone in the family way by a master to whom she had been allotted ere she returned to the Factory, but the amorous swain, who was nearly sixty, was so much struck by her black eyes and plump shape, that he expressed his readiness to take her "for better or worse;" and she had not left the place of punishment an hour, ere she was married to one of the richest settlers in the colony.*

I will tell you one more anecdote relative to Australian marriages. A very handsome woman was transported for shoplifting—her third offence of the kind. She left a husband behind her in England. On her arrival at Sydney she was allotted to an elderly gentleman, a free settler, and who, being a bachelor, sought to make her his mistress. She, however, resisted his overtures, hoping that he would make her his wife, as he was not aware that she had a husband in her native country. Time wore on, he urgent—she obstinate,—he declining matrimonial bonds. At length she received a black-edged letter from her mother in England; and, upon being questioned by her master, she stated *"that its contents made a great alteration in her circumstances."* More she would not tell him. He was afraid of losing his handsome servant; and agreed to marry her. They were united accordingly. When the nuptial knot was indissolubly tied, he begged his beloved wife to explain the nature of the black-edged letter. *"There is now no need for any further mystery,"* she said, *"The truth is, I could not marry you before because I had a husband living in England. That black-edged letter conveyed to me the welcome news that he was hanged five months ago at the Old Bailey, and thus nothing now stands in the way of our happiness."*—And that woman made the rich settler a most exemplary wife.

I have now given you an insight into the morals of the female, as well as those of the male convicts; and you may also perceive that while transportation is actually a means of pleasing variety of scene and habits to the woman, it is an earthly hell to the man. I know that transportation is spoken of as something very light—a mere change of climate—amongst those thieves in England who have never crossed the water; but they are woefully mistaken! Transportation

*Fact.

was *once* a trivial punishment, when all convicts were allotted to settlers, and money would purchase tickets-of-leave; or when a convict's wife, if he had one, might go out in the next ship with all the swag which his crimes had produced, and on her arrival in the colony apply for her husband to be allotted to her as her servant, by which step he became a free man, opened a public-house or some kind of shop, and made a fortune. Those were glorious times for convicts: but all that system has been changed. Now you have Road-Gangs, and Hulk-Gangs, and Quarrying-Gangs,—men who work in chains, and who cannot obtain a sufficiency of food! There is also Norfolk Island—a Garden of Eden in natural loveliness, rendered an earthly hell by human occupation. Oh! let not the opinion prevail that transportation is no punishment; let not those who are young in the ways of iniquity, pursue their career under the impression that exile to Australia is nothing more than a pleasant change of scene! They will too soon discover how miserably they are mistaken; and when they feel the galling chain upon their ankles,—when they find themselves toiling amidst the incessant damps of Macquarie, or on the hard roads of Van Diemen's Land, or in the quarries of Norfolk Island,—when they are labouring in forests where every step may arouse a venomous snake whose bite is death, or where a falling tree may crush them beneath its weight,—when they are exposed to the brutality of overseers, or the still more intolerable cruelty of their companions,—when they sleep in constant dread of being murdered by their follow-convicts, and awake only to the dull monotony of a life of intense and heart-breaking labour,—then will they loathe their very existence, and dare all the perils of starvation, or the horrors of cannibalism, in order to escape from those scenes of ineffable misery!

But I need say no more upon this subject. The bark, in which I worked my passage to Europe, reached England in safety; and I was once more at large in my native country. Yes—I was free to go whithersoever I would—and to avenge myself on him who had betrayed me to justice! The hope of some day consummating that vengeance had never deserted me from the moment I was sentenced in the Central Criminal Court. It had animated me through out all the miseries, the toils, and the hardships which I have related to you. It inspired me with courage to dare the dangers of an escape from Macquarie: its effect was the same when I resolved upon quitting Norfolk Island. I have once had my mortal foe within my reach; but my hand dealt not the blow with sufficient force. It will not fail next time. I know that vengeance is a crime; but I cannot subdue those feelings which prompt me to punish the man whose perfidy sent me into exile. In all other respects I am reformed—completely reformed. Not that the authorities in Australia or Norfolk Island have in any way contributed to this moral change which has come over me: no—my own meditations and reflections have induced me to toil in order to earn an honest livelihood. I will never steal again: I will die sooner. I would also rather die by my own hand than return to the horrors of Macquarie or Norfolk Island. But my vengeance—oh! I must gratify my vengeance;—and I care not what may become of me afterwards!

Notes

[1]See the Catalog to the *British Parliamentary Papers* (Shannon, Ireland: Irish UP, 1968), 69-73.

Lucy Dean;
The Noble Needlewoman
Silverpen
[Eliza Meteyard]
(1850)

Following the publication of Henry Mayhew's series on the working classes in London in the Morning Chronicle *during 1849, the living and working conditions of seamstresses again became a prime concern of Victorian reformers. The preceding year Caroline Chisholm had organized the Family Colonization Loan Society, and during 1849 four more emigration societies were founded, with Sidney Herbert's Fund for Promoting Female Emigration specifically aimed at financing the emigration of London's distressed needlewomen.*

The first example of seamstress emigration in fiction occurs in Lucy Dean; the Noble Needlewoman *written by Eliza Meteyard and published under the pseudonym "Silverpen" in* Eliza Cook's Journal *from 16 March until 20 April 1850. Meteyard's picture of emigration is based upon a blend of Chisholm's work and Edward Gibbon Wakefield's* A View of the Art of Colonization.

Meteyard prefaces her story with two epigraphs from Wakefield; the first stressing the need to inform the working classes of the possibilities offered by emigration, while the second argues the importance women play in shaping the communities formed through colonization. Through these quotations, Meteyard introduces three themes which are stressed throughout Lucy Dean: *the need for the working classes to receive information concerning emigration, preferably from others who have emigrated; the need for emigrants themselves to raise the fare necessary to emigrate; and the need for women who emigrate to be both virtuous and religious.*

But not everyone was equally impressed with the emigration scheme for the relief of needle-workers. During the latter part of 1849 and early 1850 a debate was carried out in the press as to the wisdom of Sidney Herbert's Fund. During the month of December The Spectator *ran four articles on Herbert's plan which, while not attacking the idea, showed that it would not solve the problem of unemployment or low wages for seamstresses.[1] More outspoken concerning problems in the plan were the articles which appeared in the*

Morning Chronicle, *the* Globe, *and* Reynolds's Political Instructor.[2] *Although the emigration movement was short lived, it, like the self-help movement also positively portrayed in the novel, represents an important aspect of working-class life during the mid-Victorian era.*

* * *

"The poorer classes are ignorant of what a paradise a colony is. If they only knew a colony is for people of their class, they would prefer emigrating to getting double wages here and how glad they would be to get double wages here need not be stated. I have often thought that if pains were taken to make the poorest class in this country really and truly aware of what awaits emigrants of their class, and if a suitable machinery were established for enabling them to emigrate, and get into employment by means of enabling them to emigrate, and get into employment by means of money saved by themselves here, enough of them would emigrate to cause a rise of wages for those who remained behind. At present, speaking of the class generally, they know hardly anything about colonies, and still less about what they ought to do in order to reach a colony, even if they could have wherewith to pay for the passage. The colonies are not attractive to them as a class, have no existence as far as they know, never occupy their thoughts for a moment. That they have not much inclination to emigrate should surprise nobody."--*Wakefield's Art of Colonization*, p. 137.

"In trade, navigation, war, and politics—in all business of a public nature, except works of benevolence and colonization—the stronger sex alone take an active part; but, in colonization, women have a part so important that all depends on their participation in the work. There is another proposition which I think you will adopt as readily; it is that, in every rank, the best sort of women for colonists are those to whom religion is a rule, a guide, a stay, and a comfort. You might persuade religious men to emigrate, and yet, in time, have a colony of which the morals and manners would be detestable; but, if you persuade religious women to emigrate the whole colony will be comparatively virtuous and polite. As respects morals and manners, it is of little importance what colonial fathers are in comparison with what the mothers are. It was the matrons more than the fathers of the New England Pilgrimage, that stamped the character of Massachusetts and Connecticut; that made New England, for a long while, the finest piece of colonization the world has exhibited."—*Ibid.*, p. 157.

"There are thousands now
Such women, but convention beats them down;
It is but bringing up; no more than that."
                                        Tennyson's Princess.

It twinkled dully, shot up fitfully, with a sickly glare, then sunk down into the socket of the battered candlestick; and thus the last morsel of the hard-earned candle gone, the frosty, brilliant, wintry moon shimmered in coldly through the attic window, and gleaming down (perhaps in heavenly pity) in arrowy points of light, fell on the now still needle, and the cold, half-rigid, half corpse-like, fingers of the seamstress.

There was but one; a pale thin woman of, perhaps, thirty years of age, but looking older by full ten or fifteen years; for care and sorrow had left their visible impressment on her grave and earnest face.

After bending her face awhile upon her upraised hands (upon which more pityingly, and more broadly, streamed down the rich refulgence of the heavenly moon) she rose, fetched a piece of worn brown paper from out a darkened corner of the room, tied two finished shirts within it, and then dressed herself in a very thin and rusty-coloured mourning shawl, and an old straw bonnet.

Thus dressed, with the old worn paper parcel on her arm, she had reached the door, when she abruptly paused again, and speaking, as though some one sat within the shadows of the room: "No! no! it's no use going, especially at night, when Mrs. Moss has got her son Moses there, for, if he's hard by day, she's harder then. No! no! Sweet must go,—for he's the last thing left saving Nelly's little childish locket—for Lawrence is dead, and can never hear Sweet sing again; but she————." She spoke no more, even to those shadows of the room, but only to her own soul, whose tears of anguish rained through her wasted fingers, on to the faded signs of death and burial.

When calmer, she returned again within the shadows of the miserable room, for, having a sloping roof, it was very dark, except just around the window; brought a tattered handerkerchief, or apron, from a baulk or shelf, and, going to the window, took down a bird-cage opened its little door, and put her hand within. Though cold—for that poor room was very cold—and with its little head tucked beneath its wing, the bird, in an instant, was aroused by the hand which touched it, and caressing it, and nestling to it, with a marvellous fondness and tameness, which was almost human, flew out on to her bosom. When there, it nestled again, rubbing its little bill full twenty times up and down, till, at last, it perked it up, and looked quaintly, keenly, half wistfully, into the seamstress's worn, corpse-like face.

"My Sweet," she said again, "love has saved you many times, but to-night you must go, for Lawrence can no longer hear the pretty notes he taught you, and Nelly's gone, and I am starving, without even a candle or thread to finish that which will bring a meal. So you must go—though if———." Sweet gave here such a chirp of love and goodness, which so plainly said, "sell me, or pluck me, or even stop my little cheerful notes for ever, so that it be for your good," that something new of hope and strength of resolution sprung up instantly within the woman's soul; and so, caressing the bird anew, she replaced it in the cage, tied the latter carefully up in the apron, and pinning together the corners so as to exclude the wind, was again returning to the door, when the scene from the attic window struck her sight. From this, through the gully of a narrow street, the Thames, off Lambeth, could be seen; and now on this, the broad light of the splendid wintry moon, pouring itself far down within the water's liquid depth, showed clearly upon the surface a little boat or skiff, which, urged by one rower up against the tide, seemed, whilst within such shadows as lay upon the water, to make its way slowly, and by monstrous toil; but once within the fulness of the light, though the tide roared against it, even still it shot ahead, and was easy to the rower and his scull.

Though as yet the analogy had no birth, still some inward impulse of the soul made the haggard, starving seamstress gaze long and earnestly; and when she moved away with the bundle of needlework, and locked her attic-door, her steps were quicker and firmer than they often were.

Though the sharp frosty night-wind must have been bitterly felt by one so poorly clad, the woman, after crossing Westminster Bridge, carefully avoided the more sheltered thoroughfares, and keeping along such narrow streets as were little frequented, did not emerge from out them, except when no way lay more direct. That she had some strong reason for doing this was evident by the timid, wistful, half-pitying, half-stern glances she cast before her, when any woman's lightsome step approached, or when any crowd blocked up the thoroughfare. At last, upon reaching a narrow street, lying on the eastern side of the Temple, she slacked her hitherto rapid steps, for herein was the bird-fancier's shop where she thought, as many times as the last year's extreme penury had made her think of parting with the bird, she might find it a kind master, as, in passing by, she had often observed a comfortable, smooth-looking little old man upon the door step, and in the windows such an array of clean cages sparkling tiny fountains, such lumps of sugar and ladies' fingers, such seedy plantain, and such yellow-flowered groundsel, and such a merry, pecking, pert, hopping, flitting, impudent and roguish set of linnets, blackbirds, bulfinches, thrushes, larks, and canaries, as to show that this was a sort of bird's Paradise, where carolled notes of fields and sunny skies brought summer often there, with scented flowers, with rippling brooklets, and with waving leaves.

With a beating heart, and not till she had more than once surveyed the tiny, roosting, apparently headless family of Mr. Twiddlesing, for such was the name above the door in this wise—"Brutus Twiddlesing's British and Foreign Aviary.—N.B. Birds taught Popular Airs," did the seamstress venture in, to behold Twiddlesing in person, leaning forward leisurely on his counter, a fair-sized snuff-box, in the shape of a bird's nest, just beside his right thumb and forefinger, into which he now and then dipped, or "took an egg," as he said, whilst he duly listened to a tall, thin, barber-like looking man, who, dressed in a rusty black dress-coat, monstrously wide for him in the back, whilst very short in both the arms and flaps, sat on a high stool, and graced the "Twiddlesing Aviary" with his parts in speech.

After some timely patience, the unhappy needlewoman was enabled here and there to drop in a word or two, which in a while were in amount sufficient to inform Twiddlesing that she had got a bird with her and wanted to sell it. Whereupon the cage was set on the counter, beside the snuff-box, the apron unpinned, and Sweet seen. Brutus looked gravely but at last he said, after he had glanced at his tall friend,

"But it's an edicated one—and I rarely wentur upon old birds, for you can do nothing with 'em in a singing way."

"Sing!" and the woman ejaculated this, as if a goddess had been asked where her beauty lay, or a rich rose its perfume. "Why, not one amongst hundreds could sing like it; for a poor brother I had, who was a genius in organ-building, and taught it with infinite pains, said that not one in a hundred would be found like it; and he died of decline last spring, it is therefore destitution—the last stage of destitution—which forces me to part with it; but I want bread, and such is a sad want———."

Twiddlesing was about to say something, but the tall man lifted up his finger, and asked the woman what she was.

"A needlewoman—that is a shirt, a slop, or a waist-coat-maker, just as I can get it to do, though by trade I am a better sort of dressmaker; but in winter time that sort of work is slack; and, even if not so, now I have no decent clothes in which I could seek it. Though it is only five years since I came up a healthy girl, with a mother, three sisters, and a brother, from a distant Cornwall to London, for the lad had a genius for mechanics, and wished to be apprenticed to an organ-builder; and now all that is left of us is me, and one——." She said no more, but stopped abruptly, and bent her face upon her rusty shawl.

"The old tale, the old tale," said the tall man parenthetically, rubbing as he spoke the old stained, powdered collar of his rusty coat, with a nervous sort of movement of his right thumb and forefinger— "and have, of course, been helped a bit by humane people, and are now worse off than before."

"But once only have I been helped," the woman replied, "and that was to bury my mother. But I know those who have been helped, only to feel poverty more sorely when need came again."

"Of course, of course," added the tall man, with a triumphant wave of his hand across the counter to Brutus Twiddlesing, "dear old precious master is again right; never knew him to fail, sir, never; and this is what he said when a man called one morning (knowing his bounty, God bless him) to ask his aid, and I went and explained the thing. 'Indeed, O'Flanagan! well, just feel if I have got a button to my pocket, and, if I have, button it, for not one guinea shall go to make needles rustier with human tears. No, no; but if it were twenty guineas, or if even a hundred guineas, to build ships with, to send these human women to lands where they are needed, where they might become mothers, and be blessed by the hand of nature; where they might be happy, and eat of the blessed bread of this blessed earth, they should go; but to put one penny angle in for the needful fishing of a mighty ocean, Robert Fortescue never will: so button up my pocket, O'Flanagan.' This is just what my dear old master said," continued the tall man, "and he is a good and great lawyer living hard by, and it is emigration he means—a going to other lands, where fewer folks are, and there working, and marrying, and being happy. Did you ever hear of this?"

"Something," rejoined the woman, hopelessly and vacantly, "of dreary voyages and desert countries at the end. No, I know little of this matter; some Cornish people of my native village went out across the seas I know, but, since I have been in London, life has been too sore a struggle to think of anything but bread. And if I even did, what hope is there that one like me could change the lot of earning fourpence a day by twelve hours work, and a parish coffin at the close. Hope—! I have ceased to think of that." And the woman laughed with the laugh of a broken, desperate heart.

"To look at your face," said the honest wearer of the noble lawyer's rusty black,—and here, as he was a bit philosophic, he looked profoundly at Twiddlesing, and dipt his thumb and finger in the "bird's nest," "you ain't one that ought to say that, for there's a deal in this face of yours which says you could work through a hard way, if you saw hope at the end of it; and so—"

"Well," she interrupted him, somewhat impatiently, "at least this talk won't serve me now. And so (turning to Twiddlesing) will you buy the bird or not——"

"I must have time to think of sich a piece of importance, as taking into my aviary a grown-up and edicated bird," spoke Brutus gravely, "for bad notes is bad things ma'am, and I must have time to try his woice; for, of course—"

"Try?" and there was something Siddonian in the voice with which the downcast woman spoke the word, "because I am poor, I do not necessarily lie! But keep it till I return, for I have some further way to go, and recollect that, in parting with him I part with my life's-blood." So saying, she hurried out into the cold bleak night air again, leaving Mr. Twiddlesing and his friend, O'Flanagan, to take such an amazing amount of "eggs" out of their bird's nest as to be incredible.

In a street close upon Aldgate, the needlewoman, after speaking to one or two women, ill clad and wretched like herself, who came out from the open doorway of a mean house, entered through a narrow, dirty-looking passage, into a large room lighted by a gas-jet, and across which ran some few yards from the door, a very wide counter, worn and greasy, like a tailor's board. It was piled up with made and unmade work, rolls of Calico hanks and reels of sewing cotton, waistcoating, yard measures, a great leaded pincushion, pairs of scissors, and strips of parchment. In front of this counter, four or five miserable women were grouped in the various positions of waiting for, receiving, and giving in work, whilst Mrs. Moss, a monstrously fat Jewess, very gaudily attired, was not only concluding with these women the business of the day, but casting also now and then a watchful regarding eye to a huge fire-place at the rear of the room, over which a little shrimp of a drabbled servant was frying a great pan full of fish, whilst before it, to keep hot, stood a heaped-up dish of beef-steaks and onions, previously fried. In front of this fire stood a three-legged table, covered by a dirty cloth, wiped knives, Britannia-metal forks and spoons of a sickly yellow hue, a jar of pickles, a loaf of bread, and a pewter-pot of stout; whilst, as the viands were not yet put on, nor Mrs. Moss yet ready, her only son-and-heir, Mr. Moses Moss, shopwalker in a cheap tailoring establishment near at hand, had placed his feet, whilst swinging his body back with much ease and elegance in a low chair, he showed himself off conspicuously to his admiring mother, her hungry workers, or the little wretched cowering fryer of the fish.

This young gentleman, thus elegant and self-indulgent, was beguiling the time till the herrings were done, and Mrs. Moss at liberty, by the varied divertisements of an occasional glance at a small journal or magazine he held in his hand, on every finger of which was a bright stoned ring, by pulling the hair, or viciously nipping the bare arms of the miserable little servant; whilst the labour attending on such divertisements, as they came round in rotation, was refreshed by a taste of the contents of the pewter pot. Just as his mother dismissed the other women, and turned to the last comer, the before-mentioned cheap book or pamphlet was the object of this young gentleman's attention, and a certain passage therein greatly exciting his risibility, he read it aloud, in a voice strongly nasal, and with a Jewish accent.

"Vell," he said, when he had arrived at the conclusion, "this is jolly, eh! eh! Hope and adwice to needlewimen, and creturs like this fryer here—happy and prosperous lands for 'em all—husbands, and no end to tea; and peaches by the bushel. Well, Missis Moss, the sooner you put by yard measures and needles the better, with such adwice to be had for three halfpence; vell, the end'll be, I suppose, gents'll have to make their own shirts, or else go vith-hout." And, so commenting, Mr. Moses gave an additional pull at the stout, and nipped the little servant's arm till she shrieked with pain.

"Now, vat's it you vant," spoke Mrs. Moss, addressing the woman, "I thought the dozen fine-fronted Irish vas enough for von veek, eh? or, are you come to say they're pawned? You'd best not," and Mrs. Moss, the middlewoman, shook her head in a way which accurately illustrated from whence Mr. Moss inherited his vicious nature.

Though of a strong and self-possessed character, the miserable needlewoman was so abashed by the ferocious aspect of the Jewess, as to visibly tremble whilst she stated her abject need, and, untying the parcel she had brought, she laid the two finished shirts on the table.

"You see, ma'am," she continued, "so much was taken off for the last job of waistcoats, owing to the fault you found with the match of the stripes, that but sixpence was left me for bread or rent, and, as even my last candle's end was burnt out tonight, I have brought those in the hope that you will let me have a trifle as my need is very sore."

"And vat's that to me," said Mrs. Moss, "ain't it al'lays the old tale; ain't yer al'lays here?"

"But twice, ma'am," replied the woman, "once when my mother died, and once when——" she stopped abruptly here, and burying her face again in her rusty shawl, burst into passionate tears.

"Oh! oh! oh!" laughed Mrs. Moss, with the breadth and depth of the lungs of a Dutch boor, "thy pretty sister, eh! But tears ain't the coin wanted here, so march, the shirts'll be safe till thee bring the rest, eh! eh! So put out the fish, Peg" (here she turned and spoke to her small servant in a voice like a trumpet) "and my sweet Moses" (here she uttered the most dulcet treble) "get out the case-bottle, I'm tired, and shall have rum to-night!" So saying, the middlewoman cast the two finished shirts on to a shelf at her right hand, and waving her huge fat red hand peremptorily as a sign for the woman to go, locked up her till, pocketed the key, and turned towards her ample fire-place, and the graces of her bewitching heir.

The woman had moved slowly to the door, closed it after her, and gone thoughtfully onward some few paces along the pavement, when she felt her arm touched, and turning round, beheld the miserable little object of Mr. Moss's spite at her elbow, and who, stuttering out some such remark as, "she knowed what it was to be bad off for wittles," thrust one of the fried herrings and a potatoe into the woman's hand, and disappeared as quickly back again as she had come.

This touch of pity in a creature so miserably used, as to be more like a hounded dog than one possessing human flesh and blood, begot anew the needlewoman's tears, but these not lasting ones, for her thoughts were busy with what the Jew had read, and which so strongly bore relation to the conversation in Brutus Twiddlesing's shop.

She was still full of these thoughts when she reached the bird-fancier's. His shop was now shut up, saving the little half window in the door, through which she could see that Mr. Brutus, now alone, was seated in a small inner room, about six feet square which, nevertheless, had a bright fire, and was, altogether, as snug as a wren's nest. A supper, consisting of a dish of saveloys, and bread and cheese, was cosily set forth, whilst the little old man, now adorned by a woollen night-cap, and comforted by a mug of ale, and his pipe on the hob, his "bird's nest," on a little three-cornered shelf, which just fitted it, was resting, after the daily labours of his aviary, in a capacious armchair, and with his feet outstretched on the fender. When the woman had opened the shop-door, and closing it again, advanced towards Mr. Brutus's snug retreat, she was amazed to see her bird perched on the forefinger of his left hand, whilst, in his right, he held a "lady's finger," which the bird, aroused every instant or so by the shrill chirps of Brutus, drowsily pecked, and then relapsed into that position which very much bespoke a strong inclination to tuck its head up under its wing, and be off in a nap.

"Come, young woman," spoke Brutus, cheerfully, addressing the needlewoman, "just come in here and rest a bit, and take a saveloy and a little ale, I want to talk to you uncommonly." So saying, he deposited the bird in its cage, and did the hospitable graces of his little cheerful fire-side with kindly eagerness.

"I've taken an uncommon liking to the bird already," he continued, when he had placed a portion of his meal upon the needlewoman's plate, and poured her out some ale, "and think, with a little of my tuition, he'll do. But no more o' this, just now, for you look cold, and have walked far, I daresay." He watched her eat with cheerful goodness, his own meal being a mere pretext, and, when she looked less cold and hungry, he recommenced the conversation by asking her name.

"Lucy Dean," she said.

"Lucy's an uncommon pretty name," he said, "one of my last autumn's hatch has that, so now what I mean to say is, this, as I've taken a mighty to the bird, and so has Mr. O'Flanagan, and that ain't common, for he's a special taste in my line what do ye ask for it?"

"Alas," spoke the woman, "little as I have left on earth, the bird is very precious to me, for if I only knew of certain bread, a hundred pounds wouldn't buy it, but as it is, it must go. Suppose then I say five shillings—it's worth at least five pounds, but then you'd be kind, and would perhaps let me come in and look at it sometimes."

"Five shillings would be useful, eh?" asked Brutus, evading her last question.

"A fortune," she said. "Oh God, that such a sum, so small to many, should be so large to others, as to have hanging on its possession the threads of life and death." Even as she spoke Mr. Brutus crossed his right hand over the "bird's nest," opened it, took leisurely a pinch of snuff, then gently lifting up the "nest" itself, brought from under it a veritable crown-piece, which he placed on the table before the wondering needlewoman.

"This is yours," he continued, "for my good friend O'Flanagan left it for you, as his master Counsellor Fortescue bids him take a pound's worth o' silver every now and then, and drop in a seed corn, whenever he can, in honest, profitable land. So this settled, I'll take Sweet, as I may say and board, lodge, and edicate him gratis not talking a word just at present about selling him, but hoping now you'll drop in a bit to see him sometimes, as he'll have a deal o' cheerful company, and be all alive in spirits, and there's only one thing I'd ask in return, that is . . . ."

The woman looked up eagerly here, though the tears of many mingled feelings were flowing fleetly from their fountains, so that the bird-fancier continued, by saying "that you think of what Jack O'Flanagan said tonight, as he is but the second voice of his master, who in his turn, knows an uncommon deal about sich things."

"I have, I have," spoke the woman. And she went on and described to Brutus what the Jew had read by strange coincidence; and how up to the very instant of her return to his shop her mind had been full of it. But, beyond this, she had not time to say more, for the minute he heard about the small magazine, Mr. Brutus jumped up, adjourned to his shop, and coming back in an instant with a parcel delicately done up in silk paper, cleared a space on the table and laying it reverently down, opened it as if it held cloth of gold or some holy coat of Treves.

"There, this is it," he said, when he had taken from the midst of others, the number of the magazine the Jew had read. "I know every word on't, and so does O'Flanagan, and so does the Counsellor; only that O'Flanagan goes so far as to put 'em under his pillow at night, as he likes, he says, to sleep on the thought o' this blissid little woman."

"Woman?" and the bird-fancier's questioner repeated the word many times.

"Woman, yes," replied Brutus, enthusiastically, "and one as has done more to put a heart in things sich as this, than half the men in the country. Don't she? don't she?" he continued, as his voice ascended up the scale like the notes of a blackbird, "for doesn't she say, jist what the counsellor and O'Flanagan does, that charity will never heal woeful misery like yours, not if it be the charity of half a nation; for it is but lifting a bucket out of a big ocean. But that some must brave the perils of the ocean to these far lands, must lay aside the beggared needle and its lazy bread, must cook and bake, wash and iron, sweep the house and trim the garden, become mothers, and nurse their offspring into good men and women. And some of you must get money, and collect money in that country, and come back to this, and spread the knowledge wide and far that there are blessed lands in this wide world, for them as'll strive and work, and not cling to the pauperism o' the needle; as O'Flanagan says the counsellor says, because it's 'ginteel.' So strive a bit my woman, harm never yet come o'striving after a good pint." Mr. Brutus took here an "egg" from his "nest," and seemed refreshed thereby.

"I would, I would, for I have a lion's heart," said Lucy, "if I knew how. But—" and she stopped suddenly as if at first startled by her own temerity, "but might not this rare one, who speaks so nobly from the depths of her woman's heart to her suffering sister woman, tell me how and what to do?"

"I dare to say," replied Brutus, struck by the same idea too, "though I once heard a person say, as had seen one, that authors, in and out o' their books, are very different things; and one that might be excessively pleasant in his chapters, would be excessively grumpy out on 'em. But if you'll jist wait, I'll step to my partic'lar friend, Noseby, the newsman, round the corner, and ask, for he goes as far as O'Flanagan, in his liking for the little woman, and'll tell you if any body can." So saying, admirable Mr. Brutus tied on a mighty comfortable (a present, as he hinted, from a partic'lar nice lady), put on his hat, and departed; soon returning, with not only a copy of a magazine, with Mr. Noseby's respects, but also the precious document of a strip of paper, containing the needed address.

"I assure you," spoke Brutus, " that Noseby made many inquiries before he'd give this here, sich is his weneration; and that was only after I'd twice told him that you was one o' the fair sex. For though he goes himself once a month in his weneration to look outside the door, he'd die before he'd give up this little dockiment to any one as wore a hat. And now, Lucy Dean, as you must go, you must jist have a little drop to keep out the cold, that you must." So saying, Mr. Twiddlesing produced a punchy bottle from a narrow closet, like the case of a clock, and which was nailed up against the wall by the side of his brass warmingpan. From this he poured something very red and odorous, but which Lucy would not more than put to her lips. He then suffered her to go with, as he let her out at his shop door, "a God speed," and "that, come whenever she might, she was welcome, and Sweet should not only be duly groundselled, fresh watered, sanded, sugared, and lady-fingered, but also edicated in the ways of a gentleman."

It was now late, but with a light heart how swift the feet become; so in time, that would have appeared marvellous under another state of feeling, the woman, after the purchase of some necessaries at a huckster's shop, yet open, reached the solitary garret. It looked mournful and desolate enough after the light and warmth of the bird-fancier's little parlour, but apparently regardless, or at least, unobservant of these things, Lucy lighted the candle she had with her, sat down upon the only chair the room contained, and read and read again, like some schoolboy with his task, the golden words of sound advice, set down by this sweet spirit in the shape of woman. It was a new spirit, the spirit of a new time; and as the starving, mournful, solitary woman read, all sense of weakness and of desolation passed away; and once more, united into one, the love of father, mother, and sister, seemed to be re-born with newer fervor from their perished dust; and encircling her, befriending her, sustaining her, to tell her that there is hope for all who strive with earnest will.

When at last she rose, her resolution was taken; and as if it were a good one, and a right one, she saw, as she passed the window to her lowly bed, that the heavenly moon still gleamed upon the river, to right and left, far up and down, but fullest now and sweetest in its light, where darkest shadows had been cast before.

Mr. O'Flanagan's bright crown enabled her to take a mourning bonnet, shawl, and gown, out of pawn, and borrowing a pair of shoes and gloves from the kindly mistress of a neighbouring coffee-shop, Lucy Dean, thus once more decently clad, set off on the errand she had resolved upon. The place she had to go to lay five or six miles from town, but the morning was frosty and bright, though cold.

As she cleared the outskirts of the city, and hedge rows replaced unfinished houses in all stages of progress, and fields lay far and wide, though mantled with hoar frost; her spirits, hopeful, though humble, made her for the time feel as if she could seek any presence, however great. But this only lasted whilst the little village, whither she was going lay in a degree remote, for as she neared it and turned down a sloping, grassy lane from the high road, she trembled and hesitated, and faltered in her steps. It was one of the most hidden, and quaintest of little villages, one would often see; and by its bits of common turf, its large old spreading though now leafless trees, its gabled red-bricked houses, and low garden gates, and ivied porches, it might be easily imagined to be five hundred miles away from London instead of a little more than five. After finding out the exact house, it was some minutes before she had heart enough to ring the gate bell; and when it was answered, and an old woman, clad in a monstrous high-bibbed apron, led her through a little wainscoted passage, with a glass door at the further end, which showed the bright laurels of a small garden, and a parlour door opened, and some one said, "let the person come in," Lucy Dean, breathless and trembling, passed round the door, not to behold still more to her breathless amazement, the vision she had conjured up of a middle-aged lady, very tall and very grandly dressed, and with a very distant manner and a haughty voice, but a little woman, years younger then herself, in whose face you saw the fervent, pitying, noble heart, the world had learnt to love so well; and the written thoughts of whose heart, hundreds of Twiddlesings and O'Flanagans wrapped up carefully in silk paper. The presence of a grand, proud, haughty woman, sensible of power, would have sustained the self-resolution of the needlewoman; but to see before her as the lady uprose from her chair, a little frail, childish creature, without a sign of pride or thought of self, brought back at once all her own humility of state, her sufferings, and her hoarded sorrows; and scarcely moving one step from the now closed door, she wept, with buried face, and knelt, in soul, before this little creature, without power to stay her tears or to conceal her heaving and convulsed respiration.

"Come," spoke the lady, with a gentle voice, "you have walked far, I fear. Come sit down, you will be better presently." So saying, she stirred up the fire to a bright glow, drew up a large old-fashioned chair beside her own, and then taking Lucy's hand made her sit down beside her.

The needlewoman was sufficiently educated to understand that brevity is courtesy to strangers; so as soon as she was sufficiently calm she stated her name, her age, her occupation, her sorrows, and the events of the over night, which had led to her knowledge of the lady's writings, and her desire to see her and ask her good advice.

"I am glad these things are serviceable," said the lady, "especially in reference to my own sex, for I put down on paper what my soul believes to be truth. But, beyond this, I fear I am powerless. Still, as the old word is, where there is a will there is a way, I would gladly find one in such a matter, for any woman who I think would go forth to the colonies, with the determination to work, not only for herself, but to pave a way for others of her sex, less fortunate, or less courageous. Such a woman might achieve immeasurable good. Now a few questions which lie at the root of all. Could you wash, cook, bake, do you know how to provide a comfortable dinner, and nurse a child, eh?"

"Till I went to learn dressmaking of my own choice, Madam, at the age of eighteen," answered Lucy, "I managed my parents' household for several years; and not a girl in our Cornish village, as was well known, had a better name for baking an oven of good bread, brewing clearer ale, ironing, washing, or making a Sunday shirt, or keeping the bee-hives and the flower-beds in the garden more tidily. There is many a one still living in our village who could tell you so."

"This is well, for these are chief points," continued the lady, "in all womanly life, if even no more than superintendence be needed; but much more needful ones, to those who seek a new country, and will as a moral certainty, become wives, if not mothers. To show you my own strong sense of duties like these I speak of, look at me, and at my hands! Could you fancy that these can brew and bake, wash and iron, cook a dinner from an Irish stew to a cod's head and oyster sauce?"

"I should hardly think so Madam—these hands look so frail and delicate."

"They *can*," and the writer spoke with an emphasis which startled Lucy, though the iron will expressed thereby was akin to the strongest characteristic of her own nature, "and I hold myself to be no wonder because they can. As to life in the new world, it is one of hope to a resolute and good woman; and often, and often, I feel the strongest inclination to lay down my pen, and show by action from another land, and across the widest ocean of the world, what *one* woman, resolute of heart, can do to help her sisters here. I know I should be serviceable, I know I should be happier—but then————(she stopped here for her voice was choked————) friends say, that my usefulness would be circumscribed to the principle of emigration alone, whilst here, with the same degree of usefulness I can serve a hundred things beside. So, I submit to— which is perhaps destiny—though if heavenly angels do keep chronicles of hidden human woes, and would permit men of the coming time to read them by the light they then will read by, the darkest and most mournful pages would be found, wherein what is written on human women's hearts has been the truth recorded. But we all bear a cross you see—though I—and I would fain make such as you assist me, lift it from off our sister women." The lady spoke those last words so from the soul, that, though so buoyant, and so outwardly light of heart, not long before, she now tremulously bent downwards towards the hearth, as if to hide her deep emotion from the needlewoman's gaze.

Presently, however, and still as if purposely retaining this attitude, she said gently, "I have two other things to ask—the one, are you religious? I do not mean in the sense of mere church-going, or mere outward form, but I mean in the sense of conscience and right action, that would enforce faith and duty in your household, that would teach your lisping children by your knees, those prayers which men go back to in their after years, for penitence, for faith, for hope, for good; and next, I————." The speaker stopped here; bending her face still more, for the blood now blushed there from her warm and gentle heart.

The one beside her knew intuitively what she meant, though no question had been asked; and so obeying the profound impulses which wrought upon her at the instant, she knelt as a disciple might before the holiest teacher, and said, as she buried her face in the stranger's lap, in a voice, faint and lowly, yet which bore upon it the stamp of truth: "I would teach, lady, what I was taught in my own childhood, love to God and duty to man; and, as for my life, it has been a pure and womanly one, or else I could not have come to *you* this day . . . You will believe me, I am sure."

"I will," was the firm and earnest answer; "for truth is always simple in its asseverations." And those hands, worn with work, and which, for months had felt no kindly pressure of affection or sympathy, were grasped by the dear fervent ones of this sweet nature. A thousand words could not have made declaration of a more pregnant meaning, than this same pressure of these fervent hands.

It was some seconds before Lucy rose, and when she did so, the lady said, now in her more ordinary way, "You must pardon what I implied, if I did not ask; but, a woman, useful, religious, and chaste, is more worthy of success, and more likely to succeed in a new country like Australia, whither I should advise you to go. Now, as for the means of going thither, you say you can work well at the needle?"

"I have done the finest and coarsest work, Madam."

"Well, fortunately, I have lying here, and yet unanswered, a note from a friend of mine, asking if I know of a good needlewoman, who could work for her this entire winter, as part of her family are going abroad in the spring, and need a large outfit, so that I will write a note, which you shall take to her. She is a liberal and good woman, and will pay you well I know, and thus, if you should get the work, you may, by diligence, through this winter and the spring, lay by a portion, at least, of the passage money thither. Further I can not promise, till I see what you can, and will do, though if you prove, what I hope you will, I shall ask you to do other things beside help yourself in the noble land you go to. For, here, charity, however well intentioned, does but relieve, to augment still more severely the sufferings of your class—and, if public charity still more largely steps forth to aid emigration, it can only do so partially—but if the hearts of the colonists themselves could be stirred in this matter, if the women who have gone forth, and been benefited, could be made to remember the needs of those who remain at home,—if men, who need, and ask for, good chaste, and useful wives, would help towards what is so priceless, a permanent and yearly fund might be raised for the purposes of female emigration, on such a plan, as would ensure fitting candidates here, and a fitting and moral reception for them in the colonies. This is what I mean, this is what I should like to carry out, however humbly." She said no more, and then turning to the table at her side, wrote a brief note. Lucy Dean rose to go when she saw it finished. "No," continued her earnest friend, "not till you have had some refreshment." So saying, she rang, and the old servant brought in a tray. Whilst Lucy sat and ate the savoury meal, thus brought in for her, she had time to observe the little quaint old wainscoted room, its rich old china bowls stuck on the top of little corner cupboards, its few casts and pictures, its many books, its large old chairs, its latticed window looking into the garden, and showing a mass of verdant holly, bright with clustered berries, old spreading laurels, and a thriving myrtle, and then hastily scanning all these things, fastening her gaze at last upon the sweet womanly face before her. At last Lucy rose to go.

"You will let me see you again at the end of the week," said the lady. "This is Tuesday, so come on Saturday, my friend will have made her enquiries by that time. Now good day, bear what I have said in your heart, as I think by your manner you will."

Lucy, when she had ended her thanks, hesitated in a manner, evident to the writer.

"What is it?" she asked.

Hesitatingly, Lucy answered, with trembling lips, "I am much alone, lady and I should like to have beside me or before me, some token, however small, of your goodness and your words. An old glove, or pen, a faded ribbon, anything so that you have worn it, or touched it."

Blushing and trembling as the earnest compliment met her ear, Mary Austen, for such was her name, rose, and going towards a flower-stand, took from thence a thrifty *primula*.

"It will be better," she said, "than ribbon, or pen, or glove; it will be green, and, perhaps, bear flowers."

"Like your goodness, lady, as I hope, and in another land," and saying thus, and curtseying lowlily, the needlewoman, too moved to say any more, closed the door of the little quaint country parlour, upon the sweetest nature she had ever known.

The enquiry into Lucy's character, by the lady, to whom she bore Miss Austen's note, proved so satisfactory in every respect, as not only to ensure her more than sufficient work to occupy the entire winter, but also the high trust of cutting it out from the piece. Added to this, the same kindly hand which thus intrusted her paid her a few shillings in advance, gave her some articles of warm, second-hand apparel, and such old household things for her miserable, denuded garret, as two chairs, a tea-kettle, and a pair of blankets; so that on the Saturday afternoon, when she again reached the old country house, and stepped into its parlour, the signs of the coming more womanly, more hopeful, more natural life, were already marked upon her worn and haggard face. The interview was a brief one; for Mary Austen was in some respects, as stern of will and concise of speech, as in others she was warm of heart and child-like in her nature.

"I have little time," she said to Lucy, "for frequent interviews; nor will you if you mean to work out a future course of well-being, either for yourself or others. For much rests on your own honest endeavours, particularly, as my friend writes me word, that with industry and thrift, she thinks you may contrive to put by six or eight pounds out of the sum she reckons she shall have to pay you. If you do this, say six only, I will write some paper, the price of which shall add five pounds, thus making in the whole £11 towards £15, the cost of a passage to South Australia, whither I strongly desire you to go; more especially since I have recollected that you are a Cornish woman, for many of your countrymen have settled in the mining districts round Adelaide. And by the time this sum of £11 is gathered, means may disclose themselves of obtaining the remainder of the needed sum. Till then I must commend you to your own diligence—for only prove to me, what I believe you to be, a stern, strong-willed, earnest, truthful woman, bowed down yet not debased by misfortune, and no effort, I can make to serve you, shall be wanting."

Lucy was moving away, though with her lingering gaze still fixed upon this earnest face of large humanity, when Mary, questioning her again, said, gently, "you have a sister?"

This question, so simple in itself, might have been one which involved life and death, or some fatal secret, of the confession of some guilty knowledge, for the effect which it had upon the creature questioned, as she stood for the moment incapable of speech or movement, and at last she only answered with difficulty, "Yes Madam, she will only be seventeen next July—but she's gone wrong—and I never mention her."

"Did she do so from need," asked Mary, speaking so low that her voice was a whisper, "for if so, you should be forgiving and relenting, Lucy."

"I would," replied the woman, with a sternness which startled the questioner, "if it had been so, but it was not. For Lawrence even sold the little organ he had made, that Nelly, 'our father's flower,' as she was called, might not be so pinched as were the rest; and my mother likewise parted with, one by one, such few valuables as remained, so that the beauty of our home might not know want; but all in vain. For she went wrong, and so put past hope Lawrence's recovery; for Nelly was the pride of his heart. Sometimes I am hard enough, even wrong enough, to think, aye, and to say, that it was love of finery, or dislike of such a sordid home as ours had come to be, or our cruel hours of labour which led her astray, for she had nice and delicate tastes, girl as she was; but in my more charitable moments, I believe, and indeed am certain, that it was some one of Lawrence's friends who persuaded her to quit us, under promise of marriage, and assistance to her friends, for she had a believing nature, and clung to others with instinctive faith; and thus deceived, did not dare to return. Poor child— perhaps, by what I suffer and think, the grave were better than this dream of happier lands."

"Nay, nay," added Mary, tenderly, "the grave is no fit ending to human tragedies like these, my poor one; for if we, as women, despair of helping our sister woman, what can men do? No! it is only through labour—honest self-help, that those standing can raise the fallen—and this you may do—this is what I have to do—this is what the strong in will, and what the untempted of our sex have to do. Not, not, as God is my witness, but what I would have every woman, whose destiny it is to kneel beside her infant's cradle in this newer land, be able to curtain it to rest, by the holy veil cast down of her soul's purity."

"I understand you, Madam," replied the needlewoman, weeping, though tears which flowed not from the bitterest fountain of the soul, "and from so understanding, take both counsel and stronger resolution, for it seems as if I drew fresh zeal from every word you speak. And so God bless you, Madam, the primula you gave me has not yet leaf or flower; perhaps, it may have both." So saying, she bent lowlily, and moved to go, like a disciple from before the face of his prophet.

"Good-by," said Mary Austen, cheerfully, "now both of us to work. You to your needle, I to my pen, and depend upon it, diviner flowers will spring towards heaven, than what we even think of, or dream of; for charity, and love, and faith, within the heart of woman, have not yet accomplished the millionth part of their duty, nor scarcely yet foreshadowed their destiny in the progress of the ages. Good-by—and God speed you." And with a lingering gaze on Mary's earnest face, for these last sentences she had spoken, as if partly addressed to herself, Lucy closed the door, and so began these women's services to humanity.

I shall not linger over the months of this winter. For hours before the break of day, for hours long after it was closed, the busy needle plied a ceaseless task; and it was not a weary one, for hope shone brightly at its end. The chamber too looked different than of old; though much could not be said for its cheerfulness, as such a small bit of fire burnt in the grate, as to convey a sense of coldness rather than warmth. But things were brighter at nighttime when the one dip candle was lit, and the curtain drawn across the window. As the weeks, however, went by, a new source of care and trouble arose; for as soon as it became known amongst Lucy's friends, all needlewomen, like herself, that she was in good and full work, then knowing her nature, and abject in their wretchedness, they came to beg and borrow, in the certainty that one who had found means to be kind in the hour of extreme poverty, would be so now when she had work to do, and they had not. And this fact of refusing a penny to human creatures, pleading for its gift or loan, as if for their life; or asking for a piece of bread, a candle, or a little coal, and that by those too who had often helped her in her own hour of need, were the hardest tasks of all, but Lucy recollected her promise to Mary Austen, who with her usual penetration, had foreseen this trouble, and guarded her against it. But the worst part of these daily trials was, what was soon said of her by those who had been to her in her own misery, sympathizing friends, or their averted glances, or angry looks, when they chanced to meet her at the huckster's shop, or on the staircase of the house in which she lodged. A few, however, knew her better than to dream that the narrow prosperity of the needle could change this woman's most womanly heart; and came only the oftener, when they once understood her motives, to listen to her hopeful speech, and helping her with hem or seam, or by cleaning up the room for her, so assist her to the best of their poor ability. It thus happened, as the pebble dropped into the stream widens its own circle, that Lucy Dean had many listeners; human creatures who came to her, to listen, to believe, to trust, just as she in turn had done; to return to their breadless, fireless homes, with hope re-born within their hearts, as from the icy hand of winter, the leaves and buds of Spring. Thus, as the woman plied her needle, and told the little which she knew of happier and newer lands, a Raphael would have seen within their earnest, bending faces, new graces for a New Maternity; for hope lives not within a woman's heart, without declaring its presence and existence, through those feelings, those expressions, those emotions, which

Nature, truer and diviner than man's laws, has decreed shall be the sign of woman's great prerogative, as Mother of the World.

Thus early and late Lucy plied her needle. On Sunday, however, just as the day closed in, and if it were in any degree passable weather, she might be seen on her way to the village where Mary Austen lived, and there, after a gaze upon the lighted casement panes, a moment's lingering by the garden wicket, a leaf of ivy gathered, and a blessing and a prayer, she retraced her steps, refreshed and newly strengthened for the labour of the coming week!

One evening in February, and about three months after her first knowledge of Mary Austen, and whilst sitting at her work, she suddenly recollected that her promise to visit Brutus Twiddlesing had never been fulfilled. She therefore, as the night was bright, and her eyes and fingers sore-tired with the long day's work, she put it by, dressed, and went her way thither. Everything was in its old place; the shop, the birds, the little old man, his quaint snuff-box, saving that O'Flanagan was not there, and that Brutus, instead of leaning indolently on the counter was busy at a sort of little carpenter's bench, at the rear of his shop, with an owl, chained to its perch, roosting solemnly above his head.

"This wisit," said Brutus, in a somewhat mysterious manner, when he had recognised and greeted the needlewoman, "isn't jist the thing in the way o' time; it should have bin a little afore, or a little to come. For ye see that uncommon bird o' yours is only jist——"

"Not dead," faltered the needlewoman, as she thought of the little tiny fluttering thing the poor dead lad had taught and fed, "not dead?"

"Oh, dear, no," replied Brutus, taking a pinch of snuff by way of assistance, "only changed his condition." So saying, he brought from the snuggest retreat of the "Twiddlesing Aviary" a cage as big as a large barrel-organ, in which, to Lucy's astonishment, was not only roosted Sweet, but snugly by his side another little bird, as golden as himself, though smaller, whilst on a little shelf at the rear of the cage was a tiny nest, which, though not yet complete, was already snug and warm with moss and wool, and downy feathers. The cage, too, was not only roomy enough to have accommodated a brood hen and a dozen ducklings most conveniently to their respective tastes, but was also so trimly kept as to show the love and care of the bird-fancier.

"Ye see," continued Brutus, delivering himself most gravely, "this here matter has bin o' great consideration to me; for, in the first place, it's an uncommon bird; next, it was lonely; third, as you are going far away, and O'Flanagan has taken amazingly to it, I thought it would be best with a little mate: and so, if there was a brood, there might not only be an uncommon little songster a-piece for the Counsellor, for the dear young lady, whose writings O'Flanagan and Noseby put up in silk paper, for me as may be said to be their rearer and edicater, but also one or two for you; so that in far-off lands, if one should die, you won't be quite out o' them sort o' notes, as many a sunny morning'll make ye think o' dear old England and absent friends. Ay! ay! in them far-off lands, a woice as the ear has bin used to is a precious thing. But, as I said, ye come at a wrong time; a little afore you'd have known nothing about it—a little later, and you'd've seen the little eggs, or four or five little Sweets with gaping bills above the nest, for bliss ye, little creturs like them take an uncommon deal o' nourishment, and never leave off gaping till they git sumfen." Whilst thus speaking, Mr. Brutus had been unlatching Sweet's cage door, and now disturbing the tiny house holder from its perch, placed it on Lucy's finger. Though it was then night-time, though thus disturbed from its quiet sleep, the little tiny fluttering thing recognised the seamstress in a minute, and pecking and rubbing its bill upon her finger, flitted at last to her shoulder with downy wing, there to repeat its tiny homage, as it were, to the poor dead lad who had raised it from its callow nest. As it thus perched, Brutus Twiddlesing adjourned to the place where he had been working when Lucy came in; soon returning with a half-finished cage of very large dimension, which he was constructing himself, as he informed Lucy, "for Sweet's woyage," and which he exhibited with an amount of pride quite ludicrous. It was pretty clear, however, that the greatest amount of Twiddlesing's genius was being expended on it; for a sort of movable shutter "to keep out wind, an rain, and sun" encompassed it, it had a receptacle for a great amount of bird-seed, plantains, sugar, and lady's-fingers, and a proposed fountain, large enough for an aviary. When thus this handicraft had been duly exhibited, Sweet was restored to the company of Mrs. Sweet, the cage hung up, and Lucy was invited to the inner room. Though not desirous of staying, and telling Brutus so, yet the instant he heard that she had seen Mary Austen, he not only overwhelmed her with questions, but must make her remain whilst he himself set off to fetch Noseby and O'Flanagan, and they returning with him, the fire was stirred up, the cloth laid for supper, and this quickly over, the table was drawn aside, the "bird's-nest" restored, the fat bottle produced, and the three old men, as great oddities in their way as could be, commenced a ceaseless fire of questions. "What sort of eyes had she, what sort of hair, what sort of a nose, how was she dressed, was she tall or short, what did she say?" And when Lucy with brimming eyes had answered these to the best of her ability, by relating entirely her two interviews with Mary Austen, the enthusiasm of the three old men knew no bounds; they took "birds' eggs" to an amazing extent, repeated their questions again and again, vowed severally and together, that there was not such another little woman in the whole world as this Mary, and that her writings, instead of being done up in "silk paper," deserved the very best "gilt and morocco!" Yes! thus shall it ever be with genius; it speaks from out the heart; it links soul to soul; it flows around the universe, and ascending to the heavens, man must, by the very condition of his being, worship what comes from thence, what there returns, what is there enshrined, as what is greatest and divinest in all nature!

Leaving the three enthusiastic old men to their "bird's-nest" and further discourse, Lucy returned home. The house where she lodged was, as I have said, a mean and sordid place, and the staircase used in common by many, led to the street door being often left to stand ajar for hours together. She was therefore surprised, though not alarmed, when, on the garret landing, she stumbled over something lying there. Procuring a light, and bringing it from her room, she was astounded to find a human being lying huddled up, and more so when, putting down the candle, she recognised the pinched and emaciated features of Mrs. Moss's little servant, Peg. As the girl was either insensible from cold or illness, Lucy dragged her into the room, lighted the fire, laid her before it, made some tea, and succeeded in pouring a few drops into her mouth, but with little effect for some considerable time. At length, when partly roused, she seemed suddenly to recognise Lucy, and wildly clinging round her begged to be saved.

"Oh! I thought I should never find you," she sobbed, "for since I run away, after the dreadful beating missis gave me, and Mr. Moses helped her, mum, I bin searching for you everywhere. Oh! please, and now I've found you, don't let me go again there. Oh, pray don't. I won't eat no wittles Miss; I'll go begging, and get some, only let me be with you; I'll clean the room, and do anything——."

"But I am very poor, Peg," said Lucy, "and though I have work, it is upon condition that I save as much of my earnings as I can, and besides, I am going to sail away in a ship to a far land, in a little while. So, perhaps, if I speak to your parish about you, they'd——."

"Oh no, mum, not the parish; they'd punish me, and send me back to Mrs. Moss; and I can't go there, I'd rather be drownd'd, that I would. Please let me stop, I won't eat no wittles——." Repeating these last words over and over, and over again, as if stamped upon her brain by some process of the Jewess, as iron letters on a granite rock, she relapsed into insensibility, and as to have driven into, or laid in the street the miserable child who had fed her with the herring and potatoe in her own hungry hour, was an impossibility, let the consequences be what they might, Lucy placed small Peg in her bed, fetched the parish doctor, and till she felt better, was the tenderest of nurses. By this time, habit brought about what a sense of duty might not have permitted in the first instance: and thus Peg remained from week to week—always going, to be sure—but never gone. At length Lucy found her too useful to part with, for, besides cleaning the room and going [on] errands, she began to sew tidily, and to do the plainer portion of the work in hand.

One night as they sat together, Peg said abruptly, having never mentioned the circumstance before,— "Please mum, don't Miss Nelly bring her baby here sometimes?"

"Baby," gasped Lucy, as turning pale, and faint, and sick, the work dropped from her hands. And she repeated the word many times.

"Yes, mum," continued Peg, "she came to Mrs. Moss's one dreadful snowy day with the baby in her arms and asked for work. At first, missis laughed at her, and said a many hard things as she shouldn't; but at last, when the young cretur offered to take the fine shirts at a half-penny less then the rest would, and find thread too, she gave her a dozen, with a side wink to that wicked son, who sat there making game as he always was, as much as said (for I know that woman's heart well) 'let her take them; it'll save sixpence towards my weekly rum.' I saw her but once again after this night, though I heard her tell missis she was badly off—no, 'dreadfully,'—that was the word."

"And the baby," again questioned Lucy, paler, more drooping, more agitated than before.

"A beauty," said Peg, so enthusiastic and interested as to drop on her knees beside her mistress, "as whilst Mrs. Moss went waddling up stairs for some change, I asked your sister to come across the kitchin just to warm her by the fire, and so, mum, lifting up the end o' the ragged shawl, I saw sich a little cretur, not a month old, mum, as in spite o' rags, an angel, sich as be in church winders, might'a put under its whitest wings and flown to heaven with. Big blue eyes, mum,—very blue—little golden hair, and little hands, all so pink within as to be like missis's big sea-shells which stood on the drawers—ay, mum,—it was sich a little darling as you couldn't help loving."

But Lucy, neither saying she should love or hate, sat weeping for many minutes—for it was Nelly born again: blue eyes, fair hair, small hands; and such knowledge made her weep the bitterest tears.

But all her own, and Peg's inquiries, relating to Nelly, were fruitless; for Mrs. Moss, infuriated at losing one of her best workers, in the person of Lucy, and one who added to her sins by harbouring Peg, refused to give any tidings, as to whether she now employed, or where lived, the most wretched amongst her ill-paid seamstresses.

Thus, time wore on; winter waning mildly into spring; and spring, with mild and genial face, casting her sunniest glances towards broad June; when one night in the end of May, just at midnight, and when Peg had been long asleep, so that she was alone in strictest communion with her own soul, Lucy

Dean placed the last stitch in the last garment. An ignoble thing this to make record of, but purpose can enrich the poorest circumstances; and the purpose here was very noble, though dimly seen; and the steps to it worthy, being those of labour and not charity. After sitting a long while in profound thought, for in fancy her foot seemed now to touch the newer land, she rose, and unlocking an old box, for drawers she had none, took from thence a small cotton bag, in which she had hoarded her poor savings, and brought it to the candle to tell out again, though she knew every coin, the gathered sum of £7 10 s., which, with what had yet to be paid to her on the morrow, would increase her whole savings to the amount of £8 4s., this being £2 4s. more than it was supposed she could save. Precious coins these; precious the millions of such to the mighty progress of the ages.

Her joy was so intense, that she sat down, late as it was, and wrote a letter to Miss Austen, saying her task was over, though without specifying the exact result. And when an answer quickly came, inviting her to the little country village on the following afternoon at five o'clock, her joy, as it may be well conceived, was greater still, for she had only seen Mary once, and that but for a few brief minutes, when coming to town, she called.

It was therefore with a heart lighter than it had been for years, that Lucy entered Mary's quaint and cheerful little parlour on the following afternoon, and saw again that dear face bright with smiles, that hair so beautiful, that dress so trim and rich, and yet so plain and unassuming, and that loving human heart with so little false pride in it, as to have ordered tea to be set forth, which it now was with cake and fruit, richly garnished with the freshest flowers; whilst beyond, though looking like a part of the room, by reason of the low and open casement, lay the old bowery garden, its ivy gilded by the waning sun.

After tea, and when the sun fell richer still within this little room, and all was hushed around, Lucy brought out the tiny bag, and laid forth upon the table the hard-earned money; one by one, coin by coin, till its circle was large enough, and round enough and fair enough, to be thrice enriched by the scintillating splendour of the sunbeams which fell upon it, blessing it, as it enriched. Mary was astonished at the amount of Lucy's savings.

"My friend," she said, "has told me many times of your industry, care, and excellent work, but I scarcely thought that economy, like what this is proof of, was added. But depend upon it every coin thus earned, and lying here, will teach you a truer and wiser lesson, of what has to be done, and what you can do for our sex, than any written paper, or any arguments of mine. Now let me see what I can add." So saying, she took from her purse five sovereigns (not telling or showing Lucy that but three shillings remained therein) and laid them by the seamstress's little hoard; thus making in the whole the sum of £13 4s.

"Still," continued Mary, willing to divert Lucy's deep emotion, "the matter is yet difficult. The passage money will be at the very least £14, then there is some sort of outfit needful, however poor a one it may be, and then to live whilst it is preparing. Therefore there is still something for us to do, though I scarcely see how. But come with me." So saying, and leading the seamstress by the hand, as if she were blind, for Lucy's deep feelings, true and sterling as they were, were not to be overcome or subdued, even by the angel strategy of this great heart, Mary Austen took her out of the room, up the old staircase, and into a trim bed-chamber, to the side of a small painted chest of drawers. These, one by one, she opened bidding, as she did so, Lucy to uncover her face, to see that on their well-filled tops, lay linen, and flannel, and gowns, which were to be hers. "And you will accept them, I am sure, without pain, when you thus see that with such well-filled drawers I cannot miss them," spoke Mary, with a smile, in reply to some remark of Lucy's, "and accept them with the knowledge that though past my wearing, that they are at least cleanly and in order by their lying here, and will serve till you have better." So saying, this busy, noble, loving, little creature, her face beaming with happiness, went to and fro, carrying the things to a table, so as to place them in a bundle, whilst quite unconscious that more than once as she moved away, or displaced the things, that the cloth or paper, placed between her gift and her own possesions, and turned incidentally aside for the instant, had displayed to the seamstress's quick eye the real secret, that papers, old gowns, and odds and ends, made up the show meant so kindly to deceive! Yet, as it is said by mathematicians, that the minutest cause, or particle, or principle, once set in motion, goes onward infinitely, through the ages, and through the universe, gradually augmented by a million causes, which bear to it affinity; so it may be that these self-denying charities of earth, however small, minute, or classed with humble things, may go on hymning their bright-winged way throughout the universe, till joined by a million likenesses as pure, and good, may in some world of beauty and radiance, yet undreamt of by mortal man, meet the first mover; and flocking round him, as vernal airs the spring, tend and wait on him, as ministering spirits, till heaven infuses all divine things into one!

Lucy had tact enough, however, to conceal her knowledge, and to hide it in her heart, as prophets the sacred rule they guide their souls by. Still she was deeply moved, and kneeling down, as Mary sat to rest at the foot of the bed, buried her face upon the lady's lap.

"What can I do, what can I do for you in return?" she reiterated.

"Nothing," replied Mary, as she folded the seamstress's hands within her own, "only let you and I, in such several ways as belong to us, be truthful and serviceable to our own sex; for they need it, they do indeed."

When the needlewoman was calmer, they went down stairs together; and here Lucy spoke of her trouble about Peg, and her own sister, and added, that as regarded the small balance of money now needed, Mr. O'Flanagan's master would perhaps befriend her.

"Though I am the last person to ask a favour for myself," said Mary, "I am the best of supplicators for another; and as I know Mr. Fortescue to be both a good, a kind, and a very wealthy old man, I will call and ask to see him personally, if you like, and if you will ascertain from his servant if he admits strangers. Of this, you can send me word by letter to-morrow; for I have no further means of assisting you. I am not rich; I think I have already told you so."

With many grateful tears Lucy bade this little country home farewell, and hastened to the bird-fancier's as soon as she reached town. As she expected O'Flanagan was there, taking "bird's eggs," and leaning with his one elbow on the counter, before the large family-cage, before described, in which, as Brutus had predicted, five newly fledged little Sweets were warm within the nest, Mr. and Mrs. Sweet roosting quietly by.

"There didn't I tell you," exclaimed Brutus, triumphantly, when his first greeting of Lucy was over, "ain't I a man of my word, in saying that there would be five on 'em, and there's that number on 'em exactly, as'll have woices like Sweet, as I know by their chirp already; and won't that give one to me; and one to the counsellor, and one to that dear little woman, as Noseby and O'Flanagan here reverence so amazingly, and leave two to be reared for you, so as in a far away land, what has been made dear to you by death mayn't die quite out, eh? ain't this it?"

Lucy would only bend her head in answer to the old man's kind words, for though these things were trifles now, they would be much greater hereafter; but recovering, she told O'Flanagan of Miss Austen's intention, and asked his opinion thereon. The counsellor's servant received the news, as men do that of forthcoming pleasure or good fortune.

"Of course, dear old master will be pleased," spoke the quaint, though trusty servant, "and help you for the sake of the character of such a lady, I am sure, much better than by any other means of asking, for he has been so taken in by begging letters, as to hardly even believe that one is genuine; and as for me I've too many pensioners, up and down, to like to beg too much. So let her come—let me see—yes, the morning after next, at 10 o'clock; and though I shan't say a word, depend upon it, master shall have on his best black coat, and one of his finest frilled shirts. God bless him." At this point, Mr. Brutus took up the conversation, which soon merged itself into an exciting history, relative to the five young nestlings, of much interest to those immediately concerned, but not to ourselves.

As arranged in the letter written and sent by Lucy, Mary, at ten o'clock on the appointed morning, entered the still and shady courts of the Temple, and in the stillest and shadiest found Mr. Fortescue's chambers. These were on the ground floor, and to be entered without knowing, for O'Flanagan himself stood respectively in the open doorway, and led her into a dusky little antechamber, passing, as she did so, two old men in the hall, who bowed low, looked hard, clearly being amazed as they did so; and whom the authoress, in her astonishment, took to be humble clients, and in nowise Noseby and Twiddlesing, her admirers; she having never heard of either, or in the least imagined, that the one was rearing her a fledgling, which springing from the once miserable needlewoman's bird, would cheer her solitary home, and by the gladness of its song, give her great heart, profound assurances (if such were needed), that poetry cannot die, to those whose ears are open to its great accords by worship through the several forms of good, of truth, or beauty; or that the other, though but a common newsman, wrapped up her printed thought in silver paper. But such is the power of genius; and such the power of truth when relative to truth.

Ushered into a dull, though pleasant room, by reason of its book-lined walls, and its great table covered with many books and papers, an elderly man of shrewd, though kindly countenance, and with the manners of a courtier, accosted her, led her to a seat, and at once, with well-bred courtesy, made her at ease on several points.

"Any business," he said, "relative to female emigration, is at all times interesting to me, but particularly on the present occasion. That you may feel no reluctance to speak of this needy woman, of whom my servant O'Flanagan has said much, let me assure you that I will do what I can to serve her, either through your agency or his; and lastly, you need not hesitate at the presence of this gentleman, Mr. Minwaring, a member of the bar, who is himself going out to South Australia, probably to settle there, and his business here this very morning bearing relation to the subject. Therefore his presence is like my own."

As Mr. Fortescue spoke, Mary looked and saw the stranger standing by the table, occupied with a large map stretched upon it; she therefore proceeded, and went rapidly through the short history of Lucy Dean and of her own intentions. "You can judge, Mr. Fortescue," she continued, "that I conceive colonization to be especially the function of Governments—the colonies furnishing the means—the mother-country the machinery. At present failing this, at least on any scale to warrant the name of systematic colonization, that is, the emigration of classes not of a class; and seeing that all charitable aid for my own sex can be but a palliative, which covers over, but cannot heal, the monstrous social canker, of a condition so mournful and degrading; and whilst any mere charitable emigration fund raised in this country, can do little more than give temporary relief, it appears to me, that particular cases might be so made to operate, as ultimately to effect some able plan of Government intervention. This woman is from Cornwall, as I have said, and she is going to the mining districts of South Australia, where, as I understand, are large masses of male population, with but few women amongst them. Now my idea is, that as she is of good moral character, thrifty and clear-headed, she might, in thus going amongst these men, lead to a better state of things than what now exists; and by inducing the miners to a small monthly self-taxation, raise annually a sum, which offered to such parochial boards of England, as might be willing to cooperate, the effects would be seen, on a small scale, of what colonial funds and Government system might be made to achieve. But more of this hereafter."

"Ay, Madam," spoke Mr. Minwaring, "this is the true, if new, spirit of our times. If one fraction of our middle class women could but think as you do, could but only act up to the half of such thoughts, they might be the newer Ann Hutchinsons of this age, instead of being what Wakefield too truly calls them, 'our countless miserable nuns;' and instead of wearing out a wretched existence here, as ill-paid governesses, musicians, artists, or else wasting life in the mean frivolities, and half starvation of 'gentility,' they would go forth with brave and fearless hearts to teach to sew, to cook, to be wives and mothers, and to be mighty examples to the less taught of their sex. Oh! such a crusade as *this* would carry its influences to a far time."

"I think with you," replied Mary, "and I would pioneer the courageous of my own class, if I could, but I am, unhappily, somewhat in the position of a Government, I can do more good by general action than I could by particular interference, and seeing this to be the case, I must remain content to be amongst the 'countless.'"

"Ha! ha!" laughed Mr. Fortescue, merrily, "not so, dear lady. But let us set forth our needlewoman, and put the chariot wheels thus in motion." So saying, the fine old gentleman would have written Mary a cheque upon Drummonds' for Lucy's use, but Mary stating that her time was much occupied, begged that all arrangements for the needlewoman's voyage might be intrusted to the honest care of O'Flanagan. This being agreed to, she, after some further conversation, withdrew, leaving both gentlemen in unrestrained admiration of her, and O'Flanagan to expatiate at astounding length when called into the library, particularly, as he had the matter of the primula, Mr. and Mrs. Sweet, and family, and Noseby, and the silk paper to digress upon, and then to travel back to the main road.

Matters thus put in train, proceeded rapidly, for the counsellor's servant had mounted his hobby. The sum Mr. Fortescue so kindly added to her savings, afforded Lucy an additional outfit; the parish was generous to Peg, and gave her a small sum for the same purpose; and in less than a week the ship would leave the London Docks. As this time of departure rapidly approached, for most of her outfit was already on board, Lucy's desire to see her sister Nelly grew the more intense; but though for several days she had traversed the town in all directions, and been assisted in her inquiries by the police, she could hear nothing of the unhappy girl; though from circumstances, it was presumed that she still worked for Mrs. Moss.

On this particular evening, the one before the eve of her departure, she sat expecting Mary, who had written to say, that being in town, she might possibly call and bid her farewell; but as the neighbouring clocks had now for some time struck nine, Lucy began to think that the promised visit had been unavoidably postponed till next day, and in this opinion Mr. Fortescue's old servant, who had just entered, concurred.

"But you mustn't take on, and be ill, and with such a deal before you," spoke O'Flanagan, mistaking the real fountain of the needlewoman's tears, "for that dear little lady'll be here to-morrow, I am sure. And as for the rest, think what a deal o' friends you have got. Isn't there dear old master, as is a host in himself, isn't there this dear young lady who has been thinking of you in so many ways; isn't poor Peg as kind as can be; isn't there old Brutus, who has taken care of Sweet, and reared little ones, and built them a great 'sea cage,' as he calls it, with store enough of seed, sugar, and ladies' fingers, for a voyage three times round the world. Isn't there all these, and isn't there me, though a very humble person. Dear me, dear me! you wouldn't cry so if you would only think how hundreds, ay, thousands, have to go forth to battle hardly with life, and with no resource but honest hearts and willing hands."

"Those are not ungrateful tears, Mr. O'Flanagan," still wept the woman, "as I am sure time will prove, but those of anguish for the miserable and the fallen, whom I must leave without the power to save by earnest words. The dead I have bidden farewell, the living I may not." She wept unrestrainedly; and the old man allowed those tears to flow, for he was casuist enough to know that therein lay consolation.

As she thus sat, her face buried in her hands, the door was cast suddenly open by Peg, who tottering, pale as death, and nearly speechless, came towards her mistress with something in her arms, and half-kneeling, laid it upon her lap. Before she could gasp out what she had to say, the movement of what was thus placed on Lucy's knees, a low, short cry, and her own quick ear, and quicker heart, made Lucy comprehend the whole in a moment; and looking down, and pulling rapidly aside the ragged shawl wound round it, she saw it was an infant, Nelly's infant, for it had the same golden hair, the same delicate features, the same promise of beauty which had made Nelly the flower of her home. But for many minutes she was unconscious to all around, though so tenaciously grasping the baby, as to make it impossible for either Peg or O'Flanagan to take it from her arms. As she slowly recovered, and began to comprehend her new position, and this new claim upon her love and duty, it would have been difficult, even for a profound master of the passions to tell, whether grief of joy were paramount, for she laughed and cried by turns, though never for a moment, even whilst the tears rained down, did she cease to press her own lips to the baby's face. As this half incoherent, half impulsive passion waned down, she was glad to find herself alone with little Peg, who, weeping too, was kneeling by her side.

"Won't we be good to it, mum," she sobbed, "won't I nurse it, and take care of it, and do the best I can for it; as I'm sure Miss Nelly would——"

At this name of the unhappy mother, Lucy rose as if to move to the door, but the girl, guessing her intentions, restrained her.

"It's no use you going, missis," she said, "for when the poor cretur put the baby in my arms to bring, she said it would be no use your trying to find her."

"How, when, where——" and the woman's voice was again stayed by incoherent sobs and caresses.

"Why, you see, mum," spoke Peg, "that poor cretur had been sitting on a door-step nigh here for several nights, as I passed her more than once not knowing who she was. But to-night when she had looked round and found no one to be nigh, she hurried up to me and asked if I was the girl Mrs. Moss told her about, and when I said so, she put this dear little cretur in my arms, and bid me bear it safely to you, and to tell you to love it for her sake; and to fancy, its name being Nelly, that it's her again, young, and pure, and good; and here she couldn't say more about it, she cried so, poor thing. But by-and-by, after kissing the baby again and again, she came back to say, that you mustn't try to find her out, as she had taken her path that night and must follow it, and then she bid me go in, and I did not see her again, though I know she went down the street crying a deal, mum."

In a few minutes, O'Flanagan came in again, having at the first mention of Nelly's name, gone in search of her, and now he sat down to share the counsel of the weeping woman.

"I cannot go now," said Lucy, "I cannot take this baby across the ocean, I must remain to keep it from the parish, I——" She stopped, for even in her grief, nature prompted her to what was fine and tender-souled.

O'Flanagan coughed several times, was silent for an instant or two; and then, after taking the baby in his arms, smoothing the ringlets round its forehead, kissing its sleeping eyes, and the pink sea-shell lining of its little hand, he said, "It *shall* go, sich little souls as these, Lucy, wasn't made for parishes and workhouses. No! so if it be a bit more money to pay, it shall go; for though I shouldn't like to ask too much from dear old master, as looking like a liberty taken with one of his dignity, I've got a few pounds by me, and I'll spare enough to plant this little flower in a new soil. And there's to-morrow to settle everything."

It was late that night before the kind old man withdrew, and later still when Lucy, with this new claim upon her love and care, sunk to rest. The early morning brought a hurried note from Miss Austen, to say that Lucy must embark, bear herself through all her cares with fortitude, and that she should be at Gravesend to bid her farewell at the proper time. From this, Lucy concluded that Miss Austen knew something of Nelly and the baby.

As well she might. For coming late that same night in a cab to see Lucy, and alighting at the corner of the narrow street, there approached her, as she came along the pavement, a woman, who after turning to look back several times in a supplicating attitude, hurried past Mary a step or two, and then, still with swifter step, crossed the street towards a narrow lane, which led directly to the broad and flowing river. Her momentary glance, joined with the woman's manner, and the neighbourhood to Lucy's home, led Mary to rightly guess that this was Nelly Dean; and the more convinced of this, as the woman's steps led onward to the river, she hastened after her. This narrow lane or gulley led on to a sort of open wharf or quay, deserted for the night by bargemen and labourers, though still the heavy-laden steamers and the smaller craft passed city-ward on the far-off shore, or in the middle of the stream. It was just that space of time too where evening sinks duskly into night; and little more light was seen than that cast from the steamers on the eddies of the tide, or any sound more loud was heard than the gurgle of the waves upon the wharf bank. Reaching this lonely place unperceived, as she fancied in her mad wildness, the desperate woman cast off her tattered bonnet, and waiting for the instant till a heavy-laden steamer passed by and whose light cast in a flash upon her, for the instant showed the rich golden colour of her hair, as it swept down unfastened on her shoulders, as well as the chalky pallor of her face, she attempted to spring forward as far into the rapid water as she could, but her step between life and death was stayed, and some one, one of her own sex, stood courageously between her and the surging waters.

"Woman," spoke the stern and earnest voice of truth, "the sins of this world need reparation here. What would you do?"

For a moment, the wretched girl, with a sort of blind ferocity, strove to elude the restraining arms, and in the struggle, griped them as a vice its wedge or nail; then as the voice entreated once again, crouched like a hound beneath the keeper's lash; and then at last, all woman, fell weeping down before the feet of her, who of all women, most could save and most could pity!

"My poor one, my unhappy one," spoke Mary, half kneeling too in the fervency of her extreme pity, "I know you, and those you love, and I must save you if I can—come on—"

"Not to Lucy, not to Lucy," wept the girl, "her arms are fitted for my baby, not for me."

"No! by no means that, but you are weak and ill, and must come with me." So saying, she raised up the girl, and led her from the wharf, up the narrow street, and so on till she could call a cab, into which she helped her, and then entered too. But Nelly did not speak another word, or move, except when Mary's ungloved hand touched her drooping hair, her face, or fingers; then, hastily looking up, she took, more than once, the corner of her tattered shawl, and wiped them, as a sculptor wipes a precious piece of alabaster.

Knowing a poor, though respectable person, who let her house to humble lodgers, Mary drove there, procured a room, and had the wretched, half-starved, drooping girl put to bed, and some tea made and given to her. When revived by this, she went in alone and knelt down beside her.

"Though I hope you will think over your rash attempt, and see it so far in its true light as to feel it to be one you cannot make again," said Mary, after a little pause, "though you must live, you must not see Lucy before she sails. It might weaken her resolve, it would possibly do no good, as she will have care enough in taking, and in succouring your infant. Neither could I, as a woman, holding large duties to society, sanction your accompanying your sister, even if circumstances permitted it. But if, after a time, as you are now free from the burden of your child, if when better, and you leave this, you will go for a few months' probation into an asylum, which at my request will instantly receive you; if through this probation you go steadily and well, and diligently improve yourself in such duties as may be needful, you shall come to me, and be my servant; and from every human creature I will conceal the past. Thus giving you fullest power to redeem that past; and fittingly, and womanly in that newer land, take your child, and by that very act of reparation, more nobly and more truly, to your heart. This is it, but faith and love to me must go before."

The girl raised herself feebly on her pillow, not answering for some minutes, only looking on the kneeling figure, as the sculptor in the precious alabaster before him sees the figure of an angel, till grasping Mary's hands in both her fevered ones, she said, "Madam, can you help me to a future by believing—eh?"

"I can most certainly, my poor one."

"Then Madam, believe thus much," and the girl spoke as energetically as a proud, strong man, "that all this sorrow first came about, not through an evil disposition, or a love of finery, but because I who loved all within our poor home as dearly as human creature could, wished to lift them out of the sordid, abject, debasing misery of the needlewoman's life; a life than which London city holds none more dreadful. And in going away with Lawrence's friend, the son of a wealthy organ-builder, under a promise of marriage, I thought to go back, as it was promised, a happy young wife, willing and able to assist them through my husband's goodness. You must believe this, lady—you must believe," she continued, vehemently, "or else leave me to my fate."

"I do believe you," replied Mary, with the firmest voice, "in my inmost soul I believe you, for I know too well, and, in the coming age, men will accredit thus much of mercy to us, that woman's failings spring too often from her nobler self, her weakness from her generosity; and therefore I believe you in my very woman's soul."

The girl did not answer, but bending down, kissed fervently Mary's hand, just as some penitent the garment of the priest, who has said absolving prayers.

Mary presently rose, and laid Nelly's head gently on the pillow, "now you must rest," she said, "for I must go and leave you to the friendly care of this good woman of the house. The day after to-morrow I will see you, and your child, and Lucy, and tell the latter she shall hear good news of you. Now rest, and strive to be contented."

"I am already," whispered Nelly. And, soothed by Mary's words of charity and mercy, the girl nestled to the pillow, like an infant to its rest.

On the morrow but one, the great city river bounded out freshly to the mightier sea, with flowing tide, and bathed in golden light. And, as if impatient to be onward, the stately emigrant ship, crowded by its living freight, bent its sails seaward. Amongst the boats which left the shore, filled with the leave-taking friends of emigrants was one containing Mary Austen and O'Flanagan, who had walked over to the little village the night before and offered her his escort; whilst Brutus Twiddlesing, entrusting his shop to a neighbour, preferred sailing down the river so far, to see, as he said, how "the young'uns bore the woyage."

So there, when she had climbed the ship's ladder, Mary Austen beheld on a spare space of the deck, Lucy Dean, the old bird-fancier, and the "great sea-cage," and Peg with the baby, holding its face seaward to catch the genial freshness of the summer air, whilst in an old basket, placed so as to catch full air and light, stood the primula, full of life for another year, though its stalks and leaves were now sere and drooping.

For some minutes the women stood side by side incapable of speech, leaving old Brutus to deliver much good advice concerning the treatment of the little feathered family, and to say his honest parting adieus; and for O'Flanagan to repeat what Mr. Fortescue has last said, and to falter out the farewell he could not speak. Then Mary Austen, womanly and noble in the end, as at the beginning, forgot all differences of class, of rank, of breeding; and true to the mighty hand of Nature set upon her, and whilst folding the weeping needlewoman to her heart, whispered, "of Nelly, you will hear good and hopeful words," and, then pressing her lips to the baby's face, retreated eye-blind and drooping till led by O'Flanagan. But all was not grief, for as she trod the last step of the ship's ladder, Mr. and Mrs. Sweet gave out in unison their sweetest carol, whilst the summer wind blew sweeping from the shore; and on the shore, she turned, and saw Lucy, though still bending like a Niobe, waving farewell, as some angel to a spirit of higher and diviner mould, returning on its mission of high and holy purpose!

A happy and prosperous voyage was made, with fair winds and flowing sails; and that day four months Lucy landed in Southern Australia.

Although Lucy bore no recommendatory letters, and paying for her own passage, did not come within the class of free emigrants, she was most generously and kindly received by those resident ladies of Adelaide, who, since 1847, have been formed into a Committee, for the noble purpose of welcoming strangers of their own sex to their shores, and securing them honourable treatment till situations can be obtained, or their journeys to the settled inland districts commenced. But better than recommendatory letters was the noble and unprompted character given of her by both the captain, surgeon, and steward of the emigrant ship, and also by the several emigrant women who came before the ladies. "It wasn't so much that she was good to the sick, or gave a helping-hand to the doctor, times and often," spoke the captain, with all the fervour of his honest heart, in his rough seaman's speech, "as lifting the women's hearts above board when a bit downcast, and keeping 'em to duty and regular watches. Why, with that woman at my elbow, and our surgeon as good as he is, I'd sail round the world with a ship-load of termagants, and be bound to bring 'em all, with fair-weather tempers into port. And that, without offence to you ladies, is saying much." But little did that brave seaman dream, little thought these admirable ladies, what it was that had moved and animated this stern woman's will; or that across the broadest ocean of the world, in the quaintest, the smallest, the simplest of country parlours, was the guileless, child-like creature, who had brought this stern power into force, and this divinely through humanity, through charity, and through womanly sympathy. But then, as I have said, Genius *is* divine, and what it gives birth to, eternal in action; for as it were, nature receives at once into her soul what thus is spoken through the blessed inspiration of her own matchless priesthood.

One sorrow however there was, and that was a sad one, for though Mr. and Mrs. Sweet chirped immensely, and clearly liked the new land, and their little-ones were now clothed with the most golden and downy of feathers, tiny Nelly, the little bud and flower, drooped from day to day, particularly from the time the ship had entered warmer latitudes. But even here a little seed-corn set upon the ocean brought a harvest on the land; for a poor Irish girl, to whom Lucy had been very kind on shipboard, came to her on the second evening after landing, bringing a fine sturdy young Irishwoman with her.

"And isn't it that you've been kind to me sisther Kitty here, mistress," spoke the woman, after a multiplicity of Irish curtseys, "for bad luck to the Irish parish as sint us, they put us in different ships, and isn't I in good health now I've rested three weeks on land, and isn't me little Pathric (the Lord be wid 'm) a hearty babe as can be, be sparing a drop; and isn't my own husband got a good masther in the very far-away hills ye'r going to; so give me the babe, by our Blessed Mother I'll make it like my little Pathric, as hale as an Irish shamrock, and leave the reckoning till the saints make it." So saying then and there, she took the almost dying baby from Lucy's lap, bared her breast, fed it, and from that hour, it so gradually revived, as to enable the little band of emigrants to set forth on their journey by the return bullock-drays, which had brought copper ore from the distant hills to the port of Adelaide.

Nothing could have been, or was more propitious than the season to the emigrants. They had left their own land in the prime of summer, and now the same season, or rather earlier summer, though a degree hotter and drier than their own, met them on the beautiful park-like plains and sheep-runs which lie to the north and east of Adelaide. These plains, overspread with grass, and lightly timbered with the beautiful mimosa, gum, and acacia trees, soon led to the cooler regions of that chain of hills which, stretching from the extreme southern point of Cape Jervis on the south, and extending as far north as has yet been explored, contain those vast mineral resources, which will yet make Australia not only a wonder amongst nations, but will give, through the power of using metals in architecture, an impetus to a new and forthcoming era in the arts, unseen yet but by the few who have a ken into the coming ages. These hills, more sterile than the plains, though often covered by what is locally called "scrub," or low bushes, were yet generally clothed with beautiful evergreen forests, and the stringy-bark tree and pine, enclosed valleys and plains of surpassing beauty, and where the streams and creeks flowed on, unaffected from their situation by the summer heats.

There were about forty bullock-drays in all; some piled up with merchandise for the miners, and the others devoted to the emigrants and their scanty goods; the most comfortable one, temporarily covered with canvas, as a guard against the sun, and furnished with seats, being devoted to Lucy's little company, and the Irish woman and her sister. Beyond those women and the two children, there were not more than three females in the whole band that thus made its way to the hills; the rest, consisting of the dray-drivers, five or six miners returning to their work after a week's leave of absence, and overseers had secured on the agreement of tribute and tut-work, as in the Cornish mines, or as labourers at yearly wages and weekly rations, as given to stockmen and shepherds. Lucy Dean, as it might be said, was, with the exception of a male emigrant or two, going forth alone into the wilderness, with nothing but her own stern will, her womanly resolves, and the words of that sweet soul across the widest ocean in the world, to encourage and nerve her heart; all the rest had a prop to lean upon,—Peg called her mistress—and the baby nestled to her heart. The first motive which had influenced her choice of seeking work in these remote mining districts was, that many miners of her own native Cornwall worked there, particularly one of the name of Benjamin Holdon, who had been bred in her native village, and was well known to her parents. From this man's family she had heard some weeks before she sailed, and thus furnished with the exact locality of his work, bore with her the humble letters and presents of his far-off friends, and in the full assurance, while honest Ben had a penny, he would befriend her with the whole might of his strong Cornish arms. But another cause made her journey still more definite. The agent in Adelaide, to whom she bore Mr. Minwaring's kind letter of recommendation, had immediately hired her as a sort of housekeeper and general superintendent to a mining overseer and north-countryman, named Elliott, who, with a body of expert miners, chiefly Welsh and Cornish, was now working a copper mine of unexampled richness, in a point still further north than the Burra Burra mines. To this place the chief of the bullock-drays belonged, and the chief portion of the emigrants were destined.

Whilst yet upon the plains (for a somewhat lengthened route was taken, in order to make the journey less fatiguing to the women), they found the heartiest welcome at the homesteads of the outlying colonists, whose vast extent of grazing-land, corn-fields, and orchards, gave the once-starving woman a true idea of this glorious land. The first night of the journey that she sat down to one of those hospitable tables, and saw set forth as common fare, the primest joints of beef and mutton, poultry, wildfowl, pastry, and delicious fruit, of which all present might partake in the spirit which nature destined, and saw scraps sent forth, and petted dogs fed with what, in her own land, human creatures, though they worked eternally, could never earn, nor see, nor taste, the most iron tears of her hard, earnest life, stole down, and only nerved her, by the blessing of the more prodigal bread she tasted, to strive that the sad life of many of her sex might, for the reward of labour done, eat and enjoy, and no longer curse the privilege which made them human mothers. Beyond the bounds of cultivation, there was still the same power to welcome, though with coarser fare. In the stockman's hut was always abundance of damper (the local name for the bread in common use), mutton, beef, and tea, and a good wood fire if they were cold, whilst often was added to the meal a wild turkey shot down on the adjacent plains.

At length after a somewhat toilsome ascent through the forests of stringy-bark and other trees, and the brush which covers many of the hills, the party passed the mining settlement of Burra Creek, and entered at sunset through a gorge in the hills, one of those rich valleys which lie round Mount Bryan. Some of Mr. Elliott's miners, who had heard of the approach of the drays from a passing stockman, had set forth to meet the little party, and now encountered them as the rich undulating valley opened to their sight. Few of those who have lived an entire life in old populated countries can fancy the hearty zeal with which the remote colonist greets a stranger; and this was the case at present. After the miners had hailed their comrades, and welcomed the male emigrants on foot by a hearty shake of the hand all round, the foremost of them approached the tilted dray which sheltered Lucy, for the arrival of women in these remote districts is a rare event, and one always of interest. But when the first stalwart miner, who raised the tilt, cried out with much emotion—"Here is not only women here, but one of the truest and best, out of our dear old Cornish land;" the excitement of some eight or ten of the men knew no bounds, and Lucy was forced to descend from the dray, in order to receive their welcomings, and to really let them see that she was no mere Cornish sprite, but a real living Cornish woman. At this instant, as most always, the little budding Nelly was in her arms, as beautiful as health and nature can make a baby, and on its little dimpled, lovely hand, the deeply-moved miner laid his finger. The trivial movement asked a question which his lips could not.

"No Ben, no," spoke Lucy at once, and with a firmness not to be mistaken, for she well knew that all power over these men, lawless as perhaps they might be, depended on the sense they would have of her moral worth, "not mine, I am unmarried, but my sister Nelly's child, and she being poor, I've brought it as a Cornish winter-rose to rear. No, I have come as Mr. Elliott's superintendent and servant, and the letters I have for him will testify to my character, for this is my little niece." She said these latter words loud enough for all to hear.

"Nelly, Nelly's baby," and a change stole over the face of the great-limbed miner, which even the hue of his sun-dyed face could not hide; but he said no more, only taking the baby into his arms as lightly as if it were a feather, bore it down the rich swarded mountain-side, wonderously gazing on the beauty of its infant face.

The valley was such a one as few could see unmoved, for from it stretched, both east and west, through low breaks in the hills, almost limitless ranges of the finest agricultural soil, particularly towards the east; whilst this valley itself, of considerable surface area, was threaded by several creeks of fine water, which were not only of large service to the miners for washing the ore, but, falling together into one pool, added to the beauty and value of the settlement. The hills, mostly of small elevation, were clothed with the greenest sward, only varied by belts of forest trees, above which invariably cropped out their rocky summits. The ore of the few mines yet worked lay so near the surface, as to have yet scarcely needed the sinking of shafts of any depth, and these being situated on the finest acclivity of the valley, amidst low scrub and their riches exposed wherever a lode had been struck through, gave as the setting sun fell on the ore, the vision of a magician's palace, wrought out of porphyry and gold.

In a line with the mines, and sheltered by a lovely grove of mimosa and she-oak trees which sloped to the pool were raised the miners' tents—the only buildings yet erected being some wooden sheds for the bullocks, and a long low, but roomy house, built of a sort of quartz picked out in forming the mine-shafts. This house fronted the lake, and a rude garden had already been formed at the rear. The sinking sun but faintly tinged the rocky summits of the highest hills, when the drays reached this place, and a tall, reserved-looking man, of thirty-eight or forty years of age, came out, and welcoming Lucy and her little company with a few brief words, invited her in, and ordered one of the miners, who evidently performed the office of cook, to put fresh damper on the embers, fry some beef in the ever-useful article of the colonists—the frying-pan, and brew some tea, which is invariably done in a large tin kettle—for tea in the Australian colonies usurps the place of all other ordinary beverages.

When Mr. Elliott had read the agent's letters and the recommendatory ones Lucy had brought, and found that she had been hired as his "help," he at once gave up this dwelling to her use, and that of Peg and the baby, but not before he had seen a hospitable meal set forth on the rude table of roughly-hewn wood. When, however, she was rested and refreshed, the baby washed and put to sleep in the swinging hammock which had formed his bed, and Peg gone for awhile to the tent assigned to the Irishwoman and her husband, the overseer came back again, and thrusting a fresh log of serewood in the fire, which soon blazed up like a torch, he sat down beside it.

"Well," he said, after he had sat awhile, and in a half satirical tone which grated harshly on the trembling woman's ear, "the agreement is at thirty-five English pounds yearly and your rations, eh?"

"Yes, Mr. Elliott, these were the terms settled between me and the agent to whom I took Mr. Minwaring's letter."

"Well," continued Elliott, in the same dry Scotch tone, "that man has held the commission so long, as to make your coming somewhat a surprise, for I began to think, either no useful women were left, or that no one of reputable character would venture in these far wilds. But I'm glad of it, though your life will be a hard one."

"I'm used to work, and hard work too," she innocently replied.

"I do not allude to your usefulness," he answered, with another of those Scotch smiles, which implied doubt more than trust, "but that before to-morrow sunset, there'll be a score [of] men and more, all comely and thrifty, ready to make you a wife, for reputation and decent conduct are priceless things anywhere, but especially in the wilderness."

"This is thinking meanly, nay harshly, of me, Sir," replied Lucy, hastily, in a voice which implied that the overseer had before him a more heroic-souled woman than he imagined, "before I have been tried."

"Well, well," he added, hastily, "if you are the description of woman that I think might largely influence the class of men I have around me, I shall say that I have not waited in vain. But recollect I shall be somewhat a stern judge, for time or change has not taken from my soul the influence wrought upon my boyhood by a pure and noble mother, who though dead for years, is still my better angel."

"As all mothers ought to be to the souls of men," said Lucy, "but be as stern and watchful as you will, I trust to go through unscathed, as an easy task to me, who have had the last extremity of poverty and hunger gnawing at the heart to tempt and to deceive; but I have no thought, at least at present, about marriage, and you would accept this for the honest truth, if you knew my history as Heaven knows it."

"Well, well," he said, in the same tone, "everything is in your favour as a 'help;' and your will, if truthful, shall be law, but I am sufficiently Scotch to wait for the fruit of acts, before I give heed to words; it is my way and you must not be disconcerted by it."

He said no more on this subject, but after giving Lucy somewhat an outline of the duties required of her, and the character of the people she would have to deal with, he withdrew. He had scarcely closed the door before its rude wooden latch was re-lifted, and Ben Holdon, with a timid foot, came in, and went and sat down in silence on the overseer's seat. There was a change in his manner of so singular a kind as to immediately attract Lucy's attention, and make her ask if the letters she had brought had contained ill news.

"Not a word, but what such a messenger as you should bring across the sea. But I need ask you a question, and you won't be long answering it, eh? but give a plain sort of answer: Yes or no!"

Lucy, still more surprised, looked up, and saw how earnest was his meaning. At length, hesitating and faltering in his voice, even whilst he spoke, he said abruptly, neither looking at her, but rather with his gaze fixed on vacancy, "Is Nelly married?"

For a minute Lucy hesitated. She must speak, yet the truth unfolded a degradation; she therefore, for some moments, sat with her face bent down upon her hands, and from their shelter so faintly whispered "no," that none but an ear painfully listening could have heard it. But it was heard, and wrought such an effect, that for any other reason than the true one, would have seemed marvellous; for in an instant roused from the sort of sullen fear with which he had asked the question, he had risen, and now stood before her wiping the cold sweat from his brow, but speaking cheerfully and with much feeling.

"Lucy," he said, in the broad vernacular of his boyhood, which only proved that recurrence to the past, brought with it the old tongue, "I always loved that little'un; many and many time when she was quite a baby, I, though then a little lad, crept to the cradle to look in her face; many and many time did I bring her posies i'th' spring, and lay on the garden bench for her, where she was so fond of playing, pretty thing; and many and many time an I 'ticed her, when I grew a bit bigger, down to the shore to get her pink and yellow shells, and build her a house i' the sand—ay, I loved that little'un as I never loved anything else— ay, and a sore sorrow it were when thee all packed up and went so far away. But a sorer time than that, was when some folks on our village, as had bin away, brought word that you was all on you becoming grand there away in Lond'n; that Lawrence had got apprenticed, and Nelly were to be married to the organ-master's son; so when I heard this last, I took on sadly, and couldn't settle to no'thing, for every hope in my laddish heart was gone, so wi' the bit o' money I'd bin sav'n, for ye see I'd laid in my mind, that the little'un I so dearly loved should have a tidy Cornish house to come to when we got married, I came out here, and thank God for the thought as was put into my mind to do it, for I've prospered, as I never could a done in the old country, as I and my partner got nigh £500 on the year's 'tribute,' for Elliott, though a few worded man like, is as straight for'ard as man can be, and one as you'll always get more from than you 'xpect. And so Lucy Dean, as things be this way, I'll marry Nelly; that I will, and make an honest husband, if ever [an] Englishman did."

Lucy looked up as the fine honest fellow thus spoke, and took his hand. "Ben," she said, "Nelly is, as you know a mother, and her life an unhappy one, and you can scarcely make her your wife, though it is hard for a sister to say so. But I'll be honest, Ben, though even Nelly be the sufferer—"

"Tut, tut," said the miner, impatiently, "dunna I often when I'm out in the forest, or on the hills a bit, find a bright flower, as the opossum, or may be that the wild dog has trampled under foot, and han'a I stopped and lifted it up on a branch, so as it might get sun and air once more; and han'a I, if I passed that way again, found it bright and shining, making the shady forest beautiful, as if a foot had never crushed it to the sod. And mayn't the lass come all right agin now the baby be away, for hunger and poverty be sore tempters, Lucy Dean; and thee and thine come on too honest a stock to be bad by natur."

"God bless and thank you, Ben," added Lucy, fervently, "what you say is true, and Nelly is by this time so far out of all way of sin, as to be with one of the purest and sweetest ladies in the world; and so if it be as we wish, you shall have your own way, but not without,—no, Ben, not if it saved her from the parish coffin."

"Thank, thank you," replied the miner, "all'll come right with Nelly, that I know, I'll answer for her. So that's all settled, and I'm your brother henceforth, and you shall not only have a hundred pounds to send for her, when you think the right time's come, but you must let the little'un learn to call me father—you must let me be a building a house, it shall call 'home,' and I'll make benches and tables, and dig a bit o' garden plot and rear flowers, every thing o' which, as it's made or grows, we'll both on us teach the little'un to say and think is because 'mother's coming.'"

"God bless and thank you, Ben," repeated Lucy, many times, "let us hope Nelly will deserve what you so kindly and so nobly mean. As for the baby, let it call you what it will, I shall teach it to love and reverence you for your honest truth."

This conversation proved one of large results—it gave Lucy, in the purest sense, a friend willing and able to protect her—and it gave hope, and a motive to labour, to one of the finest manly hearts which ever beat in English bosom. Lucy knew this and prayed that Nelly might deserve it.

Keenly observant and far-sighted, as a seer, Donald Elliott soon saw that Lucy Dean was both a virtuous and industrious woman, and well fitted for the work that lay before her. He therefore selected two dozen men from the body of the newly-arrived emigrants, some of whom were carpenters and miners by trade, and set them to work upon houses sufficiently large to replace entirely the use of tents, which had been only erected whilst labour was scarce. As the population now gathered together amounted nearly to one hundred persons, and space was plentiful, one large building was erected for the men to sit and take their meals in; another, somewhat raised from the ground on a framework underneath it, was built as a dormitory for the single men; a third for the purpose of a kitchen, bakehouse, washhouse, larder, and dairy; a fourth as a dwelling for such men as had wives; and a fifth, which included a business office, a room for Donald Elliott, another all nicely fitted with store closets for Lucy, a fourth room in which the men might assemble if they liked, and bedrooms above these reached by separate staircases, for Elliott and for Lucy, her little servant, and the baby.

Though wood and stone were so abundant, and every man so interested in the progress of the houses, as to give a hand's help each day after his own hard labour in the mine, even including Donald Elliott himself, these houses and such rude furniture as was absolutely necessary, in order to make them habitable, could only be barely finished by the time the rainy season set in— that is the middle of our May—which, though the winter of Australia, is yet genial, and somewhat like an English spring. When these various apartments were ready [for] her use, stores were brought from Adelaide by the return drays, and Lucy began to introduce something like order into the little settlement. It was true she was supplied with the direction Mary Austen had written for her use on almost every conceivable point; but these would have served to little purpose unless she had possessed some practical knowledge as to baking, cooking, washing, and keeping a house in order. Whilst they had to prepare them themselves, or only assisted by the two or three miserable useless women, whom some of the miners had married or brought from the convict settlements, there had been only two meals a day, one before the men left for the mine in the morning, and one on their return at night; but now, as spring went on, and Lucy became gradually possessed of the appliances of an ample kitchen, a large wood fire, and cooking utensils brought by the drays from Adelaide, a good meal was prepared, of which all in the little settlement partook at noonday. This regularity in partaking, and variety and change of food soon effected a marked change in the condition of the men; for sheep and bullocks were easily obtained from the adjacent sheep runs, wild fowl, turkeys, and kangaroos, were abundant in the district, the few fowls and pigs of the colonists increased rapidly, the four cows, three brought from the stockmen since Lucy's arrival, gave abundant milk, and now the garden, stretching far along the rich alluvial soil, and constantly added to by the labours of the miners, gave, as the spring advanced, abundance of the finest vegetables, including cabbages, peas, beans, turnips, onions, leeks, carrots, cauliflowers, broccoli, celery, beet, artichokes, Scotch-kale, horseradishes, parsley, radishes, lettuces, spinach, and many others; whilst both the sweet and water melon thrived and gave an enormous abundance of the finest fruit, when in season in the month of February. The fruit trees and vines were yet too lately planted to give other result than extreme promise when fully grown; but the raspberry canes, the gooseberry and apricot trees, and the strawberry beds, were hardly outmatched in prolificness by the growth of melons. Thus, with the exception of grain, which could be brought at a cheaper rate from the nearest outlying settlement, than grown by those whose labour was otherwise so valuable, the mining community soon possessed the blessing of varied and abundant food; which Lucy, aided by Peg, the Irish woman, and her sister, and such helps as had come to the settlement with the last batch of emigrants, used with provident care, and with much skill, as practice increased her knowledge. Previous to her arrival, and whilst living in tents, the miners had suffered more or less from cutaneous diseases, owing to the want of clean and dry linen; mining labour always inducing profuse perspiration from the skin. But one day a week was now set apart as a washing day, and aided by plenty of home-manufactured soap, and a lye made from the burnt ashes of a particular plant, abundant on the hills around, two-thirds of the day accomplished the needful labour for the week; and as the white garments dried on the mossy acclivities of the valley, an English traveller issuing suddenly from the gorges of the hills, might have mistook this for a home scene in the old country, and not one in a far outlying region of Australia. Thus progressed the bodily needs of the colonists. As these men, many as rude as the wilderness can make man, began individually to recognise the change in their life Lucy had wrought, their respect grew in proportion. The clear, fresh-smelling dormitory, their excellent comfortable meals, their clean and tidy shirts and stockings were productive of hourly fruit, and even the dozen or two, who, resting on the strength of their savings, or personal qualification, had at first been bold enough to make Lucy offers of marriage, would now have been abashed to think of such a thing. In place of this, respect and liking grew together; and it was a touching, sacred thing, as their rude nature visibly softened under the pure and blessed influence of this noble woman, and indirectly under the blessing of a nobler influence still, to see them alone or in bands go to her neat room after the day's labour was over, to beg a book, to ask advice, to talk with her, or to take her some little offering—a rare mineral from the mine, a flower from the woods, a piece of furniture of their own constructing; or to ask her, where they were poor scholars, to read to them, or write for them, "home" letters.

But as time wore on, and the rich sun of summer gleamed upon the wilderness, the greatest glories of these men's hearts were two—that was Nelly, and the thriving family of the Sweets—so thriving, that both old and young had built little nests, and reared a brood—the elder Sweets, one of six— and the younger, one of five; and as no pip or other complaint incommoded these youngsters, and the Australian climate thrived with them amazingly, there were some fifteen of this little golden family chirping and singing in the gladness of the sun, and flitting from room to room, never acknowledging their cage as home till evening cast its shadows on the valley. But Nelly was the flower; how many times each evening those little pink shell-like palms were kissed, I hardly know, or those little golden curls waved in the far-up mountain air; but though one carried her here, and another there; though one caught her gay-coloured birds, another made her a little cart to ride in, a third dolls and baby houses, she took to none of them as she did to stalwart Ben; but now constantly with him through these summer evenings (for he had commenced building a cottage on one of the sweetest acclivities of the valley), she sat on his thick jacket and chattered whilst he worked, for she began to talk, and he took upon himself the office of instructor; and when at last, after a multiplicity of attempts, the monosyllable of "dad" was accomplished, his joy knew no bounds.

Lucy had drawn the first quarter of her yearly wages, and sent it, through the agency of Elliott, to Miss Austen, for Nelly's use; and now that the whole year was expired, and she received the balance, she prepared for a journey to Adelaide, the drays going to the adjacent port of Gawler with ore. Her objects were several; first, Peg's marriage—now so changed, as would have led her to be unrecognised in the far-off region of Aldgate—with one of the miners; next, to dispatch a large sum, which she had collected amongst the miners, for the assistance of those distressed women whom she had promised to help as soon as she had power, and of whom a list had been left with Miss Austen, in case any method arose of befriending them; and lastly, to select and lay in important stores for the use of the little colony.

The journey to and fro proved a most prosperous one, Peg returning with her mistress the happiest of young wives, and with one-half of a dray filled with toys for the baby. From this time another season rolled majestically on, with the same gladness of the sun, the same eternal stars, the same blue upon the ocean, the same verdure on the sod; and the valley thrived in peace and plenty, with this only change, that whilst Ben was still furnishing his house with a great amount of chairs and tables, made of acacia-wood, and tamed tiny Nelly a whole family of little kangaroos and parrots, his comrades began to build similar tenements, here and there, as taste directed. At length, in about a year from the date of Lucy's visit to Adelaide, news was brought that some thirty female emigrants had arrived in port, and awaited their transit across the plains. The commotion in the colony can scarcely be conceived, nor was it lessened when further news came, that Elliott's agent, acting on instructions long received, had dispatched them in the care of a party who was coming on a visit of exploration to that part of Australia. At length Elliott and some stockmen, who had set forth to be their guide through the hills, returned at the head of a cavalcade of drays and horsemen; and Lucy, no long while after, welcomed into the miners' common dining-room, those famished women, who, not more than three years before, had sued from her a penny or bit of bread, as if things of life and death; and who now, weeping around her in love and joy, told her new glory of that divine heart so far away across the widest ocean of the world. How she had sought them out, and added others to their number; and how, aided by Mr. Fortescue's purse, and O'Flanagan's philanthropy, a home had been raised for them, where, whilst they had been fed and sheltered, an experienced matron had ably instructed them in cookery, housewifery, and other useful things. One only disappointment was there to Lucy's heart, and that was that Nelly was not amongst the rest; but then she had not hinted the matter to Miss Austen. Ben drooped, however, sadly under the matter; but presently he took again to his furniture, and the kangaroos, and to add to tiny Nelly's vocabulary.

It was well that the miners had followed brave Ben's example in house-building, for in about a month, thirty courtships had proceeded so harmoniously and so prosperously, as to call into force the holy offices of one of the gentlemen lately from Adelaide; and, accordingly, on the Sunday morning before his departure, the agent having fortunately forwarded to Elliott a sufficient amount of wedding rings, and a sort of rude chapel having been now for some time built, this good priest performed the onerous duty of saying thirty marriage services in one,—and prayed that olive branches might spring up around the table of the mighty land, heaped up with corn, with oil, with wine.

These marriages were so prosperous in result, and became so noised far and wide, by the agency of stockmen, that Lucy's long-held intention was half assisted into accomplishment. She, therefore, now lost no time in seeking, though miles away across the plains, or over the adjacent chain of hills, those hordes of men who wrought at the lead and copper mines of South Australia. Sometimes her journey occupied weeks; sometimes she was accompanied by Elliott or Holdon; but oftener, when the journey was remote, by some of the natives, who, in return for kindness done them by her hand, protected her as a sacred thing. She told these miners of the good done by those who worked under Elliott; that their small contributions (comparatively to their earnings) had brought to them, that in that land were countless women worthy to be such, who, setting aside hunger and misery, and destitution, drooped and pined away, and died, because their natural mission had been unaccomplished; she told them of sterility and barrenness, where both were negatives against the hand of nature; she said, "here is land where food rots, where verdant pathways are untrod, where sweet winds soothe no ear, nor waft no cheek, where cradles rock not, and where baby hands pluck not one of myriad-painted flowers; and yet where you, as men, pine in mournful solitude,—no voice to cheer you, no hand to raise you, no tear to drop for you, nothing to make you less sensual, or bring you nearer Heaven! And yet your money lies unused—much of it—so spare a little, and we will call it a HUMAN BRIDGE TAX; say sixpence a week each man—not much alone—but vast as a whole; for it will dry countless eyes, and make human mothers out of those whose only office yet has been to weep!"

Not contented with this appeal to one class of men alone, she wrote and sent letters to the newspapers of Adelaide, Port Philip, Melbourne, and Sydney; she appealed to the Colonial Government, and to the wealthy and industrious of her own sex, and so successfully, as soon to bring large aggregate sums into the colonial banks of these far-apart towns. This was accomplished in one year's time from the time of commencement; and now she prepared for a voyage to her own country, there to whisper to the dear ear and heart of genius, what woman's promise unto woman yet shall be. None liked her to go; but her slightest will was a law.

It was now the most glorious portion of the Australian spring, and the night before her departure, there rode into the settlement a gentleman, unattended except by his servant, and two natives, who had served as guides. He sought Elliott, made known his name as Minwaring, and then saw Lucy at his own request alone.

He had been cultivating, he told her, a very large tract of park-like country, lying between Sydney and Bateman Bay, on the eastern coast of Australia, that he held an official appointment, direct from the colonists themselves, and was greatly interested in the subject of emigration. That he had seen her several letters to the colonists in Sydney, Port Philip, and Melbourne papers; that he instantly recollected her name, as the person of whom Miss Austen had spoken of, so nobly in his presence, to Mr. Fortescue, and for whom he himself had written recommendatory letters. That, making inquiry, he had found this to be really the fact—he had lost no time in making the coast voyage from Sydney to Adelaide, that he had travelled from thence across the country by the dray-route, and now sought her, to see if he could aid her in any way relating to the object of her letters.

"No, Sir, thank you," replied Lucy, "by the time I reach Adelaide, the collected sum will be placed in the bank there to Miss Austen's account; and to her I shall bear the bills, untrammeled by one condition. I am but her servant, yet I will be a truthful one, though I believe the sum is destined to be divided into three portions; one of which will be offered to such populated parishes, as will consent each one to give an outfit to a certain number of pauper females; a second will be applied to the partially free emigration of middle class women, such as governesses, and the needy daughters of professional men; and the third will be applied to the establishment of a permanent school, near London, for the instruction of females of the lower class, who have asked the boon of free, or, partially free emigration."

This conversation touching Mary Austen, once commenced, proved a fertile and lengthened one; and before Elliott entered to bid his guest to supper, Lucy was possessor of a secret destined to be of importance.

There was little rest for that usually strong, self-reliant heart that night, for a few hours would separate her from the endeared scene of her happiest years. It was at the first blush of the sun that Lucy rose, and dreaming, went forth into the valley. Here stealing in the shadows of the hills before even the miners were astir, and gaining the summit of a lovely acclivity looking towards the limitless plains, she sat down upon the fragrant turf, which, enriched by the opening glory of the early sun, was tinged with softest, yet glorious light. And here so sitting, all her foregone life passed in review before her like a continuous picture; her sorrows about Nelly, the death of Lawrence, and her mother—her breadless home, sheltered poor Sweet in the tattered apron; and from that one bright and shining face ever being a portion of it; till, like her eyes, her soul went onward with the light she tracked, and resting on the far-up mountain crags, were one within the glory settled there.

How long she rested there she scarcely knew; how long her tears rained down she could not tell; but at last her hands were taken both together, and looking, she found Elliott sitting by her side. She did not wonder—there had been much in his manner, for many months, that had prepared her for this.

"What is said at last proves more than what is said at first," he spoke in his old way, "and we have acted together too long in peace, in unanimity, and trust, to misunderstand one another now—so let the image of a pure and earnest mother fade somewhat in the light of one, who of all others, will make a pure and earnest wife. We want no courtship, or what people call one—ours has been one, continuous from the beginning—we will get married Lucy, at Adelaide."

"I answer as frankly," said Lucy, "that I will be your wife, but not till I return. The tie I leave behind might take away some portion of the duty and the truth I owe to one, but for whom, Elliott, I should have never seen this land, or you, or anything of good or gladness. But I will be as much to you in heart as if we were married at this minute, and when I land at Sydney, where with Mr. Minwaring, you will meet me on my return, I will become your wife that day."

Elliott could not shake her resolution, and only gained her consent to his accompanying her to Adelaide with some difficulty.

It was a sorrowful leave-taking, particularly of tiny Nelly, but she was left in loving, trusty hands; and the journey to Adelaide accomplished, Lucy Dean embarked for England in less than a week after, bearing with her the respect and good will of thousands of the colonists.

The voyage, though long, was quicker than it usually is by several days; and landing at Liverpool, she lost no time in hastening onward to town, and from thence to the old village and the old house where she supposed Mary yet lived, for there it was she had directed her last letter. To her consternation, however, Mary was not there.

"Why, poor dear heart," spoke the mistress of the house, "her affairs have been a bit straitened of late, owing to the expenses of the Emigrant School, and the loss of money in the hands of a bookseller. I wanted her to stop and trust to better times, but she wouldn't—she was always so particular about money matters—so she moved, some six months since, to a small lodging in Camden Town, but I'll give you her direction."

"And her servant—my sister, I mean," asked Lucy.

"Why the best and faithfulest of little servants, mistress ever had, yet, for all that, I wanted Miss Austen to part with her, rather than leave her old home, but she would not; nothing I could say could persuade her."

Lucy was not long riding into town, or in finding where Miss Austen lived—she gave her name at the door, but went upstairs unannounced, and knocking, went in at once, and beheld Mary—not changed in any one respect since she had last seen her—but who, with the same pure, glad look beaming on her face, sat reading beside a table; whilst no great way off, busy with her needle, was one whom [Lucy] at a glance knew to be Nelly. But she could not speak to her, would not see her, only the one bright nature who was so true, so noble. She pressed forward, knelt beside Mary, and bending down her head, could only utter with convulsed respiration, "Madam, I am Lucy Dean."

Neither could speak, nor did one or other move till Lucy raised up her face to look upon that other face, as children kneeling by their mother's side. But this bright nature, noble in the moment of her joy, lifted one of her hands away, pressed something to her knee, drew it down even to the side of Lucy, and then passing her arms around what thus so knelt together, said, *"Be one, for you are Sisters."*

Passionately weeping, both women yet knelt on.

"Brave woman," at last said Mary tenderly to Lucy, "as the purest reward that I can give you, let me, before one other word is spoken, tell you that Nelly has proved, by our self-redemptions; and in saying that *I* love her, let it be more than sufficient absolution in your eye."

I need not paint the sequel to this picture. Hours and hours Lucy and Mary talked.

"And why not, Madam," said Lucy, "let me, though so far away, know about your strait, or if not, O'Flanagan or Mr. Fortescue?"

"I can beg for others," replied Mary, "but not for myself. Besides, Mr. Fortescue so kindly helped me in the matter of the emigration school, that I could not, with grace, ask him again; and latterly he has been in rapidly declining health, so much so, that O'Flanagan now rarely stirs abroad."

In two days Mary was comfortably settled in her old home, enriched by many comforts, through the care of Lucy. This duty performed, Lucy went and saw the old bird-fancier, whose almost first word was concerning the family of the Sweets; and when he heard that they had multiplied to a prodigious extent, he muttered something about "need of edication," and "popular airs," took an "egg" out of the veritable "bird's nest," looked astoundingly for a Twiddlesing to look, and finished by saying, "he should certainly think about it."

Her visit to O'Flanagan was of equal interest, the old man weeping and laughing between whiles, for Robert Fortescue was rapidly turning the last leaf of Life's great book. He was, however, yet perfectly sensible, and O'Flanagan not only promised to tell him of Lucy's return, but to read to him the letters she had brought him from Mr. Minwaring.

About a week from this date, a carriage was sent for Mary and Lucy, and going together, they were admitted into the old lawyer's sick room. He was propped up in bed, yet he welcomed them with interest and joy.

"I have lived," he said, "to some purpose, in thus living to see women taking an interest in actual life, particularly in relation to the amelioration of the lot of their own sex. So be not baffled, but bear onward. Return with Lucy to her adopted country, Mary Austen, and marry Mr. Minwaring; he says he has loved you from the hour he first saw you in my old study, and therefore to you both I leave my entire fortune, having executed a will to that effect, with the exception of a handsome legacy to Patrick O'Flanagan, whom it is my desire should accompany you to Australia; and smaller ones to two old men named Twiddlesing and Noseby, the one a bird-fancier and the other a newsman. The bulk of my fortune thus bequeathed, I wish some of it to be invested either in Australian mines or agriculture, as a perpetual fund for female emigration, so that the hand of Robert Fortescue, even in the grave, may dry the bitter tears of woman, and make her holy in the human privilege of mother. Now God bless you both, great women—many have united man and woman into one; let me, upon this, my dying bed, do what is wiser—unite woman and woman together—and tell them, that in unity, Divine work lies for them to do." So saying, he placed their hands together.

For a year after Mr. Fortescue's death, Mary and Lucy remained in England, achieving fully the spirit of their noble work. Their project was well received by the parishes applied to, and a large body of emigrant women sent forth. Very many of the middle classes were incited by Mary's writings to leave genteel beggary for a nobler life. The school was founded a short distance from London, and committed to laborious and trusty hands.

At this time Mary and Lucy, accompanied by O'Flanagan and Twiddlesing, and a small fraction of his aviary, including the renowned "bird's-nest," and Noseby, left England, and after a prosperous voyage landed at Sydney. Here they were met by Minwaring and Elliott, the latter having come on his errand of promise to marry Lucy, to invest his savings in mining property before his marriage, he had been making surveys since Lucy's absence, and thus discovered a tract of country, so boundless in its wealth, that imagination could hardly picture it. The secret was yet unknown; yet still the extent of land was beyond his power to purchase. As soon as Minwaring learnt this, it was agreed upon that a portion of Mr. Fortescue's fortune should be therein invested, as a perpetual fund for female emigration.

Two months after landing, Mary Austen and Lucy Dean were married in Sydney by the colonial bishop, amidst the greatest festivity and rejoicing,—the former proceeding onward to Camden County, with Mr. Minwaring, O'Flanagan, and Noseby; and the latter setting off soon after with her husband, Nelly, and Twiddlesing—the bird-fancier, being much concerned as to the long neglected edication of the Sweets, to Melbourne, where brave Ben not only met them, and got married at once, but with a proud and glowing heart, took Nelly across the plains to her far-off home; there for her to clasp once more her baby to her heart, and to hear it say, as it led her amidst tame parrots and kangaroos, and little cageless Sweets, "Mud'yer's coming."

In one year, this great block of country had been surveyed, purchased, and a copper-mine of inestimable value opened, which being at once called ROBERT FORTESCUE'S WHEAL, was set down amongst other yet unwrought mines in perpetuity, for providing a large sum for annual and equal division between the Colonial and English Governments, conjointly with the annual tax before-mentioned, for free and national emigration, under certain regulations.

Both on the same day, Mary and Lucy, became mothers of boys. As soon as she was well enough, Lucy, whose baby was born at Adelaide, took the coast-voyage to Camden to see Mrs. Minwaring; and there one evening, sitting hand in hand on the broad sands, against which swept the mighty ocean, their infants couched up one shawl beside them, the spiritual faith of both seemed to have a voice and say,— "Flow on thou mighty ocean, and tell the myriad oceans of myriad worlds, that what is boundless in them, what is deep, or what is pure, has prototype and likeness in the SOUL OF WOMAN!"

Notes

[1]See "The Great Woman Market." *The Spectator* (15 Dec 1849), p. 1184; "The Needlewomen and Their Rescue." *The Spectator* (8 Dec 1849), p.1158-59; "Needlewomen's Rescue—Ministerial Hopes." *The Spectator* (29 Dec

1849), p. 1232; "Political Economy and the Seamstress." *The Spectator* (15 Dec 1849), p. 1183-84.

²See G.W.M. Reynolds, "A Few More Words of Warning to the Needlewomen and Slopworkers." *Reynolds's Political Instructor* 1 (1849-50), p. 74; "A Warning to the Needlewomen and Slopworkers." *Reynolds's Political Instructor* 1 (1849-50), pp. 66-67.

Woman's Wrongs
Ernest Jones
(1852)

Although many scholars date the beginning of Chartism around 1836-37 with the fight against the New Poor Law, others turn to the founding, in London and Yorkshire, of trade unions during 1830-1832. The latter group argue that early Chartism developed among groups of skilled artisans, printers, and working craftsmen in various trades who were idealists strongly under the influence of Owenite or similar doctrine and who had an ardent belief in both education and the power of reason.

In May 1838 the Chartists first published "The People's Charter" in London. In this revolutionary document they called for six points of reform: manhood suffrage, a ballot, equal electoral districts, annual parliaments, removal of the property qualification for Parliament, and a salary for members of Parliament. On June 14, 1839, the Chartist petition was brought to the House of Commons, where, in July, it was rejected (235-46). A second petition was brought before the Commons in May 1842, when it was again rejected (287-49). When a third petition was brought in April 1848 it was laughed out of the Commons. Despite this harsh rejection, the Chartists continued to meet and agitate for reform. The last Chartist Convention was held in February 1858. [1]

The Chartist movement attracted a variety of people. For example, Ernest Jones, a Chartist leader and publisher, was not of the laboring classes. Born into wealth and social standing, Jones was a barrister who rejected this life and devoted himself to the cause of the Charter. In 1847 he became, with Fergus O'Connor, co-editor of The Northern Star, and that same year he began a new monthly magazine, The Labourer. In May 1851, Jones began the weekly journal Notes for the People (in May the following year it became The People's Paper) in which Woman's Wrongs appeared. [2]

Jones was an avid Socialist as well as a Chartist, and his Socialist stance is evident throughout Notes from the People, including Woman's Wrongs. In his various works Jones stresses the irreconcilable antagonism between Capital and Labor, the distribution of wealth among the privileged few, and the *need for workers to establish political power in order to unseat the landed and powerful classes. In* Woman's Wrongs, *Jones focuses on the most powerless sector of Victorian society, women. The original Charter called for universal suffrage which would include women, but this was changed to manhood suffrage because the Chartists feared that suffrage for women would be a bone of contention that could defeat passage of the Charter. Nevertheless the Chartists promoted feminism by including women's issues with those of the working class in general. Jones underscores women's general helplessness by dividing his story into four sections—"The Working-man's Wife," "The Young Milliner," "The Trademan's Daughter," and "The Lady of Title"—with each section focusing on a woman from a different socioeconomic group—lower working class, upper working class, petite bourgeois, and aristocracy. By focusing on women from all classes Jones is able to equate the corruption of power with that of poverty, and show that lack of power inevitably leads to seduction (literal or figurative) and destruction.*

In "The Working-man's Wife," the section included here, Jones deals with the undercutting of workmen's wages, the seduction and abandonment of working women by men of higher social standing, and the corrupting influence of both capital and poverty.

INTRODUCTION

To paint life *as it is*—no poet's fancy, no romancer's dream, can paint more strange or sad a picture. The romance of fiction cannot equal the romance of truth.

Well then—such I desire to portray. To reflect in simple language, the domestic wrongs and sorrows of society—such as they at present are—in a plain, simple, and unvarnished tale.

Oh! many a battle is fought by the dim circle of the household hearth, as noble, or as terrible, as that with crowned brigades on the field of "glory." Oh! many a suffering is endured in the still bosom of familiar life, as bitter or as hopeless as that of the unlaurelled martyr at the bigot's stake!

And yet—who speaks of them? Who knows of them? Who recks of them?

Down—down beneath the cold surface of society there are rankling wrongs—that fret, that fester, that destroy—and yet, they never glide over the tongue of the Reformer, the brain of the Religionist, or the heart, even of the well-wishers of mankind.

Every order of society has domestic sufferings peculiar to itself, sufferings, besides those to which "all flesh is heir"—brought on by the vile mechanism of our system. These sufferings may first strike *man*,—and that is but just, for man makes society what it is—or at least, allows it to remain so—but the evil stops not there—it reaches farther, to the breast of *woman!* What gross injustice! for society counts woman as nothing in its institutions, and yet makes her bear the greatest share of sufferings inflicted by a system in which she has not voice! Brute force first imposed the law—and moral force compels her to obey it now.

I purpose, therefore, to lift the veil from before the wrongs of woman—to shew her what she suffers at her own home-hearth—how society receives her—what society does for her—where society leaves her.

To shew it, not merely in one class or order—but upward, downward, through all the social grades. If I draw pictures at which you shudder—if I reveal that, at which your heart revolts—I cannot help it—it is truth—such is the world that surrounds you—such is the world that made you—such is the world *you help to make*—go! try to alter it, and BEGIN AT HOME.

THE WORKING-MAN'S WIFE.

I.—THE CHILDBIRTH OF THE POOR.

If, at any time, you should pass of an evening the Royal Palace of Pimlico, down the long line of pillared palaces, and thence diverge by the stately piles of governmental craft, the temples of brute force by land and sea, the pinnacles beneath which class legislates against class—the hall where justice darkles in its sideling nooks, or the proud pile where Mammon stands based upon the graves of buried fame. If you should pass down between the long lines of this stately but unequal epic of stone, and brick, and marble, interspersed with its episodes of gleaming water, and green trees, exotic birds and flowers, statues, arches and columns, fountains of water, and jets of thrice filtered flame, dotted on the margins, prosaic and yet brilliant notes! with its innumerable shops, and flooded with the long current of carriage, horse and foot; take but one step, and side by side with all this gaud and glory, you pass into the regions of darkness and dismay. Behind you lies the greatness of the present in light, and voice, and life; the glory of the past in pillar, arch, and statue; and before you, between two tall houses opens a narrow, deep ravine, winding on in gloomy, sightless lengths, a thin strip of murky sky stretched between the reeking house-tops, like dirty calico across a broken roof. The windows of Downing-street overlook the contrast!

Proceed a little way, and to the right you will see a narrow archway beneath the first floor of a mouldering house. You must stoop to enter it; some steps lead downward from the street; a fetid stench continually rushes upward through the opening; and on looking down, you perceive a narrow court, formed by a few dilapidated tenements on either side, and closed up by a dead wall at the end. The space between them is unpaved, and half-covered with pools of stagnant water, filth, and ordure. Ragged children, almost naked—the colour of their skin concealed by dirt—with pale, straggling, unkempt hair, bare feet, hollow, sunken eyes, white, shrunken, ghastly faces, and their dwindled limbs, flit over it by day. At night are heard strange sounds of strife or orgy, of tears and prayers, and hoarse murmurs, which might be taken equally for the brute-expression of a savage pleasure, or the last groaning of a dying victim.

Well nigh, side by side with this pestiferous gulf, arise the splendid mansions you have passed, the dwellings of the magnates of the land. The wretch below can see from his glassless casements the silken curtains of the rich hang fluttering in the breeze; and if pain or hunger keep him wakeful in the close, hot, summer night, he can hear the roll of carriages bearing gay fashion to its gorgeous revel, the ball-room music floating from the balconies—aye, even the voluptuous murmurs of the scene within.

His is a hell, where the damned have paradise in perspective, with the certainty of never entering.

This scene is a type of the whole neighbourhood. Some slight changes were made not long ago—when the rich opened a new street through part of the district. But it needed the cholera to come first, and radiate from this focus of infection. The rich had *pity* then, because they felt *fear*—and the ordure was removed at the same time as the corpses.

On the evening on which our narrative begins, sad, moaning cries were heard from one of the smallest houses in the court described above—cries anxious and broken, similar to those uttered by a woman about to become a mother.

It was Margaret Haspen in the pangs of child-birth.

The young woman lay in one of those close wooden boxes, recessed in the wall—opening with a sliding door, or curtain, in the room—called by courtesy a bed. What little of the fetid air of the street that entered the room, could scarcely reach the dark, unhealthy nook, in which the miserable woman writhed with agony. The door of the one room that constituted the entire home of Margaret and her husband, stood open, but it was crowded with neighbours. There was a continual running to and fro between the street-door and the bed-side—all the old gossips in the neighbourhood being desirous of seeing how the labour was proceeding; for the very poor have that, at least, in common with Queens, their births take place with open doors.

Not far from the bed-side of Margaret sat John Haspen, the bricklayer, with folded arms and outstretched legs, smoking his pipe with calm indifference.

Still nearer stood the nurse, with equal apathy.

However, after a time, the phlegm of the latter seemed to vanish—she became uneasy—the agony of Margaret became insufferable—and the neighbours began to wink at each other knowingly, and to express their fears in whispers.

"Twelve hours, and no progress! there must be something wrong! Perhaps an operation will be wanted!"

"Oh! just fancy if she was to suffer like Patty Braddis! They were obliged to cut her side open! She has just exactly the same symptoms! It's the same case precisely! How Patty suffered! When she was dead, the blood ran from her eyes, drop by drop, as from two badly closed wounds!"

Margaret, who heard all, uttered a piercing shriek.

"I told you," said an old crone, "that the child lay wrong. She won't stand it. They'll be obliged to cut it in pieces!"

Here the sufferer gave so horrible a cry, that even Haspen was troubled. He advanced to the bed-side. Margaret grew worse and worse.

"Haspen," said the nurse, "you must fetch a doctor. I cannot take the responsibility upon myself."

"She's better now,"—he answered sullenly.

"Yes! to be worse again in a moment. Go for the doctor."

"Do *I* know a doctor? Where the d— am I to get a doctor?"

"Fetch Mr. Cutter—he lives close by."

"I'll fetch him; don't budge, John!" said a neighbour, and limped off in a half-run.

The bricklayer resumed his place in an angry mood.

"A doctor too!" he muttered through his teeth, relighting his pipe. "This completes our ruin—this confinement," and he cast a look of sour displeasure on his wife.

The doctor entered with the old crone. Mr. Cutter had served long in the marines. He was a fearless practitioner, who treated his man as a sculptor does a block of marble—cutting away without remorse or scruple. Accustomed to nautical slang and jollity, he brought it into the sick-room. No one knew better than he how to crack a joke over a death-bed, or launch a pun beside a grave. This freedom of speech and callous confidence had given the poor a high opinion of his talents. Finding him always unmoved and jocose beside the bed of pain, they thought he drew his firmness from the certainty of success. Thus his reputation was soon founded, and a few reckless, fortunate cures crowned it. As to the many dead whom he had murdered, nobody talked of them: the medical assassination of the poor is a matter too unimportant for attention. Besides, amid that crowd where the one treads on the heels of the other in the run for life, a dead man is one competitor less, and one vacant place more. Once buried, his quondam comrades feel more easy; for, in our social state, which makes us *rivals* instead of *associates,* there are always more interested in each other's *death* than in each other's LIFE.

When Cutter entered, Margaret was uttering fainter cries of exhaustion.

"Well, well, my girl! What's the matter? They tell me you've a starling that won't come out of his cage! Ha, ha! that's all. We must open the door. What's the lock broken, and the key lost? Ha, ha! Well, let's see! Children are like a bottle of wine—the beginning's more pleasant than the end. Ha, ha, ha!"

He then set about his task.

"Never mind! Patience! A little steel medicine—ha, ha!—and all will be right."

The sight of his preparations terrified poor Margaret.

"No, no!" she shrieked, writhing at the bottom of her bed. "You'll kill me—I won't—let me alone!"

"Ha, ha!" giggled Mr. Cutter; "never mind—all done in a minute. No, no! eh? You didn't always say no, no, my dear! so it's too late to say it now. Ha, ha!"

"What a witty man he is!" tittered the gossips at the door.

Margaret resisted a few moments, but he commanded her harshly with an oath to be quiet, and she yielded. One hour after, a female child was born, amid terrific agony.

"Curse it, a girl!" cried the husband, dashing his pipe to pieces in his anger.

"A girl!" moaned the sufferer; "all that pain, and then to have a girl!"

Such is the child-bed of the poor—so the poor man's child was born: a curse and a sigh welcomed it into life.

"That's it," cried Mr. Cutter, gaily. "You see it's not so bad after all. Ha! ha! Now you must have rest, and peace of mind. Take light, and at the same time, nourishing food. Well: have you no towel?"

"No, sir."

"The deuce! the outfit seems to have been a little neglected. Ha! ha! No matter; well, as I was saying, broth, and light white meats—and, above all, no imprudence. Good bye; I will call in again in a few days."

We need not tell the reader that none of these recommendations were followed—because they *could not be.*

Margaret recovered, however, as all women of her class—not by tender care, not by nourishing diet, but thanks to the vigour of a healthy constitution. But, as always happens in like cases, she preserved the traces of her sufferings. There was not, as with the rich, the gentle hand of caressing love or of hired but assiduous care, to wipe the wrinkles of pain from the drawn face—there was not the resource of science, and the choice of viands, to replenish the temporary void of strength. The bright luxuriance, the buoyant freshness that embellished the young maid, was succeeded in the young mother by that faded hue, that haggard expression, that withering and decay, that characterises the matrons of the poor.

Toil, domestic duties, the painful care of her child, finished the work, and effaced the last vestige of her early beauty. She sank into that premature old age, so sadly traceable in the child of want and sorrow.

Meanwhile, the child grew, and prospered.

The bricklayer's home was like that of most others of his order—a mixture of annoyance and irritation. The first intoxication of pleasure attendant on the union of a man and woman who have not learnt to dislike each other, once past—the first fever of youthful passion once over, they sank into mutual cold indifference.

Indeed, Haspen never loved his wife. She was a servant at his employer's, and he married her because he wanted a wife, and she had saved a little money. He looked on his house merely as a resting-place—at his wife merely as a servant without wages, whom he found convenient to prepare his meals, and make and share his bed.

On the whole, he was not by nature a bad man. Sunk in utter ignorance, his principal pleasure was the satisfaction of his appetites—society had done the best to make a brute out of a man—yet he was capable of sudden generous impulse, though devoid of that gentleness and feeling which smooths the intercourse of home, and wins domestic sympathy. A machine of flesh and bone, he could be good or bad, according as the hand of circumstance might push him.

Margaret was his superior: having entered service many years, she was removed from that close contact with rude, unpolished vice, that breaking against the sharp corners of society, which deadens feeling and intelligence. She had lived neither amid the oaths of rage nor the cries of drunkenness. She had not been thus much refined, but what she could descend easily to the lower grade—a change, however, that withered the freshness of the young woman's soul, even as neglect and want had withered that of her body!—a change that left the scarce conscious recollection of a better life, and faded visions of a happier home. Thus they jogged on together—and they bore the character of a happy couple in their court, because Haspen *did not beat her.*

The years passed thus without producing any material change. The little child, Catherine, grew into girlhood, and the parents lived on under the fear of the morrow, as before. Haspen's earnings neither rose nor fell. Placed on the brink of destitution, he still contrived to cling to the rim of the precipice—a breath could knock him over—the illness of a few weeks—want of employment—fall of wage. But he had escaped all these dangers—without, however, laying anything by for the future. Indeed, his wages were too low to reserve much, and what little he might have spared was engulfed by the public-house.

Nevertheless, Margaret had little fear for the future. Catherine was strong, and could already do some work. She would soon be old enough to enter service—and her wages were a great guarantee for the future. Add to this the fact, that the young girl had received from heaven the greatest blessing it can give the poor man's child—she was a *"little eater."*

II.—AN EMPLOYER.
"Just honour enough to escape being hung."

Mr. Barrowson, Haspen's employer, was a large, open-faced, florid man—with a wide mouth, white teeth, and curly hair. He had a frank jovial manner, with a loud voice, and a large fat hand, equally ready to grasp in recognition or to strike in enmity. He passed for an excellent fellow. Though forty years old, he was still a bachelor, and seemed likely to remain so. It was certainly whispered in some quarter that he was a libertine, avaricious, and had done some things treating very closely on the limits of the criminal law; but he invariably took up his bills, paid ready money—and, in one word—acted like an "honourable man." He had just successfully completed several extensive speculations, and was enjoying a pause in business, after unusual application.

Content with his enormous recent gains, he was sitting quietly in his office, by the side of his partner, reading the *Times*.

"It's horrible!" he cried suddenly. "If government does not act with vigour, business will be ruined."

"What is it?" asked his partner.

"Nothing but combinations of working-men; everywhere a demand for a rise of wage."

"There's the law against combination."

"Certainly; but where's the use of the law, if it is not enforced?"

The partner mended a pen, and said nothing. Barrowson resumed:

"By the bye, have you seen the other masters?"

"Yes; the reduction of wages for bricklayers, plasterers, and masons, is agreed to."

"Very good. If they object, we'll turn them adrift. We have no press of work just now, and *they must soon return or die of hunger."*

"Exactly so. Of course, *they're at perfect liberty to choose,"* the partner quietly observed, wetting the nib of his pen, and resumed his calculations, while Barrowson continued his perusal of the *Times*.

That very evening, in paying his men, Barrowson told them his contracts were all finished, and he had no further need of their services. This was a thunderbolt to his hearers.

Barrowson had expected the effect of his words, but he remained deaf to their prayers to keep them on. "Go and try elsewhere," was his answer. They ran to every other employer, but they were all in the conspiracy, and all told them that they were not in want of hands. The men were forced to return to Barrowson. He repeated his old answer—"he had no work for them." At last, *as though moved by pity,* he said, that "out of kindness to them, and at a heavy inconvenience to himself, he would take a few of them on again, but at LOWERED WAGES."

They had not expected this, and they went away.

Barrowson shrugged his shoulders, and said, looking after them: "They are proud now, because their bellies are full. Wait a few days longer!"

He counted on hunger as an auxiliary, and she failed him not. The struggle cannot be long between the rich, who can afford to wait, and the poor, who must dine to-morrow. And sure enough, the men came back, begging Mr. Barrowson to take them on at the diminished wages. The wages once lowered in the one firm, the others followed the example, and a general reduction took place throughout the district. The conspiracy, of which the men were made the utterly unconscious tools, had been crowned with complete success. Instead of wages being lowered from the employer's poverty, they are lowered when he is so rich that he knows he can afford to bear a strike. The master makes his arrangements *before he begins the reduction*—the man, *not till after it is made*. The first is sure to conquer.

One workman alone refused to work at the lowered rate. Refused by every firm, he still persisted to struggle single-handed against that terrible coalition. He was told that the law was on his side, and would punish the combination of employers as well as that of the employed—a good many told him this, but not one could tell him how he could get at the law, or how he could pay for the law; and, if the truth must be told, he had no great confidence in the laws made by the rich for the protection of the poor. The law, to him, was a policeman and a tax-collector—and, embittered by fighting the unequal struggle, he suffered in silent patience. But his resources diminished with every day: he had sold all his furniture—the all but necessary clothing of his wife, his child, and himself went next—the pressure increased, the last means of prolonging the combat was gone—he had reached the confines of famine and death—nothing remained but *submission!*

Pale with rage, shame and hunger, he went to the premises of Barrowson, and asked for work on the same conditions as the others.

The employer received him with a jovial air—told him the somewhat superior place he had formerly filled was occupied by one Latchman, but that he might go and work among the crowd.

The return of Haspen was quite an event in the yard. Those among his companions who had been the first to submit, and before whom he had boasted that he would sooner die than yield, seized with avidity this opportunity for his humiliation. He was overwhelmed with a deluge of gross jests and mockeries, which he could answer only by the strength of his arm. But when he first had sent back the sarcasm down the throats of a few of his hearers, the open mockery ceased. Nevertheless a half-smothered hostility continued to growl around him. His companions could not forgive him for having shewn more spirit than themselves.

In the midst of this general aversion, one man only made up to Haspen— it was Latchman, who had supplanted him.

Latchman had the character of a commonplace, rather indifferent workman. His appearance was repulsive, and his worn and blunted features reminded you of one of those pieces of money from which long use has nearly effaced the original stamp—the noble effigy of manhood. Perhaps it had been lost beneath the wearing hand of vice—perhaps nature had but negligently struck the die; the bad money of humanity that circulates along the ranks of life! Perhaps, too, a profound hypocrisy had thrown that mask of unmeaningness upon his sallow face. Latchman was, among all the workmen, the one who attracted the least notice. He was known only for his passive obedience and obsequious servility—to which qualities he owed his new employment. His having superseded Haspen and his place did not much ingratiate him with the latter, who repelled his advances; but nothing could offend Latchman: insult glided from his bent and servile brow without leaving a single trace of anger—besides, he adopted an infallible means of conciliating Haspen—he treated him to drink—and they were quickly friends.

Meanwhile, the embarrassments of Haspen continued unabated. His wages, never large, and now less, did not permit him to recover himself from his difficulties—his debts or his losses. Vainly he struggled against the overwhelming fatality which was dragging him down into an abyss. Vainly he struggled against the poverty, which clung to him like an ulcer. He strove hard—he strove manfully—but he strove uselessly. As soon as he saw that he gained no ground in the strife, he gave up all effort, and sank into apathy and despair.

Then the real misery came—that clinging watchful misery that counts the mouthfuls and calculates the strength. It came—and with it came *the evil thoughts!* Perfidious voices seemed whispering in his ear—he felt tempted, and he trembled!

He resisted—but the very struggle weakened him: he tried to drown his thoughts in drink, and, that means once tried, he sought none other. From his home, where the picture of their misery harrowed him, he rushed to the beer-shop to forget it. The very sight of his mute, but plaintive family, threw him into the rage of helpless despair—rendered still more blind by drunkenness.

About this time, cries of pain and anger began to be heard by the neighbours, and the report ran in the court that the bricklayer was in the habit of beating his wife.

To crown their misery, Margaret was delivered of another child, whom they named Mary.

III.—A NIGHT SCENE.

About eight months had elapsed since the birth of Margaret's second child.

It was one of those nights of early spring, replete with fog and frost, so prevalent in London; while the dull sound of a half awakened tempest moaned along the sky. The Abbey clock had just struck eleven.

Margaret sat cowering over the grate, where the faint embers of a fire glimmered. The young woman had retained no traces of her pristine beauty. Her face was sallow and wrinkled—her haggard eyes shone wildly through swollen lids that tears had furrowed. Little Mary rested on her knees, but the child's hoarse, uneasy respiration, was interrupted by a deep convulsive cough. In the midst of the silent gloom of the apartment, the weak struggles of the child sounded like the rattle of the dying. At last the fire went out entirely, and the room remained in darkness.

Then Margaret heard in the corner farthest from the fire-place, a chattering of teeth, mingled with plaintive moans.

"Catherine! Catherine!" cried the mother in alarm—"What is the matter?—What makes you cry?"

An almost inarticulate voice was heard to answer in the darkness: "Mother! I die of cold!"

"Come to me, Catherine! Press yourself against me. Give me your hand, my child—your hand—I don't feel it."

"It is in your's, mother!"

"Then I, too, must be very cold."

"Oh yes! your hands freeze me!"

"Oh G—! If I had but the fever I had yesterday, I could warm her!"—cried

Margaret. "I am very wretched!"——

"Where is father?" asked the child, pressing against her mother, and folding her dress around.

"I don't know, Catherine!"

"Will he bring us something to eat?"

"Are you hungry also, child?" asked the young mother in a mournful voice.

The little girl noticed something plaintive in the tone, as of a breaking heart, and said in a low accent—

"Not very, mother!—If I could but sleep, I should not think about it."

Margaret took a handkerchief from her neck and tied it round that of her daughter, then—seeking the most sheltered nook, placed her there, gently exhorting her to sleep. The little nurse babe, Mary, had also just dropped to sleep, and once more all was wrapped in deep, funereal silence.

At this moment, a heavy, vacillating step rung on the pavement of the street without.

The door flew rudely open—and Haspen entered, drunk, and pipe in mouth.

He advanced, stumbling, to the middle of the sombre room, his sight yet unaccustomed to the transition from the gassy glare without, and sought with outstretched arms, the fire-place that showed no signs of warmth.

"Margaret!" he cried in a voice evidently indicative of irritation.

He called her thrice without receiving an answer.

At last a voice was heard as harsh as his, "Well?"

"Why, you child of the devil! is there neither fire nor light?"

"Because I have none!"

"And why have you none?"

"Because John Haspen drinks and sings at the public-house, while his children die of cold and hunger."

"That'll do, Margaret!"—cried the bricklayer, dashing his foot upon the floor—"that'll do, unless you wish me to stave in your skull like an empty barrel."

"John Haspen, the children are starving!"

"Then give them your tongue to eat, viper! and be silent! So there is no wood here to light a fire. Where's the hatchet?"

He took a hatchet from the floor, and at a blow smashed one of the two only chairs remaining in the house—threw the fragments on the grate, and a few sparks communicating with the dry wood, soon kindled it into flame, and cast their lurid light on the melancholy scene.

Margaret had never left her place, and sat motionless, with fixed eyes, her child pressed in her arms, and but feebly concealing beneath an assumed indifference the indignation that boiled in her veins, stretched her nostrils, and flashed from her eyes. Haspen, standing before the grate, held his feet alternately over the flame, that lit up the evil aspect of his harsh and hardened features.

All the rest of the room was lost in darkness.

For a time, the actors in this strange scene were silent—then Haspen, taking his pipe out of his mouth said, turning to his wife: "to-morrow they'll come and sell all we have to pay the rent. That scoundrel Stonage, won't let us remain here any longer."

"And, pray, where shall we go to?"

"To the street. That will be good enough for your ape and you. Besides, we must quit London. I have no more work. I left Barrowson's three days ago, and could not get a job anywhere else."

"Serve you right, Haspen. What's the use of a man who's not fit for anything—whose hand trembles with gin, and who can't see where he lays his trowel?"

"Silence, woman!" cried the bricklayer, in ungovernable fury, and crushing his pipe between his fingers; "silence! or I'll teach you that my hand is strong enough for you still."

The woman tossed her head in scornful defiance.

"That's not what you promised me, John, when you came of evenings to speak with me at master's gate. If I drew back from your hand, then, it was to avoid a caress, and not a blow. I thought I married one who had the arms of a workman, and the heart of a man. Why did you not tell me then, that you could not work well enough to keep two little children? You want us to leave London! And pray, what for? Do you suppose I'll go, with two girls around my neck, begging from door to door for you? You want to make a trade of the misery of your wife and children, do you? You're out in your reckoning, sweetheart! Follow you I will—but it shall be to cry to the passers-by: 'Do you see this man? He is strong—he is well—but he will not work to give us food.'"

"Have you done, Margaret?"

"Presently, Haspen! I must tell you all. I've held my tongue too long— but mark you! I suffered too much hunger in the hunger of these poor little innocents. Go and swill in the beer-house if you like, but I'll not quit its door. While you drink, you shall hear us cry for bread—when you come out drunk, you shall have to stagger over the bodies of your children that I'll cast in the mud before the threshold. Its time you shared a little of our misery. They're not my children only. Do you think my arms are strong enough to carry them always, without you taking your turn? I've had my share of suffering—the rest shall be for you."

Haspen had listened to this long tirade, at first with a scornful indifference, then with fast rising wrath. His features became inflamed, his chest heaved, his breath hissed in his throat that tried to compress its fury. He advanced one step towards Margaret with clenched hands—then drew back—containing himself still.

"I, too—I've had my share to put up with—and with you," he said, at last, in a low, dull, stifled voice. "Silence! unless you wish to see blood flow to-night. I hate you, woman! for since I took to you, my miseries crowded on me. Before—I never wanted—I worked all the week, and I played all the Sunday— but you—you have come, you, and your children! Do you understand me now? You are a nest of vipers that I'll crush under my feet!"

In speaking these last words with the rise of thunder in his voice, he stamped his heavy foot upon the remnants of the burning chair that laid before the grate with such a terrible force that the blazing splinters showered about the room.

A sudden cry was heard, and little Catherine darted up from the chimney corner towards her mother—her clothes had caught fire.

The terrified Margaret raised her in her arms: "John! John! water! for the love of Heaven! water; the poor child is burning!"

But the angry man never moved.

His foot upon a brand—his head erect—with the delirious excitement of rage—he looked rigidly and terribly silent upon the child writhing in its mother's arms—and the mother trying to extinguish the flames.

During three minutes the struggle lasted—it was a fearful sight to see those two weak creatures wrestling for life amid a circle of fire—and the impassive stillness of the strong man who stood gazing on them.

At last, Margaret surrounded the child with an embrace so close and so complete, that the smothered flames expired.

"G——! my G——! she is burnt! burnt to the bone!"—and then turning to Haspen, whose angry quiet goaded her to madness: "look here, villain! look—this is your work!"

She raised her wretched daughter, yelling with pain, in her arms, and held it close before the face of its father.

"Back, woman—back!"

"Finish your murder, then!"

"Margaret! *won't* you be silent?"

"Kill her, then—assassin! Look—see!—don't her blood make you thirst?"

The hideous wounds of the victim nearly touched the face of the man—he could no longer master his passion.

"Back! I tell you, Satan!" and, quicker than the word, a blow was given. It was aimed at the mother, but it hit the forehead of the child, who fell on the floor with a fearful moan.

That moan was followed by a hoarse and savage cry, as the mother's eyes wandered round in search of something; she stretched her hands—stooped— and suddenly rising—the husband felt the sharp, cold blow of a hatchet strike his cheek, and glide off into his shoulder.

Pain made him utter an oath—he was about to dart on Margaret, but with the agility of a tigress, she had already darted into the darkest corner of the room, her child in one arm, the hatchet in her hand. The gleam of her hatchet and of her angry eyes was alone visible in the darkness—the hoarse hissing of her quick breath was alone audible in the silence.

The man paused suddenly before that fury of the tigress defending its young—he felt fear.

For a time there was silence such as might make one's blood creep!

It was interrupted by the noise of someone pushing open the badly closed door.

Latchman entered.

"What's all this?" he said. "I passed before your door, Haspen; I thought I heard cries, and feared some misfortune had happened."

"Yes—two great misfortunes! The one, to have been born—the other, not to have drowned myself twelve years ago! Go away; this is a matter between me and that viper there!"

"What are you going to do?" cried Latchman, who had just perceived Margaret amid the darkness, and understood all at a glance. "Haspen, leave your wife alone."

"I'll crush her head between my fists!" he roared. "She has struck me— she has raised her hand against me!"

"I defended my child," said a dull voice.

"I'll throw you on your knees to ask my pardon."

"Try it!" said the same voice—and the eyes and the hatchet glistened in their dark corner.

Latchman saw it was time to interfere, or the scene would turn to blood: he seized Haspen, struggling with rage and drink, with his wiry arm—and, soothing him all the while, dragged him to the door, and then over the threshold, despite his struggles.

Margaret hastened to bolt the door inside. For some time the struggles of Latchman and Haspen, who wanted to re-enter, were heard outside; but at length the latter appeared to yield to the representations of his companion, and their voices were lost in the distant street, in the direction of Whitehall.

IV. TEMPTATION
"Poverty is the mother of Crime."

Whitehall was a blaze of racing meteors, when Haspen and Latchman entered from the dark gulley-like street that opened out into it from the slimy depths of Westminster. There was a party at the Duchess of Buccleugh's and some hundred equipages, with their shining lamps, were drawn up in glittering rows, or flitting about with rival speed along the broad pavements of Whitehall and Palace-yard. The waiting lines around the Lords and Commons increased the gaudy bustle, and groups of spectators stood here and there upon the causeway. From the Duchess's windows came streams of light; wide, variegated awnings stretched over the porticoes and across the street; the shining liveries of tinselled, powdered lacqueys shone on every side; the bayonets of the sentinels bristled over the throng; the harness sparkled on the stately steeds, whose fiery pawing and indignant tossings scattered the white, snow-like foam of their hot mouths as though in scorn upon the passers-by. The windows of Downing-street were silent and lightless, but from the opposite side, from the Duchess's mansion, floated strains of low, voluptuous music, now and then maddening up into the thrilling whirl of the electric waltz. A rich faint odour came from the princely portico and the light draperied windows, while a subdued murmur of gentle, animated converse, or the light musical ring of a silvery laugh stole amid the pauses of the minstrelsy. What a pomp of riches, might, and pleasure! But like the skeleton at a Roman feast, the poor stood here and there shivering in rags, and hunger, and cold upon the pavements. Squalor, wretchedness, misery were writing their silent protest on the pageant. The skeleton was at the rich man's feast!

"Move on! move on!" cried the policeman, for rags must slink into their hiding-place when riches walk abroad. They are offensive—phoo! away with them!—how dare they parade their misery! Go, vanish into corners, till the bone and sinew you cover is wanted to do some work for your master. There, away with you—away with you; you have no business in the pleasure-light of life. "Move on! move on!" but the liveried slave might keep his post, and the young debauchee might stand upon the watch for falling innocence in some fair child of toil.

"Move on! move on!" Yes, we will move, and onward!

As Haspen and his friend advanced, the scene became more lively. One by one, and two by two, Peers and Commoners hurried from St. Stephens, leaving the nation's business undone, to dance at the Duchess's and waltz the more.

In Downing-street work had ceased eight hours ago—or, rather, the mockery of work had ceased since then—the care of government seemed lost, its brute force lived alone in bayonet and bludgeon, guarding its bright outrage against God and man.

"The fashion's out to-night," said Latchman.

Haspen answered not, but moved on.

"Stop," continued Latchman, "let's look at it. What a beautiful sight! It must be very splendid inside there—I should like to see it."

"Come on! What's it to us?"

"Well, nothing; only there's no harm seeing how others enjoy themselves."

"Isn't there; well, I don't want to see it."

"I wonder what your wife and child are doing now?"

"Devil! will you hold your tongue? What's that to you?"

"Why, I was thinking if some of these people would give you something for them——"

"Ah!"

"Why don't you ask them?"

"What—*beg?*"

"And why not? They're so very rich—they're wasting so much—they'd never miss it. You musn't be proud, John; it won't do for one like you; it's not your place."

"And why not? Proud!—I'm not proud; but by —— I'm as good a man as any of these in——l flunkies, or their masters either. Beg!—I'll see them —— first."

"But, John, if you could get a shilling,—you know you're starving—they're starving at home—nobody'll know anything about it. Think now, if you could go back with a big loaf—there's your little Catherine, and Mary, poor things!—it would save their lives. Now try—nobody'll ever know—it's done in a moment. Look at that old gentleman there—it's only speaking a word, and—just think now, to go home and give them a meal!"

The bricklayer's countenance grew troubled; he looked down, and never marked the sinister, leering look, that bespoke scorn and triumph, in the eyes of Latchman. The thought seemed to grapple his heart, and involuntarily he moved towards the man Latchman had pointed out. Just then there was a commotion around them.

"What's that?" asked a bystander, as a stalwart policeman dragged a poor little boy of about ten brutally by the arm.

"Oh, he's only taking that young vagabond to the station-house."

"What's he done—*robbed?*"

"No; he's *begged* of that old gentleman."

"Come on, John Haspen," said Latchman; "begging won't do, after all;" and the twain were once more engulfed in the dark streets of Westminster.

They stopped at a low dilapidated house—numberless in a nameless alley—it was an asylum of thieves, deserters, and fugitives from the arm of the law. There the unskilful were trained to rob—the the initiated met to plot, or to divide the spoil. After Latchman had knocked in a peculiar way, he and Haspen were admitted. A fat-lamp burned in the foul passage—the house was silent. Latchman ushered his companion into a low, large room, furnished with tables and benches. A mute attendant placed a bottle of gin and two glasses on the table, and left them. The two men seated themselves at one of the tables.

"What the deuce was the matter with you and your wife, Haspen? When I left you, you seemed to be in a very good humour."

"Haven't I told you she struck me?"

"But what for?"

"What for? Because she's a ——! whose complaints drive me mad. I've nothing to give the children—I'll never go home again!"

"Well, it's a hard case to be sure, to see one's child want bread. Let alone, that it'll go from bad to worse with you. That's been a bad job for you with Barrowson. You were wrong to strike him."

"Do you suppose, then, I'd allow him to raise his hand against me, without returning it? Pooh, what do I care! I've lost my employment—I know no other master'll take me now; but I don't care that for it. They shan't think they're going to trample on me, I can tell them! They always had a spite against me, because I didn't consent at once to the reduction, as you did. You've feathered your nest pretty well. You were an infernal coward, Latchman!"

"Stuff!" replied the latter, emptying his glass very quietly, "as though they had not a right to lower wages whenever they chose!"

"No, by ——! they have not the right. Have they the right to kill a man, eh? I tell you from that time bread fell short—my children fell sick—they'll never recover it! It's the life of my wife and children the thieves have robbed me of!"

Latchman shrugged his shoulders with a most provoking indifference.

"What would you have? They're rich—they're the masters. What is it to them if you rot alive!"

"But, by ——! I don't choose to rot!" cried the bricklayer, starting up, and striking his heavy fist upon the table that the glasses jingled. "Have I not got as good a right to live as they? If they won't give me food, by G—, *I'll take it!*"

"Why have you not done so, then?"

This question was asked in a very calm tone, but in so direct a manner—

so full of meaning—that Haspen felt embarrassed.

"Why?—Why?——"

"Yes, *why?* Have you a right to the same pay, if you give the same work?"

"Why of course I have."

"Well, then, if your wages are cut down, why don't you take back what is stolen from you. *Would you allow* one of your fellow-workmen to seize on a portion of your wages on pay day?"

"Thunder and lightning, I should think not!"

"Then why do you let your master do it? When a rich man robs us, Haspen, we can't seek justice, as if it was a poor one; but one can take it—one seizes on one's stolen property as one can best get it. Do you understand? What do you say to that?"

"I?—Nothing!" replied Haspen, thoughtfully and sullenly.

Latchman called for more gin.

"I say! hark'ye, Haspen! the question is, whether you mean to live in misery, or to live at your ease, with a bob in your pocket, and a bottle before your nose."

"And how should I manage to live so?"

"I told you already. If you hadn't your ears at your elbows, a month ago, when we were in Barrowson's counting-house, you wouldn't have been in this plight now."

"But prison!"

"Prisons are for the stupid. Besides, d'ye see, you if you don't get any work, you will be obliged to beg, and you will be sent to prison all the same as a vagrant. So, you see, you must go to prison at any rate."

"By G—! that's true!" cried the bricklayer, dropping his hat upon the ground. "When one's down, everybody gives one a kick."

"Then help yourself on to your legs again."

"Silence!" roared Haspen, "or you'll make me do something wrong."

"Pooh, you're too frightened. Well, have your own way. Go again to Morley, or Achren, or Shell and Co., to ask them to let you work, or perhaps Barrowson——"

"Latchman! haven't I told you to hold your tongue!" cried Haspen, grinding his teeth with rage.

"And if I did hold my tongue, would that make things better? You want to work—do you know you have not even got any tools?"

"Tools! no tools? why my tools are at the premises."

"Aye; but master said he'd keep them for the deductions that were due from your wages. You was a week in arrears. Do you hear?"

"He said that? the thief!"

"And this morning your tools were sent to the forge, along with a lot of others."

"Is it true?—Is that true? By G—, I'll tear him into mince-meat!"

"And a nice meal you'll have of it!" said Latchman, smiling with provoking coldness. "Besides that won't last you two days;" and he quietly lighted his pipe.

"Don't forget, my boy, that to-morrow you'll be without work, without tools, and without lodging!"

Haspen answered not a word. His head sunk on his chest, his eyes were fixed on the ground; his heart and brain, worn out with the angry storms that had been wracking them so many hours, at last gave way, and when Latchman turned on him his cunning side-long glance, *the hard, strong workman cried!*

A gleam of joy passed over the face of the tempter; he advanced to the bricklayer—he took his large hand in his own skeleton grasp, and whispered:

"They've stolen your tools, Haspen! but there are others at the warehouse. To-morrow evening come here, at nine o'clock, and we will arrange it all."

Haspen raised his head without speaking, heaved a sigh, deep, harsh, and bitter, emptied his full glass at a draught, and casting around him a wild, savage glance, said:

"I'll come!"

The two working-men went out and parted.

V.—A NIGHT ROBBERY
"The world calls that man a robber, who presumes to take another man's property, without, himself, possessing a thousand pounds a year."

Some months after the above scene had occurred, on a cold November night, just as eleven o'clock had pealed from the tower of the Abbey, two men might be seen gliding along the wall that encompassed the premises of Barrowson.

The night was dark and rainy, the wind whistled through the few leafless trees that dotted the muddy quays of the Thames, and the roll of the river came up at times, like the sad and solemn voice of some strange warning.

"Wait here, John," said one of the men to his companion. "The rest will soon be here."

"You're sure you told them of the hour?"

"Never fear!"

"Are you sure he keeps the money in the counting-house?"

"Yesterday evening, when I gave him the keys, they were busy counting the rouleaux."

"Hush, here's some one!"

In truth, two men were seen advancing through the gloom. They soon made themselves known, and, after a short and whispered consultation, all four proceeded towards an angle of the wall. One leant against its base, another climbed on his shoulders, and the third, with the assistance of the two first, reached the summit. Once there, he helped his three companions up—they glided down into the yard, and proceeded among piles of timber and building-materials toward the interior of the premises. There the foremost halted.

"Two of you here, plant the ladder; above all, be mum—the Governor sleeps in that room overhead."

"But the dog?"

"Never mind the dog—I'll manage him."

Latchman, for it was he who had spoken, waited till his companions had secured the ladder, and then advanced at their head.

At the corner of the shed he stopped.

"Now silence! Stop there, Castor's about to wake up."

A low and angry growl was heard, such as precedes the open bark of a huge watch-dog.

"Well, Castor! Old boy, Castor, don't you know me?"

These words were spoken in a subdued and cautious tone, which, probably, was the reason why the dog did not recognise the speaker, for he darted towards Latchman, but suddenly his head was bowed to the ground.

"Here, Castor—here, my boy!"

The noble animal raised its head without misgiving; the next moment it uttered a faint, broken cry, and rolled over dead.

"On!" said the robber to those behind.

"Is it really dead?"

"Look!" Latchman had cut its throat.

They were now under the window of the counting-house, which was on the first floor.

"Plant the ladder," continued the same voice that had hitherto issued every order; "and you, Jack, mount first, because of the glass."

One of the three men mounted forthwith.

"You remain on watch, Peter. Give the alarm at the least danger."

"Never fear."

"Lest you should be seen, hide yourself in the that tool-house. You can see all about you, from there. You, Haspen come with me."

They mounted the ladder, Haspen first. Jack had in the meantime reached the window, and a pane of glass was taken out by him with marvellous dexterity.

"None but a glazier could have done that!!"

"Silence, Haspen!"

The glazier had entered the room through the window, the other two followed in their turn, and vanished in the interior. The window was forthwith closed behind them.

During several minutes the yard remained in complete silence, save the perpetual dropping of the rain from the roofs, and the whistling of the wind around the deserted sheds.

The clock struck one.

Suddenly the sound of hurried footsteps reverberated against the walls— a key grated in a lock, and a man entered the yard.

A quick and slight whistling resounded from the shed where Peter watched, and straightway human shadows appeared against the casement of the first floor; a head even became visible,—leant, listened, and as swiftly disappeared.

All sunk in the same silence as before.

Meanwhile the man who had entered the yard passed across it, in the direction of the house. The human shadows reappeared at the window, but another whistle as slight and wild, it might have been taken for the wintry wind, was heard from the shed, and the shadows vanished.

The stranger had now arrived in a line with the tool-house where Peter was concealed. It was Barrowson's partner, who lived on the premises, returning from a party.

"The careless scoundrels!" he muttered, seeing the door of the tool-house open; "there are tools there that the rain would rust," and he locked the door, and put the key in his pocket.

A few steps further on, he knocked against the ladder by which the robbers had mounted.

"A ladder too! Haven't I told them always to put them away? Leant against the wall too, as though it was to show thieves the road!"

With these words he took the ladder down, laid it flat upon the ground, and entered his lodgings to retire for the night.

More than ten minutes now elapsed without any signs of life, when a quick, short whistle again sounded from the tool-house. Forthwith the window of the counting-house opened.

"Curse it, the ladder is gone!" said Haspen, leaning over the wall.

"And Peter is shut in—we can't get down."

"Then we're taken!" exclaimed the glazier.

"Twenty feet at least—we can't jump it."

"We're lost!"

"What shall we do?"

The three men looked at each other in utter stupefaction.

"It's you—you cursed glazier, who planned our coming here," cried Haspen, clenching his fist. "If we're nabbed, you shall die by my hand."

"Don't I risk as much as you? Why did you come, if you're such a chicken-hearted rascal?"

"Silence!" said Latchman, who was the first to regain his presence of mind. "Is this a time to quarrel? Let's sooner see if we can't save ourselves."

"How? there's no chance!"

"One—and one only. This wall forms one side of the store-room, which runs up two storeys. If we break through it, we can jump down on the heap of stores piled against the side, and we can let ourselves out that way—the outer door fastens on the inside."

"But how shall we break through the wall?"

"There are always tools kept in the little room there; give me the glim. There—d'ye see—we can set to work now."

"Shall we have time?"

"Three hours before us, at least. Quick—to work."

"And Peter?"

"We can open the door of the tool-house, when we're once below. But quick—not a moment's to lose!"

The three thieves set to work in good earnest. The loosened stones began to give way, but, for fear of making a noise, they were obliged to progress but slowly. An hour was spent thus, in nervous, anxious terror; at last, a huge stone, the removal of which seemed to ensure a passage, was pushed too heavily, and fell down into the store-room with an appalling noise.

The three men stood panic-stricken.

"It's nothing! everybody's sleeping," said Latchman. "Let's see if we can pass."

"I'll try," replied the glazier, and put his head through the opening.

Without losing time in disputing precedence, his companions began to push him by the legs, but the narrow opening refused passage to the stout and thick-built robber, who struggled in vain to extricate himself.

"He'll never get through," said Latchman.

"But he must," growled Haspen, pushing him with his colossal strength.

"Help! help! you're crushing me!" exclaimed the unhappy man.

"Through! through!" cried Haspen, jamming him with terrible force.

The stones which held the glazier's body wedged, were loosened by so many efforts, and the wall from above suddenly giving way, half buried the wretched victim in the narrow opening.

"Good G—! he's crushed!" the two men cried simultaneously.

The glazier uttered no sound—his limbs became motionless.

Latchman and his companion looked at each other in silence—a terrible silence, compassing all that man can feel of agony and terror.

The legs of the body protruded into the counting-house, but the trunk and bust were hidden and wedged in the wall. The two workmen tried to release it by removing some stones, but the vice-like grasp of the masonry remained, and they vainly sought to draw the body back toward them.

More than an hour again passed, in a frenzy of despair and fear.

And already the morning twilight began to whiten in the air, and the first soft effulgence streamed across the casement, while a delicate rose colour fell upon the distant spires.

A blind fury seized Latchman and the bricklayer; the foam flaked from the mouth of the latter, the blood trickled from his hands, bruised with his long and useless efforts.

"Latchman!" he cried, mad with rage and fear, "if I dash my brains to pieces against the stones, I'll get through."

Latchman was silently busy in removing the loose masonry. His efforts shewed the more plainly their position. A large mass had formed a sort of keystone that supported the remainder. To move it, would bring down the whole, and rouse the house. Sufficient space remained for a man to pass, but that space was entirely occupied by the body of the glazier.

The two workmen saw, at a glance, that they must either withdraw the body, or wait there to be taken. But every effort to withdraw the body proved vain.

The thieves drew back discouraged.

"Impossible to get him out whole!" said Latchman, with a frenzied look. "Haspen! our life's at stake! that man is dead! *we must get him out in pieces!*"

"What do you mean?"

"There's nothing else can save us. Take you knife, and help me!"

"I cannot—No! Latchman."

"Then I must alone."

The knife flashed in the hand of the robber, and plunged into the body.

But scarcely had the blade gashed the flesh, ere a smothered shriek burst from beneath the ruin,—the body writhed convulsively, and, at a bound, disappeared through the opening.

Roused from his swoon by the sudden pain, the glazier had made one of those almost supper-human efforts, attempted only in the hour of agony, and had succeeded in forcing his way.

Haspen and his companion uttered a cry of joy, and precipitating themselves through the aperture, were soon in the store-room below. There a horrible sight awaited them. The glazier was seated on the floor, half naked and bleeding, and trying to fold up the skin of his head, which had been entirely torn down over his face. But no time was to be lost in idle pity, and the two workmen, assisting their comrade to walk, unloosened the door of the store, and were soon standing in the open yard.

Already Haspen was advancing toward the tool-house where Peter was imprisoned, his repeated signals becoming dangerously loud, as his anxiety increased with the delay—when a cry burst from the street without—a rattle was sprung—a sudden commotion arose in the house. The bricklayer paused in fear; he looked back—the counting- house was in flames!—they had left the lantern behind them, and it had fired the wood-work.

The tread of many feet was close at hand—the keys were turning in the great gates—Latchman, Haspen, and the glazier had barely time to glide behind a shed, and escape across the wall at one end of the yard, as the police and workmen entered at the other.

But Peter remained a prisoner in the tool-house.

VI.—THE ASSIZES

It was the middle of the assizes. The court was re-opened after an adjournment of an hour—and a dense crowd was assembled to hear the trial of the burglars who had broken into Barrowson's counting-house. The jury were resuming their places, after having copiously replenished their inner man with the relics of a substantial meal—and a throng of workless workmen, of curious loungers, and of interested thieves, were congregated on all sides.

The judge was a fat good-natured looking man, of about sixty, with a fresh colour, and a frolic-some eye; very fond of cracking a joke, and passing even sentence of death so pleasantly, as though the criminal ought to feel excessively obliged to him. He was the perfect type of that fat, round, easy, middle-class justice, that most complacently sets about vindicating public morals, and avenging public order, with the most comfortable calm of conscience, on four thousand pounds per annum.

Baron Snobtape was born of a legal family—his father, grandfather, and great-grandfather had been lawyers before him—and he was considered the cleverest man upon the bench. No one, like him could disconcert hardihood, or throw artifice off its guard! His great, jolly, good-natured face disarmed suspicion. No one, like him, could feign an interest in a prisoner, or put a captious question with seeming careless indifference.

There was a great rivalry at this time between Snobtape and Baron

Papergules—and, accordingly, the former had exerted all his ability on this occasion. As he shone in proving guilt, not innocence, the fate of the prisoner was certain.

In vain was the assumed stupidity of innocence—so difficult to convict of hypocrisy. In vain Latchman, who defended himself with the most brilliant cunning, had upset one piece of evidence after another, and explained away the most damning circumstances. Snobtape succeeded in making the witnesses contradict each other. In vain Peter, with heroic constancy, refused to turn queen's evidence! (what heroism and self-sacrifice there is in the world, and wasted—wasted worthlessly!)—Snobtape disconcerted cunning and courage alike—link by link he soldered the manacles around the limbs of the prisoners, and in this race between the cunning of justice and the cunning of crime—the former was gaining rapidly a victory.

An intense interest was excited by the trial—but what was its effect upon the public? That interest went with the accused, and not with the accuser! The public came to hear this struggle of intellect against despair—for life on the one side, for gain upon the other—with feelings kindred to those that take it to the playhouse. Justice was strong—and impulsive generosity took the weaker side. The narration of that night of agony in the counting-house, the thrilling tremor of the hair-breadth escape—the subsequent capture—the refusal of Peter to implicate his comrades—all caused greater interest in the criminals than horror of the crime. *Did justice gain here?* No! public feeling, like a retributive conscience, avenged in its impulsive sympathy on the stern justice of the rich, the social injustice that had forced the poor to sin. This feeling was heightened by the presence of Margaret with her two children—and grew more deep as one by one the folds were raised from that dread drama of domestic misery. But the evidence of little Catherine sealed her father's fate. The poor child was placed in the witness-box. It was a terrible sight to mark the keen, cold, long-practised intellect of the hardened lawyer, wrestling with the fond innocence of the faithful child who strove to save her father. It was hideous to hear the bland, singing tones of the old man, surprising her unguarded innocence, and breaking through her weak and fragile caution. Every confession wrested from the young girl's ignorance tied the halter closer round her father's neck.

That evidence decided the case. It is true the judge and court listened to the defence with complacent kindness. Indeed, a young barrister had received his maiden brief to defend Haspen. He was a friend and protege of Snobtape. Descended of a rich family, with large expectations, he danced and sung with the Misses Snobtape—he was a good match—and Snobtape was pushing him. Some ladies were accommodated with private seats to hear him—they were members of both families—Laura Snobtape was among them! The young lawyer made a truly pretty speech—he spoke for the ladies—he awakened tender sympathies—he delivered himself of rhetorical passages, but as to anything that could save his client's neck, not one word of the kind did he utter—or ever think of uttering. On concluding, his friends gathered round him—he was complimented on his excellent debut, and Laura Snobtape tapped him with her fan, while the jury said, "guilty," and the strong heart-broken man was called up for judgment in the presence of his wife and children.

The sentence of the court was transportation for life—and hard labour at the hulks for the first ten years. The convicts heard the sentence in motionless silence, and the public—the play once over—went away in careless hurry to seek other pastime or profitable employment.

One woman, with two children, remained alone of all that crowd of strangers, besides the officers of the court, and one or two lawyers arranging for the next case. The prisoners were removed at once to the hulks. In an ante-room they were allowed to see their friends once more.

Margaret advanced to Haspen with little Mary in her arms.

"John," she said, kindly, "here are your children. Kiss them."

"Leave me alone, Margaret!" the bricklayer replied, hurriedly without raising his eyes. "Get away! Don't think about me!"

"Haspen—for the love of heaven! kiss your children!" and she pushed Catherine and Mary into their father's arms.

The latter raised his head—a savage glare shot from his eyes—the muscles of his face worked, and his large hand roughly repulsed his little children.

"Get away, woman! You have been my ruin! Away with you, all! It was to stop your cries for bread that I robbed. You have been my black angel! Get away—get away, I say! Leave me ! Go—go!"

And he staggered out with his goalers.

The counsel who had defended Haspen, had entered during this scene, and beheld it with astonishment. He thought it would make a capital article for the *Legal Times,* to show "the depravity and heartlessness of the poor"—for he was a literary man as well as a lawyer. Accordingly, to glean more, he approached Margaret, who had remained, erect and motionless, before the vacant space where Haspen had just stood.

"Your husband seems to be rather rough, my good woman," said the young lawyer, carelessly twirling his golden eye-glass.

"That's true, sir," she replied, as one half-stunned, "Haspen has a rough tongue and a heavy hand."

"Then you need regret it the less, that society takes him from you, and screens you from his brutal treatment."

Margaret raised her dark eyes on the young lawyer.

"Oh! then it's society that takes my husband from me, sir?"

"Yes, my good woman—to punish and reform him."

"Then society will take care of my children, won't it?—as it takes away Haspen, who alone enabled us to live, it will replace him to us, won't it."

The lawyer smiled.

"You don't understand, my good woman; society means all the world. All mankind are united like one great family —this family is called society,—and punishes any one of its members who injures another, the same as you would punish your little girl if she hurt her sister. Haspen has hurt a member of society, by robbing him of his rightful property, and to punish him he is sent to the hulks. Do you understand it now?"

"Oh, yes sir. But then why are my children and I punished, who never did any harm to anybody? For now we're without bread. Haspen will be in prison, and there he will get plenty of food; we shall be at liberty, and there we shall die of hunger. D'ye see, we shall be worse punished than he!"

The lawyer kept twirling his eye-glass—but seemed rather at a loss for an answer.

At last he said, "It's an unavoidable misfortune."

"But, sir, if we're all one family, as you said just now, surely this shouldn't be. If I punish my little girl because she's done wrong, I don't throw a part of the punishment on her sister. For, d'ye see, sir, taking my husband away from me for life, is the same as if he died. It would have been better had you killed him, for then I might, perhaps, have found another father for these children."

"Your husband *is* civilly dead," rejoined the lawyer, delighted at having found a means of turning the question. "You may look on yourself as a widow. If you had children by him now, they would be bastards. If he earns money before he dies you wouldn't inherit it. Henceforth, society looks on him as dead."

"Oh, then I can marry again, sir, can't I, if I find anybody who'll work to give these children bread?"

"No! not a bit—of course not," cried the lawyer, impatiently. "How stupid these working-people are!" he added, in an undertone. "They can't understand anything."

And, in truth, Margaret was too simple to understand the justice of our laws. Her learning was only COMMON SENSE!

VII.—RESULTS

The trial of Latchman, Haspen, and their accomplices, had revealed the underhand dealings of Barrowson—had brought many things to light, of which nothing was publicly known—and shewn the various infamous means by which he robbed the earnings of his men. He had received many public slights on this account, and altogether, a very disagreeable impression was made on the public mind.

Barrowson saw the necessity of doing something to efface it. He had not lived so long in the world without having learnt that it was necessary to sacrifice, at times, a little to appearances. He well knew that public opinion looked on virtue as a very troublesome lady, but one, nevertheless, with whom it would never do to break entirely—and with whom it was necessary to be at least on bowing terms.

Accordingly he offered Margaret the place of porteress on his premises—which favour conferred on the wife of the man who had robbed him, was looked on by all the world as an act of the most sublime generosity, and perfectly re-established him in the good graces of society.

Margaret, pursuant to this arrangement, took up her abode on Barrowson's premises.

But the name of a convict's wife marked her like the brand of a red-hot iron. She had to suffer every humiliation that could reach so humble and obscure a life. The people have their nobility of honesty,—the noblest that can be!—but alas! just as haughty, as exclusive, and as unjust as all the others!

Margaret was placed in a position superior to that she had hitherto known; but, obliged to renounce her old acquaintance, she found no countenance from the new; gone were her pleasant chats at the street corner—as attractive to her as the ball-room and *converzatione* to the child of fashion. And the children! No more sports and games—the very children, glad to have a triumph over a weaker sister, insulted the children of the convicted burglar. All was lost for that unhappy family. If Catherine or her little sister tried to mingle in the sports of their former playmates,—all hands closed before theirs outstretched to form the merry round—and they were forced to sit on a stone at the opposite side of the yard, seeing, with big tears on their cheeks, the others laughing in the sunlight, free, unstained, and frolicsome. It was long before Margaret could accustom herself to her new fate, and accept her badge of misery. As to Catherine, she fitted herself into her new position with greater courage. The first tears once shed, she determined to take life as she found it. The child inherited much of the firm, haughty, nature of her father—much of that disposition to brave public opinion, which makes either a hero or a criminal, according to the force of circumstances. Meanwhile, as she grew up, she became more and more careless of the scorn of others—more hardened against the censures of the world. Her strong, bold spirit soon persuaded itself that, where honour was once gone, virtue was an unnecessary luxury. Repulsed for a fault not her own, she made up her mind at once—and instead of useless fretting against the prejudices that destroyed her, she accepted her disgrace complacently, and placed herself at ease amidst her shame.

This callous and depraved reasoning was but strengthened by the intercourse of dissolute young men and abandoned women, *the only society the prejudice of the virtuous allowed her!* Her heart was prostituted by the impure contact—long before she had committed any actual sin; she needed now but an opportunity for the latter. That opportunity soon offered.

Catherine was beautiful—with that rich, full, solid beauty, so enticing to the sensualist. Barrowson had not failed to notice her. She was exactly to his taste. He had little difficulty in succeeding with his victim.

The situation of Catherine soon demanded secrecy—and Barrowson, who was a most punctilious observer of the decencies—sent her off privately to a village a short way out of town.

Her mother heard of her dishonour and of her departure at the same time.

She uttered no reproaches—she knew they would have been laughed at—but she determined on forthwith quitting the neighbourhood, and going somewhere where her misfortunes would not taunt her in the public street.

A year, however, had elapsed, before she could realize her intention.

During this time, Catherine had followed her course, and had arrived at the goal: *she was on the streets!*

This was too much. Margaret Haspen sold all the little she had gathered together since her husband's "death," and set off for the country, where Barrowson granted her a lease of a little public-house, halfway between town and his country seat.

The worthy man placed the crown on all his kindness by giving her a letter of recommendation to his brewer and spirit dealer, and promised to bait his horse at her door whenever he passed that way. This was, indeed, remarkably convenient to him, for he was in the habit of riding or driving down to this house of a Saturday evening—and frequently either alone, or in very questionable company—this half-way house being a place of rendezvous—not used for the most laudable purposes by our worthy merchant. It happened just to be vacant, and he thought he could not place a more ready tool to keep it than Margaret, the convict's wife.

After all, Barrowson was an excellent creature!

VIII.—THE HALF-WAY HOUSE.

It was six o'clock in the evening; the weather was sultry; a grey mist covered the sky—and a hot wind lifted the sand fitfully along the broad and dusty road. A little girl of eight stood at the door of a lonely public-house, some ten miles on the road from London, and about a mile distant from the nearest village. She had been gathering some wild flowers in the fields, and they drooped withering in her hand, while, singing a monotonous song, but with a sweet and mournful voice, she stood intently gazing down the long and arid highway, and evidently expecting someone. In the distance down the road, the granite spire of a market town just beckoned over the trees. At last, with a cry of pleasure, she let her flowers drop, and bounded forward.

"Good evening, mother—mother!" and Margaret Haspen was obliged to stop, as little Mary dashed against her in her exuberant joy.

"Get out of the way, you plague! or I shall throw you down," said Margaret; but in a kindly tone, at variance with the words, and taking little Mary in her arms, pressed her fondly to her breast.

"What news, Mary? Has anybody been?"

"Oh, yes; lots of people! Three men and a woman—all at once!"

"Did you give them to drink?"

"Yes. But they'd drank too much already—for they could scarcely walk."

"Did they pay you?"

"Oh, yes. Then the woman asked my name; and when I said Mary Haspen, I don't know what was the matter with her—she grew quite white—and then began to cry."

"What's that you say?"

"And after having cried a good deal, she took me in her arms and kissed me. Then she asked me if we were all well, and if we were poor."

"And did she tell you who she was?"

"Oh, no. She would have said more, but the men came, and laughed at her because she cried. Then she began to laugh and sing. She drank a great deal of gin, and then they all left together. Oh! I'd nearly forgot—*she said she would come back to-night to see you.*"

Margaret grew thoughtful, and asked no more questions. She soon recognised, by a description which the child had given, her long-lost daughter Catherine. The men were evidently strangers she had enticed away to the public house. Bitter thoughts crowded on her brain, and she sighed heavily, and then mechanically set about setting the house in order.

———

Margaret Haspen had put little Mary to bed—the sun had set—it was growing dark—she sat alone before the fire, listening to the hollow, melancholy wind that moaned sadly through the dry foliage of the sunburnt trees, when suddenly the sound of steps were heard before the door.

Margaret Haspen turned round, and saw by the indistinct twilight, the figure of a labouring man pass the window, hesitatingly, and looking around him, as one who feared discovery. Having assured himself that no one but the bricklayer's wife was in the bar-kitchen, he entered.

"Good evening to ye! Can you give us a light, missus?"—and he took an unkindled pipe out of his mouth.

"There's the fire!"—said Margaret.

The newcomer walked to the fire-place, slowly twisted a piece of paper, lit it, and held it to his pipe still, after it had gone out, for his eyes were busy scanning the premises. Feeling sure, at last, that Margaret was quite alone, he took off his waggoner's slouch-hat, and said—

"Don't you know me again, Margaret Haspen?"

The woman uttered a cry of surprise.

"You! Latchman!"

"Hush! silence!—don't speak that name!—are you alone in the house?"

"Yes! quite alone!—But why?"

Without giving an answer—Latchman gave a wild, peculiar whistle.

Immediately heavy footsteps were heard, and another man, dressed like a labourer, entered.

"There's no one here but Margaret,"—said Latchman, and the new visitor also uncovered his head—it was Haspen!

Latchman stopped another exclamation of surprise on the part of Margaret—

"Great ——! Is it you?"—said the poor woman trembling in every limb.

"It's us, Margaret—shut the door—and now—quick! give us some grub—for we've had nothing for twelve hours!"

The woman never moved. Her faded eyes could not stray from those two pale, hardened faces, gleaming through the fire-light of the room like some threatening apparition from the past.

"Well!—Moggy! d'ye hear me?"—said Haspen, pushing her gently.

The sound of that voice, whose harsh, metallic tones were but too well remembered, made her start, as though beneath the touch of a half-closed wound. However, mechanically, and with a kind of fear, she proceeded to the cupboard, and placed some food and drink before her sullen guests.

There was silence for several minutes—the two men ate with eager haste—Margaret had withdrawn to a remote dark corner, and sat watching them, as the red fire-light fell upon their Cain-like foreheads.

At last Haspen turned, and said— "you don't seem over-joyed to see us, Margaret!—yet it's not so very short a time since we parted."

"It's a pity, John, that we ever met!"—sighed Margaret—but not reproachfully.

"I know, Margaret!" and his tone was softened— "and yet, it might have been different—*it's a pity,* Margaret!—Where are the children?"

The wretched woman was more startled at the tone, than she had been at the first appearance of that evening's visitors. Her hand trembled much, and her cheek was very pale, as she took the candle and led the outcast to the bed-side of his child.

Opening the slide of the recessed bed, she fainted. The stalwart felon stepped to the bed, with the soft footfall of a slender girl.

Little Mary lay lapped in careless sleep. The roses sparkled on her dimpled cheeks—her long lashes drooped peacefully over her closed eyes—her bright, brown, curly hair wantoned around her little neck—and one pretty hand, hanging listlessly open, shewed the innocence of her unconscious slumber. Haspen looked at her some moments, in utter silence—then he slowly bent, and pressed one gentle kiss upon her pure, calm forehead. Recording angels!— there was a tear left there!

The felon turned round abruptly—and walked with long, quick strides, to the door; Margaret re-closed the slide.

At last, he said, in a rough, hurried tone—

"Where's Catherine?"

The poor mother bowed her head.

"Catherine has left me."

"Left you? Why?"

"She got into bad ways—and"—

"And—what?—Well?"

"She was with child."

"Ah!"—

Haspen folded his arms across his breast, with a gloomy look—and remained silent a long time.

"Who was she with child by?"—he said at length, as though struck by a sudden thought.

"By Barrowson."

The name had scarce escaped the lips of Margaret—before the felon had started up with clenched fists, and flashing eyes.

"*Barrowson* and *Barrowson*—and always BARROWSON!"—he hissed through his closed teeth. *He* always—and HE— and HE alone upon my path!— and I can't crush his head between these two hands"— and he made a terrible gesture.

He sat down again, his whole body trembled with ungovernable rage.

Three was a long pause, which no one ventured to interrupt. Latchman had the true tact of knowing when to speak and when to keep silent. He had not uttered a word during the conversation between Haspen and his wife, and he, therefore, waited now, without shewing either impatience or uneasiness. At last, when he thought his companion sufficiently cool to listen to him, he reminded him of the dangers that surrounded them, and of the priceless value of the passing moments.

Both the fugitives formed part of a widely spread metropolitan association of thieves, of whom strong numbers resided here and there about the country, affording asylum, assistance, and concealment to the imperilled brothers of the community. This commonwealth of thieves has remained immutable, while kingdoms and republics, empires and constitutions have melted away from over and around it.

The two fugitives had, accordingly, depended for concealment on the wide ramifications of their union, and relied for evading the police on the secret resting places they could meet in the crowded solitudes of London, and the denuded solitudes of the country.

In the village near Margaret's abode, lived one of their accomplices. Him they now sought to reach. After a whispering conversation with Haspen, Latchman turned to Margaret.

"Do you know Plotchild?"

"What—the beer-house keeper in the next village?"

"Yes, I know him."

"We must get to his house. How shall we find it?"

"If you go there, you'll be taken. The police 'use' the house now."

"The ——! What shall we do now, Latchman?"

"We must send for him to come here."

"Moggy, will you go for us?" said Haspen.

"If it is necessary to save you."

"Well, then, go—go quick! Tell him his friends of the dark glim' want to see him."

"And if he refuses to come?"

"You tell him that, and he'll come."

Margaret went.

The two felons were alone in the house—alone, save the sleeping Mary.

Latchman fastened the door behind her, and sat down at the table by the side of his companion.

"If this cove will but shell out."

"Perhaps he'll put us in the way of cribbing something. There are plenty of bens here to get into."

"There are the travellers* too—their pockets are well lined."

"We'll do what we can—but as for the stone-jug, I'll have no more of it. I'd sooner be scragged. The first who tries to grab me I'll cook his goose for him with this," and the bricklayer drew a formidable knife, sharpened into a point by the patient laboriousness peculiar to a prisoner preparing for escape.

"Mind you don't miss fire, then, and let out some tin with the claret."

Haspen made no answer, but he clutched convulsively that arm of death, and his eyes glared savagely, as some fearful but enticing picture seemed to rise before his mental sight. Latchman thought he was merely responding to his sanguinary jest.

"We must have blunt, one way or another, that's clear," said the latter, "for without a tanner or two we should be nabbed in four-and-twenty hours."

"I tell you, Latchman, I won't go back there, and stand so, any longer, with a chain on my leg, and be made a sight of to the stray visitors who pass a pleasant hour looking at the wild beasts in their cage. No, I'll hang—so, I'll make sure of that, before they catch me."

Latchman nodded approval, and the two felons lit their pipes, and smoked in silence.

Some little time had elapsed thus, when a horse's steps were heard in great distance along the road, coming in the direction from London.

The two men raised their heads, and listened.

"Who can that be?" whispered Haspen, with the confused suspiciousness of trembling guilt.

"We can stag him thro' here," and Latchman climbed on the dresser, to look through a small hole at the top of the closed shutter.

"It's a swell on horseback."

"Hallo! He stops."

"What's he doing?"

"He's fastened his horse—he's taking off a portmanteau—he's coming to the door."

At the closed door, the traveller let his portmanteau drop on the ground, and a jingling, as of money, was distinctly audible.

The two thieves looked meaningly at each other.

Meanwhile the traveller had knocked at the door, and receiving no answer, cried in an angry voice:

"Well, Margaret, are you asleep or dead? Why don't you let me in?"

"By my soul, I know that voice," said Haspen. "Listen, Latchman, haven't you heard it before? Look, if you know him."

"It's too dark. Oliver's got his nightcap on.* But, at any rate, there's no

* Commerical travellers

harm in opening, we're two, and he's alone."

"But, if he knows us, Latchman, he'll tell."

"One can easily prevent his doing that," said the convict, with a soft smile that had something horrible in it.

"Margaret, you infernal ——! why don't you let me in?"

"Who's there?" answered Latchman, mimicking Margaret's voice.

"Who the deuce should it be? I—BARROWSON."

"BARROWSON!" cried the bricklayer, darting forward, and seizing the knife he had laid on the table. "Let him in! Quick! Let him in!"

The door opened—and Barrowson walked in.

"The D— seize you! I thought you meant to let me shiver there all night. There's a fog enough to soak you to the bone—Ha! where's Margaret?"—he added, on perceiving what he had neglected to notice at first, that it was not Margaret who had let him in. He had proceeded right across the room to the fire-place. In looking round for the absent hostess—his eyes encountered the face of Haspen—who stood erect, motionless, and terrible, before him.

Barrowson uttered a cry of half surprise, half fear,—and involuntarily made a step towards the door.

Latchman had closed it, and stood with his back leaning against it.

Barrowson's ruddy face turned very pale—its expression became anxious. However, he tried to resume his usual jovial manner, and exclaimed:

"The deuce, friends! who would have thought of seeing you here."

"Or you either," rejoined Latchman, taking off his hat, and bowing with deliberate irony— "we are quite delighted to see you in good health, and especially with a well-filled portmanteau."

The rich man looked at his treasure with trembling—he still held it in his hand.

"What?—that?—oh nothing! that's nothing, only a few shirts,—that's all.—But where's Margaret?"

"She's gone—Barrowson!—and—*you are alone with us!*"

Haspen uttered these words in a tone so deep and dread—that the merchant started at every syllable.

"Then,"—said the latter—stammering, and advancing to the door— "we'll—we'll ride on home—good-night—friends?—"

"Why do you want to go," interposed Latchman, "you'll sleep very comfortably here. We'll make do all right in Margaret's absence, depend upon it—you shan't want for anything we can do for you. To begin—let me relieve you of this load"—and he laid his hand on the portmanteau.

"No! No! Not a bit! Don't trouble yourself, I'll let nobody have it."

---

* The moon's behind a cloud.

"Pooh! only some shirts! that's all," resumed Latchman—shaking it and making the money jingle.

"What a deuced odd sound these shirts of yours have! Come, my boy! sit down by the fire, and make yourself at home."

The miserable merchant felt his heart fail him. His eyes wandered from Latchman to the bricklayer—and found no encouragement from either. The face of the latter, especially, literally flashed with hate. Barrowson once more moved to the door with undisguised terror.

"For the love of heaven, let me go! Gentlemen!"

"We are no gentlemen!"—interposed Haspen, in a hoarse, dry tone, in which the desire of prolonging the scene, struggled with the almost irresistible impulse of his fury—"thanks to you—to you—who forced the felons' chain upon our legs!"

"My friends!—don't blame me—I was not the cause—rest assured—my good friends!—Let me go!—and I swear by all that's sacred, I'll never tell a soul that I have seen you!"

"We're not afraid—for you won't go from here!" sneered Latchman.

"What do you mean? my friends!" and the faltering merchant could scarcely articulate. "Haspen!—my friend!"

"I your friend!"—thundered the bricklayer, every muscle of his frame suddenly starting into convulsive action "—I?—I?—I whom you ruined? I! who would tear you with my bare hands!"

And he strode towards Barrowson,—his eyes on fire, his arms stretched forward, his fingers curved to seize their prey.

The unhappy merchant completely lost his presence of mind.

"Where am I—Oh my God!—am I in a den of cut-throats?"

"For you, at least! Barrowson!" cried Haspen, as he seized the portly merchant with his muscular arm, and threw him backwards over a bench before the hearth. The victim raised himself upon his knees—a hideous and a pitiable sight. His wild, unmeaning eyes were starting from their sockets, his hands were raised in supplication, his body bent in the attitude of the most humiliating abjectness—his whole appearance exhibited what villainy has most vile, and fear most cowardly. He tried to speak, but his teeth chattered together, and he could scarcely make himself heard.

"For the love of heaven! Haspen!—let me go!—I always did good to your family; it was I who placed your wife here. Don't take advantage of this place. Let me go."

"Ha! you did good to my family! did you?" hissed the bricklayer. "Tell me, was it in lowering my wages, to drive me into want? Was it in turning me out of work, forcing me to steal from sheer hunger? Was it in sending me to the hulks? Was it in ruining Catherine, whom you have turned upon the streets? Oh! you have done my family much good, Barrowson! And I! I'll pay it you back now! I won't be ungrateful, one good turn for another! one by one! See, Barrowson!—there's for lowering my wage!" and the heavy shod foot of the bricklayer smote the merchant's head, that he flew back crashing against the fire-place wall.

"That's for turning me adrift! That's for sending me to the hulks! That's for my child, Catherine! D'ye hear, Barrowson! for my child!—Catherine! Kate! Pretty little Kate!—There!—There!—There!—Ha! ha! ha!"

At every word the foot of the convict came down with a terrible blow, and the bruised and bloody head of the merchant rolled round upon the hearth-stone. He still uttered suppressed cries of agony, and once, he even succeeded in half raising himself, streaming with blood, and crying:

"Mercy, Haspen, mercy! forgive me, oh my God! don't kill me, Haspen! mercy! don't kill me!"

He then fell forward on his face, grovelling, like a serpent, on his belly, before his former workman, and embracing his legs in abject supplication, tears and blood together fell from his face.

But Haspen was frenzied. "You never had pity on me! I want your blood, Barrowson!"

With one hand he held the merchant writhing at his feet; with the other he stretched towards the table, trying to reach the knife he had laid there. He grasped it at length.

But scarcely had Barrowson seen the glimmer of the blade by the fire-light, ere, with one of those sudden returns of strength that the last agony and the last despair confer, he tore himself away—dashed the bricklayer back, and darted to the darkest corner of the kitchen, where he remained, uttering piercing cries.

"Cut his throat! silence him, Haspen, or we're lost!"

But Haspen had already bounded after him, and seizing the merchant by the hair, had thrown him upon his knees—his head thrown backward, and the long blade of the knife disappeared to the very hilt down the throat and breast of the victim.

Barrowson fell from him without a sigh. Haspen placed a foot upon his forehead, and drew out the knife jammed firmly in the bones.

Latchman drew near. He looked on the body with perfect indifference, and turned the head round with his foot, as if to see whether life really were extinct. The body never moved.

"That's well done. He'll tell no tales!"

"Water!" cried the bricklayer, whose hands were dripping with blood.

"There! But what shall we do with him now?"

"Follow me, and you'll see."

At this moment a key turned in the lock of the house door—it opened gently—and Margaret stood upon the threshold.

IX.—CATHERINE.

On the afternoon of the fatal night, the occurrence of which we have just recorded, Catherine, as the reader will recollect, had called at the half-way house, in company with two men, light companions of her fallen days, whom she had lured on an excursion in the country. It will, moreover, be remembered, that she had promised little Mary to return in the evening.

Separated from her mother during two years, she had lost sight of her early home, and wandered hither and thither, without knowing the dwelling-place of her deserted mother. Chance had now thrown that knowledge in her way. Although sunk in the lowest stages of vice, this poor young girl had not lost all her better nature; in the midst of her degradation she cherished a remembrance of maternal love, and above the gangrene of foul lusts, some feelings of pure love still rose, like the sweet flowers that sometimes cluster over a corrupt and pestilent swamp.

She had, therefore, resolved to return to the half-way house that very night, once more to see her mother, to obtain her forgiveness, and to embrace her once again.

Unfortunately, her loose companions had detained her to a very late hour, and when she left them, she was so far gone under the influence of the drink they had forced her to partake of, that she had great difficulty in recognising and pursuing the road to her mother's house.

She tried, nevertheless, to find her way, but felt herself so stupefied, that she entered a field and sat down to rest. Scarcely had she done so, ere sleep overpowered her.

Several hours must have passed before she awoke. The darkness was very great; a mist lay reeking on the ground and trees, and a mournful wind crept moaning through the branches.

Catherine passed her hands across her eyes, stretched her cold, stiffened limbs, and began to look round for her onward path.

She was on the side of a large field of furze that ran on one side of a cross-road; the moon was behind a great black cloud; but a gleam that fell through a break in the mass, disclosed a white strip in the distance (while all else was lost in gloom); it was the highway leading from the village past the half-way house.

Towards this she endeavoured to direct her steps. Rising with difficulty, she was skirting along the ditch, when she thought she heard, not far off, a confused whispering of voices. Then she saw some indistinct shadows advancing through the mist.

She stood motionless and observant.

Soon, two men became distinctly visible, stealing along the hedge, and carrying an apparently very heavy burden. At a short distance from the young girl they stopped, and let their load drop to the earth, which it did with a dull, cushion-like sound.

"This is a good place," said the least of the two men, who were dressed in the garb of labourers; "by throwing him here, they'll think it's some chap who's been 'spoken to' on the highway."

Catherine trembled, as she heard these words, and conceived their meaning.

"Besides which, nobody'll come here in a hurry," replied the other. "This furze is only two years old, and nobody'll touch it yet a bit."

"Have you the mattock?"

"Yes; and the pick. Stand out there a little more."

The two men set to work, and Catherine heard their violent and hurried labour, as they were hewing out a trench.

Her eyes now wandered to the burden which the men had laid down at some little distance from her. It was wrapped in a large piece of sacking, and as far as she could judge by the feeble light of a solitary star that stepped forth amid the darkness, two or three large black-looking streaks appeared to have sweated through the surface. Who could the victim be? Where could it have been stricken? She determined to do her best towards discovering the murderers.

Catherine's nature was not easily susceptible of fear—and, moreover, the remaining excitement of drink gave her that audacity which, at such times, takes the place of courage even with the most timid. She therefore determined not to attempt flight, but to remain and watch; and accordingly crouched down behind a tuft of furze.

The two labourers had soon completed the trench, whereupon they each lifted an end of the sack.

"Take care!" said the taller; "mind that no spots get on your clothes."

"That's not so easy," rejoined the other. "His head is at my end, and the blood runs like beer when the spiggot's drawn."

They dropped their load into the hole, threw the earth back over it, and Catherine heard them trampling on the heap, to flatten down the surface. They then carefully replaced the sod, and stuck some furze here and there into its old place.

"It's all over now!" observed the lesser of the two men; *"he'll* never complain of the face-ache again!"

"Yes!—it is over!" rejoined the other, in a voice so slow and solemn, that his companion started.

The last speaker then stood bareheaded and silent, for a moment, ere he added—

"We are quits now. Good-night, Barrowson!"

A faint sound, like a half-stifled shriek, was heard from amid the furze.

"Hush! List! Jack! did you hear that?"

"What?"

"I thought I heard a cry!"

"Where? Where?"

"Here—close by—*from the earth!*"

"Pooh! the wind in the furze. You're funking! Come on."

The two men advanced straight towards Catherine.

"This time it's no funking. Do you hear that? Look to the road!"

They stopped, and the measured pace of the rural police sounded from the lane.

"It's the peelers! Down! quick!" and they both lay flat upon the grass. They almost touched Catherine. She hardly dared to breathe. The police passed by—they were saved.

"Now, Jack—run! They made my heart go like a dog's tail."

The two men rose, and rapidly hurrying across the field, soon disappeared behind the hedge.

Cautiously Catherine rose, too—crept, more than walked, to the ditch, and peered through the bushes. The moon burst forth, and shone full upon the road,—and by its keen, cold, pursuing beam, the watcher distinctly saw two men emerge on the high road, and hurry on in a direction leading from the village already noticed as lying at some distance from the half-way house.

She, also, then crossed the hedge, and hurried towards the village on which the fugitives had turned their backs.

————

Catherine had been at the police-station about half an hour. The sleeping sergeant had been rousted up—and a statement of all she had witnessed during the night had been taken down from the lips of the young girl.

The deposition was almost finished, when the gallop of a horseman was heard in the street, and a mounted policeman alighted at the office.

He deposed as follows:—

"This evening, late, Plotchild, who, as you know, sir, holds with the hare and runs with the hounds, told me that two runaway convicts were at a house in the neighbourhood. I at once got some of my men, and then proceeded to the spot. Though very late, there was light in the house—the house door was fastened, we knocked, but no one answered, so we forced the door, and what should we see, but this woman busy washing out the marks of blood from the floor and walls. As soon as she saw us, she almost fainted, and cried: 'I'm lost!' I arrested her at once,—left the house in charge of one of my men, and here we are."

Catherine had listened to the inspector's report with a strange and unaccountable anxiety; some vague foreboding shook her. She leant forward to look at the face of the female prisoner, but the latter stooped, and a large bonnet, and drooping handkerchief laid over it, concealed her features.

"This is important," said the sergeant, "Just as you came, this girl was deposing that she had seen two men bury a body in a field."

Scarcely had the sergeant spoken the words, ere the prisoner looked up, and fixed her eyes on Catherine: a piercing shriek announced the mutual recognition.

"My mother! Oh, my mother! My God! what have I done?" and Catherine sank senseless in the arms of Margaret Haspen!

X.—A CAPTURE.

A few days afterwards Haspen and Latchman were drinking in the ale-house of an obscure village, they had entered towards dusk. A change had been coming over Haspen during the last few days—he had had his revenge on Barrowson—his one great thirst was slaked, and he kept growing more and more reckless of concealment—more and more unfriendly every day, to the great horror of Latchman. While seated, exhausted, haggard, and broken down in mind and body, in the humble bar, a man entered, apparently a tramp like themselves. He called for beer, and while drinking it, cast his sinister and prying eyes over the rim of the pot, furtively upon the wayworn fugitives. After a sly and lengthened scrutiny, the stranger rose with an unconcerned air, whispered to the landlord, and went out.

Latchman turned and said something to Haspen.

"I don't care—I'm tired of this at last—I'll die!" rejoined the latter, in a scarcely suppressed tone.

"I'm not, then," whispered Latchman; "come—look at that man! for God's sake—don't speak so loud!"

"For God's sake! What have you to do with God?" answered Haspen, with a cold, bitter, retributive irony, as conscience or common sense stirred in his stormy, rude brain. He took no pains to subdue his voice.

Latchman trembled in every limb.

"John! you're mad—don't be a fool! come, quick! we shall be taken, I'm sure, if you don't! Look at that man! It's dark—there's time still, we can both take different sides, and meet again in——"

"Hell! We go together—we part company no more."

"Haspen! you've the money—give it me."

Haspen had kept the profit of the last plunder—a new thing for him to do, since he knew Latchman had always been the purse-bearer. Was there a secret cunning in the act, by which he bound the seducer down to the standard of his own extremities. Latchman lingered on the spot of danger for the money—he feared to fly without it, for the money afforded him his only chance of escape from the encircling and quick pursuit. The path was still clear; the one man could not venture to arrest them—it was dark—the country was wooded and thinly peopled—there was a certainty of escape, if attempted before the other stranger returned with the local police and assistance from the village.

"Haspen—come—quick—the money!"

Haspen remained looking on his companion with a grim smile of delight, but answered nothing.

Hurried steps as of several men were heard coming in the direction of the street.

"Are you mad, John? Do you hear,—— Well then! I'm off——go to the devil by yourself."——and he was about to dart through the open door—but before he could realise his intention, the strong hand of the bricklayer was fixed with a vice-like clutching upon his arm—but he uttered not a word!

"Are you mad? are you mad? Haspen! Let me go"—and he writhed his thin form like a serpent in the grasp of a fallen Hercules!

The wretched felon shrieked, implored, threatened, fought—but the strong man stood impassable—it was fate, seizing its prey.

Suddenly the fugitives were surrounded by the police and a large crowd of people. The time of flight was gone. In that war of two against the world, the world had conquered. Latchman ceased struggling, and cowered down like a re-captured hound before a cruel master.

"There! take him!" roared Haspen, with a sound of triumphant joy in his voice; "there, take him;" he cried, as he lifted the wretch from the ground, and hurled him into the arms of the surrounding law; "that is Latchman, who taught me my first robbery—that is Latchman, the thief and *murderer*. And I'm John Haspen, who *killed* Barrowson, the scoundrel—take him; and now take all you'll get of me."

With the shriek of a fiend, the doomed Latchman flew into the arms of his recoiling captors, who then closed round to seize their remaining prey; but, with the rapidity of lightning, Haspen drew forth the knife that had slain Barrowson, and the first of his assailants fell dead at his feet. "Come on, come on!" he yelled; but the bravest shrank back before his terrible despair. At last, closing in on him from all sides, they beat him down with long staves and the forms that stood in the bar. Half stunned, and brought to the ground, he struggled still, streaming with blood at every pore, with gnashing teeth and foaming mouth. The man was turned into the wild beast, fighting not for life or for revenge, but in the fierce paroxysms of dying fury. At last his assailants rushed close in upon him, prostrate as he lay, his broken arm had fallen by his side—his heaving heart panted with exhaustion—and the heavy truncheons of the police dealt the crashing blows with impunity upon his now unguarded head. When silence was restored in the wrecked bar, shattered by the terrible conflict, the still form of the felon was borne out upon a shutter, one mass of wounds, bruises, and blood. He still breathed a few times, but never recovered consciousness, and expired before he could be carried to the station.

XI.—AN EXECUTION

An execution was to take place at Newgate. It had been announced long beforehand, as an instructive and national solemnity. The press had been pointing attention to it, day by day. Before daybreak, the people began to assemble—the people, so anxious for anything that will tear them out of the dull monotony of their cheerless, routine life! They came, as they would to the public-house, seeking something to drown thought for a few hours. They came, as they had gone the previous evening to the playhouse, to get the amusement of one excitement more!

The pomps of the olden days are gone, with their magic of song and scent, of velvet and gold, of plumes and steel, of minstrelsy and war. The glorious pageants of popular freedom are not yet come—nothing is left in the meantime, but a Queen's visit and an execution.

And you should have seen how the people thronged! Two necks to be dislocated for the sake of public morals! What a delicious, interesting sight. Women came with their children, as to a holiday spectacle. A little girl cried at home. "Will you be still?" said the mother, "or you shan't go and see the woman hung this morning!" and the little girl was still, and went.

Meanwhile, busy, bustling conversation was going on among the crowd. Thieves pursued their avocations, boys and girls were "larking," some were playing at marbles and chuck-farthing; practical jokes were played in every direction; and the hoarse laugh and the delighted scream, testified of the general pleasure. Here and there, knots were engaged in more earnest, interesting conversation. This man had known the murderers, the other had lived in the next house, a third could tell all about their birth, parentage, and education; every one of these at once felt himself, and became in the eyes of the bystanders, a man of very considerable consequence. There was a sort of rivalry between them: he who could boast the greatest intimacy with murderers, reached the highest dignity. It seemed a great honour to have known them.

Strange that the great crime "honours," while the lesser one degrades. They, who would not have associated with a convicted thief, were proud of having been intimate with a convicted murderer.

One man, only, among the mass, seemed to shrink with horror from the sight. It was one of the jurymen who had passed the verdict guilty, knowing the penalty—DEATH.

Whilst this was going on in the open air, the heavy tolling of the church bell, timing, as it were, the pulse of popular excitement with its electric throbs, a harrowing scene was enacting in the prison—in a dull, dead, cell, lay Margaret. The door opened, and a young woman entered, bearing a child in her arms.

"Mother! Mother!" cried an agonising voice! "My poor mother!"

Margaret trembled—and opened her arms—it was Catherine and little Mary!

Oh! it was pitiful to see the latter clinging around the neck of the doomed woman. She grasped in her trembling, tiny hands, the gaunt, pale, form of Margaret, she twined her little legs and arms around her—she glued herself to her mother's breast, till she could scarcely breathe—and, amid the inarticulate words and cries, and convulsive sobs, the gaoler came and parted them—for life and death!

Meanwhile, the crowd without became impatient for the sight—some wanted their breakfast—some had to go to work—some felt cold and tired—and the show delayed. At last, Latchman appeared. Hopelessness and certain death had given courage to his craven heart. He advanced with a firm step; bowed gracefully around; talked unconcernedly to the hangman; and, with a theatrical pronunciation, turning to the multitude, said—

"Ladies and gentlemen! I trust I have made my peace with earth and heaven! I forgive all my enemies! and I die full of hope!"

Whereupon something like an approving murmur ran along the crowd; isolated cries were raised of, "Well done, old boy!" "Spoken like a trump!" and then his neck was broken—the people being edified by his behaviour, and learning to believe that after all murder could not rest very heavily upon the conscience—that hanging was not so very bad, and that a murderer could die in a very comfortable manner.

But the next act of this dread drama was approaching. Intense, breathless attention riveted the crowd, when Margaret appeared! Suffering and agony had ennobled her otherwise common face—death clothed it with interest—sorrow touched it with beauty! She spoke no word! Innocent of murder, innocent of any crime, except the more than questionable one of not denouncing her own husband—she merely rested her eyes for a few moments reproachfully on the multitude below, and then raised them mournfully to heaven.

At this moment a piercing shriek rang over the crowd, and below, close in front of the drop, stood Catherine and Mary. The latter was raised high in her sister's arms, and stretched her little hands upward to her mother.

"Mother!" cried the child, "you must not die! Stay with me, mother, mother! What will become of me? What shall I do without you?"

"God pity you!" cried Margaret, and writhed her pinioned arms in vain; but she leant forward—all the mother came rushing to her face—an involuntary blessing hovered on her lips—Oh! despite years of hardship and hunger—despite grief and age—she looked beautiful—very beautiful—that moment! "God bless you! He knows I don't deserve to die. Hush!—Mary!—Don't cry so, Mary!" and the soft cajoling tenderness of the mother turned her choking tones into angelic music.

Another moment, and her lifeless corpse was dangling in the air before that careless myriad of spectators.

****

A thick soft rain was now falling—the crowd dispersed rapidly in all directions. The busy monotony of life began to ring on every side: every one went his own way on his own business, few caring for God, and fewer for their neighbour.

****

Half an hour afterwards, a group of girls of the town were seen passing up Smithfield, supporting one of their companions. One walked behind, carrying a little girl, whose eyes were swollen, whose cheeks were wet, with tears.

Two young shopmen passed by.

"Is that the child of the woman that has just been hung?"—one of them asked the girl who carried Mary.

"Yes, sir!"

"Poor thing! What will become of it?"—said the other.

"Luckily for her, she's pretty!"—rejoined the first.

Both smiled knowingly, twirled their clouded canes—and entered a shop.

Notes

[1]For more information on the Chartists, see Dorothy Thompson, *The Chartists: Popular Politics in the Industrial Revolution* (New York: Pantheon, 1984).

[2]For further information on Jones, see John Saville, *Ernest Jones, Chartist* (London: Lawrence and Wishart, 1952).

A Night in a Workhouse
James Greenwood
(1866)

*Though poorhouses existed before the Victorian Era, a new attitude
toward them arose with the increased influence of Political Economy and
Utilitarianism.* Incorporating ideas from Jeremy Bentham's Pauper Management, *poorhouses were transformed into workhouses where the poor who
sought refuge would "be put to some kind of gainful labor and made to yield
a profit above the cost of board."¹ Bentham's plan called for the living
conditions of the inhabitants of the workhouses to be "less desirable than that
of the poorest person outside."² While Bentham's plan was not adopted, its
influence can be seen in the New Poor Law of 1834 which decreed that indigent
people live in workhouses where conditions were so bad that they were called
"Poor Law Bastilles."*

In The Condition of the Working Class in England, *Frederick Engels
reports that "the workhouse has been made the most repulsive residence which
the refined ingenuity of a Malthusian can invent." ³ He cites cases where the
sick were mistreated, one sick man being put in bed with "a fever patient,
violently ill, in a bed teeming with vermin." Engels also discusses the fact that
in one workhouse the sheets hadn't been changed in thirteen weeks so the beds
were "swarming with vermin" and "the tableware was washed in the slop-
pails." Such outrages provoked investigative reports like James Greenwood's
"A Night in A Workhouse."*

*Conditions in workhouses had improved substantially by 1866 when
Greenwood visited, but he was still appalled by the filth, danger and discomfort. Greenwood's report was very well received and launched his successful
career in investigative journalism. Heavily influenced by Mayhew, Greenwood's
reports are factual, but are informed by the humanitarianism that is characteristic of the late Victorian "urban explorers" who called attention to the
continuing problems of the poor.⁴*

* * *

At   9 o'clock on the evening of Monday the 8th inst., a neat and
unpretentious carriage might have been seen turning cautiously from the
Kennington road into Princes road, Lambeth. Approaching a public house
which retreated a little from the street, he pulled up; but not so close that the
lights should fall upon the carriage door, not so distant as to unsettle the mind
of anyone who chose to imagine that he had halted to drink beer before
proceeding to call for the children at a juvenile party. He did not dismount, nor
did anyone alight in the usual way; but any keen observer who happened to
watch his intelligent countenance might have seen a furtive glance directed to
the wrong door—that is to say, to the door of the carriage which opened into
the dark and muddy road. From that door emerged a sly and ruffianly figure,
marked with every sign of squalor. He was dressed in what had once been a
snuff-brown coat, but which had faded to the hue of bricks imperfectly baked.
It was not strictly a ragged coat, though it had lost its cuffs—a bereavement
which obliged the wearer's arms to project through the sleeves two long
inelegant inches. The coat altogether was too small, and was only made to meet
over the chest by means of a bit of twine. This wretched garment was
surmounted by a "bird's eye" pocket handkerchief of cotton, wisped about the
throat hangman fashion: above all was a battered billy-cock hat, with a
dissolute drooping brim. Between the neckerchief and the lowering brim of the
hat appeared part of a face, unshaven and not scrupulously clean. The man's
hands were plunged in his pockets, and he shuffled hastily along in boots, which
were the boots of a tramp —indifferent to miry ways.

The mysterious figure was that of the present writer. He was bound for
Lambeth Workhouse, there to learn by actual experience how casual paupers
are lodged and fed, and what the "casual" is like, and what the porter who admits
him, and the master who rules over him; and how the night passes with the
outcasts whom we have all seen crowding about workhouse doors on cold and
rainy nights. Much has been said on the subject—on behalf of the paupers—
on behalf of the officials; but nothing by anyone who, with no motive but to
learn and make known the truth, had ventured the experiment of passing a night
in a workhouse and trying what it actually is to be a casual.

The day had been windy and chill—the night was cold; and therefore I fully
expected to begin my experiences among a dozen ragged wretches squatting
about the steps and waiting for admission. But my only companion at the door
was a decently dressed woman, whom, as I afterwards learnt, they declined to
admit until she had recovered from a fit of intoxication from which she had the
ill fortune to be still suffering. I lifted the big knocker, and knocked; the door
was promptly opened, and I entered. Just within a comfortable-looking clerk
sat at a comfortable desk, ledger before him. Indeed the spacious hall in every

way was as comfortable as cleanliness and great mats and plenty of gaslight could make it.

"What do you want?" asked the man who opened the door.

"I want a lodging."

"Go and stand before the desk," said the porter, and I obeyed.

"You are late," said the clerk.

"Am I Sir?"

"Yes. If you come in you'll have a bath, and you'll have to sleep in the shed."

"Very well, Sir."

"What's your name?"

"Joshua Mason, Sir."

"What are you?"

"An engraver." (This taradaddle I invented to account for the look of my hands.)

"Where did you sleep last night?"

"Hammersmith," I answered—as I hope to be forgiven.

"How many times have you been here?"

"Never before, Sir."

"Where do you mean to go to when you are turned out in the morning?"

"Back to Hammersmith, Sir."

These humble answers being entered in a book, the clerk called the porter, saying, "Take him through. You may as well take his bread with you."

Near the clerk stood a basket containing some pieces of bread of equal size. Taking one of these, and unhitching a bunch of keys from the wall, the porter led me through some passages all so scrupulously clean that my most serious misgivings were laid to rest. Then we passed into a dismal yard. Crossing this, my guide led me to a door, calling out, "Hillo! Daddy, I've brought you another." Whereupon Daddy opened unto us, and let a little of his gaslight stream into the yard where we stood.

"Come in," said Daddy very hospitably. "There's enough of you tonight anyhow! What made you so late?"

"I didn't like to come in earlier."

"Ah! That's a pity, now, because you missed your skilly (gruel). It's the first night of skilly, don't you know under the new act?"

"Just like my luck," I muttered dolefully.

The porter went his way, and I followed Daddy into another apartment, where were ranged three great baths, each one containing a liquid so disgustingly like weak mutton broth that my worst apprehensions crowded back. "Come on, there's a dry place to stand upon up at this end," said Daddy kindly.

"Take off your clothes, tie 'em up in your hank'sher, and I'll lock 'em up till the morning." Accordingly I took off my coat and waistcoat, and was about to tie them together, when Daddy cried, "That ain't enough, I mean everything." "Not my shirt, Sir, I suppose?" "Yes, shirt and all; but there, I'll lend you a shirt," said Daddy. "Whatever you take in of your own will be nailed, you know. You might take in your boots though. They'd be handy if you wanted to leave the shed for anything, but don't blame me if you lose 'em."

With a fortitude for which I hope someday to be rewarded, I made up my bundle (boots and all), and the moment Daddy's face was turned away shut my eyes and plunged desperately into the mutton broth. I wish from the bottom of heart my courage was been less hasty, for hearing the splash, Daddy looked round and said "Lor now! there was no occasion for that; you look a clean and decent sort of man. It's them filthy beggars that want washing. Don't use that towel—here's a clean one! That's the sort! and now here's you shirt" (handing me a blue striped one from a heap), "and here's your ticket. No. 34 you are, and a ticket to match is tied to your bundle. Mind you don't lose it. They'll nail it from you if they get a chance. Put it under your head. This is your rug—take it with you."

"Where am I to sleep, please Sir?"

"I'll show you."

And so he did. With no other rag but the checked shirt to cover me, and with my rug over my shoulder, he accompanied me to a door at which I entered, and, opening it, kept me standing with naked feet on the stone threshold, full in the draught of the frosty air, while he pointed out the way I should go. It was not a long way, but I would have given much not to have trodden it. It was open as the highway—with the flagstones below and the stars overhead, and as I said before, and cannot help saying again, a frosty wind was blowing.

"Straight across," said Daddy, "to where you see the light shining through. Go in there and turn to the left, and you'll find the beds in a heap. Take one of 'em and make yourself comfortable." And straight across I went, my naked feet seeming to cling to the stones as though they were burning hot instead of icy cold (they had just stepped out of a bath you should remember), till I reached the space through which the light was shining, and I entered.

No language with which I am acquainted is capable of conveying an adequate conception of the spectacle I then encountered. Imagine a space of about 30 ft. by 30 ft. enclosed on three sides by a dingy whitewashed wall, and roofed with naked tiles which were furred with the damp and filth that reeked within. As for the fourth side of the shed, it was boarded in for (say) a third of its breadth; the remaining space being hung with flimsy canvas, in which was a gap 2 ft. wide at top, widening to at least 4 ft. at bottom. This far too airy shed was paved with stone, the flags so thickly encrusted with filth that I mistook it first for a floor of natural earth. Extending from one end of my bedroom to the other, in three rows, were certain iron "cranks," of which I subsequently learnt the use, with their many arms raised in various attitudes, as the stiffened arms of men are on a battlefield. My bedfellows lay among the cranks, distributed over the flagstones in a double row, on narrow bags scantily stuffed with hay. At one glance my appalled vision took in 30 of them—thirty men and boys stretched upon shallow pallets with but only six inches of comfortable hay between them and the stony floor. These beds were placed close together, every occupant being provided with a rug like that which I was fain to hug across my shoulders. In not a few cases two gentlemen had clubbed beds and rugs and slept together. In one case, to be further mentioned presently, four gentlemen had so clubbed together. Many of my fellow-casuals were awake,—others asleep or pretending to sleep; and, shocking as were the waking ones to look upon, they were quite pleasant when compared with the sleepers. The practised and well seasoned casual seems to have a peculiar way of putting himself to bed. He rolls himself in his rug, tucking himself in, head and feet, so that he is completely enveloped; and, lying quite still on his pallet, he looks precisely like a corpse covered because of its hideousness. Some were stretched out at full length; some lay nose and knees together, some with an arm or a leg showing crooked through the coverlet. It was like the result of a railway accident; those ghastly figures were awaiting the coroner.

From the moral point of view, however, the wakeful ones were dreadful still. Towzled, dirty, villainous, they squatted up in their beds, and smoked foul pipes, and sang snatches of horrible songs, and bandied jokes so obscene as to be absolutely appalling. Eight or ten were so enjoying themselves—the majority with the check shirt on and the frowzy rug pulled about their legs—but two or three wore no shirts at all, squatting naked to the waist, their bodies fully exposed in the light of the single flaring jet of gas fixed high upon the wall.

My entrance excited very little attention. There was a horse pail three parts full of water standing by a post in the middle of the shed, with a little tin pot beside it. Addressing me as "old pal," one of the naked ruffians begged me to "hand him a swig," as he was "werry nigh garspin." Such an appeal of course no "old pal" could withstand, and I gave him a pot full of water. He showed himself grateful for the attention. "I should lay over there if I was you," he said, pointing to the left side of the shed; "It's more out of the wind then this 'ere side is." I took the good-natured advice and (by this time shivering with cold) stepped over the stones to where the beds of straw bags were heaped and dragged one of them to the place suggested by my comrade. But I had no more idea of how to arrange it than of making an apple pudding, and a certain little discovery added much to my embarrassment. In the middle of the bed I had selected was a stain of blood bigger than a man's hand! I did not know what to do now. To lie on such a horrid thing seemed impossible; yet to carry back the bed and exchange it for another might betray a degree of fastidiousness repugnant to the feelings of my fellow lodgers, and possibly excite suspicion that I was not what I seemed. Just in the nick of time in came that good man, Daddy.

"What! not pitched yet?" he exclaimed; "here, I'll show you. Hallo! somebody's been bleedin'! Never mind; let's turn him over. There you are you see! Now lay down, and cover your rug over you."

There was no help for it. It was too late to go back. Down I lay, and spread the rug over me. I should have mentioned that I brought in with me a cotton handkerchief, and this I tied round my head by way of a nightcap, but not daring to pull the rug as high as my face. Before I could in any way settle my mind to reflection in came Daddy once more to do me a further kindness and point out a stupid blunder I had committed.

"Why, you are a rummy chap!" said Daddy. "You forgot your bread! Lay hold. And look here, I've brought you another rug; it's perishing cold tonight." So saying, he spread the rug over my legs and went away. I was very thankful for the extra covering, but I was in a dilemma about the bread. I couldn't possibly eat it; what then was to be done with it? I broke it, however, and in view of such of the company as might happen to be looking made a ferocious bite at a bit a large as a bean, and munched violently. By good luck, however, I presently got half-way over my difficulty very neatly. Just behind me, so close indeed that their feet came within half a yard of my head, three lads were sleeping together.

"Did you hear that, Punch?" one of them asked.

"'Ear what?" answered Punch, sleepy and snappish.

"Why, a cove forgot his toke! Gordstruth! you wouldn't ketch me a forgettin' mine."

"You may have half of it, old pal, if you're hungry." I observed leaning up on my elbows.

"Chuck it here, good luck to yer," replied my young friend, starting up with an eager clap of his dirty hands.

I "chucked it here," and slipping the other half under the side of my bed, lay my head on my folded arms.

It was about half-past 9 when, having made myself as comfortable as circumstances permitted, I closed my eyes in the desperate hope that I might fall asleep, and so escape from the horrors with which I was surrounded. "At 7 tomorrow morning the bell will ring," Daddy had informed me, "and then you will give up your ticket and get back your bundle." Between that time and the present full nine long hours had to wear away.

But I was speedily convinced that, at least for the present, sleep was impossible. The young fellow (one of three who lay in one bed, with their feet to my head) whom my bread had refreshed, presently swore with frightful imprecations that he was now going to have a smoke; and immediately put his threat into execution. Thereupon his bedfellows sat up and lit their pipes too. But oh! if they had only smoked—if they had not taken such an unfortunate fancy to spit at the leg of a crank a few inches from my head, how much misery and apprehension would have been spared me. To make matters worse they united with this American practice an Eastern one; as they smoked they related little autobiographical anecdotes—so abominable, that three or four decent men who lay at the further end of the shed were so provoked they threatened that unless the talk abated in filthiness, to get up and stop it by main force. Instantly the voice of every blackguard in the room was raised against the decent ones. They were accused of loathsome afflictions, stigmatised as "fighting men out of work" (which must be something very humiliating I suppose) and invited to a "round" by boys young enough to be their grandsons. For several minutes there was such a storm of oaths, threats, and taunts—such a deluge of foul words raged in the room—that I could not help thinking of the fate of Sodom; as, indeed I did several times during the night. Little by little the riot died out without any of the slightest interference on the part of the officers.

Soon afterwards the ruffian majority was strengthened by the arrival of a lanky boy of about 15, who evidently recognized many acquaintances, and was recognized by them as "Kay," or perhaps I should write it "K." He was a very remarkable looking lad, and his appearance pleased me much. Short as his hair was cropped, it still looked soft and silky; he had large blue eyes set wide apart, and a mouth that would have been faultless but for its great width; and his voice was as soft and sweet as any woman's. Lightly as a woman, too, he picked his way over the stones towards the place where the beds lay, carefully hugging his cap beneath his arm.

"What cheer, Kay?" "Out again, then, old son!" "What yer got in yer cap, Kay?" cried his friends to which the sweet voice replied, "Who'll give me part of his doss (bed)?___ my ___ eyes and limbs if I ain't perishin'! Who'll let me turn in with him for half my toke" (bread)? I feared how it would be. The hungry young fellow who had so readily availed himself of half my "toke" snapped at Kay's offer, and after a little rearrangement and bedmaking, four young fellows instead of three reposed upon the haybags at my head.

"You was too late for skilly, Kay. There's skilly, nights as well as mornins."

"Don't you tell no bleeding lies," Kay answered incredulously. "Blind me, it's true. Ain't it Punch?"

"Right you are," said Punch, "and spoons to eat it with, what's more. There used to be spoons at all the houses, one time. Poplar used to have 'em; but one at a time they was all nicked don't you know."

"Well, I don't want no skilly, leastways not tonight," said Kay. "I've had some rum. Two glasses of it, and a blow out of pudding—regler Christmas plum puddin'. You don't know the cove as give it me, but thinks I this mornin' when I comes out, blessed if I don't go and see my old chum. Lordstruth, he was struck. 'Come along,' he ses, 'I saved you some puddin' from Christmas.' 'Whereabouts is it?' I ses. 'In that box under my bed,' he ses, and he forks it out. That's the sort of a pal to have. And he stood a quartern, and a half an ounce of hard up—tobacco. That wasn't all neither; when I come away, ses he, 'How about your breakfus?' 'Oh, I shall do,' ses I. 'You take some of my bread and butter,' and he cuts me off four chunks buttered thick. I eat two on 'em comin' along."

"What's in your cap, Kay?" repeated the devourer of "toke."

"Them two slices," said Kay, generously adding, "there, share 'em amongst yer, and somebody give us a whiff of 'bacca."

Kay showed himself a pleasant companion; what in a higher grade of society is called "quite an acquisition." He told stories of thieves and thieving, and of a certain "silver cup" he had been "Put up to," and that he meant to knick afore the end of the week, if he got seven stretch—seven years—for it. The cup was worth ten quid—ten pounds, and he knew where to melt it within ten minutes of nicking it. He made this statement without any moderation of his sweet voice, and the others received it as serious fact. Nor was there any affectation of secrecy in another gentleman, who announced, with great applause that he had stolen a towel from the bathroom; "And s'help me, it's as good as new, never been washed more'n once."

"Tell us a rummy story, Kay," said somebody; and Kay did. He told stories of so rummy a character that the decent men at the further end of the room (some of whom had their little boys sleeping with them) must have lain in a sweat of horror as they listened. Indeed, when Kay broke into a rummy song with a roaring chorus, one of the decent men rose in his bed and swore he would smash Kay's head if he didn't desist. But Kay sang on till he and his admirers were tired of the entertainment. "Now," said he, "let's have a Swearing Club, you'll be in it."

The principle of this game seemed to rest on the impossibility of either of the young gentlemen making half a dozen observations without introducing a blasphemous or obscene word; and either the basis is a very sound one, or for the sake of keeping the "club" alive the members purposely made slips. The penalty for "swearing" was a punch on any part of the body, except a few which the club rules protected. The game was highly successful. Warming with the sport and indifferent to punches, the members vied with each other in audacity and in a few minutes Bedlam in its prime could scarcely have produced such a spectacle as was to be seen on the beds behind me. One rule of the club was that any word to be found in the Bible might be used with impunity, and if one member "punched" another for using such a word, the error was to be visited upon him with a double punching all round. This naturally led to much argument, for in vindicating the Bible as his authority, a member became sometimes so much heated, as to launch into a flood of "real swearing," which brought the fists of the club upon his naked carcase as thick as hail.

These and other pastimes beguiled the time until, to my delight, the church chimes audibly tolled 12. After this the noise gradually subsided, and it seemed as though everybody was going to sleep at last.

Nearly one o'clock. Still quiet and no fresh arrival for an hour more. Then suddenly a loud noise of hobnailed boots kicking at a wooden gate, and soon after a tramping of feet, and a knocking at Daddy's door, which, it will be remembered, was only separated from our bedroom by an open paved court.

"Hallo!" cried Daddy.

"Here's some more of 'em for you—ten of 'em," answered the porter, whose voice I recognised at once.

"They'll have to find beds, then," Daddy grumbled, as he opened his door. "I don't believe there are four beds empty. They must sleep double or something."

This was terrible news for me.

As soon as these wrathful men had advanced to the middle of the shed, they made the discovery that there was an insufficient number of beds—only three beds, indeed, for ten competitors.

"Where's the beds? D'ye hear, Daddy? You blessed, truth-telling old person, where's the beds?"

"You'll find 'em. Some of 'em is lying on two, or got 'em for pillows. You'll find 'em."

With a sudden rush our new friends plunged among the sleepers, trampling over them, cursing their eyes and limbs, dragging away their rugs; and if by chance they found some poor wretch who had been tempted to take two beds, or bags, instead of one, they coolly hauled him out and took possession. There was no denying them and no use in remonstrating. They evidently knew that they were at liberty to do just as they liked, and then took full advantage of the privilege.

One of them came up to me, and shouting, "I want that, you ____," snatched at my birdseye nightcap, and carried it off. There was a bed close to mine which contained only one occupant, and into this one of the newcomers slipped without a word of warning, driving its lawful owner against the wall to make room. Then he sat up in bed for a moment, savagely venting his disappointment as to "toke," and declaring that never before in his life had he felt the need of it so much. This was my opportunity. Slipping my hand under my bed, I withdrew that judiciously hoarded piece of bread, and respectfully offered it to him. He snapped at it with thanks.

By the time the churches were chiming 2, matters had once more adjusted themselves, and silence reigned, to be disturbed only by drinkers at the pail, or such as, otherwise prompted, stalked into the open yard. Kay, for one, visited it. I mention this unhappy young wretch particularly, because he went out without a single rag to his back. I looked out at the rent in the canvas, and saw the frosty moon shining on him. When he returned, and crept down between Punch and another, he muttered to himself, "Warm again. Oh, my G—d! Warm again!"

Whether there is a rule which closes the casual wards after a certain hour I do not know; but before one o'clock our number was made up. The last comer, his rug over his shoulders, waltzed into the shed, waving his hands, and singing in an affected voice as he sidled along—

"I like to be a swell, a-roaming down Pall-mall,
        Or anywhere—I don't much care, so I can be a swell."

—a couplet which had an intensely comical effect. This gentleman had just come from a pantomime (where he had learnt his song, probably.) Too poor to pay for a lodging, he could only muster means for a seat in the gallery of "the Vic," where he was well entertained, judging from the flattering manner in which he spoke of the clown. The columbine was less fortunate in his opinion. "She's werry dicky, ain't got what I call 'move' about her." However, the wretched young woman was respited now from the scourge of his criticism; for the critic and his listeners were fast asleep; and yet I doubt whether anyone of the company slept very soundly. Every moment someone shifted uneasily, and as the night wore on the silence was more and more irritated by the sound of coughing. This was one of the most distressing things in the whole adventure. The conversation was horrible, the things in the tales that were told more horrible still, and worse than either (though not by any means the most infamous things to be heard—I dare not even hint at them) was that song, with its bestial chorus shouted from a dozen throats; at any rate they kept the blood warm with constant hot flushes of anger; while as for the coughing, to lie on the flagstones in what was nothing better than an open shed, and listen to that hour after hour, chilled one's very heart with pity. Every variety of cough that ever I heard was to be heard there; the hollow cough, the short cough, the hysterical cough, the bark that comes at regular intervals, like the quarter chime of a clock, as if to mark off the progress of decay; coughing from vast hollow chests, coughing from little narrow ones—now one, now another, now two or three together, and then a minute's interval of silence in which to think of it all and wonder who would begin next. One of the young reprobates above me coughed so grotesquely like the chopping of wood that I named him in my mind the Woodcutter. Now and then I found myself coughing too which must have added just a little to the poignant distress these awfully constant and variable sounds occasioned me. They were good in one way; they made one forget what wretches they were, who, to all appearance were so rapidly "chopping" their way to a pauper's graveyard. I did not care about the more matured ruffians so much, but though the youngest, the boys like Kay, were unquestionably among the most infamous of my comrades, to hear what cold and hunger and vice had done for them at 15, was almost enough to make a man cry, and there were boys there even younger than these.

At half-past two, everyone being asleep, or at least lying still, Daddy came in and counted us—one, two, three,—four, and so on in a whisper. Then, finding the pail empty (it was nearly full at half past 9, when I entered) he considerately went and refilled it, and even took trouble in searching for the tin pot which served as a drinking cup and which the last comer had playfully thrown to the further end of the shed. I ought to have mentioned that the pail stood close to my head, so that I had peculiar opportunities of study, as one after another of my comrades came to the fountain to drink, just as the brutes do in those books of African travel. The pail refilled, Daddy returned and was seen no more till morning.

It still wanted four hours and a half to 7 o'clock—the hour of rising—and never before in my life did time appear to creep so slowly. I could hear the chimes of the parish church, and of the Parliament Houses, as well as those of a wretched tinkling Dutch clock somewhere on the premises. The parish church was the first to announce the hour (an act of kindness I feel bound to acknowledge). Westminster came next, the lazy Dutchman declining his consent to the time of day till fully sixty seconds afterwards. And I declare I thought the difference of sixty seconds an injury—if the officers of the house took their time from the Dutchman. It may seem a trifle, but a minute is something when a man is lying on a cold flagstone, and the wind of a winter night is blowing in your hair. 3 o'clock, 4 o'clock struck, and still there was nothing to beguile the time but observation, under the one flaring gaslight, of the little heaps of outcast humanity strewn about the floor, and after awhile, I find, one may even become accustomed to the sight of one's fellow creatures lying around you like covered corpses in a railway shed. For most of the company were now bundled under the rugs in the ghastly way I have already described though here and there a cropped head appeared, surmounted by a billycock like my own or by a greasy cloth cap. Five o'clock, six o'clock chimed, and then I had news—most welcome— of the world without, and of the real beginning of day. Half a dozen factory bells announced that it was time for working men to go to labour; but my companions were not working men and so snored on. Out through the gap in the canvas the stars were still to be seen shining on the black sky, but that did not alter the fact that it was six o'clock in the morning. I snapped my fingers at the Dutchman, with his sixty seconds slow, for in another hour I fondly hoped to be relieved from duty. A little while and doors were heard to open and shut, yet a little while, and the voice of Daddy was audible in conversation with another early bird; and then I distinctly caught the word "bundles," blessed sound. I longed for my bundle, for my pleasing brown coat, the warm, if unsightly jersey, which I adopted as a judicious substitute for a waistcoat, for my corduroys and liberty.

"Clang!" went the workhouse clock. "Now, then, wake 'em up!" cried Daddy. I was already up, sitting up that is, being anxious to witness the resurrection of the ghastly figures rolled in the rugs. But nobody but myself arose at the summons. They knew what it meant well enough and in sleepy voices cursed the bell, and wished it in several dreadful places; but they did not move until there came in at the hole in the canvas, two of the pauper inhabitants of the house, bearing bundles. "Thirty two," "Twenty eight!" they bawled, but not my number, which was thirty four. Neither thirty two nor thirty eight, however, seemed eager to accept his good fortune in being first called. They were called upon several times before they would answer. Then they replied with a savage "Chuck it here, can't you!" "Not before you chucks over your shirt and ticket," the bundle holder answered, whereon "Twenty eight" sat up and, divesting himself of his borrowed shirt, flung it, with his wooden ticket, and his bundle was flung back in return.

It was some time before bundle No. 34 turned up, so that I had fair opportunity of observing my neighbours. The decent men slipped into their rags as soon as they got them, but the blackguards were in no hurry. Some indulged in a morning pipe to prepare themselves for the fatigue of dressing, while others, loosening their bundles as they squatted naked, commenced an investigation for certain little animals which shall be nameless.

At last my turn came, and "chucking over" my shirt and ticket, I quickly attired myself in clothes which, ragged as they were, were warmer than they looked. In less than two minutes I was out of the shed and in the yard where a few of the more decent poor fellows were crowding round a pail of water and scrambling after something that might pass for a wash. Finding their own soap, as far as I could observe, and drying their faces on any bit of rag they might happen to have about them, or upon the canvas curtain of the shed.

By this time it was about half past 7, and the majority of the casuals were up and dressed. I observed, however, that none of the younger ones were as yet up, and it presently appeared that there existed some rule against their dressing in the shed; for Daddy came out of the bathroom, where the bundles were deposited, and called out "Now four boys!" and instantly four little wretches, some with their rugs trailing about their shoulders and some quite bare, came shivering over stones and across the bleak yard, and were admitted to the bathroom to dress. "Now four more boys," cried Daddy, and so on.

When all were up and dressed, the boys carried the bed rugs into Daddy's room, and the pauper inmates made a heap of the "beds," stacking them against the wall. As before mentioned, the shed served the treble purpose of bedchamber, workroom, and breakfast room; it was impossible to get fairly at the cranks and set them going until the bedding was stowed away.

Breakfast before work, however, but it was a weary while to some of us before it made its appearance. For my own part I had little appetite; but about me were a dozen poor wretches who obviously had a very great one,—they had come in overnight too late for bread, and, perhaps may not have broken fast since the morning of the previous day. The decent ones suffered most. The blackguard majority were quite cheerful, smoking, swearing, and playing their pretty horse play, the prime end of which was pain or discomfiture for somebody else. One casual there was with only one leg. When he came in overnight he wore a black hat, which added a certain look of respectability to his worn suit of black. All together his clothes had been delivered up to him by Daddy, but now he was seen hopping disconsolately about the place on his crutch, for the hat was missing. He was a timid man with a mild voice, and whenever he asked some ruffian whether he had seen such a thing as a "black hat," and got his answer, he invariably said "Thank you," which was regarded as very amusing. At last one sidled up to him with a grin, and showing about three square inches of some fluffy substance, said, "Is this anything like wot you've lost, guvner?" The cripple inspected it. "That's the rim of it!" he said. "What a shame!" and hobbled off with tears in his eyes.

Full three quarters of an hour of loitering and shivering, and then came the taskmaster, a soldierly looking man, over six feet high, with quick, gray eyes, in which "No trifling" appeared as distinctly as a notice against trespassing on a wayside board. He came in among us, and the gray eyes made out our number in a moment. "Out into the yard, all of you," he cried, and we went out in a mob. There we shivered for some 20 minutes longer, and then a baker's man appeared with a great wooden tray piled up with such slices of bread as we had received overnight. The tray was consigned to an able-bodied casual who took his place with the task master at the shed door, and then in single file we re-entered the shed, each man and boy receiving a slice as he passed in. Pitying, as I suppose, my unaccustomed look, Mr. Taskmaster gave me a slice and a large piece over.

The bread devoured, a clamour for "skilly" began. The rumour had got abroad that this morning, and on all future mornings there would skilly for breakfast, and "Skilly, skilly!" resounded through the shed. No one had hinted that it was not forthcoming, but skilly seems to be thought an extraordinary concession, and after waiting only a few minutes for it, they attacked the taskmaster in the fiercest manner. They called him thief, sneak, and "crawler." Little boys blackguarded him in gutter language, and looking him in the face, consigned him to hell without flinching. He never uttered a word in reply, or showed a sign of impatience, and whenever he was obliged to speak it was quite without temper.

There was a loud "hooray!" when the longed for skilly appeared in pails, in one of which floated a small tin saucepan, with a stick thrust into its handle by way of a ladle. Yellow pint basins were provided for our use, and large iron spoons. "Range round the walls!" the taskmaster shouted. We obeyed with the utmost alacrity; and what I should judge to be about three fourths of a pint of gruel was handed to each of us as we stood. I was glad to get mine because the basin that contained it was warm and my hands were numb with cold. I tasted a spoonful, as in duty bound, and wondered at the esteem in which it was held by my *confreres*. It was a weak decoction of oatmeal and water, bitter, and without even a pinch of salt or flavor in it—that I could discover. But it was hot, and on that account, perhaps, was so highly relished, that I had no difficulty persuading one of the decent men to accept my share.

It was now past 8 o'clock, and, as I knew that a certain quantity of labour had to be performed by each man before he was allowed to go away, I was anxious to begin. The labour was to be "crank" labour. The "cranks" are a series of iron bars extending across the width of the shed, penetrating through the wall and working a flourmill on the other side. Turning the crank is like turning a windlass. The task is not a severe one. Four measures of corn—bushels they were called but that is doubtful—have to be ground every morning by the night's casuals. Close up to the ceiling hangs a bell, connected with machinery, and as each measure is ground the bell rings, so that the grinders may know how they are going on. But the grinders are as lazy as obscene. We were no sooner set to work than the taskmaster left us to our own sweet will, with nothing to restrain its exercise but an occasional visit from the miller, a weakly expostulating man. One or twice he came in and said mildly, "Now then, my men, why don't you stick to it?" and so went out again. The result of this laxity of overseeing would have disgusted me at any time and was intensely disgusting then.

The consequence of all this was that the cranks went round at a very slow rate, and now and then stopped altogether. Then the miller came in, and the loungers rose from their couches, the tailors ceased stitching, the smokers dropped their pipes, and every fellow was at his post. The cranks spun round furiously again, the miller's expostulation being drowned amid a shout of "Slap, bang, here we are again!" or this extemporised chorus—

We'll hang up the miller on a sour apple tree,
We'll hang up the miller on a sour apple tree,
We'll hang up the miller on a sour apple tree,
   And then go grinding on.
         Glory, glory, hallelujah, etc.

By such ditties the ruffians enlivened their short spell of work. Short indeed! The miller departed, and within a minute afterwards beds were reoccupied, pipes lit, and tailoring resumed. So the game continued—the honest fellows sweating at the cranks, anxious to get the work done, and go out to look for more profitable labor, and the paupers by profession taking matters quite easy.

I had seen the show—gladly I escaped into the open streets. The sun shone brightly on my ragged, disreputable figure, and showed its squalor with startling distinctness, but within all was rejoicing. A few yards, and then I was blessed with the sight of that same vehicle—waiting for me in the spot where I had departed from it 14 weary hours before. Did you observe, Mr. Editor, with what alacrity I jumped in? I have a vivid recollection of you, Sir, sitting there with an easy patience, lounging through your *Times*, and oh! so detestably clean to look at. But, though I resented your collar, I was grateful for the sight of a familiar face, and for that draught of sherry which you considerately brought for me, a welcome refreshment after so many weary hours of fasting.

And now I have come to the end, I remember many little anecdotes which escaped me in writing the previous articles. I ought to have told you of two quiet elderly gentlemen who, amid all the blackguardism that went on around, held a discussion on the merits of the English language, one of the disputants showing an especial admiration for the world "kindle," "fine old Saxon word as ever was coined." Then there were some childish games of "first and last letters," to vary such entertainments as that of the Swearing Club.

The moral of all this I leave to you. It seems necessary to say something about it, for the report which Mr. Farnall made after visiting Lambeth Workhouse on Saturday seems meant to suggest an idea that what has been described here is merely an irregularity.

One word in conclusion. I have some horrors for Mr. Farnall's private ear (should he like to learn about them) infinitely more revolting than anything that appears in this pamphlet.

Notes

[1]See Gertrude Himmelfarb, *The Idea of Poverty: England in the Early Industrial Age* (New York: Vintage, 1985), p. 80.

[2]See Himmelfarb, *Idea of Poverty*, p. 80.

[3]See Frederick Engels, *The Condition of the Working Class in England* (London: Granada, 1981), p. 312.

[4]See P.J. Keating, *The Working Classes in Victorian Fiction* (London: Routledge, 1971), p. 38.

The Record of Badalia Herodsfoot

Rudyard Kipling
(1890)

In the 1880s the slum areas of the East End of London became the central focus for middle class philanthropic activities among the poor. One result of the increase in religious and social interest in the East End was a spate of novels, short stories and non-fiction examining the social conditions of the urban poor. Though many of these works are in the tradition of Mayhew, some considered the social theory of the philanthropists who were working in the East End. Of these, Rudyard Kipling's "The Record of Badalia Herodsfoot," published in the Detroit Free Press (London) in 1890, examines the ideas of Samuel Barnett and William Booth. Barnett, the founder of Toynbee Hall, maintained that philanthropists had to know the real needs of an area to help alleviate problems, and Booth's Salvation Army initiated a policy wherein the poor themselves ministered to the needs of their fellows under the aegis of middle class philanthropists.[1] Kipling combines the two ideas by having his protagonist, Badalia Herodsfoot, distribute charity on the basis of her knowledge of her neighbors. Ironically, Kipling subverts these philanthropic ideas by showing that destructive social forces were so strong in the East End that even well-considered philanthrophy could not succeed in transforming the populace.

The influence of French naturalism is also evident in "The Record of Badalia Herodsfoot." The French naturalists found much of their subject matter in the lower classes because the poor of the Nineteenth Century directly contended with the forces of not only a brutal cosmos but of an oppressive social system. In "The Record of Badalia Herodsfoot," Kipling examines the attitudes that degrade the citizens of the East End, and he arouses a sense of compassion as he portrays Badalia's struggle to improve the circumstances of her fellows.[2] Despite Badalia's success in her task, she ultimately falls victim to the senseless brutality that pervades her world. Kipling's social message, that despite their own and others' best efforts the poor are doomed, appears to preclude further attempts to alleviate social problems. But the strong sense of compassion leavens the nihilistic impulse in the story and transforms it into a *protest against both the cosmos and the social system.*

* * *

The year's at the spring
And day's at the morn;
Morning's at seven;
The hill-side's dew-pearled;
The lark's on the wing;
The snail's on the thorn:
God's in his heaven—
All's right with the world!

Pippa passes.

This is not that Badalia whose spare names were Joanna, Pugnacious, and McCanna, as the song says, but another and much nicer lady. In the beginning of things she had been unregenerate; had worn the heavy, fluffy fringe which is the ornament of the costermonger's girl, and there is a legend in Gunnison-street that on her wedding-day she, a flare-lamp in either hand, danced dances on a discarded lover's winkle-barrow, till a policeman interfered, and then Badalia danced with the Law amid shoutings. Those were her days of fatness, and they did not last long, for her husband after two years took to himself another woman, and passed out of Badalia's life, over Badalia's senseless body; for he stifled protest with blows. While she was enjoying her widowhood the baby that the husband had not taken away died of croup, and Badalia was altogether alone. With rare fidelity she listened to no proposals for a second marriage according to the customs of Gunnison-street, which do not differ from those of the Barralong. "My man," she explained to her suitors, "'e'll come back one o' these days, an' then, like as not, 'e'll take an' kill me if I was livin' 'long o' you. You don't know Tom; I do. Now you go. I can do for myself— not 'aving a kid." She did for herself with a mangle, some tending of babies, and an occasional sale of flowers. This latter trade is one that needs capital and takes the vendor very far westward, in so much that the return journey from, let us say, the Burlington Arcade to Gunnison-street, E., is an excuse for drink, and then, as Badalia pointed out, "You come 'ome with your shawl arf off of your back, an' your bonnick under your arm, and the price of nothing-at-all in your pocket, let alone a slop takin' care o' you." Badalia did not drink, but she knew her sisterhood, and gave them rude counsel. Otherwise she kept herself to herself, and meditated a great deal upon Tom Herodsfoot, her husband, who would come back some day, and the baby that would never return. In what manner these thoughts wrought upon her mind will not be known.

Her entry into society dates from the night when she rose literally under the feet of the Reverend Eustace Hanna, on the landing of No. 17, Gunnison-street, and told him that he was a fool, without discernment in the dispensation of his district charities.

"You give Lascar Loo custids," said she, without the formality of introduction; "give her pork-wine. Garn! Give 'er blankits. Garns 'ome! 'Er mother, she eats 'em all, and drinks the blankits. Gits 'em back from the shop, she does, before you come visiting again, so as to 'ave 'em all handy an' proper; an' Lascar Loo she sez to you 'Oh, my mother's that good to me!' she do. Lascar Loo 'ad better talk so, bein' sick abed, 'r else 'er mother would kill 'er. Garn! you're a bloomin' gardener—you an' yer custids! Lascar Loo don't never smell of 'em even."

Thereon the curate, instead of being offended, recognised in the heavy eyes under the fringe the soul of a fellow worker, and so bade Badalia mount guard over Lascar Loo, when the next jelly or custard should arrive, to see that the invalid actually ate it. This Badalia did, to the disgust of Lascar Loo's mother and the sharing of a black eye between the three; but Lascar Loo got her custard, and coughing heartily, rather enjoyed the fray.

Later on, partly through the Reverend Eustace Hanna's swift recognition of her uses, and partly through certain tales poured out with moist eyes and flushed cheeks by Sister Eva, youngest and most impressionable of the Little Sisters of the Red Diamond, it came to pass that Badalia, arrogant, fluffy-fringed and perfectly unlicensed in speech, won a recognised place among such as labour in Gunnison-street.

These were a mixed corps, zealous or hysterical, faint-hearted or only very wearied of battle against misery, according to their lights. The most part were consumed with small rivalries and personal jealousies, to be retailed confidentially to their own tiny cliques in the pauses between wrestling with death for the body of a moribund laundress, or scheming for further mission-grants to resole a consumptive compositor's very consumptive boots. There was a rector that lived in dread of pauperising the poor, would fain have held bazaars for fresh altar cloths, and prayed in secret for a new large brass bird, with eyes of red glass, fondly believed to be carbuncles. There was Brother Victor, of the Order of Little Ease, who knew a great deal about altar cloths but kept his knowledge in the background while he strove to propitiate Mrs. Jessel, the Secretary of the Tea Cup Board, who had money to dispense but hated Rome—even though Rome would, on its honour, do no more than fill the stomach, leaving the dazed soul to the mercies of Mrs. Jessel. There were all the Little Sisters of the Red Diamond, daughters of the Horseleech, crying "Give" when their own charity was exhausted, and pitifully explaining to such as demanded an account of their disbursements in return for one half-sovereign, that relief work in a bad district can hardly be systematised on the accounts' side without expensive duplication of staff. There was the Reverend Eustace Hanna who worked impartially with Ladies' Committees, Androgynous Leagues and Guilds, Brother Victor, and anybody else who could give him money, boots, or blankets, or that more precious help that allows itself to be directed by those who know. And all these people learned, one by one, to consult Badalia on matters of personal character, right to relief, and hope of eventual reformation in Gunnison-street. Her answers were seldom cheering, but she possessed special knowledge and complete confidence in herself.

"I'm Gunnison street," she said to the austere Mrs. Jessel. "I know what's what, *I* do, an' they don't want your religion, Mum, not a single ____. Excuse me. It's all right when they comes to die, Mum, but till they die what they wants is things to eat. The men they'll shif' for themselves. That's why Nick Lapworth sez to you that 'e wants to be confirmed an' all that. 'E won't never lead no new life, nor 'is wife won't get no good out o' all the money you gives 'im. No more you can't pauperise them as 'asn't things to begin with. They're bloomin' well pauped. The women they can't shif' for themselves—'specially bein' always confined. 'Ow should they? They wants things if they can't get 'em anyways. If not they dies, and a good job too, for women is cruel put upon in Gunnison-street."

"Do you believe that—that Mrs. Herodsfoot is altogether a proper person to trust funds to?" said Mrs. Jessel to the curate after this conversation. "She seems to be utterly godless in her speech at least."

The curate agreed. She was godless according to Mrs. Jessel's views, but did not Mrs. Jessel think that since Badalia knew Gunnison-street and its needs as none other knew it, she might in a humble way be, as it were, the scullion of charity from purer sources, and that if, say, the Tea Cup Board could give a few shillings a week, and the Little Sisters of the Red Diamond a few more, and, yes, he himself could raise yet a few more, the total, not at all likely to be excessive, might be handed over to Badalia to dispense among her associates. Thus Mrs. Jessel herself would be set free to attend more directly to the spiritual wants of certain large-limbed, hulking men who sat picturesquely on the lower benches of her gatherings and sought for truth—which quite as precious as silver, when you know the market for it.

"She'll favour her own friends," said Mrs. Jessel. The curate refrained from mirth, and, after wise flattery, carried his point. To her unbounded pride Badalia was appointed the dispenser of a grant—a weekly trust, to be held for the benefit of Gunnison-street.

"I don't know what we can get together each week," said the curate to her. "But here are seventeen shillings to start with. You do what you like with them among your people, only let me know how it goes so that we shan't get muddled in the accounts. D'you see?"

"Ho yuss! 'Taint much though, is it?" said Badalia, regarding the white coins in her palm. The sacred fever of the administrator, only known to those who have tasted power, burned in her veins. "Boots is boots, unless they're give you, an' then they ain't fit to wear unless they're mended top an' bottom; an' jellies is jellies; an' I don't think anything o' that cheap pork-wine, but it all comes to something. It'll go quicker 'n a quartern of gin—seventeen bob. An' I'll keep a book—same as I used to do before Tom went an' took up 'long o' that pan-faced slut in Henessy's Rents. We was the only barrer that kep' regular books, me an'—'im."

She bought a large copy-book—her unschooled handwriting demanded room—and in it she wrote the story of her war; boldly, as befits a general, and for no other eyes than her own and those of the Reverend Eustace Hanna. Long ere the pages were full the mottled cover had been soaked in kerosine—Lascar Loo's mother, defrauded of her percentage on her daughter's custards, invaded Badalia's room in 17, Gunnison-street, and fought with her to the damage of the lamp and her own hair. It was hard, too, to carry the precious "pork-wine" in one hand and the book in the other through an eternally thirsty land; so red stains were added to those of the oil. But the Reverend Eustace Hanna, looking at the matter of the book, never objected. The generous scrawls told their own tale, Badalia every Saturday night supplying the chorus between the written statements thus:—

Mrs. Hikkey, very ill brandy 3d. Cab for hospital, she had to go, 1s. Mrs. Poone confined. In money for tea (she took it I know, sir) 6d. Met her husband out looking for work.

"I slapped 'is face for a bone-idle beggar! 'E won't get no work this side o'___excuse me, sir. "Won't you go on?" The curate continued—

Mrs. Vincent. Confid. No linning for baby. Most untidy. In money 2s.6d. Some cloths from Miss Evva.

"Did Sister Eva do that?" said the curate very softly. Now charity was Sister Eva's bounden duty, yet to one man's eyes each act of her daily toil was a manifestation of angelic grace and goodness—a thing to perpetually admire.

"Yes, sir. She went back to the Sisters' 'Ome an' took 'em off 'er own bed. Most beautiful marked too. Go on, sir. That makes up four and thruppence."

Mrs. Junnett to keep good fire coals is up. 7d.

Mrs. Lockhart took a baby to nurse to earn a triffle but mother can' d pay husband summons over and over. He won' t help. Cash 2s. 2d. Worked in a ketchin but had to leave. Fire, tea, and shin of beef, 1 s 7 1/2 d.

"There was a fight there, sir," said Badalia. "Not me, sir. 'Er 'usband, o'
course 'e come in at the wrong time, was wishful to 'ave the beef, so I calls up
the next floor an' down comes that mulatter man wot sells the sword-stick
canes, top o' Ludgate-'ill. 'Muley,' sez I, 'you big black beast, you, take an'
kill this big white beast 'ere.' I knew I couldn't stop Tom Lockart 'alf drunk,
with the beef in 'is 'ands. 'I'll beef 'm,' sez Muley, and' 'e did it, with that pore
woman a-cryin' in the next room, an' the top banisters on that landin' is broke
out, but she got 'er beef-tea, an' Tom 'e's got 'is gruel. Will you go on, sir?"

"No, I think it will be all right, I'll sign for the week," said the curate. One
gets so used to these things profanely called human documents.

"Mrs. Churner's baby's got diptheery," said Badalia, turning to go.

"Where's that? The Churners of Painter's-alley, or the other Churners in
Houghton-street?"

"Houghton-street. The Painter's-alley people, they're sold out an' left."

"Sister Eva's sitting one night a week with old Mrs. Probyn in Houghton-
street—isn't she?" said the curate, uneasily.

"Yes, but she won't sit no longer. *I've* took up Mrs. Probyn. I can't talk
'er no religion, but she don't want it; an' Miss Eva she don't want no diptheery,
tho' she sez she does. Don't *you* be afraid for Miss Eva."

"But—but you'll get it, perhaps."

"Like as not." She looked the curate between the eyes, and her own eyes
flamed under the fringe. "Maybe I'd like to get it, for aught you know."

The curate thought upon these words a little time till he began to think of
Sister Eva in the grey cloak with the white bonnet ribbons under the chin. Then
he thought no more of Badalia.

What Badalia thought was never expressed in words, but it is known in
Gunnison-street that Lascar Loo's mother, sitting blind drunk on her own
doorstep, was that night captured and wrapped up in the war-cloud of Badalia's
wrath, so that she did not know whether she stood on her head or her heels, and
after being soundly bumped on every particular stair up to her room, was set
down on Badalia's bed, there to whimper and quiver till the dawn, protesting
that all the world was against her, and calling on the names of children long
since slain by dirt and neglect. Badalia, snorting, went out to war, and since the
hosts of the enemy were many, found enough work to keep her busy till the
dawn.

As she had promised, she took Mrs. Probyn into her own care, and began
by nearly startling the old lady into a fit with the announcement that "there ain't
go God like as not, an' if there *is* it don't matter to you or me, an' anyhow you
take this jelly." Sister Eva objected to being shut off from her pious work in

Houghton-street, but Badalia insisted, and by fair words and the promise of favours to come so prevailed on three or four of the more sober men of the neighbourhood that they blockaded the door whenever Sister Eva attempted to force an entry, and pleaded the diphtheria as their excuse.

"I've got to keep 'er out o' 'arm's way," said Badalia, "an' out she keeps. The curick won't care a ___ for me, but—he wouldn't any'ow."

The effect of that quarantine was to shift the sphere of Sister Eva's activity to other streets, and notably those most haunted by the Reverend Eustace Hanna and Brother Victor, of the Order of Little Ease. There exists, for all their human bickerings, a very close brotherhood in the ranks of those whose work lies in Gunnison-street. To begin with, they have seen pain—pain that no word or deed of theirs can alleviate—life born into Death, and Death crowded down by unhappy life. Also they understand the full significance of drink, which is a knowledge hidden from very many well-meaning people, and some of them have fought with the beasts at Ephesus. They meet at unseemly hours in unseemly places, exchange a word or two of hasty counsel, advice, or suggestion, and pass on to their appointed toil, since time is precious and lives hang in the balance of five minutes. For many, the gas-lamps are their sun, and the Covent Garden wains the chariots of the twilight. They have all in their station begged for money, so that the freemasonry of the mendicant binds them together.

To all these influences there was added in the case of two workers that thing which men have agreed to call Love. The possible chance of Sister Eva's catching diphtheria did not enter into the curate's head till Badalia had spoken. Then it seemed a thing intolerable and monstrous that she should be exposed not only to this risk, but any accident whatever of the streets. A wain coming round a corner might kill her; the rotten staircases on which she trod daily and nightly might collapse and maim her; there was danger in the tottering coping-stones of certain crazy houses that he knew well; danger more deadly within those houses. What if one of a thousand drunken men crushed out that precious life? A woman had once flung a chair at the curate's head. Sister Eva's arm would not be strong enough to ward off a chair. There were also knives that were apt to fly. These and other considerations cast the soul of the Reverend Eustace Hanna into torment, that no leaning upon Providence could relieve. God was indubitably great and terrible—one had only to walk through Gunnison-street to see that much—but it would be better, vastly better, that Eva should have the protection of his own arm. And the world that was not too busy to watch might have seen a woman, not too young, light-haired and light-eyed, slightly assertive in her speech, and very limited in such ideas as lay beyond the immediate sphere of her duty, where the eyes of the Reverend Eustace Hanna turned to follow the footsteps of a Queen crowned in a little grey bonnet with white ribbons under the chin.

If that bonnet appeared for a moment at the bottom of a courtyard, or nodded at him on a dark staircase, then there was hope yet for Lascar Loo, living on one lung and the memory of past excesses, hope even for whining, sodden Nick Lapworth, blaspheming in the hope of money over the pangs of a "true conversion this time, s'elp me Gawd, sir." If that bonnet did not appear for a day, the mind of the curate was filled with lively pictures of horror, visions of stretchers, a crowd at some villainous crossing, and a policeman — he could see that policeman—jerking out over his shoulder the details of the accident, and ordering the man who would have set his body against the wheels—heavy dray wheels, he could see them—to "move on." Then there was less hope for the salvation of Gunnison-street and all in it.

Which agony Brother Victor beheld one day when he was coming from a death-bed. He saw the light in the eye, the relaxing muscles of the mouth, and heard a new ring in the voice that had told flat all the forenoon. Sister Eva had turned into Gunnison-street after forty-eight hours' eternity of absence. She had not been run over. Brother Victor's heart must have suffered in some human fashion, or he would never have seen what he saw. But the law of his Church made suffering easy. His duty was to go on with his work until he died, even as Badalia went on. She, magnifying her office, faced the drunken husband; coaxed the doubly shiftless, thriftless girl wife into a little fore-thought, and begged clothes when and where she could for the scrofulous babes that multipled like the green scum on the water cisterns.

The story of her deeds was written in the book that the curate signed weekly, but she never told him any more of fights and tumults in the street. "Mis' Eva does 'er work 'er way. I does mine mine. But I do more than Mis' Eva ten times over, an' 'Thank yer, Badalia, 'sez 'e—'that'll do for this week.' I wonder what Tom's doin' now long o' that—other woman. 'Seems like as if I'd go an' look at 'im one o' these days. But I'd cut 'er liver out—couldn't 'elp myself. Better not go, p'raps."

Hennessy's Rents lay more than two miles from Gunnison-street and were inhabited by much the same class of people. Tom had established himself there with Jenny Wabstow, his new woman, and for weeks lived in great fear of Badalia's suddenly descending upon him. The prospect of actual fighting did not scare him: but he objected to the police-court that would follow, and the orders for maintenance and other devices of a law that cannot understand the simple rule that "when a man's tired of a woman 'e ain't such a bloomin' fool as to live with 'er no more, an' that's the long an' short of it." For some months his new wife wore very well, and kept Tom in a state of decent fear and consequent orderliness. Also work was plentiful. Then a baby was born, and, following the law of his kind, Tom, little interested in the children he helped to produce, sought distraction in drink. He had confined himself, as a rule, to beer, which is stupefying and comparatively innocuous: at least, it clogs the legs, and though the heart may ardently desire to kill, sleep comes swiftly, and the crime often remains undone. Spirits, being more volatile, allow both the flesh and the soul to work together—generally to the inconvenience of others. Tom discovered that there was merit in whiskey—if you only took enough of it— cold. He took as much as he could purchase or get given him, and by the time that his woman was fit to go abroad again, the two rooms of their household were stripped of many valuable articles. Then the woman spoke her mind, not once, but several times, with point, fluency, and metaphor; and Tom was indignant at being deprived of peace at the end of his day's work, which included much whiskey. He therefore withdrew himself from the solace and companionship of Jenny Wabstow, and she therefore pursued him with more metaphors. At the last, Tom would turn round and hit her—sometimes across the head, and sometimes across the breast, and the bruises furnished material for discussion on doorsteps among such women as had been treated in like manner by their husbands. They were not few.

But no very public scandal had occurred till Tom one day saw fit to open negotiations with a young woman on the subject of matrimony according to the laws of free selection. He was getting very tired of Jenny, and the young woman was earning enough from flower-selling to keep him in comfort, whereas Jenny was expecting another baby and most unreasonably expected consideration on this account. The shapelessness of her figure revolted him, and he said as much in the language of his breed. Jenny cried till Mrs. Hart stopped her on her own staircase and whispered: "God be good to you, Jenny, my woman, for I see how 'tis with you." Jenny wept more than ever, and half dazed with the sickness that makes the banisters swim in the morning, gave Mrs. Hart a penny and some kisses, while Tom was conducting his own wooing at the corner of the street.

The young woman, prompted by pride, not by virtue, told Jenny of his offers, and she spoke to Tom that night. The altercation began in their own rooms, but Tom tried to escape; and in the end all Hennessy's Rents gathered themselves upon the pavement and formed a court to which Jenny appealed from time to time, her hair loose on her neck, her raiment in extreme disorder, and her steps astray from drink. "When your man drinks, you'd better drink too! It don't 'urt so much when 'e 'its you then," says the Wisdom of the Women. And surely they ought to know.

"Look at 'im!" shrieked Jenny. "Look at 'im, standin' there without any word to say for himself, that 'ud smitch off and leave me an' never so much as a shillin' lef be'ind! You call yourself a man—you call yourself the bleedin' shadow of a man? I've seen better men than you made outer chewed paper and sput out arterwards. Look at 'im! 'E's been drunk since Thursday last, and 'e'll be drunk s'long's 'e can get drink. 'Es took all I've got, an' me—an' me— as you see—"

A murmur of sympathy from the women.

"Took it all, he did, an' atop of his blasted pickin' an' stealin'—yes, you, you thief—'e goes off an' tries to take up long o' that"—here followed a complete and minute description of the young woman aforementioned. Luckily, she was not on the spot to hear. "'E'll serve 'er as 'e served me! 'E'll drink every bloomin' copper she makes an' then leave 'er alone, same as 'e done me! O women, look you, I've bore 'im one an' there's another on the way, an' 'e'd up an' leave me as I am now—the stinkin' dorg. An' you may leave me. I don't want none o' your leavin's. Go away. Get away!" The hoarseness of passion overpowered the voice. The crowd attracted a policeman as Tom began to slink away.

"Look at 'im," said Jenny, grateful for the new listener. "Ain't there no law for such as 'im? 'E's took all my money, 'e's beat me once, twice an' over. 'E's swine drunk when 'e ain't mad drunk, an' now, an' now 'e's trying to pick up along o' another woman. 'Im I give up a four times better man for. Ain't there no law?"

"What's the matter now? You go on into your 'ouse. I'll see to the man. 'As 'e been 'itting you?" said the policeman.

"'Ittin' me? 'E's cut my 'eart in two, an' 'e stands there grinnin' as tho' 'twas all a play to 'im."

"You go on into your 'ouse an' lie down a bit."

"I'm a married woman, I tell you, an' I'll 'ave my 'usband!"

"I ain't done her no bloomin' 'arm," said Tom from the edge of the crowd. He felt that public opinion was running against him.

"You ain't done me any bloomin' good, you dorg. I'm a married woman, I am, an' I won't 'ave my 'usband took from me."

"Well, if you are a married woman, go into the 'ouse," said the policeman soothingly. He was used to domestic brawls.

"Shan't—thank you for your impidence. Look 'ere!" She tore open her dishevelled bodice and showed such crescent-shaped bruises are made by a well applied chair-back. "That's what 'e done to me acause my heart wouldn't break quick enough! 'E's tried to get in an' break it. Look at that, Tom, that you gave me last night; an' I made it up with you. But that was before I knew what you were tryin' to do long o' that woman—"

"D'you charge 'im?" said the policeman. "'E'll get a month for 't, per'aps."

"No," said Jenny firmly. It was one thing to expose her man to the scorn of the street, and another to lead him to jail.

"Then you go in an' lie down, and you"—this to the crowd—"pass along the pavement, there. Pass along. 'Taint nothing to laugh at." To Tom, who was being sympathised with by his friends, "It's good for you she didn't charge you, but mind this now, the next time,"&c.

Tom did not at all appreciate Jenny's forbearance, nor did his friends help to compose his mind. He had whacked the woman because she was a nagging nuisance. For precisely the same reason he had cast about for a new mate. And all his kind acts had ended in a truly painful scene in the street, a most unjustifiable exposure by and of his woman, and a certain loss of caste—this he realised dimly—among his associates. Consequently, all women were nuisances, and consequently whiskey was a good thing. His friends condoled with him. Perhaps he had been more hard on his woman than she deserved, but her disgraceful conduct under provocation excused all offence.

"I wouldn't 'ave no more to do with 'er—a woman like that there," said one comforter.

"Let 'er go an' dig for her bloomin' self. A man wears 'isself out to a skeleton shovin' meat down their mouths, while they sit at 'ome easy all day; an' the very fust time, mark you, you 'as a bit of a difference, an' very proper too for a man as is a man, she ups an' 'as you out into the street, callin' you Gawd knows what all. What's the good o' that, I arx you?" So spoke the second comforter.

The whiskey was the third, and his suggestion struck Tom as the best of all. He would return to Badalia, his wife. Probably she would have been doing something wrong while he has been away, and he could then vindicate his authority as a husband. Certainly she would have money. Single women always seemed to possess the pence that God and the Government denied to hard-working men. He refreshed himself with more whiskey. It was beyond any doubt that Badalia would have done something wrong. She might even have married another man. He would wait until the new husband was out of the way, and, after kicking Badalia, would get money and a long absent sense of satisfaction. There is much virtue in a creed or a law, but when all is prayed and suffered, drink is the only thing that will make clean all a man's deeds in his own eyes. Pity it is that the effects are not permanent.

Tom parted with his friends, bidding them tell Jenny that he was going to Gunnison-street, and would return to her arms no more. Because this was the devil's message, they remembered and severally delivered it, with drunken distinctness, in Jenny's ears. Then Tom took more drink till his drunkenness rolled back and stood off from him as a wave falls back and stands off the wreck it will swamp. He reached the traffic-polished black asphalt of a side street and trod warily among the reflections of the shop-lamps that burned in gulfs of pitchy darkness, fathoms beneath his bootheels. He was very sober indeed. Looking down his past, he beheld that he was justified of all his actions so entirely and perfectly that if Badalia had in his absence dared to lead a blameless life he would smash her for not having gone wrong.

Badalia at the moment was in her own room after the regular nightly skirmish with Lascar Loo's mother. To a reproof as stinging as a Gunnison-street tongue could make it, the old woman, detected for the hundredth time in the theft of the poor delicacies meant for the invalid, could only cackle and answer—

"D'you think Loo's never bilked a man in 'er life? She's dyin' now—on'y she's so cunning long about it. Me! I'll live for twenty years yet."

Badalia shook her, more on principle that in any hope of curing her, and thrust her into the night, where she collapsed on the pavement and called upon the devil to slay Badalia.

He came upon the word in the shape of a man with a very pale face who asked for her by name. Lascar Loo's mother remembered. It was Badalia's husband—and the return of a husband to Gunnison-street was generally followed by beatings.

"Where's my wife?" said Tom. "Where's my slut of a wife?"

"Upstairs an' be ____ to her," said the old woman, falling over on her side. "'Ave you come back for 'er, Tom?"

"Yes. 'Oo's she took up while I've bin gone?"

"All the bloomin' curicks in the parish. She's that set up you wouldn't know 'er."

"'Strewth she is!"

"Oh, yuss. Mor'n that, she's always round an' about with them sniffin' Sisters of Charity an' the curick. Mor'n that, 'e gives 'er money—pounds an' pounds a week. Been keepin' her that way for months, 'e 'as. No wonder you wouldn't 'ave nothin' to do with 'er when you left. An' she keeps me outer the food-stuff they gets for me lyin' dyin' out 'ere like a dorg. She's been a blazin' bad 'un has Badalia since you lef'."

"Got the same room still, 'as she?" said Tom, striding over Lascar Loo's mother, who was picking at the chinks between the pave-stones.

"Yes, but so fine you wouldn't know it."

Tom went up the stairs and the old lady chuckled. Tom was angry. Badalia would not be able to bump people for some time to come, or to interfere with the heaven-appointed distribution of custards.

Badalia, undressing to go to bed, heard feet on the stair that she knew well. Ere they stopped to kick at her door she had, in her own fashion, thought through several volumes of the book of human life.

"Tom's back," she said to herself. "An' I'm glad...spite o' the curick an' everythink."

She opened the door, crying his name.

The man pushed her aside.

"I don't want none o' your kissin's an' slaverin's. I'm sick of 'em," said he.

"You ain't 'ad so many neither to make you sick these two years past."

"I've 'ad better. Got any money?"

"On'y a little—orful little."

"That's a ____ lie, an' you know it."

"'Tain't—and, oh, Tom what's the use o' talkin' money the minute you come back? Didn't you like Jenny? I knowed you wouldn't."

"Shut your 'ead. Ain't you got enough to make a man drunk fair?"

"You don't want bein' made more drunk any. You're drunk a'ready. You come to bed, Tom."

"To you?"

"Ay, to me. Ain't I nothin'—spite o' Jenny?"

She put out her arms as she spoke. But the drink held Tom fast.

"Not for me," said he, steadying himself against the wall. "Don't I know 'ow you've been going' on while I was away, yah!"

"Arsk about!" said Badalia, indignantly, drawing herself together, "'Oo seez anythink agin me 'ere?"

"'Oo sez? W'y, everybody. I ain't come back more'n a minute 'fore I finds you've been with the curick Gawd knows where. Wot curick was 'e?"

"The curick that's 'ere always," said Badalia, hastily. She was thinking of anything rather than the Rev. Eustace Hanna at that moment. Tom sat down gravely in the only chair in the room. Badalia continued her arrangements for going to bed.

"Pretty thing that," said Tom, "to tell you own lawful married 'usband— an' I gav five bob for the weddin' ring. Curick that's 'ere always! Cool as brass you are. Ain't you got no shame? Ain't 'e under the bed now?"

"Tom, you're bleedin' drunk. I ain't done nothing' to be shamed of."

"You! You don't know wot shame is. But I ain't come 'ere to mess with you. Give me wot you've got, an' then I'll dress you down an' go to Jenny."

"I ain't got nothin' 'cept some coppers an' a shillin' or so."

"Wot's that about the curick keepin' you on five poun' a week?"

"'Oo told you that?"

"Lascar Loo's mother, lyin' on the pavement outside, an' more honest than you'll ever be. Give me wot you've got!"

Badalia passed over to a little shell pincushion on the mantelpiece, drew thence four shillings and threepence—the lawful earnings of her mangle—and held them out to the man who was rocking in his chair and surveying the room with wide-opened rolling eyes.

"That ain't five poun'," said he, drowsily.

"I ain't got no more. Take it an' go—if you won't stay."

Tom rose slowly, gripping the arms of the chair. "Wot about the curick's money that 'e guv you?" said he. "Lascar Loo's mother told me. You give it over to me now, or I'll make you."

"Lascar Loo's mother don't know anything about it."

"She do, an' more than you want her to know."

"She don't. I've bumped the 'eart out of 'er, and I can't give you the money. Anythin' else but that, Tom, an' everythin' else but that, Tom, I'll give willin' and true. 'Tain't my money. Won't the dollar be enough? That money's my trust. There's a book along of it too."

"Your trust? Wot are you doin' with any trust that your 'usband don't know of? You an' your trust! Take you that!"

Tom stepped towards her and delivered a blow of the clenched fist across the mouth. "Give me wot you've got," said he in the thick, abstracted voice of one talking in dreams.

"I won't," said Badalia, staggering to the washstand. With any other man than her husband she would have fought savagely as a wild cat; but Tom had been absent two years, and, perhaps, a little timely submission would win him back to her. None the less, the weekly trust was sacred.

The wave that had so long held back descended on Tom's brain. He caught Badalia by the throat and forced her to her knees. It seemed just to him in that hour to punish an erring wife for two years of willful desertion; and the more, in that she had confessed her guilt by refusing to give up the wages of sin.

Lascar Loo's mother waited on the pavement without for the sounds of lamentation, but none came. Even if Tom had released her gullet, Badalia would not have screamed.

"Give it up, you slut!" said Tom. "Is that 'ow you pay me back for all I've done?"

"I can't. 'Tain't my money. Gawd forgive you, Tom, for wot you're—" the voice ceased as the grip tightened, and Tom heaved Badalia against the bed. Her forehead struck the bed-post, and she sank, half kneeling, on the floor. It was impossible for a self-respecting man to refrain from kicking her: so Tom kicked with the deadly intelligence born of whiskey. The head drooped to the floor, and Tom kicked at that till the crisp tingle of hair striking through his nailed boot with the chill of cold water, warned him that it might be as well to desist.

"Where's the curick's money, you kep' woman?" he whispered in the blood-stained ear. But there was no answer—only a rattling at the door, and the voice of Jenny Wabstow crying ferociously, "Come out o' that, Tom, an' come 'ome with me! An' you, Badalia, I'll tear your face off its bones!"

Tom's friends had delivered their message, and Jenny, after the first flood of passionate tears, rose up to follow Tom, and, if possible, to win him back. She was prepared even to endure an exemplary whacking for her performances in Hennessy's Rents. Lascar Loo's mother guided her to the chamber of horrors, and chuckled as she retired down the staircase. If Tom had not banged the soul out of Badalia, there would at least be a royal fight between that Badalia and Jenny. And Lascar Loo's mother knew well that Hell has no fury like a woman fighting above the life that is quick in her.

Still there was no sound audible in the street. Jenny swung back the unbolted door, to discover her man stupidly regarding a heap by the bed. An eminent murderer has remarked that if people did not die so untidily most men, and all women, would commit at least one murder in their lives. Tom was reflecting on the present untidiness, and the whiskey was fighting with the clear current of his thoughts.

"Don't make that noise," he said. "Come in quick."

"My Gawd!" said Jenny, checking like a startled wild beast. "Wot's all this 'ere? You ain't——"

"Dunno. S'pose I did it."

"Did it! You done it a sight too well this time."

"She was aggravatin'," said Tom, thickly, dropping back into the chair. "That aggravatin' you'd never believe. Livin' on the fat o' the land among these aristocratic parsons an' all. Look at them white curtings on the bed. *We* ain't got no white curtings. What I want to know is—" The voice died as Badalia's had died, but from a different cause. The whiskey was tightening its grip after the accomplished deed, and Tom's eyes were beginning to close. Badalia on the floor breathed heavily.

"No, nor like to 'ave," said Jenny. "You've done for 'er this time. You go!"

"Not me. She won't hurt. Do 'er good. I'm going' to sleep. Look at those there clean sheets! Are you comin' too?"

Jenny bent over Badalia, and there was intelligence in the battered woman's eyes—intelligence and much hate.

"I never told 'im to do such," Jenny whispered. "'Twas Tom's own doin'—none o' mine. Shall I get 'im took, dear?"

The eyes told their own story. Tom, who was beginning to snore, must not be taken by the law.

"Go," said Jenny. "Get out! Get out of 'ere."

"You—told—me—that—this afternoon," said the man very sleepily. "Lemme go asleep."

"That wasn't nothing. You'd only 'it me. This time it's murder—murder—murder! Tom, you've killed 'er now." She shook the man from his rest, and understanding with cold terror filled his fuddled brain.

"I done it for your sake, Jenny," he whimpered feebly, trying to take her hand.

"You killed 'er for the money, same as you would ha' killed me. Get out o' this. Lay 'er on the bed first, you brute!"

They lifted Badalia on to the bed, and crept forth silently.

"I can't be took along o' you—and if you was took you'd say I made you do it, an' try to get me 'anged. Go away—anywhere outer 'ere," said Jenny, and she dragged him down the stairs.

"Goin' to look for the curick?" said a voice from the pavement. Lascar Loo's mother was still waiting patiently to hear Badalia squeal.

"Wot curick?" said Jenny, swiftly. There was a chance of salving her conscience yet in regard to the bundle upstairs.

"'Anna—63, Roomer-terrace—close to 'ere," said the old woman. She had never been favourably regarded by the curate. Perhaps, since Badalia had not squealed, Tom preferred smacking the man to the woman. There was no accounting for tastes.

Jenny thrust her man before her till they reached the nearest main road. "Go away, now," she gasped. "Go off anywheres, but don't come back to me. I'll never go with you again; an', Tom—Tom, d'you 'ear me?—clean your boots."

Vain counsel. The desperate thrust of disgust which she bestowed upon him sent him staggering face down into the kennel, where a policeman showed interest in his welfare.

"Took for a common drunk. Gawd send they don't look at 'is boots! 'Anna 63, Roomer-terrace!" Jenny settled her hat and ran.

The excellent housekeeper of the Roomer Chambers still remembers how there arrived a young person, blue-lipped and gasping, who cried only: "Badalia, 17, Gunnison-street. Tell the curick to come at once—at once—at once!" and vanished into the night. This message was borne to the Rev. Eustace Hanna, then enjoying his beauty sleep. He saw there was urgency in the demand, and unhesitatingly knocked up Brother Victor across the landing. As a matter of etiquette, Rome and England divided their cases in the district according to the creeds of the sufferers; but Badalia was an institution, and not a case, and there was no district-relief etiquette to be considered. "Something has happened to Badalia," the curate said, "and it's you affair as well as mine. Dress, and come along."

"I am ready," was the answer. "Is there any hint of what's wrong?"

"Nothing beyond a runaway knock and a call."

"Then it's a confinement or a murderous assault. Badalia wouldn't wake us up for anything less. I'm qualified for both, thank God."

"I'd give much if our Church insisted on decent medical training. I've subscribed to the Thirty-nine Articles, but it would be better if I had subscribed to the *Lancet* intelligently from the beginning. Come along."

The two men raced to Gunnison-street, for there were no cabs abroad, and under any circumstances a cab fare means two days' good firing for such as are perishing with cold. Lascar Loo's mother had gone to bed, and the door was naturally on the latch. They found considerably more than they had expected in Badalia's room, and the Church of Rome acquitted itself nobly with bandages, while the Church of England could only pray to be delivered from the sin of envy. The Order of Little Ease, recognising that the soul is in most cases accessible through the body, take their measures and train their men accordingly.

"She'll do now," said Brother Victor, in a whisper. "It's internal bleeding, I fear, and a certain amount of injury to the brain. She has a husband, of course?"

"They all have, more's the pity."

"Yes, there's a domesticity about these injuries that shows their origin." He lowered his voice. "It's a perfectly hopeless business, you understand. Twelve hours at the longest."

Badalia's right hand began to beat on the counterpane, palm down.

"I think you are wrong," said the Church of England. "She is going." "No, that's not picking at the counterpane," said the Church of Rome. "She wants to say something; you know her better than I."

They bent very low.

"Send for Miss Eva," said Badalia, with a cough.

"In the morning. She will come in the morning," said the curate, and Badalia was content. Only the Church of Rome, who knew something of the human heart, knitted his brows and said nothing. After all, the law of his order was plain. His duty was to watch till the dawn while the grey worn moon went down.

It was a little before her sinking that the Rev. Eustace Hanna said, "Hadn't we better send for Sister Eva? She seems to be going fast."

Brother Victor made no answer, but as early as decency admitted there came one to the door of the house of the Little Sisters of the Red Diamond and demanded Sister Eva, that she might soothe the pain of Badalia Herodsfoot. That man, saying very little, led her to Gunnison-street, No.17, and into the room where Badalia lay. Then he stood on the landing, and bit the flesh of his fingers in agony, because he was a priest and a man and knew how the hearts of men and women beat back at the rebound, so that Love is born out of horror, and passion declares itself when the soul is quivering with pain.

Badalia, wise to the last, husbanded her strength till the coming of Sister Eva. It is generally maintained by the Little Sisters of the Red Diamond that she died in delirium, but since one Sister at least took a half of her dying advice, this seems uncharitable.

She tried to turn feebly on the bed, and the poor broken human machinery protested according to its nature.

Sister Eva started forward, thinking that she heard the dread forerunner of the death-rattle. Badalia lay still conscious, and spoke with startling distinctness, the irrepressible irreverence of the street-hawker, the girl who had danced on the winkle-barrow, twinkling in her one available eye.

"Sounds jest like Mrs. Jessel, don't it? Before she's 'ad 'er lunch an' 'as been talkin' all the mornin' to her classes."

Neither Sister Eva nor the curate said anything. Brother Victor stood without the door, and the breath came harshly between his clenched teeth. He was in pain.

"Put a cloth over my 'ead," said Badalia. "I've got it good, an' I don't want Miss Eva to see. I ain't pretty this time."

"Who was it?" said the curate.

"Man from outside. Never seed 'im no more'n Adam. Drunk, I s'pose. S'elp me Gawd that's truth! Is Miss Eva 'ere? I can't see under the towel. I've got it good, Miss Eva. Excuse my not shakin' 'ands with you, but I'm not strong, an' it's fourpence for Mrs. Imeny's beef-tea, an' wot you can give 'er for baby-linning. Allus 'avin' kids, these people. I 'adn't oughter talk, for *my* 'usband 'e never come nigh me these two years, or I'd a-bin as bad as the rest; but 'e never come nigh me. . . . A man come and 'it me over the 'ead, an' 'e kicked me, Miss Eva; so it was just the same 's if I had ha' had a 'usband, ain't it? The book's in the drawer, Mister 'Anna, an' it's all right, an' I never guv' up a copper o' the trust money—not a copper. You look under the chist o' drawers—all wot isn't spent this week is there. . . An', Miss Eva, don't you wear that grey bonnick no more. I kep' you from the diptheery, an'—an' I didn't want to keep you so, but the curick said it 'ad to be done. I'd a sooner ha' took up with 'im than anyone, only Tom he come, an' then—you see, Miss Eva, Tom 'e never come nigh me for two years, nor I 'aven't seen him yet. S'elp me—

I haven't. Do you 'ear? But you two go along, and make a match of it. I've wished otherways often, but o' course it was not for the likes o' me. If Tom 'ad comeback, which 'e never did, I'd ha' been like the rest—sixpence for beef-tea for the baby, a shilling for layin' out the baby. You've seen it in the books, Mister 'Anna. That's what it is; an' o'course, you couldn't never 'ave nothing to do with me. But a woman she wishes as she looks, an' never you 'ave no doubt about 'im, Miss Eva. I've seen it in 'is face time an' agin—time an' again . . . Make it a four pound ten funeral—with the pall."

It was a seven pound fifteen shilling funeral, and all Gunnison-street turned out to do it honour. All but two, for Lascar Loo's mother saw that a Power had departed, and that her road lay clear to the custards. Therefore, when the carriages rattled off, the cat on the doorstep heard the wail of the dying unfortunate, who could not die—

"Oh, mother, mother, won't you even let me lick the spoon!"

Notes

[1]See P.J. Keating, *The Working Classes in Victorian Fiction* (London: Routledge, 1971), pp.111-115.

[2]See Bonamy Dobrée, "Rudyard Kipling" in *Kipling and the Critics*, ed. Elliot L. Gilbert (New York: New York UP, 1965), pp. 37-58.

Bibliography

Primary Sources

Brown, John. "A Memoir of Robert Blincoe." In *The Lion* 1828: 119-256.

Fielden, John. *The Curse of the Factory System.* London: Cobbett, 1836.

Galt, John. "The Seamstress." In *Stories of the Study.* Vol. III. London: Cochrane and M'Crone, 1833. 250-267.

Greenwood, James. "A Night in a Workhouse." In *The Fashionable Science of Parlour Magic; Being the Newest Tricks of Deception, Developed and Illustrated. To which is added, An Exposure of the Practices made use of by Professional Card Players, Blacklegs, and Gamblers.* 8th ed. Ed. J.H. Anderson. Bloomsbury: R.S. Francis, 1866.

Jones, Ernest. "Woman's Wrongs." In *Notes to the People* 2 (1851-52): 515-1028.

Kipling, Rudyard. "The Record of Badalia Herodsfoot." In *Detroit Free Press Christmas Number* (London) 1890: 3-9.

Martineau, Harriet. *The Turn-Out.* Wellington, Salop: Houlston, 1829.

Reynolds, G.W.M. *The Mysteries of London.* Vols. 1-3. London: John Dicks, 1850.

Silverpen [Eliza Meteyard]. *Lucy Dean; the Noble Needlewoman.* In *Eliza Cook's Journal* 2 (16 Mar to 20 Apr 1850): 312+.

Toulmin, Camilla. "The Orphan Milliners." In *Illuminated Magazine* 2 (Apr 1844): 279-85.

Secondary Sources and Suggested Readings

Altick, Richard. *The English Common Reader: A Social History of the Mass Reading Public, 1800-1900.* Chicago: Chicago UP, 1967.

Avery, Gillian. *Victorian People.* New York: Holt, 1970.

Aydelotte, William O. "The England of Marx and Mill as Reflected in Fiction." In *Journal of Economic History.* Sup. B, 1948.

Baker, Joseph E., ed. *The Reinterpretation of Victorian Literature.* Princeton: Princeton UP, 1950.

Banks, J.A. "Population Change and the Victorian City." *In Victorian Studies* 11 (Mar 1968): 277-89.

Bell, Florence [Lady]. *At the Works: A Study of a Manufacturing Town.* London: Virago, 1985.

Bergman, Helena. *Between Obedience and Freedom: Women's Role in the Mid-Nineteenth Century Industrial Novel.* Gothenburg Studies in English

45. Goteberg, Sweden: Goteberg UP, 1979.

Best, Geoffrey. *Mid-Victorian Britain*. London: Weidenfeld and Nicolson, 1971.

Bodenheimer, Rosemarie. *The Politics of Story in Victorian Social Fiction*. Ithaca: Cornell UP, 1988.

Booth, Bradford Allen, ed. *The Gathering of the West*. Baltimore: Johns Hopkins, 1939.

Booth, Charles. *On the City: Physical Pattern and Social Structure*. Chicago: U of Chicago P, 1967.

Brantlinger, Patrick. "The Case Against Trade Unions in Early Victorian Fiction." In *Victorian Studies* 13 (1969): 37-52.

___. *The Spirit of Reform*. Cambridge: Harvard UP, 1977.

Briggs, Asa. *Chartist Studies*. London: Macmillan, 1977.

___. *Essays in Labour History*. London: Macmillan, 1960.

British Parliamentary Papers. Shannon: Irish UP, 1968.

Burt, Daniel I. "A Victorian Gothic: G.W.M. Reynolds' *Mysteries of London*." In *New York Literary Forum* 7 (1980): 141-58.

Butt, J. and I.F. Clarke, eds. *The Victorians and Social Protest: A Symposium*. Hamden, CT: Archon, 1973.

Butwin, Joseph. *"Hard Times:* The News and the Novel." In *Nineteenth Century Fiction* 32 (1977): 166-87.

Calhoun, C. *The Question of Class Struggle: Social Foundations of Popular Radicalism During the Industrial Revolution*. Chicago: U of Chicago P, 1982.

Carlyle, Thomas. *Thomas Carlyle: Selected Readings*. Ed. Alan Shelston. Harmondsworth: Penguin, 1980.

Cazamian, Louis. *The Social Novel in England, 1830-1850*. Trans. Martin Fido. London: Routledge, 1973.

Chadwick, Edwin. *Report on the Sanitary Conditions of the Labouring Population of Great Britain*. Ed. M.W. Flinn. Edinburgh: University Press, 1965.

Chapman, Raymond. *The Victorian Debate: English Literature and Society*. London: Weidenfeld, 1968.

Chinn, Carl. *They Worked All Their Lives: Women of the Urban Poor in England, 1880-1939*. Manchester: Manchester UP, 1988.

Clark, G. Kitson. "Hunger and Politics in 1842." In *Journal of Modern History* 25 (Dec 1953): 355-74.

Clarke, Allen. *The Effects of the Factory System*. Littleborough: Kelsall, 1985. Rpt. of 1899 ed.

Colby, Robert. *Fiction with a Purpose*. Bloomington: Indiana UP, 1967.

Cole, G.D.H. *British Working Class Politics, 1832-1914*. London: Routledge, 1941.

___. *Chartist Portraits*. London: Macmillan, 1965.

___. "Fiction and the Rising Industrial Class." In *Essays in Criticism* 17 (1967): 64-74.

___. *The Real Foundations: Literature and Social Change*. New York: Oxford, 1974.

___. *Studies in Class Structure*. London: Routledge, 1964.

___ and A.W. Filson. *British Working Class Movements: Selected Documents, 1789-1875*. New York: St. Martin's, 1967.

Colls, Robert. *The Pitmen of the Northern Coalfield: Work, Culture and Protest, 1790-1850*. Manchester: Manchester UP, 1987.

Crossick, Geoffrey. "The Labour Aristocracy and Its Values." In *Victorian Studies* 19 (1976): 301-20.

Crowther, Margaret. *The Workhouse System*. London: Batsford, 1981.

Dalziel, Margaret. *Popular Fiction 100 Years Ago*. London: Cohen and West, 1957.

Deacon, Jane. *Hard Lessons: The Lives and Education of Working-Class Women in Nineteenth-Century England*. Minneapolis: U of Minnesota P, 1989.

Dobrée, Bonamy. *Rudyard Kipling: Realist and Fabulist*. London: Oxford UP, 1967.

Eagleton, Mary and David Pierce. *Attitudes to Class in the English Novel*. London: Thames and Hudson, 1979.

Edelstein, T.J. "They Sang the Song of the Shirt: The Visual Iconology of the Seamstress." *In Victorian Studies* 23 (Winter 1980): 183-210.

Engels, Frederick. *The Condition of the Working Class in England*. London: Granada, 1981.

Epstein, James and Dorothy Thompson, eds. *The Chartist Experience: Studies in Working-Class Radicalism and Culture, 1830-60*. London: Macmillan, 1982.

Evans, Eric J. *The Forging of the Modern State: Early Industrial Britain 1783-1870*. London: Longman, 1984.

Faber, Richard. *Proper Stations: Class in Victorian Fiction*. London: Faber and Faber, 1971.

Fishman, W.J. *East End 1888: A Year in a London Borough Among the Labouring Poor*. London: Duckworth, 1988.

Flick, Carlos. *The Birmingham Political Union and the Movements for Reform in Britain 1830-1839*. Hamden, CT: Archon, 1978.

Fried, Albert and Richard M. Elman, eds. *Charles Booth's London: A Portrait of the Poor at the Turn of the Century, Drawn from His "Life and Labour of the People in London."* New York: Pantheon Books, 1968.

Gallagher, Catherine. *The Industrial Reformation of English Fiction, 1832-1867.* Chicago: U of Chicago P, 1985.

Gammage. R.G. *History of the Chartist Movement, 1837-1854.* New York: Kelley, 1969.

Gash, Norman. *Reaction and Reconstruction in English Politics, 1832-1852.* New York: Oxford, 1965.

Gaskell, Peter. *The Manufacturing Population of England.* London: Baldwin and Craddock, 1833.

Gilbert, Eliot L., ed. *Kipling and the Critics.* New York: New York UP, 1965.

Gillespie, Francis E. *Labor and Politics in England, 1850-1867.* Durham, NC: Duke UP, 1927.

Ginswick, Jules, ed. *Labour and the Poor in England and Wales 1849-1851* London: Cass, 1983.

Glenn, Robert. *Urban Workers in the Early Industrial Revolution.* London: Croom Helm, 1984.

Goodway, David. *London Chartism.* Cambridge: Cambridge UP, 1982.

"The Great Woman Market." *The Spectator* 15 Dec 1849: 1184.

Hammond, J.L. and Barbara Hammond. *The Age of the Chartists: 1832-1854.* Hamden, CN: Archon, 1962.

Harrison, J.F.C. *The Common People.* Totowa, NJ: Barnes and Noble, 1984.

Helsinger, Elizabeth K., Robin Lauterbach Sheets, and William Veeder. *The Woman Question: Society and Literature in Britain and America, 1837-1883.* 3 vols. Chicago: U of Chicago P, 1989.

Himmelfarb, Gertrude. *The Idea of Poverty: England in the Early Industrial Age.* London: Faber, 1983.

Hobsbawm, Eric J. *Labouring Men: Studies in the History of Labour.* London: Weidenfeld and Nicolson, 1964.

Hollis, Patricia. *Class and Conflict in Nineteenth-Century England: 1815-1850.* London: Routledge, 1973.

Houghton, Walter E. *The Victorian Frame of Mind: 1830-1870.* New Haven: Yale UP, 1978.

Hughes, Winifred. *The Maniac in the Cellar.* Princeton: Princeton UP, 1980.

Humpherys, Anne. "Geometry of the Modern City: G.W.M. Reynolds and the *Mysteries of London.*" In *Browning Institute Studies* II (1983): 69-80.

___. "G.W.M. Reynolds: Popular Literature and Popular Politics." In *Victorian Periodicals Review* 16.3-4 (Fall/Winter 1983): 79-89.

James, Louis. *Fiction for the Working Man, 1830-1850.* London: Oxford UP, 1963.

Jones, Gareth Stedman. *Outcast London.* Oxford: Clarendon, 1971.

Kanth, Rajani Kennepalli. *Political Economy and Laissez-Faire: Economics and Ideology in the Ricardian Era.* Totowa, NJ: Rowman, 1986.

Keating, P. J. *The Working Class in Victorian Fiction.* London: Routledge, 1971.

Kestner, Joseph. *Protest and Reform: The British Social Narrative by Women, 1827-1867.* Madison: Wisconsin UP, 1985.

Kirk, Neville. *The Growth of Working Class Reformism in Mid-Victorian England.* London: Croom Helm, 1985.

Kovalev, Yuri V., ed. *An Anthology of Chartist Literature.* Moscow: Izd-vo Literatury na inostrannykh Azykaskh, 1958.

Lubenow, William C. *The Politics of Government Growth: Early Victorian Attitudes Toward State Intervention 1833-1848.* Hamden, CT: Archon, 1971.

Lucas, John. *Literature and Politics in the Nineteenth Century.* London: Methuen, 1971.

Ludlow, J.M. and Lloyd Jones. *Progress of the Working Class 1832-1867.* New York: Garland, 1984.

Maccoby, Simon. *English Radicalism.* Vols. III, IV. London: Allen and Unwin, 1935-61.

Marcus, Steven. *Engels, Manchester and the Working Class.* New York: Random House, 1974.

Marshell, Dorothy. *Industrial England 1776-1851.* 2nd ed. London: Routledge, 1982.

Martineau, Harriet. *Autobiography.* Vol. I. Boston: Osgood, 1877.

Mather, F.C. *Chartism and Society.* London: Bell and Hyman, 1980.

Mayhew, Henry. *London Labour and the London Poor.* New York: Dover, 1968.

Meacham, Standish. *Toynbee Hall and Social Reform, 1880-1914: The Search for Community.* New Haven: Yale UP, 1987.

Melada, Ivan. *The Captain of Industry in English Fiction, 1821-1871.* Albuquerque: U of New Mexico P, 1970.

Milne, John Duguid. *Industrial Employment of Women in the Middle and Lower Ranks.* New York: Garland, 1984.

Neale, R.S. "Class and Class-Consciousness in Early Nineteenth-Century England: Three Classes or Five?" In *Victorian Studies* 12 (September 1968): 5-32.

"The Needlewomen and Their Rescue." *The Spectator* 8 Dec 1849: 1158-59.

"Needlewomen's Rescue-Ministerial Hopes." *The Spectator* 29 Dec 1849: 1232.

Neff, Wanda. *Victorian Working Women.* New York: Columbia UP, 1956.

Pinchbeck, Ivy. *Women Workers and the Industrial Revolution, 1750-1850.* London: Routledge, 1930.

"Political Economy and The Seamstress." *The Spectator* 15 Dec 1849: 1183-84.

Purvis, Jane. *Hard Lessons: The Lives and Education of Working-Class Women in Nineteenth-Century England.* Minneapolis: U of Minnesota P, 1989.

Radical Periodicals of Great Britain. New York: Greenwood Reprints, 1969.

Reynolds, G.W.M. "A Few More Words of Warning to the Needlewomen and Slopworkers." *Reynolds's Political Instructor* I (1849-50): 74.

___. "A Warning to the Needlewomen and Slopworkers." *Reynolds's Political Instructor* I (1849-50): 66-67.

Rose, Mary B. "Social Policy and Business: Parish Apprenticeship and the Early Factory System, 1750-1834." In *Business History* 31.4: 5-32.

Saville, John. *1848: The British State and the Chartist Movement.* Cambridge: Cambridge UP, 1987.

___. *Ernest Jones, Chartist.* London: Lawrence and Wishart, 1952.

Scheckner, Peter. *An Anthology of Chartist Poetry: Poetry of the British Working Class, 1830s-1850s.* Cranbury, NJ: Fairleigh Dickinson UP, 1989.

Smith, Harold, ed. *The British Labour Movement to 1870.* London: Mansell, 1981.

Smith, Sheila N. *The Other Nation.* Oxford: Clarendon, 1980.

Storch, Robert D., ed. *Popular Culture and Custom in Nineteenth-Century England.* London: Croom Helm, 1982.

Thomas, Maurice. *The Early Factory Legislation.* London: Thames Bank, 1948.

Thomis, Malcolm I. *Responses to Industrialization: The British Experience 1780-1850.* Hamden, CT: Archon, 1976.

Thompson, Dorothy. *The Chartists: Popular Politics in the Industrial Revolution.* New York: Pantheon, 1984.

Thompson, E.P. *The Making of the English Working Class.* New York: Vintage, 1963.

Tillotson, Geoffrey and Kathleen Tillotson. *Mid-Victorian Studies.* London: London UP, 1965.

Vicinus, Martha, ed. *The Industrial Muse.* London: Croom Helm, 1974.

Walkley, Christina. *The Ghost in the Looking Glass: The Victorian Seamstress.* London: Peter Owen, 1981.

Ward, John Trevor. *The Factory Movement, 1830-1855.* New York: St.

Martin's, 1962.

Weaver, Stewart Angas. *John Fielden and the Politics of Popular Radicalism, 1832-1847.* Oxford: Clarendon, 1987.

Webb, Igor. *From Custom to Capital: The English Novel and the Industrial Revolution.* Ithaca: Cornell UP, 1981.

Webb, R.K. *The British Working Class Reader.* London: Allen and Unwin, 1955.

West, Julius. *A History of the Chartist Movement.* New York: Kelley, 1968.

The Locust Hill
Literary Studies Series